"WHAT DO THEY KNOW?"

YOUTH, CULTURE AND CRIME

"WHAT DO THEY KNOW?"

YOUTH, CULTURE AND CRIME

L.A. Visano

de Sitter Publications

Published by de Sitter Publications
1288 Ritson Road North
Suite 417
Oshawa, ON, L1G 8B2
Canada

All remuneration from this book to the author shall be donated to the *Toronto Youth for Humanity*.

Library and Archives Canada Cataloguing in Publication

Visano, L. A

    What do they know? : youth, crime and culture / Livy Λ. Visano.
ISBN 1-897160-22-4

    1. Youth—Social conditions—21st century. 2. Youth—Attitudes.
    3. Juvenile delinquency. I. Title.
    Includes bibliographical references and index.

HV9076.5.V57 2006   305.235'09'0511   C2005-907683-6

de Sitter Publications
1288 Ritson Road North
Suite 417
Oshawa, ON, L1G 8B2
Canada
www.desitterpublications.com
sales@desitterpublications.com

To the enlightened consciousness,
A space so bitterly criticized and poorly understood,
Where creative curiosity, confusing change and community
compassion connect,
When life, loyalty and love are learned

For Doug, Franco and Greg

Table of Contents

Acknowledgements

Clearly, this book is the result of numerous emotional, spiritual and intellectual connections with a large number of youths, far too many to identify. As they know all too well, this inquiry would never have been possible without their generous assistance. To all of them–the street kids, high school students and former gang members, I will always remain deeply indebted and owe my utmost gratitude.

To the government and non profit youth serving agencies (administrators, staff, volunteers and clients), and to the primary and secondary schools (teachers, principals and students), far too many to mention and many of whom wished to remain anonymous, I extend my deepest respect and appreciation. I extend to Paul Brienza my deepest gratitude not only for his immediate willingness to act as the project's Research Associate but for his intellectual acumen and his incredible ability to draw upon his inestimable insights to guide this research. I am fortunate to have on the original Youth Project Team as Research Assistants: Corey Nishio Robin Sooklal Adrian Szaszkiewicz and Aliki Yorgiadis, as well as the more recent additions to the team: Hamza Dawood, Garfield Garwood, Alpha King, Rehab Renie, Damian Bailey, and Dwight Bleary. Thank you to all.

Many others have provided helpful advice throughout the last five years. I thank all of them equally: Furat Al Yassin, Claudius Alexander, Damian Bailey, Dwight Bleary, Damian Cyr, Allana Cyr, Jasvir Dhillon, Mauva Freckleton, Hannibal Gairey Ya Ya, Purcell Green, Raj Hardev Janice Henry, Elizabeth Johnson, Steve Loreiro, Andy Ly, Jeremy Meaghan-Cargill and Rabia Siddiqi. From the beginning of this project in 2001 Christopher Spotton and Courtney Rossi educated me; to both of them I owe a special debt of gratitude. Likewise, over the long life of this enterprise a large number of graduate and undergraduate students have made this project conceivable by injecting a sense of bold imagination and uncompromising integrity into the politics of learning and teaching.

I am grateful to Andreas Georgiou who shared so generously his intellectual wisdom, let alone his hospitality. He has always stimulated my critical imagination, forging new possibilities in the blending social and philosophical studies.

A special note of thanks is extended equally to those who have been instrumental in shaping my early interests in children and youth. John Visano, "my big brother" who not only provided unflagging support but has always inspired me to pursue humanistic approaches from an early age. I owe a long-overdue debt to my twin Fulvia for her generosity of spirit; she has always been the living expression of loyalty. My sister Franca oriented me to charity and the community for which I am grateful. I am especially indebted to my parents, Maria and Gino, who continue to keep my academic pursuits firmly rooted in culture, class and ethnicity.

I remain indebted to the many from whom I have gained scholarly confidence, critical insights and continued personal encouragement.

I thank the following colleagues and friends who as conference organizers invited me to present aspects of this study. They include Wesley Crichlow (Department of Justice and Carleton University, Ottawa), Robert Doyle (Naresuan University, Phitsanulok), Francesca L'Orfano (AICW Conference), Kevin McCormick (CAATS, Kempelfelt), and Masani Montague (Cycle of Violence Seminar, York University).

Sharron Rosen's personal insights are always challenging. Her formidable questions and intuitive grasp are always boldly courageous, painfully honest and endlessly encouraging. I have learned much from her dedication to teaching and from her community work.

For this and other projects Lisa Jakubowski's ongoing support has been instrumental. From our early projects on learning, from her generous assistance in initiating the study's early contacts with London's youth serving agencies to her constant appreciation, encouragement and pedagogical directions, I fully appreciate Lisa's many contributions.

I am fortunate to work with Mavis Griffin who grounded this inquiry especially in reference to the Toronto Youth for Humanity. To my work family: Paula Yanofsky, Loretta Fiorini, Mavis Griffin, Joni Kingsley, Rosanna Moretti, thank you for your constant support and enthusiasm.

A special note of gratitude is extended to the Dean Lenton and the Dean's Office of the Atkinson Faculty of Liberal and Professional Studies for both the travel support and the Atkinson Minor Research Grant. The travel grants facilitated the dissemination of results to a number of conferences. A note of gratitude is extended to the Office of Vice President, Research for Supplementary Research Grant. I thank York University and YUFA for the research support especially the Research Development Fellowship of York University. This study aacknowledges with gratitude the financial support of the Social Sciences and Humanities Research Council, the principal sponsor of the project. The opinions expressed in this report are those of the author and do not necessarily represent the views of SSHRC.

To Shivu Ishwaran and de Sitter Publications I am extremely grateful for the quick and enthusiastic response, for the invaluable advice and above all for their courage in undertaking this project. Throughout, de Sitter maintained a standard of professional integrity that remains unmatched as well as a profound commitment to innovative and progressive projects.

I would like to thank Brenda once again for her critical reading of the manuscript. Brenda assisted me in preparing the manuscript in all stages of this SSHRC project. Her insightful comments, her editing, her depth of focus and her interdisciplinary breadth were extremely helpful. Her inexhaustible intellectual commitment and emotional support ensured the completion of this project. Words can never capture my profound gratitude.

To our children Anthony and Tammi thank you for your exciting interests and encouragement especially during our many many dinner conversations on youths.

CHILDHOOD

I watched from afar
His innocence, curiosity and spirit could not be tarnished
His movements were carefree, his enthusiasm infectious.
He is oblivious to the worries and dangers around him.
How I envy him.
A puddle from the evening rainstorm remains glistening in the morning sun.
Splash!! He chooses not to go around it.
Dare I take the risk and join him? Is anyone watching,
judging, ready to label me?
Our eyes meet. Connections, a spark … trust evolves. Splash!!!
A moment of true authenticity and empowerment
A spiritual enlightenment of complete autonomy.
A risk worth taking and reliving forever.
Shaking the water from my shoes I watch his innocence, curiosity and
warmth strengthen in the morning sunlight.
He chases a monarch butterfly through the leafy field.
His giggles, freedom and desire to connect with his
environment are breathtaking.
Do I call out to prevent him from straying too far from my grasp?
Taking a deep breath I choose rather to join him on this adventure.
Casting aside my soaked shoes and all my fears, I too journey into the
field of innocence and wonder.
How I have learnt from the spirit and dynamics of a child.
—*Sharron Rosen (2004)*

"Those who seek wisdom seek power,
Those who cherish ignorance will dwell in their own destruction"
—*Garfield Garwood (2005)*

Chapter 1

Introduction:
Understanding Youth Identity

The study of crime begins with the knowledge of oneself. All that you despise, all that you loathe, all that you reject, all that you condemn, and seek to convert by punishment springs from you.

—Henry Miller (1891-1980). *The Air-Conditioned Nightmare, The Soul of Anaesthesia* (1945).

Introduction: Certitude as Servitude

The study of youth crime is a formidable inquiry into conformities and confrontations with conventional cultural narratives of coercion. This challenging enterprise requires an honest interrogation of how one interprets both the familiar and the foreign, that is, how one transforms the familiar into the foreign and the foreign into the familiar. Informed by critical social and critical criminological theories, this study analyzes the construction of youth crime by examining the differential impact of layered carceral contexts of culture and political economy on the individual and collective consciousness. In problematizing the relationship between control and culture, the following questions are considered: first, what are the mechanisms through which the dominant culture impacts on the control of crime? In reference to this crime-control nexus, the dominant culture mediates social relations and focuses attention away from fundamental injustices and inequalities, promoting instead the celebration of ego centric distortions such as individualism, possessiveness, materialism and the reproduction/consumption of narcissism. Further, cultural symbols contribute to the transformations of the prevailing imaginary, sentiments and emotions into significant inducements or dispositions to the regulation of youth. Consequently, youth existence, as conditioned by culture and history, constitutes youth's essence, being, and connections to crime. Second, how do youths consent, resist or accommodate, that is, "make sense" of the above power relations? Given that youths form and inform identities in relation to conflicting social narratives of the self and subjectivity, they mediate culture and character by challenging and reworking their respective stories of identity, individually and collectively. What is the social construction of their subjectivities within processes of identity production, discursive displays of experience and histories of selfhood? Youths, it will be demonstrated, interpret cultural narratives of regulation as ignoring their respective capacity to understand the manifold and ever-changing ways that authorities appropriate communication. In response to this imposed relationship between discourse and social subjectivity, youth social identity and practical consciousness are organized through a specific articulation of images, objects and words, as well, as techniques replete with desire and emotions that are not necessarily rational, logical, subliminal and unconscious. Third, how does the character of criminal attributions shape and is shaped by the quality of this culture? Given that textually mediated social relations become hegemonic narratives in everyday lives, how do youths articulate their experiences? What are the limits of these interpretations? How do discourses and practices create ideologically appropriate subjects? What is the relationship between youth identity and self?

These questions are directed towards what may be called ontology of the present that asks the Foucauldian question, who are we *now*? These questions demonstrate the *relationality* of social control as a serious substantive and generic site for investigating often overlooked and yet fundamental issues of inequality, for unravelling the connectedness of concepts and applied practices, and for questioning dominant modes of discourse. Despite the proliferation of different canonical texts, a number of issues remain unresolved. Moving beyond common sense and popular interpretations of youth crime, usually based on distorted official statistics and biased media accounts, the above questions proffer a different set of perspectival and substantive materials; that is, a more critical selective rendering of the assortment of different "facts." Obviously, to the threatened, these questions will be easily discarded as rancorously polemical and rhetorically provocative. But as expressions of dissatisfaction with extant texts, the above questions will facilitate the relocation of theoretical frontiers especially since the loose journeys of mainstream criminological textbooks fail miserably to stimulate, let alone, confront foundational and analytical criminological curiosities.

What Do *We* Know? Understanding Youth: Moving Beyond Moralizing Traditions

Before one can hope to investigate what youths know, it is essential to know what informs *our* understanding of youth crime which tends to be fragmented, frequently distorted and typically bereft of both memory and imagination. This study provides a fertile framework for appreciating prevailing cultural enclosures inherent in the preponderance of ontological presuppositions about youth criminality. It is incumbent upon all of us, as learners, to move beyond the convenient practice of debunking or disparaging the orthodoxies of conventional texts and begin instead to grapple with the subtext of our own credulities, especially the fixated nature of our own subjectivities. Thus, this journey begins with a reflection about the ways in which hegemonic claims inhibit thinking, let alone, understanding. From Antonio Gramsci (1971), we discover that the *social*, especially *our* social and concrete locations, contextualizes ideological commitments. In addition, the consciousness of our knowing selves is not simply an imposed illusion glibly appropriated and manipulated—reduced as rehearsed echoes and reproduced showpieces. Rather, our respective subjectivities consists of self awareness (intrapsychic) and mutual recognition (intersubjectivity) that should be challenged to move beyond atrophied cultural roles and expectations, incubated within resources like law, bureaucratic rationality, media, manufactured common sense, education, employment, etc. An awareness of one's own interpretive framework as part of a negating hegemonic force will lead to forms of consciousness that expose various mediations which interconnect subjectivity and convention within a dialectics of empowerment. Typically, too much is deferred to the capacity of criteria (exchange values, utility of instrumental logics) that institutionalize both meaning and authority. As the culture of impoverished or at best mediocre ideas triumph, thought is held hostage to a conceptual imperialism that distorts, alienates and coerces into compliance an all too ready susceptible general consciousness. Dominant modes of mental production succeed in dividing, invading and colonizing according to fundamental imperatives of capitalism. Any thought that challenges or "really makes a difference" is too readily silenced into submission. Regrettably, ideas are frequently celebrated only after they have been calibrated and re-routed successfully according to the market-driven mechanics of instrumentalism and the optics of rational materialism. Likewise, crime is often explicated and understood in relation to titivating debates moulded by titillating chatter impugning foreign values and thoughts. Prevailing ideas about crime are not only institutionally sponsored but are interpreted popularly as valued and legitimate information. Embedded in all tiers of domination and unequal relations are cultural mythologies (law, justice and morality), cultural colonizers ("the experts") and cultured consent (vulgar co-optation and a generalized manufactured consensus) that succeed in further marginalizing the "disadvantaged." In addition to the roles played by the law and the criminal justice system in protecting "individual" rights and the rights to "property," major cultural institutions like the family, education, media, work, etc trivialize the helpless and dispossessed by invoking a dubious benevolence of dependency and a persuasive appeal to citizenship. Just as crime has become a discursively constituted phenomenon that patterns and reproduces agency, conformity is elevated as real, functional and normative. Admittedly, a commitment to a pedagogy that confronts the deficit of autonomous thought and the surplus of alienating talk is never a facile accomplishment; that is, any process of bringing to our consciousness the lived experiences of injustices and their inexorable reproductions will, of course, be criticized as ideologically cacophonous and dismissed as inappropriately controversial.

Prior to understanding how youth interests intersect with the dominant practices of society, it is equally critical to examine the social organization of our own thinking and experiences. This hermeneutic attempt to appreciate the world of youths assumes that it may be possible to freely and courageously reflect and interpret our own intellectual limitations, biases and ignorance. To do so, one must then view foundational categories such as crime not as existing "out there" as an objective fact reported by authorities, but as radically constructed through authentic, historical and cultural practices at the everyday level. In brief, *"What do*

4

they know?" is essentially about suspicion and scepticism regarding the myths, illusion and deceptions that cloak misunderstanding and ethnocentric conventional criminological thought.

Conventional criminological and contemporary popular approaches reduce youth crime to monolithic, totalized and essentialist conceptions within a narrow theoretical vision that informs an overarching conceptual closure. In order to move beyond liberal orthodox ideas that socialize "common" experiences, this study asks, how is one's knowledge constructed? What grounds the experiences of knowing anything about youth? Epistemologically all "knowledge" is rooted in experience. The processes of education, formal and informal, direct and indirect, are major sites of ideological reproductions (Althusser 1971) which influence more than our opinions of youth but rather firmly entrench a certain consciousness. Conventional learning imposes silence and inhibits the development of intellectual curiosities which confront extant contradictions. The morality of our everyday knowledge is taken for granted; prevailing moral rules are rarely problematized and invariably routinized. It is only by encountering the *real life experiences* of youth that one can fully realize the insidious ways in which hegemony operates to control thinking. Ideological blinders often prevent us from challenging our own basic values and assumptions. The pursuit of knowledge is, in large part, an escape from the dark and yet comfortable cave of ready made opinions which continue to judge differences, colonize compliance and shackle the imagination.

Self consciousness is liberating. By transcending the locus of illusory "knowledge," one is more free to focus on the rootlessness of knowledge and move towards a commitment to an enabling authenticity that exercises the hitherto paralysis in analytic thinking, that enables the knowing subject to create a less depersonalized or "deindividuated" environment, and that questions the well rewarded role of the anonymous subject forever obedient to alienating authorities. But how then does one deconstruct codes of thinking and critically elaborate on the conditions and consequences of delinquency? Again, the answer rests with consciousness, knowing ourselves and our location, temporal and spatial (Gramsci 1971). First, youths must be understood in their own language, a style of intrinsic tension, which is dialectical in form and content. A more transformative potential of both teaching and learning grounded in struggle is required. In other words, as Giroux (1983:151) argues, the goal of developing an appreciation of the immanent possibilities for a radical critique and mode of social action are based on the creation of a culture of critical discourses that enhance a more developed and sustained conscientization. But, an empowerment of subordinate groups through a shared understanding of the construction and reproduction of dominant forms of knowledge has seldom been the programme of socializing agencies. Empowerment and not just the banality of idle chatter about crime will serve to focus attention on the often-ignored structures and processes of injustice. A more critical criminology uncovers "our" assumptions; enables us to learn more about our own learning; self-consciously challenges the dominant ethos; and, develops oppositional currents. Guided by an emancipatory intent, ***What do they know?***" refuses to acknowledge youth as reducible to any fixed set of proscriptions governed by forms of cultural domination. Second, the corpus of extant criminological texts provides too much reductionism that fails to transcend local and situated politics to consider the *relatedness* of silencing, exclusion and inequality. The movement beyond a rudimentary exposition of basic concepts to formulate fundamental questions about the nature of youth crime is long overdue. That is, this study encourages criminologists to become strangers, that is, to be "in" but not "of" the dominant culture in order to problematize relationships and bring to the forefront questions that have been too blithely ignored. Criminologists are asked to be brazen in deconstructing traditional texts by exploring the contradictions and closures inherent in conventional commentaries on crime. Knowledge ought not to be solely packaged to satisfy market conditions and careerist ambitions but to also respond to critical faculties, to struggle in documenting our experiences, consciousness, intention, and their relational contexts. The concept of relatedness, the opportunity to transcend disciplinary frontiers and the challenges of synthetic convergence of diverse intellectual perspectives contribute enormously to the conceptual and substantive promises of a nascent critical cultural criminology. As Skinner (1956:1066) advises:

> We can choose to use our growing knowledge to enslave people in ways never dreamed of before de-personalizing them, controlling them by means so carefully selected that they will perhaps never be aware of their loss of personhood.

The Concept(s) of Youth

Youth identity is central to the crime-cultural nexus. Cultural studies examine the contexts within which and through which youths, whether as individuals and as groups construct, negotiate and defend their identity or self-understanding. Cultural studies draw heavily on approaches that question what may be called orthodox accounts of identity. Orthodoxy assumes that the self is something autonomous (being stable and independent of all external influences). Cultural studies, however, do not hold identity as a response to something external and different from it. Youth identity is located culturally and selfhood is constructed in part from a wide array of transactions and relationships.

Indeed, crime and culture enjoy a symbiotic relationship—the nature of crime shapes and is shaped by the quality of culture. Discourses on youth crime are not fixed especially since these discourses are related to various permutations of power. A study of youth crime benefits from the necessity of relating youth crime to the interpretations of youth cultural discourses. Clearly, institutions of control (youth criminal justice), although shifting and fragmentary, are linked ideologically to the political economy of youth such that prevailing stereotypes of youth crime are fundamentally related to well established images of youth. In this regard the study of delinquency is significant precisely because of its *referential* character, an index of the affiliation of youth. As will be elaborated later, delinquency has always been the lens through which youths are understood, validated and repudiated. Delinquency incorporates the relational and tentative elements of youth. Accordingly, the standpoint of youth acquires unequivocal meanings imposed by statistics, laws and the media that promote myths, symbols and metaphors that not only situate youth but insert what Lyotard (1984) regards the "language of the game." Since youths are considered simply as people "disconnecting as children" or as "becoming adults," the self identity of youths is understood as fragile and fragmented, therefore susceptible to trouble. Youths are suspect and forever under surveillance, confined to the world of play or simply expected to "act their age" and "grow up." Historically, as a result of diverse push-pull factors youths have often been required to become that which they were defined—underdeveloped and potentially the dangerous "others." From the early classical periods through the middle ages, the Enlightenment, industrialization to late modernity, the concept of youth has been socially constructed in reference to normalizing and pathologizing projects of regulation. For centuries dominant forms of thought and practices have reified youth as an ideological category appropriated by the apparatuses of predatory cultures that succeed in selectively communicating and legitimating the immutability of socialization as a commodity form of instrumentalism. The minds and bodies of youth have been "territorialized," inextricably tied to the institutional trends of the political economy. Adolescents and youths were conferred with sets of universally recognized values, a certain "way of behaving" or even a "way of being." Today, and for a long time, youths continue to be exploited despite a few incremental gains determined always by an adult agenda. The adult image of "kids," founded on an agonal displacement of its own unknown, rests on "othering" practices such as creating the youth's economic or emotional dependencies (food, shelter, clothing), which spell a loss of voice and fluency thereby making meaningful status attainment difficult. Although the subject of youth crime continues to be a central focus of empirical and theoretical research in criminology, the concept of youth continues to be problematic. Mainstream criminology fails to recognize that youth is much more than a fixed and fixated adult construction but rather youth constitutes an incredibly complex field of interpretive inquiry that opens up the theoretical space "of" and "for" youths to challenge and re-negotiate the identities that have been forced upon them in the process of domination.

Youth Identity and the Character of Self

This study examines the impact of the dominant culture on youth in terms of the often overlooked issue of youth reflexivity. How do youths (individually and collectively) organize their respective thoughts, feelings and motives? How do they engage in reflexive and dynamic interactions that are consistent with the cultures of their physical and psychological experiences? Interpretations of the self especially, the self as social, mental and philosophical provide a more complete appreciation of how youths ground their delinquency and resistance. The following section surveys various perspectives on the self that will facilitate a more complete understanding of the vicissitudes and vagaries of the subject matter—youth.

Self as Social: Sociological Approaches

For many thinkers from Marx to Mead, the "social" is the most formative force in developing character. Values and attitudes are products of economic, political and cultural relations. Regrettably, traditional approaches support the fallacies of either determinism or inessentialism, that is, an emphasis on the duality of objects and subjects. Lamentably, traditional texts on youths are stylized in well respected formulae that continue to stress the primacy of these binary codes; an encyclopaedic recipe in which identities, relations and activities are reduced to bifurcated notions of either deviant or conformist, victims in trouble or troublesome offenders. This artificially polarization, replete with fictive logic, misrepresents the multi-layered identities of youth and the complex phenomena of youth crime. This binary method of analysis, this false "either/or" dichotomy obfuscates and erroneously reduces subjects (actors) to objects (structures) or alternatively, objects to subjects. Instead of limiting the phenomenon of youth in terms of an either/or framework, a priority of agency or structure, it is conceptually more compelling to adopt, as Marx (1956) suggests, the "totality," the interconnectedness of events and activities, the intersections of history, culture and political economy.

The social organization of youth consists of a wide spectrum of differentially constituted events. The concept of youth character refers to the progression of related experiences and identity changes, a relatively orderly sequence of movements. Choice, development, and transformation are marked by various contingencies and stages. Stages are characterized by identifiable and organized sets of relations and social meanings that provide perspectives or classificatory schemes. The social structure of youth identity consists of various forms that typically plot biographies and relationships. They include different features of: a) the initial "getting connected" or "becoming" stage which involves various aspects of exposure, exploration, entry (recruitment or induction), trial and initiation, or training and apprenticeship; b) the "staying connected" or "being" established in roles that concerns the maintenance of identity, achievement, stability and clarification and also advancement, promotion or specialization; and, c) the "disconnecting" or decline stage of a pursuit characterized by graduation, expulsion, termination, retirement as well as "re-connecting," transformation, conversion or greater induction into another orientation. Stages, in turn, are used to justify degrees of involvements.

9

Passing through these stages is never an automatic process: participation in and commitment to a stage depend upon several specific adjustments. These contingencies appear both as conditions and consequences of inter- actions. At each stage a number of tightly interwoven contingencies operate and assume different meanings. They do not necessarily operate "simulta- neously" (Becker 1963:24) nor sequentially but become important influences during different stages of development. Three related factors are fundamental in building and maintaining the symbolic worlds of self: constituting resources/skills, reactions of others and a self-identity (self- concept, self-esteem). The logic of this self development model suggests that there are a number of situational and subjective contingencies which youths confront, interpret and select at various stages of the maturation process. These contingencies are not objectively given; a study of youth, therefore, is not limited strictly to "affinities" which preordain or to "affil- iations" which convert. Stages involve varying degrees of overlap, negotiations and compromise that accompany shifting relations and mean- ings that emerge in order to cope with affinities and affiliations. The concept of the "developing self" is a valuable tool kit precisely because of its "two-sidedness." On the one hand, this concept is linked to internal matters—the demography, the image of self, felt identity and its shifts. On the other hand, it is related to "social"/cultural identities, to the dominant society with which the former interacts. Therefore, youth identity is a complex amalgam of resources/skills; leadership; identification (ideologies with a history); networks of communication; reactions of others, etc. In reconstructing and coordinating their biographic identities, youths rely on factors that "push" them out of the dominant culture and factors that "pull" them towards the seemingly more attractive alternatives of the dominant culture. The premise of these accounts is contingent upon the available stock of information and the relevant socialization. But since there is not one particular youth identity, but many, reflecting differentially rooted cultural contexts, that is the interplay of different experiences and problem- atics related to gender, class, race, sexual orientation, education, to name a few, it is argued that the construction of youth identity is both complex, contingent and differentially negotiated. Self knowledge for youths is not only ideologically situated, but is also articulated as a legitimate response to felt exclusionary practices that generate institutional dependency. For youths their voices are silenced and rendered inauthentic: they are not encouraged to be aware of themselves as knowing beings. The so-called adult social world, as defined by prevailing cultural and legal categories, inferiorizes their respective and collective self concepts within a mystifying calculus that manufactures youth as a marginalized "other" who then is easily transformed into a prospective alien, a parasitic object of economic dependence, an aggressive agent of consumerism and a pitiful casualty of a cycle of violence.

Youth relations are indeed characterized by identifiable and organized sets of social meanings. As they emerge from social interactions youths learn who they are by having appraisals of the self reflected back to them from others. The normative characterization of youth as given and static consistently suggests that youths are constructed by external forces alone which in turn propel criminal behaviour. Youths as skilful actors are creators of their environments, engaged in a continual process of meaning construction in relation to their social realities. As agents, they actively and reflectively shape their experiences and the experiences of those with whom they routinely interact, therefore, negotiating and reconstituting their meanings. The only way to contextualize youth is to know how their actions are guided by subjective meanings, how their social worlds are constructed out of shared symbolic universes and how youths have the capacity to represent themselves symbolically because of their unique ability to use their words and language which shape their interactions.

The hallmark of this process of selfhood is *reflexivity*, the on-going activity of interpreting the concrete social world. This emphasis on the construction of social action requires a concern for those empirical moments of connections. To know how and why youth behave it is essential to understand what the situation means to them. Towards this end, the study of interpretations becomes particularly significant. For Mead (1934:173), the "essence of the self is cognitive; it lies in the internalized conversation of gestures that constitute thinking." Role taking is the act of entering into the perspective of others to become aware of one's own perspective (p.4). Taking the role of the other towards the self underlies the construction of self, that is, the self emerges in reference to others, in projections and rehearsals of roles. But, social identities are not only created by immediate actors; they are also reflections of how symbolic and distant others see them. Goffman (1959, 1963), analyzes the process of taking the role of the other toward self, how one looks at oneself as one thinks others see him/her and as one would see oneself if one were the other. Similarly, Charles Cooley's notion of the looking glass self presents the idea that actors manage their identities and interact with social objects as reflected by interpretations of others. In Cooley's (1956) "looking glass self," the self is multiple and ever changing depending on the social situations in which one finds oneself. The looking glass self consists of the actor's response to the responses of others. Actors interpret what their actions mean and what the actions and reactions of others mean in this ongoing process. Goffman (1959) suggests that the self is a product of particular interactions, as far as the individual's capacities, attitudes and ways of behaving change just as much as the people around also change. Goffman further adds that the self "does not derive from its possessor, but from the whole scene of his action" suggesting that the self is a product of such scenes not the cause of them (p.252). Goffman's dramaturgy suggests that the self and social interaction are more like performances based on settings, scripts, scenes, and props. He further develops both the back stage and front stage to discuss the concept of impression management—a technique used in social interaction in which the actor attempts to project a desired concept of self. Depending on locations and situations, actors will behave differently, display different selves or take on different identities. As Mead (1934:xxv) noted, the "individual constitutes society as genuinely as society constitutes the individual." The self is an ongoing social construction; it is never a finished project. As agents, youths make or create a role by making behavioural choices and decisions and by engaging in negotiation and compromise as well as conflict.

Thinking emerges from interpretations of ongoing social interactions. One's interpretations of encounters (activities), actors (relations) and situations (settings) managed and modified meanings, which in turn define one's identity. The social construction of subjectivity and the history of selfhood exist within the continuous production of socializing relationships (the social) and the discursive displays of experiences (the biographical).

Mental Selves: Psychoanalytic Approaches

As noted above, identity as culturally constituted is externalized according to social interpenetrations that eclipse or even deform authentic self-formation. What is the impact of the social on the self and the self on the social? Where is the innate capacity for enlightenment, freedom of thought and action? Subjectivity (self-understanding) is related to consciousness, which in turn makes the self-accessible. The cultural or collective and the individual or authentic identities, however, are not necessarily compatible or equally represented in the self. These intrapsychic conflicting self-concepts interfere with the conscious, intersubjective socialized self-image just as much as the intersubjective conflicting self concepts interfere with intrapsychic self concepts.

Psychoanalytic theories argue that one's respective history and one's inherent personality attributes define the self. Central to the conception of the self is the idea of the unconscious. In this regard, psychoanalysis enhances an understanding of how the self is constructed, by exploring the role of the unconscious in these self-conflicts. Psychoanalysis is especially valuable for it seeks to discover, for example, the hidden sources of youth identity and behaviour (conformity, resistance and delinquency). Psychoanalysis questions the extent to which the self can ever be fully conscious. A focus on instincts, as the unruly and essential passions of the personality, complements theories of the socially constructed individual by highlighting the tensive relations between the instinctual individual self and the "normalized" social self.

In his examination of the impact of social order on human nature, Sigmund Freud (1856-1939) notes that the self, as the soul, incorporates the whole of an individual—conscious and unconscious, mental and emotional, intellectual and moral. For Freud, passion and desire are acquired biologically based instincts that are also learned. The self is structured through the relationship of id and superego as mediated by the ego. Briefly, *the ego* is that part of us that is conscious, associated with logic/reason and is oriented towards perceptions in the real world. The ego presents the outer world to the id through a series of identifications with objects external to the self and carries out the commands of the reality. Deriving from the id, the ego tends to maximize instinctual gratification while minimizing punishment. In so doing, the ego functions to deal effectively with external world and to behave defensively, that is, to translate instinctual demands into expressions that is consistent with the demands of the superego (Freud 1930, 1985).

Unlike the ego, both the id and superego are unconscious. Concerned with the pleasure principle, the *id* is oriented towards internal instincts that belong to the passions. The id, as the set of instinctual desires of the libido, constantly expects gratification from which the ego seeks to discern itself through various mechanisms of repression. These instincts (original contents of the mind) are experienced as foreign rather than part of ourselves include both life and death ("thanatos"), that is, sex ("eros") and self-preservation respectively. The pleasure principle seeks to maximize instinctual gratification (feel good) without regard to external reality. The ego, however, is never able fully to distinguish itself from the id, of which the ego is, in fact, a part. Because of repression, the id seeks alternative expression for those impulses that we consider evil or excessively sexual. The id represents the inheritance of the species, which is passed on to us at birth while at the same time it is the dark, inaccessible part of our personality.

The *superego* is the reaction-formation faculty that strives toregulate unacceptable desires thereby representing moral restrictions and promoting perfection. Caught up in this conflict with the id's primitive object-choices, the superego presents itself as a sense of guilt, the internal version of punishment. This disciplining moral consciousness consists of conscience (cultural bans or prohibitions) and ego ideal (positive acts—the ought). To reiterate, the internalization of prohibitions cedes to repression (under the influence of discipline, schooling and reading) in the form of an unconscious sense of guilt. The superego may become *excessively* moral and destructive. In brief, for Freud the ego is constantly struggling to defend itself from the demanding superego, the unruly libido of the id and the external world. Consequently, the conflicts between the ego-superego and the id may help to analyze delinquent behaviour, that is, the internal costs of external adaptations. Freud (1930, 1985) explains that external social controls and basic repression may be needed for the maintenance of social order but cautions that more excessive or surplus repression contributes tragically to individual disorders. For youths, this stifling of individuality by all major institutions are injurious. In turn, their unconscious, fueled by libidinal drives, is produced through repression. The unconscious, revealing itself in dreams and slips (parapraxes), is a force in all lives that remains unconscious because it is unbearable, therefore further repressed, and seldom confronted.

Jacques Lacan (1977) revisits Freud's psychoanalytic projects to clarify a number of concepts related to the unconscious. Lacan's identity and being (subjectivity) are inextricably linked to discourses, which shape the unconscious, that is, language as the mirror of the unconscious mind governs all factors of human existence. Following Freud, Lacan describes two mechanisms of unconscious processes, condensation and displacement, two linguistic phenomena, where meaning is either condensed (in metaphor) or displaced (in metonymy). For Lacan, there are three major stages of self or psyche development: the imaginary, the symbolic, and the real. The first stage is the mirror or *imaginary* stage, characterized by unity, coherence and control despite the presence of dependence, alienation and fragmentation. The "thinking being" is situated in a symbolic universe wherein self-consciousness emerges and ego is formed. This imaginary order is the psychic the domain of the specular image ("imagos"), the outcome of mirroring development and ideal likeness. These primordial images, manifested in everyday interactions and in the constitution of self, are illusory. According to Lacan (1977, 1988) the mirror stage is a drama whose internal thrust is precipitated from an insufficient anticipation. This stage manufactures a succession of fantasies for the subject who is lost in the lure of spatial identification. The mirror stage cements a self/other dichotomy, where previously the child had known only "other," but not "self." But for Lacan, the identification of the "self" is always in terms of the "other." This is not the same as a binary opposition, where "self" = what is not "other," and "other" = what is not "self." Rather, "self" = "other," in Lacan's view; the idea of the self, that inner being we designate by "I," is based on an image, an other. The concept of self relies on one's misidentification with this image of an "other." The "other" becomes "me" in the mirror stage. Lacan uses Other, with a capital "o," to distinguish between the concept of the other and actual others. The Mirror Stage concerns the emergence of the capacity of infants before they are able to speak, and before they have control over motor skills, to recognize their own image in the mirror. This act of recognition is not self-evident, for infants have to see the image as being both itself (their own reflection), and not themselves (only a reflected image). The image is not identical with the infant subject—to become a human subject (that is, a social being) means coming to terms with this. The formation of an ego (the centre of consciousness), like the child's entry into language, is entirely dependent on this recognition. Language and symbolic (cultural) elements now become fundamental, whereas before, it was generally held that biological (natural) factors were the basis of human subjectivity. The ego seeks to confirm its identity by attempting to express itself and gain the acknowledgment of others through language. At the level of the Imaginary or the realm of necessary illusions, the subject mis-recognises the nature of the symbolic. To repeat, when the child sees its own image, it mistakes this shape for a superior self. The child identifies with this image, internalizes it as an "ideal ego" and this process forms the basis for all later identifications, which are imaginary in principle.

15

In the second, *symbolic stage*, the self surrenders to a "social" language. It is represented by the idea of the Other (the unconscious) wherein signifiers (words) unique and integral to one's being are located. This symbolic order is always ready locate identity through a shared language that embodies desire, which privileges communal meaning at the expense of personal being (Arrigo 1998). The symbolic is not simply another dimension; it emerges from the interplay(s) between subject / Other and imaginary/real as an unfolding of the "category of thirdness." Meaning emerges because of the relationship subject / Other and this relational category, once created, overrides and determines the entities or objects that constitute it.

The ego seeks to confirm its identity by attempting to express itself and gain the acknowledgment of others through language, the intersubjective medium of discourse and social interaction. The dominant factor in symbolic interaction is the unity of signification, which always refers to another signification, making it impossible to fix permanently or reliably the meaning of concretely pronounced discourses. The Symbolic realm is the structure of language itself, which we have to enter into in order to become speaking subjects, in order to say "I" and have "I" designate something that appears to be stable. The Symbolic order is the structure of language itself; we have to enter it in order to become speaking subjects, and to designate ourselves by "I." The foundation for having a self resides in the Imaginary projection of the self onto the specular image, the other in the mirror, and having a self is expressed in saying "I," which can only occur within the Symbolic, which is why the two coexist. While the unconscious decentres the subject because it introduces division, at the level of the Imaginary especially in the discourse of everyday life, the effects of the unconscious are not acknowledged. The Symbolic is a substitute for what is missing from its place. The symbol, word, etc. always entails the absence of the object or referent.

In the third *real* stage, the world is beyond signification and never attainable. The Real is a place (a psychic place, not a physical place) where there is original unity; no absence or loss; no language; only fullness and completeness satisfying all needs. One formulation of the Real given by Lacan is that it is always in its place because only what is missing (absent) from its place can be symbolised, and therefore formalised. In summary, for Lacan, it is not that humans learn to speak in the language and customs of our particular culture, rather actors are in fact spoken by the culture

16

itself. The perception and language of others forms the self even at the deepest levels of the unconscious. In other words, we can only speak using a language that is foreign to us when we come into the world. Someone else gives us our names, and we learn who we are through the responses of others.

Likewise, meaning or "exists in the framework of language. Thus, for Derrida, an ethics of responsibility (pursuit of truth) requires alterity. By penetrating the "otherness of the other," we are better able to grapple with the tensions between an absolute and irrecoverable notion of alterity and a simultaneous insistence that the other is somehow always within the self. The notion of alterity, this relational aspect (being other than myself), maintains that the other precedes, invokes and provokes the subject (Derrida 1976, 1981). Human beings require the mediation of consciousness, or the mirror of language, in order to know themselves and the world; but this mediation or mirror (these impurities) have to be excluded from the process of knowledge; they make knowledge possible, and yet are not included in the knowledge process.

Carl Jung's (1875-1961) "self" represents the totality of the personality, the balance between the opposing forces of personality where the conscious and unconscious are not necessarily in opposition to one another. Jung (1966) also refers to the self as an "unknowable essence" that transcends our powers of comprehension. The self's transcendence integrates the activities of the self, joining opposing forces into a coherent middle ground. A person's unconscious is supplemented by a "collective unconscious" consisting of universal images. The goal of self-development is both balance and wholeness. The unconscious consists of socially unacceptable mental content that was at one time conscious but later driven by various defences. The collective unconscious, the most profound and inaccessible layer of the psyche, refers to a communal memory representing the accumulated experiences or predispositions used to grasp the world.

For Jung, the ego is the center of the individual's consciousness usually characterized by one dominant attitude (introversion / extraversion) and by the dominant functions of thinking or feeling and sensing or intuiting. The ego or individually differentiated consciousness is that aspect of the self, which is experienced as personal and self-reflexive. It is the felt center of consciousness, while the self is the center of the total psyche (Jung 1966, 1968). The ego and the self are in a dialectical relationship with each other—the "ego-self axis," based on the attempt of the conscious personality to respond to the manifestations of the unconscious. Without ego consciousness, the self cannot realize itself in the world; and with the self, the ego has no depth or source of meaning and integration. The ego stands to the self as the moved to the mover (Jung 1969) and through the process of individuation, as consciousness of the self increases, the ego increasingly experiences itself as the object of a supra ordinate subject (Corbett 1989).

The self is purposive, acting as an organizing center that tries to maintain the integrity of the personality by maintaining intrapsychic homeostasis. The personality operates according to archetypes, inherited predispositions which govern perception, and affective experience. As an archetype, the shadow is the dark side of one's personality that contains the animal and sexual instincts. The shadow reveals itself in dreams, fantasies, repressions and slips of the tongue. Suppressing the shadow leads to a civilized life, but at the expense of spontaneity, creativity, and strong emotions. It's opposite the persona – the mask is the conscious part of personality, the public face (mask) that one presents to the world and provides compromises necessary for social interaction. The self and its a priori (archetypal) categories represent Jung's fundamental ontological ground. According to Jung, the self depicts its own processes within the psyche by producing specific imagery, in dreams and fantasy and is thus an experience-near concept when felt as immanent through such symbols, but is also experience-distant when used as a theoretical concept. Symbolic experiences of the self (in relation to self-state dreams) typically range from the most abstract to the most human, depending on which aspect of the totality of the self needs to be stressed. The particular content of a self-symbol found in a person's imagery is determined by whatever is being ignored by ego consciousness, because such experience of the self is a homeostatic attempt to correct for a one-sided or incomplete conscious attitude. According to Jung (1968, 1971) typical symbols that mediate the intrapsychic experience of the self are (a) symmetry, wholeness, and completion, (b) figures that are idealized or transcendent; (c) figures representing the union of opposites, since the self is a complex of opposites with a paradoxical, antinomial character (Corbett 1989). Adolescence is the true psychic birth, because it is the first time one can really be out of balance. Parents commence this imbalance by forcing youths to develop their unnatural attitude and functions. The conscious part of all opposite pairs stays in the persona and the rejected part goes into the shadow. With older youths, the process of separation from the family begins and personality and work can become fused ("inflated persona") with a greater focus on the external world.

Likewise, for Kohut (1977) the self cannot be fully described ("unknowable essence" or cognitive impenetrability) given that it is a supra ordinate intra psychic structure. Kohut's (p.xv) self is the way a person experiences himself as himself, a permanent mental structure consisting of feeling, memories, and behaviors that are subjectively experienced as being continuous in time and as being "me." The self is also a felt center of independent initiative and an independent recipient of impression—the center of the individual's psychological universe and not simply a representation. Kohut's concept of the self-object implies that selfhood is most fully experienced within a relationship that provides for the person that which is otherwise missing. The self-object is an intra psychic phenomena and not simply an interpersonal process. Lastly, for Kohut, the virtue of relationships achieves wholeness of the person.

Similar to Freud, Erik Erikson (1902-1994), considers the ego innate but stresses the psychosocial features of the conflict between child and parents. Development, divided into stages, extends over the life span. The amount of conflict in each stage determines whether the positive or negative pole is learned for adolescents who go school to become more "social." Industry (artisanship or skill learning) is contrasted with school performance inferiority. For youths, development mostly depends upon what is done to you. Thereafter, development depends primarily upon what you do. This is the stage when you are neither a child nor an adult. Identity is contrasted with role confusion. In the search for identity, many adolescents go into a period of withdrawing from responsibilities which Erikson called a "moratorium" (1963, 1968). Youths establish their philosophies of life and think in terms of ideals despite their limited experiences. Peer groups constitute the significant relations and tend to substitute ideals for experience.

According to Carl Rogers (1902-1987), humans possess an ability to actualize themselves. The self, a conscious sense of who and what one is, emerges through experiences with verbal labels such as "I" or "Me." Experience is the highest authority. Rogers does not specify any developmental stages but notes that that one's inherent potentialities are genetically determined, while the self-concept is socially determined. The important influences are conditional positive regards the granting of love and approval only when behaving in accordance with parent's wishes, or when parents withdraw love if the child misbehaves. This leads to self worth (similar to superego): the individual's belief that he/she is worthy of affection only when expressing desirable behaviours. Incongruence exists whenever there is a split between organismic experience and self-concept, a rupture that prevents self-actualization, leading to defensive behaviour such as denial (repression) and distortion. Congruence occurs whenever the self-concept agrees with inherent potentialities and there are minimal conditions of worth resulting in an openness to experience and a fulfil oneself. The human organism's "phenomenal field" includes all experiences available at a given moment, both conscious and unconscious (Rogers 1959). As development occurs, a portion of this field becomes differentiated and this becomes the person's "self" (Rogers 1959, 1961, 1965). The "self," a central construct in this theory, develops through interactions with others and involves awareness of being and functioning. The self-concept is the organized set of characteristics that the individual perceives as peculiar to himself/herself, based largely on the social evaluations he/she has experienced.

Others have been more explicit in addressing the theme of bounded and embodied consciousness. For William James (1890), the material, social, and spiritual selves have the powers of consciousness which are directed by the evolutionary goal of survival. The "sense" of self is thus bound into the life and capabilities of the body. The self is a unique identity, biologically limited, logically bound, and functionally reflexive. The self embodies the knower; knowledge logically depends on the self's two formally opposed categories, knower and known. The form of the categories is the very experience and the existence of the knower's subjectivity. By this form, the self articulates the agency that divides the person from others. Free will, the individual's recognition of agency, is a function of natural categories, their bounds, and their limitations. There is no free will without a series of internal determinants. For James (1890), there are several selves: the material, social, and spiritual.

In addition to the above perspectives, scholars have referred to the "self" as a collection of: a) continuing behaviors as kindness or aggressiveness toward others and such cognitive products of self, as self-worth and self-efficacy (Bandura 1986); b) social and political injunctions, invented and disseminated for the control of the individual (Taylor 1989); c) cognitive operations, conceived as "mind" (Boden 1977); d) events that fit in an actor slot in the person's schematics of action and outcome—a viewpoint promoted by cognitive linguists (Rosch 1997); e) the organism's exploratory actions and capabilities—its non-conceptual reactions to and representations of ecological arrays encountered in its navigation of the environment; and, f) series of dynamic interactions and junctions, contextually determined within the larger macro-system. The self could be an illusion that represents nothing observable except for one's thinking that it is a unique entity unifying constituent identities.

Interestingly, existential psychology represents a synthesis of philosophy and psychology and frequently articulated according to the belief that "existence precedes essence." Being signifies the special quality of human mentality (aptly called intentionality) that makes life a series of decisions, each involving an alternative that precipitates persons into an unknown future and an alternative that pushes them back into a routine, predictable past. Choosing the future brings ontological anxiety (fear of the unknown), whereas choosing the safe status quo brings ontological guilt (sense of missed opportunity). Authenticity involves accepting this painful state of affairs and finding the courage or hardiness to persist in the face of ontological anxiety and choose the future, thereby minimizing ontological guilt. Being-in-the-world emphasizes the unity of person and environment, since, in this heavily phenomenological position, both are subjectively defined. Being-in-the-world has three components: the natural world of biological urge and drive; the social, interactive, interpersonal aspects of existence; and, the subjective, phenomenological world of the self. Briefly, this psychological framework emphasizes the following: the meanings placed on the self, the responsibility for affirming the existence of the self, the importance of others, the threats to identities, and an awareness of thinking and feeling at different moments. The human being as a conscious self, makes choices concerning the life's paradoxes, confronting potentialities for the natural function to take over the whole person, power (significance or powerlessness of the self), love (self and other feelings), intentionality (capacity to know), freedom and destiny (acted upon or acting), and courage and creativity (capacity to move ahead). The development of adolescence is the beginning of self-initiated learning from experiences of failure. With this self-definition or learning of a role player, the phase of authenticity (self-definition) or individuality begins.

Meanings of Self: Philosophical Approaches

Instead of restricting the inquiry to "who is the self," philosophy asks, "what is the self?" That is, what is the relationship between mind and body?

21

In the *Republic* (1901) and in *Gorgias* (1920) Plato, (c. 380 BC) presents the soul (mind) and the body as distinct. The mind/soul, the essential elements of the self never changes whereas the body belonging to the empirical world of experiences changes. Modern philosophy has further developed this mind/ body duality in a number of interesting ways. The mind is a product of the (material) brain that receives messages from other organs. It is conscious and non-spatial while the body is spatial but not conscious. Moving beyond the binary, current approaches view the mind as the brain and consciousness is the individual experiences of the brain.

Immanuel Kant (1724-1804) claims that the mind of the knower makes an active contribution to the experience of objects. By demonstrating the limitations of our knowledge, Kant's analysis of the faculties of the mind reveals the transcendental structuring of experience. In his analysis of sensibility, he argues for the necessarily spatio-temporal character of sensation. Kant (1998) analyzes understanding, the faculty that applies concepts to sensory experience and concludes that categories provide a necessary, foundational template for our concepts to map onto our experience. In addition to providing these transcendental concepts, understanding is the source of ordinary empirical concepts that make judgments about objects possible. Understanding provides concepts as the rules for identifying the properties in our representations (Kant 1996). Kant's concern with the faculty of judgment is expressed as follows, if understanding as such is explicated as our power of rules, then the power of judgment is the ability to subsume under rules, that is, to distinguish whether something does or does not fall under a given rule. A further stage in Kant's project is the analysis of formal or transcendental features of experience that enable this judgment-transcendental structure of cognitive judgement.

As a product of the eighteenth century, Kant often writes in an unhistorical way and consequently overlooks the layer of traditions in which identities are formed. He tacitly assumes that in making moral judgments each individual can project himself into the situation of everyone else through his own imagination. But participants can no longer rely on a transcendental pre-understanding grounded in more or less homogeneous conditions of life and interests (Habermas 1998). Kant's deontological, cognitivistic, formalistic, and universalistic justifiable normative judgments forces us to choose a narrow concept of morality. This deontological ethics conceives the rightness of norms and commands. Although Kant opts for the grammatical form of an imperative ("Act only according to that maxim by which you can at the same time will that it should become a universal law"), his categorical imperative, in fact, plays the part of a principle of justification that discriminates between valid and invalid norms in terms of their universalizability. The result is that what every rational being must be able to will is justified in a moral sense (ibid).

In traditional philosophy, the experiencing self defines "subjectivity." For Kant, it must be possible for the "I think" to accompany all of conscious representations. Subjectivity is not viewed as impossible to understand; the self begins in the radical reformulation of the relationship of the object of sense to the cognitive faculties. Kant establishes the power and authority of reason, that faculty of mind that marks the individual. Reason has as its sole object, the understanding and its effective application in structuring consciousness such that freedom and its association with mastery becomes the condition of the self's entire being in the world. For Kant, the self, built upon the principle of strength in unity, remains untried in the world of human affairs. It is thus significant that in the threat posed upon the self by an excessive might, Kant speaks of "resistance," "courage," and the "superiority" of the self in relation to the immensity of the object which paves the way for autonomy.

Can human beings learn to understand conscious experience, even in its subjective aspect? For many philosophers like Gayatri Spivak (1985), Michel Foucault (1970) and Franz Fanon (1967), the discourse of development is always juxtaposed against the colonized mind in order to reveal the implications of hegemony.

As Martin Heidegger (1889-1976) confirms, a person is not a thing, substance, nor an object independently subsisting, but a subject. Mental consciousness is experienced, as an ongoing sensations and perceptions of material and immaterial objects, events, states, ideas and concepts etc. Intentionality is the unique peculiarity of experiences, the consciousness of that which characterizes consciousness. A person exists only in the performance of intentional acts. Since every subject is what it is only for an Object and vice versa, the subject remains ontologically indefinite. Humans are existentially inseparable from the world because their presence is embodied or embedded within it (as Being-in-the-world or Dasein). In Heidegger's early work the subject is reinterpreted as *Dasein*—a non-autonomous, culturally bound (or thrown) way of being, that can yet change the field of possibilities in which it acts. Thinkers alone have the power to disclose a new world and anyone is free to step back from the current world,

23

to enter one of a plurality of worlds, and, thereby, facilitate a change in the practices of one's society. Heidegger (1977a, 1977b, 1988) rejects the Enlightenment idea of an autonomous subject since the history of being shows how in the modern world things have been turned into objects. Heidegger opposes the claim that a person's relation to the world and the things in it must be mediated by something in the person's mind: beliefs, desires, experiences, etc.—what philosophers call intentional content. In *Being and Time*, Heidegger describes this general coping as familiarity. And just as in ordinary cases of coping, where Dasein is absorbed in its activity with no experiences of itself as an action-directing subject, so when Dasein is simply at home in its situation, there is no separation between Dasein's disclosing comportment and the world disclosed. That is, the self and world are not two entities, like subject and object but self and world are the basic determination of Dasein itself in the unity of the structure of being-in-the-world. Heidegger argues that this familiarity with the world constitutes Dasein's understanding of being. This understanding of being provides a background understanding of what matters and of what it makes sense. In addition, since individual Daseins can act only within a background that determines what can show up as making sense to do, Dasein can never be the fully lucid source of its actions postulated by the modern understanding of the subject and of autonomous agency of Being and Time. There is a structural limit to Dasein's autonomy. Despite the tendency of current practices to co-opt all deviation, one can modify, in small ways, the current understanding of being. Edmund Husserl (1859-1938) maintains that it is only through reflexion that consciousness can become known. Reflection distinguishes the experience itself from the content of experience especially subjectively and an objectively oriented aspects. For Husserl (1962, 1970), the mind has no spatial extension and no location, and is neither sense experienceable nor an immaterial object. Like the two poles of a magnet the subjective and objective poles of experience, experiencer and experienced, self and other, though epistemologically distinguishable, are existentially inseparable, their identities as subject and object each being dependent, upon their relation to, or difference from, the other (ibid). The self, for Søren Kierkegaard (1813-1855), is always already embedded with others in a socio political matrix. This is why he defines it as a relation of the necessary and the possible. To attempt to extricate oneself from one's socio political situation would simply intensify the dread despair, for one would be surrendering oneself to possibility at the expense of necessity (Nordentoft 1978; Rée and Chamberlain 1998).

For Emmanuel Levinas (1906-1995), moral consciousness resides not in the sense of experiencing values—whatever the current cultural values are—rather, a *moral consciousness* is beyond ontology and value as such and wholly otherwise-than-being. Levinas proffers a specific relationship where the I and the You encounter each other, that is, where the I is given meaning by the You, and it is this very importance of the You where the idea of good emanates there, in the beginning. The You urges the I to be responsible by acting in a way that is meaningful to the human subject. Without the You, the I does not exist. The Self has meaning through the Other's call to responsibility. The Self, bound up within a dialogue of immanence, enclosed in its own interestedness, needs a rupture. The 'who I am' of the I is the connection the I has to the Other through the responsibility to the exteriority of the Other. For Levinas, the I-You relationship is one that wholly transcends the relationship of intentionality. The solitude of Self responses sets up a dysfunctional Self/Other relationship, one that is out of balance and without reciprocity. The Self remains in service of the self/other, obligated to subjectivity goes to the point of substitution for the Other, Passivity and patience become the initial focus upon the Self (Levinas 1997). Levinas emphasises that a responsibility to strangers, to the afflicted and to the wretched prevents the self from shirking responsibility. Thus, the self is confirmed by virtue of the fact that the Other requires the self for its support. Levinas attempts to explain that the inadequacy of the subject to its own phenomenality lies in the existence of others who continually call me into question, reveal to me a life beyond my world of possessions. Levinas' notion of the I-You relationship, as a place for the Good, is situated in a specific context of communicative praxis (Leahy 1994; Davis 2004).

Since modernity has destroyed the self, modernity needs to be the focus. To Zygmunt Bauman (1993, 1995), modernity is the beyond any doubt the less human stage in history, a real dark age of alienation and repression. Post-modernity means recognizing that human reality is messy and ambiguous—and so moral decisions, unlike abstract ethical principles, are ambivalent (1993:32). This is because post-modernity gives us the chance of rediscovering the human moral capacity as it truly is" (p.34), as the fundament on which societies are build and by which they survive, as that which makes ethical negotiations and consensus possible, although without guaranteeing any happy ending. Post-modernity means for Bauman the "re-personalization" of ethics and morality, showing that in human beings moral responsibility was "from the start," somehow rooted in the very way we humans are (p.34); it is not the outcome of a ethical process. Heteronomy is an evil in itself, autonomy conversely something to cherish. The moral self can be self-confident and sure about its inherent morality; that is precisely because the moral self is very well aware of this fact that it is so hard to bear when it does not live up to its own standards of moral responsibility. Likewise, Horkheimer and Adorno (1989) question why and how mankind has sunken into barbarism instead of developing a human society.

Jean-Paul Sartre's (1905-1980) "being" is presented as "doing," a view reiterated by Maurice Merleau-Ponty (1908-1961), who writes that consciousness is in the first place not a matter of "I think that" but of "I can." By distinguishing existence from essence, he claims that for humans "existence precedes essence," or individual identity, which is a consequence, rather than a precondition, of the choice of end or "fundamental project" which defines them. In other words, according to Sartre, it is not "the" subject, nor even "a" subject, that exists independently of and prior to this choice and its accompanying acts. Rather the pre personal being or existence constitutes subjectivity by virtue of what emerges as the / its ability to make choices per se, its particular essence or identity being defined, and redefined, by the choice, and changes, of fundamental project, and the volitional acts concomitant therewith; a view which, notwithstanding its rather abstract formulation, seems to accord with the phenomenological evidence. Subjective identity is thus cast as an insubstantial and impermanent product of the desires and/or attachments which, presumably, occasion any such choice, with the consequence that, in the complete absence of desires or attachments, and their concomitant projects to which they give rise, the illusion of individual identity would dissolve altogether, resulting in escape from samsara or reincarnation. Sartre's (1956[1943]) early existentialism, although in one sense rejecting over socialized views of human nature, appears to succumb, like certain trends within psychoanalysis in a rather different way, to the opposite fallacy and to present an under socialized conception of man: in its view of society or the other as mainly thwarting, objectifying or tempting man to bad faith rather than in some way also nurturing and constituting him as human, this perspective, however insightful in other respects, seems one-sided. For the early Sartre (1936, 1943, 1946), if a prisoner confesses when his interrogator holds a gun to his head and threatens to shoot him unless he complies, he is in bad faith if he claims he had no choice. While his positive or practical freedom ("freedom to" do, be, or have whatever he wants) is radically restricted in such a situation—as it is in the lives of most persons owing to the limitations of poverty, ignorance, disease, social powerlessness and the like—the prisoner's negative or psychological freedom ("freedom from" mechanical determination) remains absolute: he could have chosen to die rather than confess. Although he never abandoned this insistence upon man's psychological (negative) freedom from mechanical determination, the later Sartre (1960) came to recognize the overwhelming power of our psychological conditioning in childhood by family, class, and culture—all of which constitute for us a kind of "predestination" he concluded. Nevertheless, Sartre continued to believe that, to the extent that we remain human, capable of the complex symboling processes entailed in minding and selfing, we retain an "I" in addition to a "me"—a degree of subjective freedom to reflect upon our conditioned selves and in this way purchase some degree of liberating distance from them. Estrangement, the alienation of the "me" from the "I" leads to what Sartre' (1943) describes as "bad faith"—the disavowal of the "I," the existential self—as well as an ignorance to the possible existence of a range of unconscious "me's." As Mcrleau-Ponty (1964) recommends, perception represents sedimented contextual knowledges. So the process by which peoples are differentiated and categorized is a process preceded by concepts of developmental stages. The colonization of the imagination depends on the creation and maintenance of several powerful ideologies which allow, perpetuate and justify the oppression of certain groups over others.

Interestingly, Friedrich Nietzsche (1844-1900), in *Beyond Good and Evil* ([1886] 1966) maintains that there is no necessary connection between thinking and the self, doubting whether the self is the agency behind the activity of thinking. For Nietzsche, the self is always to be comprehended as being situated within particular contexts and, indeed, as the product of human culture, rather than an ontological category which grounds the basis of experience and therefore knowledge.

Kenneth Gergen (1991, 1994) notes that the decline of the individual self has led to the emergence of "multiphrenic" or conflicting multiple selves as a result of the incredible saturation of numerous and various forms of interaction which create simultaneous and multiple selves. The net effect of the intense stimulation and saturation of different interactions contribute to a crisis of the self, to a loss of the perceived sense of an "authentic self."

Instead multiple selves are routinely constructed and readily experienced simultaneously. The self becomes agonal, fragmented, confusing and contradictory, resulting in "multiphrenia," a condition in which no self is privileged over another and the self becomes no self at all but a representation of multiple expressions of self (Gergen 1991, 1994).

Jean-François Lyotard (1984, 1991) also challenges the notion of a self apart from language. Intentions, dispositions and interests are realized in and through language. Michel Foucault conceptualizes the notion of the self in terms of the relations between discourses of power. Discourse constructs subjectivity. Discourse, as "social," is a form of governmentality—a moral and social control on individual actions. Social and political discourses constitute definitions of the (re)actions of others and one's own actions. The meanings inherent in this ubiquitous discourse of regulation, framed in signs and signifiers, are exchanged in interactions and clearly affect self-understanding. For Foucault, we are governed by our own discursive social practices, which are always on display and rendered instrumental to advance their constitutive power. In *The Order of Things*, Foucault (1970) undermines the tendency to think of the self as a self-sufficient and meaning-conferring cogito. The subject is not only a "warped" product but has actually disappeared. For Foucault, the subject is a function of normalizing discourses and not simply a consequence of the socialization of norms and ways of understanding being or power. Normalization regulates all aspects of life. For Baudrillard (1983), there is no experiential reality behind self-identity representations. Representations constitute the self. Since as Baudrillard argues reality is a simulation which generates a belief in reality and experience, there is no reality and no truth. In fact simulation is hyper-real—more real than real. Baudrillard's study on the impact of the system of representation (signs and signifiers as simulations) on the definition of the situation traces the "order of simulacra," the increasing circulation of signs through history. Since the social self is simulated, experiences or self-definitions are all mediated images. The self, therefore, is a technique of representation.

Postmodern works on gendered selves—notably the valuable studies of Judith Butler (1991), Patricia Hill Collins (2000), Jane Flax (1998), Donna Haraway (1991), bell hooks (1984) and Trinh T. Minh-Ha (1992) not only reconsider gender identity but succeed in giving voice to women of color, poor women, lesbian and bisexual women. They expose the dangers in approaching gender collectives as homogeneous entities and urge careful

28

consideration of the complex, often contradictory, nature of the collective existence. In contrast to the social constructionist, postmodern gender theorists challenge the dualistic, oppositional nature by which gender is traditionally framed. Patricia Hill Collins (2000), for example, remarks that elements such as race and social class produce multiple variations of "women" and "men," distinctions that many societies use to build complex hierarchical stratification systems.

Phenomenology of Youth Crime and the Polytextures of Identity

The above overview of rich competing and complementary interpretations of the self facilitates an appreciation of the complex phenomenology of youth as polytextures of identity. The relationship of the self and the social highlighted in the above perspectives are extremely relevant in asking: What is intentional? What makes something intentional? Is the actor/ subject conscious while engaging in certain activities, however defined? If there is consciousness, what then is its content?

Phenomenology critically examines the notion of social order by *challenging* culturally learned beliefs, values and ideas by *encouraging* an analysis of the underlying forms of experience and objects of consciousness such as intentionality, that is, first, the intentional aspects of consciousness, the "noesis" (for example, "I commit crime") and the building up or constitution of consciousness; second, the objective component of consciousness, the "noema" (for example, that which crimes I commit). Specifically, phenomenology asks us not to take the notions we have learned for granted, but to question them instead, to question our way of looking at the world in order to study how youths, for example, define their social situations. Once learned cultural notions are suspended or "bracketed," a more correct representation of how the phenomenon is constituted emerges. This process of constitution examines, for example, how "facts" are interpreted as events and analysed as phenomena. This social investigation diverts attention away from more deterministic theories towards intentional action. The meaningful constituting activities of subjects under study ground knowledge by correctly representing the phenomenon under study and by emphasizing the subjective experiences and perceptions of relevant social actors. Understandably then, in relation to youth crime, phenomenology rejects perspectives that attribute the application of a deviant designation to external forces impinging upon the individual. It is more concerned with *how* individuals construct meanings of things *for* themselves, in their own respective consciences, that is, how things seem to youths. But, the process by which a social world is available to us or constructed for us is always a problematic object of inquiry. Consequently, we suspend belief in the existence of that world as an objective social reality and question our everyday worlds (Schutz 1964). Phenomenologists focus on the actor's account of an event—an actor's personal interpretation of a situation as it is "announced" to others in interaction. Given the subjectiveness of this process, previously taken-for-granted notions of crime can be interrogated. That is, traditional conceptions of crime acquired through socialization can be suspended as individuals begin to dispute the normatively imposed criminal labels attached to certain actions or behaviours. As an example, consider the occurrence of "bullying" among youths which is traditionally characterized as a "deviant" act. However when upper class, "respectable" individuals partake in this activity, the action can take on a different, and more positive connotation such as a form of competitive business practice or an entrepreneurial code. The intricate process by which crime is defined is directly related to the ways in which behaviour and experiences are constructed by social actors.

Matza (1969), for example, maintains that only the deviants themselves can provide a true account of the nature of deviant phenomena and how they come into being. Towards this end, the major theme in his work is "naturalism": the constant attempt to remain true to the phenomenon one is studying. In his book, *Becoming Deviant*, Matza (1969) explains how beliefs and actions are related in the mind of social actors via the process of constructing meaning. He alludes to the "naturalistic perspective," a methodology that provides an accurate and truthful presentation of phenomena in their own right rather than a description or explanation in order to correct, reform or eradicate them (correctional perspective).

Garfinkel's (1967) insightful ethnomethodology examines the common-sense knowledge that emerges in the everyday interpretation of social reality. To fully appreciate everyday commonsense interpretations that govern social realities, that is, rules that make everyday life meaningful (p.6), he treats as fundamentally problematic that which was taken for granted. A study of the methods people use to accomplish a reasonable account of what is happening in social interaction extends the phenomenological perspective to the study of everyday social interaction and provides a structure for the interaction itself. Again, ethnomethodology inquires into the everyday activities, that is, the construction of meanings that actors use and account for their activities by asking, how does the constituted world present itself as if it were external or independent? How do we go about seeing and describing a situation that is presented for many as an objective fact? According to Garfinkel (1967:vii), an orderly and artful way of making sense of the objective reality of social facts as ongoing daily accomplishments of concerted activities requires a methodical scrutiny of how social actors invoke taken for granted rules in order to interpret situations and build procedures to accomplish events. For Garfinkel (1967:76), the investigation of the rational properties of indexical expression, the context and construction of meanings, seeks to explain the social constitution of knowledge. Given that social situations are not independent of lived experiences, ethnomethodology is an organizational study of a members' knowledge of their ordinary affairs, of their own organized enterprises (Garfinkel 1967). The concepts of indexicality, reflexivity and interaction are especially significant in understanding how the world is experienced inter-subjectively, as a world common to all. These concepts are integral to the interpretive process, a process of constructing the taken-for-granted (common sense) by which outsiders (media, police, schooling, work, family, etc) and youth themselves understand other youths to be criminal.

Indexicality

The world is experienced inter-subjectively, as a world common to all. Language and other gestures, for example, are "indexical"—they contain taken for granted elements. Meanings of situations are embedded within larger contexts of biographies (the experiences and expectations we bring to the situation) and the contingent elements of the situation. The term *indexicality* refers to the fact that all human interpretive work is bound to the *context* in which it occurs. The "reality" of youth crime will be conceived very differently, depending on whether it is viewed by suspicious police officer on a routine patrol or by partying teenagers in a speeding vehicle. For example, the importance of indexicality to youth crime could describes how political pressure or moral stereotypes compel governments to "act tough" on youth and how much is actually related to the practical demands of respective institutions of the criminal justice system. Such contextual or indexical demands significantly influence the shape of societal reaction (Pfohl 1985).

Refexivity

Reflexivity is the notion that every act is at once both in the setting and simultaneously creates the setting refers to the social activities whereby members create and maintain the very situations in which they act (Churchill 1971:185). Within the constitutive process or the ongoing (re)construction of meaning neither the contents (substance) nor the contexts (methods) are independent of each other. The process of constitution is reflexivity, the examination of which enables the ethnomethodologist to realize the lived experiences and the organization of meanings for the actors. This inquiry recognizes individual consciousness only as an essential plane of social reality. What is understood is never fixed and meanings are always fragile in interactions. Typically, once defined, a situation or person "becomes" the understanding, the "thing" that has been defined. And the "objective reality" of that person or situation becomes an indexical feature of the next interaction and interpretive process. This paradoxical characteristic of human existence whereby objects only exist in relation to the interpretive meaning they have for the people who behold them. In other words, for all practical purposes, one is never independent of the way in which the I constructs and expresses an understanding of the you. There is neither pure objectivity nor pure subjectivity. Everything is in relation to everything else. By the principle of indexicality one understands one's own interpretations of you to be bound by the social and material context in which they are related. Thus, one's grasp of you is never purely subjective. Yet, since the I must make an interpretive use of the context to arrive at a certain knowledge of you, it is also impossible for knowledge to purely objective (Pfohl 1985: 294).

Retrospective justifications for decisions which that have already been made, looking backward in producing a quasi-legal rereading of the available evidence after having already decided upon a person's guilt or innocence is problematically distorted. Once we arrive at a particular "account" (explanation) of a situation or person (decision-making based on typifications and commonsense categories indexically tied to the context of the situation), we reflexively reconstruct our understanding of the process so that our *decision or definition* appears commonsensical, "real" and normal. The rules that people use in organizing information to construct social reality are based on consistency (the logic of organizing past information and future assessments consistently with these categories) and logics of economy (conveniently locking in categories in the interest of utility and convenience). Retrospective accounts highlight biased beliefs and practices that serve accounting purposes. For outsiders and youths themselves, indexicality and reflexivity are structures, interpretive processes through which youth identity and criminality are produced and "understood" as "objective" and as taken for granted.

Interpretation and Interaction

Indexicality requires a documentary method of analysis for the actors and the analysts. This necessitates the treatment of actual appearances as "documents of" presupposed underlying patterns. Individual documentaries are interpreted on the basis of what is known about the underlying pattern. Indexicality is a process through which immediately given information (documents); appearance, police reports, past records, and typifications are used to infer meaning and motive in the behavior of others. Appearances are treated as documents, as expressions of deep or underlying patterns or structures (Pfohl 1985:295-296). Information, presented informally in interaction and information from "official record" are analyzed to construct a reasonable account of the individual.

Ethnomethodology concentrates on face-to-face *interactions*. Social interactions are analysed in terms of processes of sociation. An explanation of rules and background expectations which authorities use in negotiating appropriate sanctions are investigated as constructions of organizations and as procedures that regulate within the contexts of definitions in order to ascertain how the institutions and actors determine delinquency. The meanings available to the both the actor and the researcher, the encounters, reports etc. are researched to understand the creation of official documents on delinquency. How researchers decide what they know and how the studied actors do their tasks are equally significant. For example, how excuses and justifications are selectively presented, evaluated, negotiated are important.

Excuses are verbalizations which mitigate responsibility for an action. As Lyman and Scott (1970:112-114) observe, excuses are accounts in which one admits, using socially approved vocabularies, the act in question is bad, wrong, or inappropriate, but denies full responsibility. On the other hand, justifications are verbalizations, which emphasize the positive consequences of an act, particularly under certain situations, while recognizing its negative consequences in principle. These accounts become part of the indexical reality of the situation and reflexively shape the definition we apply to make sense of other people and their behavior. Accounts, however distorted, partial and biased, are assigned an actuality (Holzner 1968) or objective facticity within one's own interpretive framework. These constructions are shaped by efficiency and accountability. Efficiency requires a stable and simple categorical system in terms of which the complex world can be organized and described.

To ignore what youth consider to be crucial factors invites facile or more aptly lazy interpretations that often border on crude reductionism. Thus, what they say, imagine, or believe is an integral part of their real life experiences Youths, for example, attribute their criminality to deterministic causal factors, such as faulty personal relationships or difficulties at school which allegedly propel them to move outside their formerly familial environments. Family violence and/or school failures often become badges that some youths flash in trying to demonstrate that they have paid their dues and rightfully belong on the street. Biographies are easily manipulated (Willis 1977). Thus, favourable impressions of the present can be constructed by advancing unfavourable accounts of the past. Background factors alone contribute little to our understanding of how youths come to perceive themselves. But, their concern with these factors, as causes of this dislocation, is relevant to any understanding of their general social orientation. Family and school involvements in particular are presented as contextual experiences from which an initial assessment of career options and the shaping of self emerge (Visano 1987). Not only will they present themselves as victims of misunderstanding, neglect, and/or violence, they also engage in active, ongoing appraisals of their difficult circumstances.

Just as with accounts in which one admits, using socially approved vocabularies, that the act in question is not bad, wrong, or inappropriate, and admits responsibility, youths develop a distinct set of justifications for violating conventional norms. Neutralization is a social psychological perspective used to justify their deviance according to more morally and socially acceptable standards (conditions, contexts or qualifications). When individuals deny responsibility, they claim that they cannot be held liable or faulted for unlawful acts. The perpetrator would argue that these acts did not occur through his or her fault. Individuals deny personal responsibility for their actions. They maintain that the crime was an accident or equally assert that it was caused by factors well beyond their control such as negligent parents, broken homes, poverty, minority status or failure in the economy. With ***denial of injury***, individuals claim that their actions do not really harm anyone. Similarly, car thieves may justify their offences by saying they were only borrowing the car temporarily, as in the cases of carjacking. Gang fights are also presented as private quarrels that do not really concern others. Again, these and other crimes are justified as socially useful rather than injurious. Stealing from the wealthy is not injurious given that they can afford some loss. The ***denial of a victim*** involves the process of ignoring the rights of an absent or unknown victim. Here "invisibility" precludes respect or sympathy for the target. One might further rationalize one's actions by arguing that the victim was "offensive," that is, in some way he or she "had it coming"—as often happens with typical homophobic and anti lesbian bashing, misogyny, racism, etc. There are no victims, some would argue, because their prey is viewed as offensive. That is, victims are transformed as offenders; people who are "out of place" and deserve to be punished. Those who use the technique of ***condemnation of the condemners*** view the world as corrupt and hypocritical. Given this cynical logic, it is ironic, if not inappropriate for authorities to claim a right to condemn deviance. Blame is shifted to others whose motives are condemned or classified as equally derisive. Accordingly, authority figures are viewed as deviants in disguise and ought to be condemned for their corrupt, brutal or self-serving behaviour. An ***appeal to higher loyalties*** typically describes situations where offenders are caught in a dilemma between competing loyalties. They are required to make choices, for instance, between their respective reference groups or societal norms. Here, one weighs the demands of society and its laws against the needs of smaller groups. When one uses this technique, the needs of the peer group (loyalty and respect) are usually given precedence over the rules of society.

In summary, ethnomethodology examines precisely the relationship between beliefs and action. The social world is merely an ongoing practical achievement of its members but not always in circumstances of their own choosing. Conceptually, "totalities" in the world and the "completeness" of individuals are questioned especially since experience and perceptions are explicable in terms of accounts that must be reducible to the actor's meanings and intentions—practically constituted, and intentionally created phenomena.

Conclusions: The Imposed Implications of Deference and Difference

Clearly, from aggressive sexual consumerism, the economic dependence of youth, and the oppressive ideology of the family to the eroticization of violence (to name only a few contexts), youth as a group constitute a minority class. That is, in our society the concept of a youth is a social construction of contempt whereby the actual experiences and language of youth seldom constitute the central agenda. Youth is an ideology of development, physical, mental and emotional—an ideology of inferiority that denies the meaningful participation of the designated "other." It is important to emphasize that "youth" is a concept created to further justify domination, fear and ignorance. This pathology is deeply embedded and protected by the practices of the powerful other. This dominant culture is replete with illusions which further enhance the alienation of youth.

As will be discussed, youth is refashioned within a culture that is encouraged to express itself through material consumption as a concretized form of existence. Youths are expected to be acquisitive and not inquisitive, to celebrate possessive individualism and an insatiable appetite for material gains. The "social" in youth is constituted in the context of cultural controls. The relationship between youth and culture is marked not only by the corrosive politics of difference but more significantly by a pathological history of dependency. Despite the rich literature on youth, only recently has the discussion shifted to address the connections between youth, culture and crime by exploring the limits of law in liberal democratic societies. Typically, the concept of youth has been covered by many Western scholars from relatively similar vantage points that rehearse and quibble about the relative banal benefits of youth in familiar, homogenized and comfortable contexts. Accordingly, mainstream or normative approaches to youth focus on what are merely the reductivist consequences of the development of particularized youth identities (criminal) while woefully failing to confront the fundamental character of the Canadian culture—inequality. This study, however, informed by critical theory, a perspective that seeks to ameliorate social conditions rather than reproduce existing structures by directing attention to various predatory mediations that inform the governance of youth. Critical theory invites interdisciplinary orientations that challenge dominant ideologies and encourage a commitment to social justice. In theorizing about this nexus, this study highlights the contexts and consequences of the culture of (neo) liberalism that reproduce an insidious hegemony of

36

privilege. First, this analysis sketches a method for constructing an appreciation of youth that enables an honest confrontation with one's own ethnocentric biases and the development of an ethical critique of wider cultural contradictions. By moving beyond standard fetishes and by articulating the boundaries of state practices within the legal framework of youth crime, one can more fully understand how youths are leveraged / brokered and how both the ideology and the behaviour of the law institutionalize a calculated compliance if not a consuming complacency. An exploration of the implications and applications of liberal orthodox models that promote convenient and common sense assumptions about "adult" way of life as a moral imperative suggests that youth, an integral symbol of care and control is a diversion that satisfies the increasing neo liberal appropriation of difference. This study highlights conceptually the cultural bases of coercion directed at youths. In addition to the centrality of antagonistic relations, there are discrepancies between the familiar images about youths and the alien realities of youth. Within the phenomenology of youth the concept of *"distance"* provides a compelling coherence. Within this relational perspective of "law and society," delinquency is not solely confined to individual or institutional constructions but rather delinquency is a consequence of complex configurations within the political economy and culture. In short, delinquency (the text) constitutes and is constituted by relations of power (subtext) that are mediated by cultural forms of the media (intertexts). Unlike the subtext of privilege, there is no integrated text of delinquency, only fragmented narratives that distance youth. For instance, the normative notion of delinquency is a text constituted according to numbing numbers, bureaucratic babble and legal traditions.

Traditionally, criminological canons depict delinquency as a text located within the corpus of the juvenile laws, practices and policies that respond to trouble according to a dubious and decontextualized ethos of "care." The problems of deference and difference are the central issues confronting contemporary debates on youth identity. Socialized individuals are only sustained through a group identity that understands the dominant distancing ideological and cultural structures. These identities are constructed, within and upon the interplay of normative strategies which govern subjective experience. It is necessary to understand the conditions that produce conscious experience, viewed as essential to communityhood. Both the spatial and temporal structures of experience determine the intrinsic character of youth narratives, personal and collective. Moving beyond

37

the convenient and accessible notions of content in youth performance and youth products, this study grapples with (de)formation of meanings (production, interpretation and transformation) in space and time. That is, in addition to content, the morphology of youth identity communicates key symbolic messages. Fundamental to contemporary critical studies on youth is the recognition that the formation of the meaningful value of identity cannot be separated from the consequences of social contexts and conditions.

Everyday practices are replete with significant ceremonies, signs, symbols, cues and clues that pattern gestures, rituals, or performances that in turn stage degrees of cultural affiliations. Social membership has become "naturalized" such that responding to delinquency is commonsensical. For Lemke (1988:158), the structure of a text (youth) is created by structured social practices. Processes of interactions shape and are shaped by the nature of structures wherein meanings constitute and are constitutive. Language, as a cultural code, relates to a world of meanings. All knowledge and language are culturally coded. Thus, knowledge or even a consciousness about delinquency is a social product. It is precisely here in the realm of knowledge that ideologies are contested, resisted or accepted. Knowledge is coded within a language that obfuscates as well as clarifies. Ideology refers to a complex of linguistic meaning making processes which are observable and describable in instances of discourse. Clearly, ideology is constructed through discourse and it is in discourse that every determination of the subject depends, including thought, affect, enjoyment, meaning and identity. As noted earlier, the subject is determined by language (Lacan 1977: 298-300); the subject disappears in his or her discourse and becomes embodied in the spoken word. To further reproduce meanings certain, "master signifiers" that represent the subject for another signifier are implicated (p.316). Thus, a signified is empty until given form by the use of a signifier. This signifier is the "other," the element that 'lacks', the part that was not fully expressed or fully known. For de Saussure (1986:100), the link between signal and signification is arbitrary. Since we are treating a sign as the combination in which a signal is associated with signification, we can express this more simply as: the linguistic sign is arbitrary. Clearly, the concept of youth exists as a discoursal practice that is socially situated. That is, an identity is simultaneously a product and a process linked to situationally relevant contextual codes, namely, culture. For instance, for centuries youths were made to feel "lacking" and could only be signified through another signifier—the adult. Youths were always construed to be the property that existed at the pleasure of adults.

Without addressing the obvious strengths or weaknesses of recent postmodernist formulations and without delineating their relative compatibility with the above perspectives, suffice it to note that there are a number of fruitful conceptual exercises of postmodernist contributions in reference to ideology and culture. Interestingly, the logic of postmodernist perspectives suggest that youth as the subject is fractured and complexly articulated within a plurality of discourses that are never stable, static nor fixed. The foundationalism of law and order are undermined through practices of deconstruction and reflexivity. Indeed, there is an incredulity towards the metanarratives (Lyotard 1984) especially when the unity of knowledge is rejected in favour of diversity and an overlap of meanings (Manning 1991). The dissolution of grand narratives has sparked interest in more context-based, pragmatic, problem solving reform-minded political efforts. In the metanarrative of traditional law, there is a discursive production of the essential subject. The legal subject is constructed within structural inequalities. With the post modern interpretation, however, there is no bedrock of ultimate truths or deep structures. But neither is postmodernism simply an empty frame, "a free-for-all" where everything goes in defiance of a normative order. Coupled with the above cultural insights, an interrogation of the text (delinquency) allows us to analyze the prevailing essentialist ideologies of privilege-power, the mutually constructing and constraining capacity of structure, and the multiplicity of subject-positions offered by enablement and resistance (subtexts). As Lyotard (1984:15) describes:

> A self does not amount to much, but no self is an island; each exists in the fabric of relations that is now more complex and mobile than ever before. Young or old, man or woman, rich or poor, a person is always located at "nodal points" or specific communication circuits, however tiny these may be. Or better: one is always located at a post through which various kinds of messages pass. No one, not even the least privileged among us, is ever entirely powerless over the messages that traverse and position him [sic] in relation to the sender, addressee, or referent.

In brief, this study encourages an interrogation of the character, foundation and enclosures of western modernity. By interrogating these structures one uncovers how modernity and dominant forms institutionally marginalize those designated as "the other"; that is, how delinquency is normalized. In this regard, identities are habitually constructed by setting up differences and specifying distance. Deconstructionism reads the margins (youths) in the centre (law); decentring and de-essentializing the subject by pointing out that the subject (youth) is constructed in contradictions. Law superimposes the subject as de-essentialized while the media entertains these different forms of legal inferiorization. We encounter youths by transporting and internalizing fears of some onto others. In the popular media productions "for" children there are such crass contrasts of "life on the street" for disadvantaged youths and the reality of community comforts on the fictive "Sesame Street"; or similarly the "violence in the 'hood'" contrasted with the safety of "Mr Rogers' Neighbourhood." This study positions the emergent, processual, tentative, relative and agentic set of selves within the contexts of imposed forms of identity—ideology and institutions. In summary, the concept of youth is inseparable from the study of identity, individual and collective. Accordingly, identities are always in the ongoing process of becoming; transforming, open to re-positioning and forever relational. That is, how we see each other and ourselves is fixed and yet in flux.

The study of culture seeks to introduce us to the world of youth identity, especially the domains of their multiple subjectivities that are seldom mined. Moreover, the relationships of *youth identity and knowledge production* are central to understanding what they know and what we know about culture, youth and crime. The concept of crime in turn is an expression of cultural authority that reproduces both domination and resistance. This study, therefore seeks to make sense of the "saturated self" (Gergen 1991 1994) in light of what Giddens (1991:198) refers to as the creation and the continual reordering of a self-identity against the backdrop of shifting experiences of day-to-day life and the fragmenting tendencies of modern institutions.

Chapter 2

Youth and Criminal Cultures

The Corrosive Character of Culture

In general, the dominant culture embedded in prevailing ideologies and articulated in major institutions, is both a contemporary and an historical project constituted in conflict. Symbolically, the structure of culture is a partisan expression of powerful societal interests that produces and reproduces power relations. Clearly, as will be argued, culture is a set of ideological forces that are reflective and derivative of socio-economic structures and expressed in forms of consciousness. This constellation of shared or more appropriately imposed meanings, moral expectations and understanding is manifested in symbolic communication—language, customs, myths, signs as well as material artefacts, is the channel through which social relations are constituted and conducted. More significantly, culture consists of ideas that are selectively communicated, believed and legitimated quite often as a well established and living knowledge. This "collective" or "common" conscience articulates a moral binding force that tends to ignore and even resist differential levels of commitment and communication to multi-cultures, subcultures and counter cultures. Stated differently, the dominant culture is the fabric that clothes and protects the body of privilege especially by disguising and dehistoricizing selectively exclusionary practices based on age, gender, sexual orientation, religion,

41

race, class, mental, emotional and physical challenges. As Homi Bhabha (1992:235) clarifies:

> The dangers inherent in the concept of a contemporaneous "common" culture are not limited to politically conservative discourses. There is a pervasive, even persuasive presence of such a paradigm in the popular rhetoric of multiculturalism...lip service is paid to the representation of the marginalized. A traditional rhetoric of cultural authenticity is produced on behalf of the "common culture" from the very mouths of the minorities.

In addition, Bhabha (1992) adds that this common culture, even though it promises "individual" emancipation, is the ideological purveyor of this impersonal order of things (p.242). Marx and Engels (Marx 1930) reveal how this system of ideas as historical products is both illusory and socially regulating. To elucidate, one's mental labour, or the production of ideas, is structured by one's material conditions, that is:

> The ideas of the ruling class are, in every age, the ruling ideas: that is, the class which is the dominant material force in society is at the same time its dominant intellectual force. The class which has the means of material production at its disposal has control at the same time over the means of mental production, so that in consequence the ideas of those who lack the means of mental production are, in general, subject to it. The dominant ideas are nothing more than the ideal expression of the dominant material relationships, the dominant material relationships grasped as ideas, and thus of the relationships which make one class the ruling one; they are consequently the ideas of its dominance. (Marx and Engels 1962: 93)

As this quotation clearly argues, the ruling class is extremely influential in the production of ideas since it has a "monopoly" over the means of both material and mental production and will "regulate" the production and distribution of ideas in a way that is consistent with privileging its own interests especially in the field of capital accumulation. Morality, law, religion, art, metaphysics and corresponding forms of consciousness may project a semblance of independence even though they are all manifestations of common ideas.

Ideology, a *representation* of a configuration of particular interpretations of relations and often presented as a set of unstated beliefs is expressed symbolically in metaphors, myths, and images. The latter are constructed to mirror concrete reality, from individual reflexivities to social, economic and political collectivities. For Althusser (1971:66), ideology anchored in historical existence is a ubiquitous set of cultural practices that form the medium through a society experiences the world. Obviously, ideology does not represent the real world per se, but rather operates at the imaginary and symbolic *presentation of relationships of individuals to their real conditions* of existence, representations *of* relations *to* relations of production, *representations of relations* to perceptions.

These "systems of representations" are not just *vague and specifically noncommittal*; they are distorted ideas, that is, *presentations of misrepresentation*, illusionary representations of the relations. Ideologies recast various ways by concealing their unacceptable aspects of reality and glorifying other elements. These discrepancies between what is represented for the benefit of a few to the disadvantage of the many serve to condition a consciousness of deference that is founded in distortions. Moreover, this consciousness of misunderstanding discourages any transcendental thought and refuses to recognize itself as a socially and historically constituted subject. This collective consciousness masquerades itself as reasoned thought, suppresses social conflicts and relinquishes authority to the imaginary. Herein, action and words mask social contradictions on behalf of dominant classes or groups that parade themselves in misleading but binding ideals that further classify and integrate requisite rules and roles. This instrumentality facilitates social cohesion and seldom needs to rely on external concatenations of control. Following Gramsci and Foucault, one could argue that the dominant ideology cultivates helplessness by acting more locally through the consenting and docile individual. Essentially, ideology as the social control of common-sense contributes to the construction of homogenized selves which further inscribe regulation. Note how Gramsci's "consent" complements Foucault's (1979) "docile body" that is "a body that may be subjected, used, transformed and improved" (Foucault 1979:136) fabricated by institutions of power (p.194). Ideology, with its rhetoric, language and symbols, creates stable social and cultural environments within which beliefs are propagated in the service of nurturing a natural cultural climate conducive to the interests of power relations. This propagation invites greater investments in the status quo. Ideology is constituted through processes *of interpellation, reification and alienation, common sense and naturalized beliefs*, which invert the relations between an individual and the social whole.

Ideology works largely on the "social" unconsciousness, that is, the common sense of all individuals. Ideologies enlist individuals as subjects in a specific belief system through the mechanism of *interpellation*, a process whereby subjects are constituted as the effects of pre-given structures. Interpellation is the spontaneous identification, naming and calling upon individuals (recognizing and singling them out) as symbolically constructed social categories (for example, as legal subjects). In other words, a subject self identifies his or her respective place within a particular discourse. Althusser (1971:127) states: "the peculiarity of ideology is that it is endowed with a structure and a functioning such as to make it a non-historical reality, an omni-historical reality, in the sense in which that structure and functioning are immutable, present in the same form throughout what we can call history" (p.128). Lacan's (1968) subject is subject only from being subjected to the field of the Other. Ideology is not the reality in which we exist but becomes our imaginary explanation of our social conditions. Ideology's materiality exists in represented institutional practices that *constitute individuals as "subjects."* Subjects recognise themselves as subjects who reproduce their self-identities.

Interestingly, ideology transforms the self into a subject by having individuals adopt versions of the truth for themselves. This sophisticated means of domination succeeds in creating processes of self imposed subordination. As Habermas (1974) indicates, the meanings and symbols of the dominant ideology prevent critical thinking by penetrating deeply social processes, language and individual consciousness. On the one hand, the actor learns to repress, deprive and deny self-autonomy by projecting a billiard-ball or assembly line conception of self which in turn advances the vulnerability and credulity of the individual. For Karl Mannheim (1936), the word "ideology" insinuates that in certain situations the collective unconscious of certain groups obscures the real condition of society both to itself and to others thereby unable to see how certain facts which would undermine their sense of domination. On the other hand, ideology supports an all embracing rational autonomy. Georg Lukács (1971) exposes *reification* as the phenomenon where relations between people take on the character of a thing and acquires a "phantom objectivity," which conceals fundamental relations of inequality. This all-embracing process is grounded in principles of modernity such as mechanization, calculation and rational-isation. Modernization "technicises" society. Lukács deems reification to be the *historically generated incapacity of consciousness* to see the totality of social life. Instead, the mind gets lost in the realm of the concrete, the particular, and the reified. The world does not present itself as a whole to the damaged consciousness, nor as the product of human activities. The world reveals itself only in the form of isolated, quantitative and reducible commodities that are in fact detrimental to the individual. In *A Contribution to the Critique of Political Economy and Capital*, Marx (1969a:72) portrays the basic phenomenon of reification as follows:

> A commodity is therefore a mysterious thing, simply because in it the social character of men's labour appears to them as an objective character stamped upon the product of that labour; because the relation of the producers to the sum total of their own labour is presented to them as a social relation existing not between themselves, but between the products of their labour. This is the reason the products of labour become commodities, social things whose qualities are at the same time perceptible and imperceptible by the senses...It is only a definite social relation between men that assumes, in their eyes, the fantastic form of a relation between things.

Marx's reification is exemplified in the phenomenon of commodity fetishism.

The subliminal seduction manipulated by the media and the youth criminal justice system cultivate the dominant ideology, mould mindless ways of understanding, and homogenize the everyday life experiences of youths. These values function ideologically, as Marcuse (1955:32-34) elaborates, surplus repression imposes discipline from the inside. As mentioned earlier, the dominant ideology monopolizes the means of mental production to such an extent that the objective dimension of self, the "me," consists of mass-mediated images, and the "I" arises through the process of meaning deconstruction and reconstruction, that is, signifying practices (Kristeva 1982, 1991). The dominant discourse in the popular culture, consistent with official conceptions of youths redefines crime as a productive entity occupying a space between dominant discourses.

Reification is a particular and especially revealing case of *alienation*, affecting the way people think of the world in a society based on the production and circulation of commodities. Marx uncovers and ponders first the reality of alienation in his Economic-Philosophical Manuscripts and only after that formulates the concept of commodity fetishism (Tihanov 1995, 2000). For Lukács, reification and fetishism are immediate realities from which alienation emerges. Reification is a real social process of estrangement in a world in which social relations take on the mystifying form of "the violence of things." Simmel (1950) encapsulates the problematic of alienation in his concept the "tragedy of culture," that is, the "tragic necessity" for cultural forms to be strengthened by way of objectification and, eventually, rigid solidification. Objectification is at the same time a reflection of alienation. Simmel's "tragedy" is the ideological reproduction of objectification, the denial of freedom and personal enlightenment. Material alienation of real conditions corresponds to mental representations which distance (alienate) them from real conditions. As Carlsnaes (1981:43) explicates, an alienative structure results in both the objectification of the products of human labour and the reification of consciousness.

Ideology is an interpretive scheme for making sense of phenomena. But, this dominant discourse must be expressed in the lived experiences of subjects in order to establish consent through common sense understandings. Antonio Gramsci (1891-1937) develops an extremely perceptive awareness of ideology as a constitutive dimension of structure and agency. Humans enjoy the capacity to will, "potentiate" and develop themselves. This historical driving force incorporates both subjective and material elements. How does ideology, for instance, interpellate individuals as subjects? In the discussions to follow, we analyze internalised discipline—various panoptic sites of youth surveillance and control that are established to serve state and economic bloc interests. But, the social organization of self-imposed dependency relations are experienced, objectified and resisted in a manner that structures agency. The Gramscian concept of hegemony is central to an analysis of identity, cultural practices, and responses to domination, as people live out the subject positions available to them. *Hegemony* is the viewpoint of the dominant classes that incorporates subordinate groups who come to rationally negotiate advantages and ultimately reflect ruling class perspectives. But, a dominant discourse must be expressed in the lived experiences of subjects in order to establish *consent through common sense* understandings. Controlled groups have difficulties in trying to locate the source of their unease, let alone remedy it. Consent for Gramsci, involves a complex mental state, a "contradictory consciousness," mixing approbation and apathy, resistance and resignation (Jackson 1985:590). Again, this prevailing consciousness is internalized and becomes part of a "common sense." Gramsci utilizes the concept of hegemony to explain the manner in which institutions of the state occupy a powerful position within society—ideological domination. This is fundamental given the need of the capitalist state to "win consent." Hegemony influences people's perceptions precisely because it is a leadership based on the consent of the ruled, consent secured by the diffusion and popularization of ruling class views. Consent of the ruled to their ongoing exploitation flows from prevailing hegemonic practices in all institutions of the state and civil society. This permeation of an entire system of values, attitudes, morality, or beliefs supports controlling class interests. This dominant value system and its integrative effects penetrate everyday practices—all aspects of the social order. That is, hegemony, achieved through (neo) liberal institutions of civil society, is the predominance of one class over other classes through consent rather than force. This consent is manifested through a generic loyalty to ruling ideas by virtue of their position in society, a position that entails the upholding of prevailing traditions and mores of the period. Ruling ideas (governmentalities) are developed through levels of homogeneity, self-consciousness and organizations based on economic, ethical, social, philosophic and political interests. For Gramsci, hegemony cannot be purely ideological, since it must have as its foundation the domination of a particular social bloc in economic activity (Hall 1988:54). Hegemony not only fulfils a role that brute coercion could never hope to perform but also justifies deprivation and encourages passivity. Although hegemony is secured for example in law in everyday events, Gramsci (1988: 211-212) advises, however:

> though hegemony is ethico-political, it must also be economic, must necessarily be based on the decisive function exercised by the leading group in the decisive nucleus of economic activity.

Hegemony is always constructed, renewed and re-enacted through a complex series or process of struggle (Hall 1988:54). General and dominant views become acceptable, reproduce themselves and become hegemonic. Not only do views become accepted but are fiercely defended as part of one's common sense, as part of one's autonomy. Consequently, the coercive aspects of hegemonies remain hidden. Stated differently, hegemony means moral and philosophical leadership, attained through the active consent of major groups in society (Bocock 1986:11). Mouffe (1988:103), in scrutinizing the Gramscian "hegemonic principle," as the articulation of demands coming from different groups, explores the two ways in which demands can be articulated. One is hegemony by neutralization: a process in which demands are considered to resolve antagonisms without transforming society. Second, there is "expansive hegemony," a process that links demands with other struggles to establish a chain of equivalence while respecting the autonomy and specificity of the demands of different groups.

Hegemony is an order in which certain ways of life and thought are dominant, an order in which one concept of reality is diffused throughout the society in all institutional and private manifestations, governing all tastes, morality, customs, religion, political principles and all social relations (Merrington 1968:21). Ideologies are used as filters through which people are encouraged to make sense of everyday routines. On the other hand, ideologies are governmentalities of discipline that give meanings to the normative content of law.

Common sense, as Hall (1988:55) expounds, is itself a structure of popular ideology, a spontaneous conception of the world; thoughts sedimented into everyday reasoning. Ideology becomes part of a general "knowledge." The dominant sectors not only transmit that which will legitimize their interests, but also deprive the dominated sectors of access to other knowledges. What passes as the dissemination of information is sufficient to satisfy only elementary levels of popular curiosity which ensures that resistance remains limited. The ideological hegemony of the ruling classes is received by the masses as common sense, which blinds them to their own experiences (Counihan 1986). Oddly, belief becomes intellectualized. As it affects social behaviour ideology functions cognitively as a mode of self-interpretation. Interestingly, ideology overwhelms in its persuasion rather than in its prescriptions. This complex normative belief system reflects instrumental, symbolic and constitutive elements of the relations between consciousness and state power.

To repeat, the meanings and symbols of the dominant ideology prevent critical thinking by penetrating social processes, language and individual consciousness (Habermas 1974). This means we must inevitably view the consciousness of those who have been persuaded by this ideological world view as a "false consciousness," insofar as they accept this world view as a *"natural" or "inevitable"* way of seeing and understanding things, and therefore not as an "ideology" at all. The appropriation of interpretations and the promotion of "one's own opinion" are pervasive practices that sustain and legitimate current power differentials. Power legitimates itself by promoting beliefs and values congenial to the self and the dominant order; by naturalizing and universalizing such beliefs to render them self-evident and apparently inevitable; by denigrating ideas that might challenge it; and, by excluding rival forms of thought. Hegemony appears to be spontaneous—*natural*, but it is a historical result of the privilege by virtue of its position and function in the world of production. This principle of "naturalness" transforms history into a natural state that depoliticizes and dehistoricizes socially constructed reality. Universalizing and *naturalizing* processes serve to render as inevitable and self-evident those beliefs that are and have been injurious to class, gender, race, to name a few. This logic becomes more than a convenience or distortion; paradoxically these forms of thought provide certitude (clarity and consistency) thereby eventually diminishing the need for thinking, let alone critical thinking. Ideas are taken for granted, experienced as natural facts and inevitable reality. They become part of a common sense that defines the self and its relationships with others. Moreover, it therefore becomes human nature to enjoy values, however ideologically contrived. Ironically, egoism, materialism, and inequality are natural and common sense hallmarks of a civilized society that respects rights, freedom and democracy.

Text-Narrative Relations

Avoiding the reductivist tendencies inherent in the dominant culture, we argue that the category of youth cultures are connected to race, gender, homophobia and class inequalities that should be analyzed in terms of narrational trends that reproduce oppression. Culturally, a text refers to the arrangement of constituent parts which include *inter alia*, exact or original expressions of a speaker or author, the forms, versions or editions in which a written work exists whereas the narrative is the larger account, story, or recital within which texts are situated. The cultural narrative transcends situated texts. The narrative is a shrine for the maintaining the transcending values of certain canonicities. Various forms of cultural stretch, continuous and episodic, trigger passivity; the connective tissues of narrative of ideology allow the control fibres considerable elasticity or range of motion. Wiseman (1989:88) adds, "challenging the modern text (youth delinquency) gives consciousness, new meanings and abolishes exclusions" (p.133). Unlike the narrative, texts offer a panoply of discourses and competing values. The "text" subject is segmented and articulated within a variety of discourses that succeed in abstracting, mystifying and decontextualizing the narrative. Within the marketplace of rhetoric, jargon slogans and clichés, the text has become a negotiable commodity the value of which is conveniently determined by the overt or covert functions it performs vis à vis the narrative. The text, as a dialogic, provides more than ideological legitimacy; rather as currently manipulated, the text is designed to discipline participation, pre-empt criticism and discourage much needed critical dialogue. The meaning of the text emerges out of its narrational interactions which are not always clear. Since interpreting is a "social" event, reading is equally interconnected and conditioned. Just as processes of interpretation constitute structures of the text; structures simultaneously constitute interpretations. In other words, texts and narratives are shaped conjointly.

Clearly, the meaning of any text emerges out of narrational interactions Just as processes of interpretation constitute and structure the text; structures simultaneously constitute interpretations. Texts, as everyday practices and policies articulating hegemonic processes, are both contradictory and complementary; texts resist as well as accommodate. But, how are these antagonistic positions made possible? The situated reality of any text is negotiated by the corpus of diverse texts that constitute the narrative. The focus of a text, as an expression of ideology, should be examined in terms of its locus in producing, distributing and consuming practices of encoding and decoding. The text exists within cultural contexts, temporal and spatial. More precisely, textual engagements are "situated" within certain identifiable settings, indices of appropriate relations, identities and settings. The text is advanced as habitualized or institutionalized, assuming a life independent of its constituent elements. Accordingly, traditional texts are typically de-contextualized by words or lines (myopic accounts) that conceal narrated relations of control. What is revealed instead is the appropriateness of control. But, the text, as a localized script, is always written within a larger narrative that mediates cultural awareness and conditions language. This reproduction of cultural practices governs the manner in which the world is experienced. The focus, therefore, is on the relationship between the narrative (dominant ideologies of modernity, liberalism and capitalism, structures of historical trends, systems of institutions) and the text (youth cultures, media, criminal justice).

Narratives have an extensive capacity to adapt to challenging perturbations by proffering preferred meanings and readings of dominant culture which youth can claim as their respective own. Many questions need to be asked in order to confront a number of issues which remain unresolved despite the proliferation of different canonical texts. For example, we are urged to ask: how is the text received? How is meaning transferred to the reader? To what extent does the narrative shape and in turn is shaped by the nature of the text? Notably, the quintessential debate concerning the relationship between the text and the narrative continues to loom large in all conventional criminological encyclopaedic overviews. Criminology has been reluctant to move beyond its textual features. The narrative is silenced, misread or just ignored. Critical cultural theory, however, provides methods which clarify coding practices, that is, alternative approaches to framing the form and content of popular culture, the historical development of ideologies and the communication of privilege—the narrational properties of the text.

Texts of Materialism

Essentially, everyday life for youth is colonized by corporate capitalism. Corporate capital propagates consumption, narcissism and material fetishes not as rewards in affluent societies but essentially as continued investments in a consuming and producing force. In this discursive production of the essentially material subject, youths, as subjects, are articulated as fractured, fragile and complexly constituted within a plurality of discourses which position their identities. Interestingly, the eccentricities of youth are projected as serious indicators of the civil decay and manipulated as smoke-screens that distract attention away from more pressing social, cultural and political problems thereby maintaining colonial texts of identity and the convenient logics of commodification.

In short, the text constitutes and is constituted by relations of power (subtext) that collaborate with other disciplining sites (intertexts). Unlike the subtext of privilege, a narrative of resistance is missing, only fragmented texts that distance and marginalize. Resistance, therefore, remains limited as long as we are fed, in Emperor Nero's words, some bread and a

51

circus. In contemporary Canadian, the dominant culture is expressed through material consumption. But, materialism is not simply the product of socialization but more importantly, an imperative of the economic order. The conditions of our materialism constitute concretized forms of existence. Materialism, as a ubiquitous feature of our culture, speaks on our behalf; that is, our sense of self emerges from material dependence. It is a code that guides and classifies coherently the ways in which we display our experiences, imagination and consciousness. As a condition, materialism subjugates, enslaves and binds. Much effort is invested in conforming to the ways we appear, what we possess, fixated through materialism, resulting in self-enclosure. Identities and self-worth are carved by an enslaving materialism. As a society, we invest much in carving out conformity as measured according to our possessions. Fixation becomes self-enclosure. Materialism overwhelms as it mediates mental, emotional and social expressions. Although people living in advanced capitalist societies are not forced to be material, they consent and agree to be acquisitive. Materialism is personal to the extent that the dominant culture celebrates possessive individualism. Materialism manipulates especially as actors are expected to have an insatiable appetite for material gains. Those who do not have impressive material goods feel responsible for their sense of failure. Materialism is individualized—assessed in reference to individual efforts. The sanctity of the marketplace symbolises advanced capitalist societies. Within series of exchanges in the marketplace of social relations, people treat each other as objects with prospective material value. Society is atomized as people are respected as individualized, independent, self-reliant "winners or losers" competing for more material. Wholesale consumerism objectifies the individual who is shaped according to material results of production and reproduction. Individuals are transformed into objects allied to products. Notice the incredibly convenient acceptance of models proffered by Wal-Mart's value of thrift, the McDonald's value of immediacy or Microsoft's value of commonality.

Material consumption operates in the realm of ideas, thereby depoliticizing explosive class relations. As ideas are appropriated and distributed within the cultural sphere, there is considerable deference to social engineers who, as "experts," translate and advance the material needs especially of multinational corporations. Credentials, technology and corporatism generate informational capital and cultivate a general consumption that relies on the compliance of the marginalized. Essentially, everyday life is colonized by corporate capital which propagates consumption, narcissism and material fetishes not as rewards in affluent societies but essentially as continued investments in a consuming and producing force. The consumer culture is a social production that is inextricably tied to political and economic concatenations of power. It is precisely because the content of the culture of capitalism is material that profit is assigned primacy; materialism embodies both the morphology and content of culture.

Discipline, Delinquency and Distance: Between the Lines, Beyond the Text and Behind the Narrative

Language, a central feature of the text-narrative nexus, is both ideological and illusory. Language commoditizes control by structuring dependency relations. The process and structure of language as well as lexicons and vocabularies are anchored in particular histories that circumscribe acceptable expressions and marginalize differences. In other words, both the spoken and written language reflect limitations. Only when the actor surrenders to a codified and lethargic language is he or she considered to be both "in" and "of" society. Even the everyday chatter of familiar banter reflects cultural scripts. Language objectifies, stultifies and disciplines expressions of self awareness. The regularization of language is culturally necessary if talk is to be meaningful within this corporate landscape. These normative dimensions assign privilege to stereotypic language enabling the impoverishment of vocabularies and the domination of the technical, the efficient and the objective. Language presupposes a context of rules which cannot be contradicted (Gellner 1959:56). For Barthes (1973), language contributes to myth making; language politicizes myths by claiming reference to signifying signs; and, the clarity of language is misleading. Language is a performance that renders the more articulate as more legitimate and hence more knowledgeable. How then is it possible to transcend this cultural code? What facilitates the articulation of a critical consciousness that would eradicate the self paralysis of servitude inherent in ideology and its attendant the seductive illusions?

Language, as a cultural code, relates to a world of meanings. All knowledge and language are culturally coded. Thus, knowledge or even a consciousness of language is a social product. It is precisely here in the realm of knowledge that ideologies are contested, resisted or accepted.

Knowledge is coded within a language that obfuscates as well as clarifies. Ideology refers to a complex of linguistic meaning making processes which are observable and describable in instances of discourse. Clearly, ideology is constructed through discourse. As noted in chapter one, it is in discourse that every determination of the subject depends, including thought, affect, enjoyment, meaning and identity. The subject is determined by language (Lacan 1977: 298-300); the subject disappears in his or her discourse and becomes embodied in the spoken word. In order to reproduce meaning certain, "master signifiers" represent the subject for another signifier (Lacan 1977:316). Thus, a signified is empty until given form by the use of a signifier. This signifier is the "other," the element that "lacks," the part that was not fully expressed. For de Saussure (1986:100):

> The link between signal and signification is arbitrary. Since we are treating a sign as the combination in which a signal is associated with signification, we can express this more simply as: the linguistic sign is arbitrary.

Language is a situated and generic display, a site where evidence is reified. Language facilitates fetishization, objectification and colonizing. Words represent exhibitions as impartial and factual; truth is integrated with wider language games; and legitimacy is based on wholesale and retail misrepresentations. It is in the socio-linguistic moment that we encounter the formations of privilege and one's participation in that process becomes evident (Gramsci 1971). Texts are read incrementally and linearly in a language that constructs and is constructed to pacify agency and a will to knowledge. For de Saussure (1986), language supplies the conceptual framework for the analysis of reality but the established language is inherently social. His recognition that written language represents and hence obscures one's view of language opened the space for an inquiry into the relationship between actual practices and representation (de Saussure 1959). For example, official crime facts are like sacks that fall to the ground if not firmly held.

The media of communication is overwhelmingly clear in scripting a language configured in seductive symbols urging an obsessive deference to materialism. Thus, materialism succeeds in becoming personalized and possessed. Loyalties to this pervasive value system are passionately defended and generationally anchored. The institutionalization of language entrenches power as memories of superimposition fade. Language in use acquires legitimacy and becomes the natural language. Communication is convoluted; meanings are degraded; debates remain limited; and, rituals that exalt privilege are respected. Moreover, specialized vocabularies conceal the "services" rendered to the dangerous classes and justify further interventions. But this emerging personal prison or incarcerated self is fundamentally related to narrational practices. Structures of conformity are constituted through discursive disciplines. Juridic texts are designed to reproduce control and confer object-like realities to crime. Privilege channels thought within conformist boundaries (Chomsky 1989:vii). As a mode of discourse, the patho-centric script of crime objectifies challenges by invoking existing codes. Notably, legal, scientific and professional discourses dominate the language of control. As professionals adhere to a privatized, mystifying and techno-bureaucratic language, a cornucopia of meaningless jargon and mythologies dominate.

Youth crime, as a localized script of predatory subjectivities, does however exist within a larger narrative as a challenge that signifies subversion—a defiance of normative and integrative efforts ostensibly designed to "conform" actors, groups or communities. Alternatively, control shapes youth crime while ignoring how violence is the fibre that weaves the very fabric of everyday lives. As objects of exchange and constituted as convenient commodities, actors from the criminal subject to the subjected reader are forever pacified, transformed and controlled by the censorial gaze of institutions. As Gramsci (1971:31) develops:

> The demagogy, the trickery, the untruth, the corruption of capitalist society are not accidental by-products of its structure; they are inherent in the disorder, in the unleashing of brutal passions, in the ferocious competition in which and by which capitalist society lives.

Culture mediates, provides rationality and articulates a language that magically renders conformity by imposing a familiar context and generates universal commitment. Those, not belonging are "out of place" according to the strictures of culture. Wiseman (1989:42) calls to mind the "suspicion is that culture and tradition have transmuted the institutionally chosen into the naturally given." This emphasis on the socio-cultural and social fully incorporates the significant forces of economic and political structures.

Control is ideologically situated within institutions that shape self-identity. These protective cocoons, filter trouble, funnel interpretations, and marginalize differences according to universalized framed experiences and inoculated reflexivities (Giddens 1992:3). A priori conditioning incites intolerance. In this study the common-sense, knowledge and beliefs about conformity are problematized. Culture manipulates sanctions by defining disturbances as local accommodations to contests or as totalizing narratives of trouble that warrant closure, containment and coercion. Culture transforms subjects into social objects, "demonizes" differences or deviantizes the devalued "other." This cultural subject is not analyzed as the totalizing consequence of structure nor the simply reduced situated agent. Rather, this construction of control reflects a dialectics of consent framed both within power relations and the logic of the resisting knowing subject. Culture is a panoply of discourses and competing texts. The "deviant" subject is segmented and articulated within a variety of discourses that succeed in abstracting, mystifying and decontextualizing social control. Figure 2.1 highlights the location of control.

Figure 2.1

IDEOLOGIES

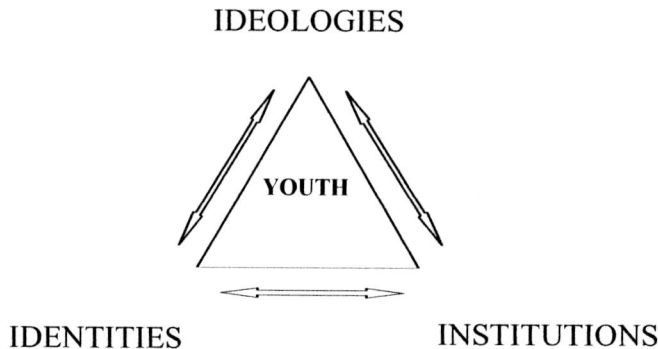

IDENTITIES   INSTITUTIONS

The reproduction of crime is a cultural practice; a way of experiencing how the world persists, preserves and universalizes inequality. Notwithstanding the rhetorical banter of liberalism, the dominant culture ignores differences and denies authenticity. The authentic, especially the concrete resistance or the risks of one's own situation, is replaced by forms of pseudo community communication.

56

Any project committed to cultural analysis interrogates the character of social order, locates this interrogation inside and outside the bounds of conventional rules, stepping back and looking into dominant institutional forms that marginalize those deemed to be the other—the criminal, the deviant. Accordingly, our cultural approach relocates that which has occupied the margins to the centre, decentres and de-essentializes the subject by highlighting how the subject is constructed in contradictions. The deference to "essential" elements of criminality (normalized exercises of power) is repositioned and negotiable—always involving recourse to transformation. Culture has an extensive capacity to adapt to perturbations, conflict and resistance.

This dominant culture is replete with illusions which enhance alienation. Foucault (1979, 1980a) notes that the micro mechanisms of power (mediated through the schools, hospitals, barracks, factories, cities, families, etc) since the late 18th century have played an increasing role in the regulation of people's bodies. This control comes not through a code of law, but through Atechnologies A of normalization which act not in a downward fashion but "from below" in localized relations within a force-field of existing and unstable power relations "analytics" of power. How then does morality come to pacify and transform human subjects within the censorial gaze of institutions? Culture mediates, provides rationality and articulates a language that magically defines conformity by imposing a familiar context and generates universal commitment. A priori conditioning incites intolerance. Youth is represented as a risk. Discourses of deviant designations are derivative of cultural conditions.

By analysing the culture-crime nexus, we are able to re-evaluate what constitutes a "criminal" and thus redefine exclusive, normative strategies which govern and manipulate subjective experience. Critical legal studies as well as critical cultural approaches interrogate dominant ideological and cultural structures in an effort to resist customary narratives and open up possibilities of resistance and change. The project of legal studies as cultural studies sets forth a series of intersecting and often conflicting interrogative possibilities more so than firmly settled answers or solutions.

Various discourse analytic tools, such as the ethics of viewing and reading, are used to examine the influence of ethical stances in these narrations. To what extent is there an impositionalist conception of the narrative on the concept of "understanding"? That is, how do youths try to make various texts their own (self referential)? Alternatively, how do the practices of reading and viewing involve entering the world of the text, thereby assuming perspectives it provides

Moreover, youth is constructed within a framework of sophisticated surveillance, characteristic of late industrial and late capitalist societies. This ubiquitous moral regulation is legitimized by institutions of the law, media, work and education that articulate the sanctity of discipline. The prevailing legal-materialist values based on the sovereignty of individualism destroy the dignity of those individuals, organizations and communities deviantized as the "others," especially youths. It is argued that the "official" versions of delinquency are manipulated by the numerous stakeholders for self-serving reasons. Lastly, the processes and structures of delinquency are indistinguishable from forms of representation of youth. In the production of these texts, the concept of youth disappears or is reduced to the presentation of trouble. Accordingly, the culture of youth is mediated through stunning statistics and enslaving images that privileges the sanctity of individualism, corporate power and the authority of the state.

Since culture has become institutionalized within absolutist and corporate interpretive frameworks, culture is a barrier to communication given its allegiance to state machinations of power and concentrated corporate capital. Critical cultural approaches consider cultural processes as connected to class, gender, sexuality, and racial relations. These various asymmetries are partially reproduced through cultural practices. The complex understanding of youth cultures and representation are central to any inquiry into the discursive and material fields of contestations and struggles over the meaning of social difference. Again, it is conceptually more fruitful to examine, as Marx (1956) suggested, the "totality," the interconnectedness of events and activities, the intersections of history, culture and political economy.

Youth Cultures

To understand any cultural phenomenon—whether an artistic creation, a social problem, an organizational practice, or any other cultural object—it is essential to analyze the characteristics of cultural objects, as well as their creators and recipients. Culture is far too frequently decontextualized and too readily extricated from the larger narrational processes such as property relations or the transformation of space, which loom large in structures of social relations. Simply stated, social order emerges within "a nexus of

58

multiple involvements" of narrational networks promoting particular interests and concerns. What warrants further empirical investigation, therefore, is not only social order and its often neglected structural embeddedness (see Figure 2.2) but, more precisely, the nature of competing orders, inevitable intersections and structural linkages of cultures in conflict or those simply different.

Youth cultures are also constructed expressions of enigmatic journeys that piece together the cultural puzzle of youth identity and social engagements within the over-arching canopy of a dominant culture that contextualizes the youth affiliations or subcultures. Any study of the youth "sub"cultures-dominant culture nexus is often presented as ideological exercises in discredit, inquiries into cultural confrontations. Fundamentally, any investigation into youth experiences ultimately challenges a particular socially constructed and historically rooted social order. The concept of the "adult" culture is an extremely elusive concept that defies simple definition. This culture defers to the (neo)liberal-democratic idea of invited engagement while retaining its foundational principles and strategies of coercion. Likewise the equally elusive concept of a youth culture is problematic, suffering from distorted images. We, therefore, are charged with the difficult task of unravelling the intersections of both concepts. We are asked to be inquisitive in deconstructing comfortable traditions by highlighting various contradictions and closures inherent in conventional adult and youth speak. One's knowledge of youth cultures ought not to be solely

Figure 2.2

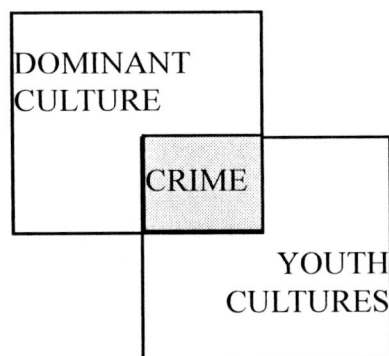

packaged to satisfy current political markets but to respond to our critical faculties; to struggle in documenting our experiences, consciousness, intention, and their relational contexts. Undoubtedly, this struggle will forge new directions, perspectives and substantive material.

Youth values are transformed within homogenized and hegemonized "objective" frames of reference, usually as criteria for assimilation. Youth contributions are distorted to protect dominant values of the privileged classes which create illusions that demand deference. Contributions by youth alternatively are simply presented as temporary or transitional life stages. The dominant cultural frames as calculable devices, as enshrined in various institutions seek to "de-politicize," "cool-out" and demystify by dignifying adult-youth differences.

Youth cultures are recast as "many ways" of life, as mosaics of subcultures, that fractionate a normative order into varieties of danger, resulting in "ordered segmentation" within society. Nonetheless, considerable order underlies this supposed social disorder. Routine interactions are not necessarily unordered, temporary and non-existent even in the "world of strangers." Attention to subcultural collectives and the establishment of their identities has re-energized criminological interests in the identification process itself. A growing literature explores the mechanics by which collectivities create distinctions, establish hierarchies, and renegotiate rules of inclusion. In addition, symbolic boundaries are important for the construction of identities across space and time. Boundary strength refers to the generation of values within group identities. In order to work function, and survive in the modern world, subcultures instil ideas and develop sentiments and feelings of right and wrong. Consequently, youths herein develop the abilities to see themselves and recognize themselves as meaningful in similarly circumstanced interactions.

As youths band themselves together in real and imagined ways, they stress the indissoluble relation between self and their others. Specifically, youths come to regard themselves as their significant others see them. Images they have of themselves are reflections of meanings assigned by their primary groups—peers. The self does not exist in isolation but always remains directly connected with others. Most of what they know about themselves is derived from others as a result of ongoing self- and group-appraisal processes. In brief, the group serves as the foundation for the construction of consciousness, continuously created and re-created. Members appreciate their selves in routine interaction with others. The mutable self is made possible by the symbolic community of the individual with significant others. Individuals make choices and construct actions that shape the self. Actors reflect upon their activities and upon the relationship of such activities to their identity. The views of the self are not given by simple self-reflection, they are acquired from others. For example, symbolic interactionism stresses the importance of others in shaping self-concept and draws attention to the central role of self-evaluation in development of self-conception. This reference to others is strongly influential in validating and sustaining one's self-concept; it is the audience in which an actor claims his/her self-worth. By attending to others, for example, youths learn both favourable definitions of self and guides for interaction. This "cojoint action" of the collective unit is the fitting together of different members. This frame of reference aids in organizing experiences. This self-indication is central to their idea of human agency; active in bestowing meanings on every situation, in interpreting ideas and activities. In reference to crime, the subculture becomes particularly significant in highlighting the way(s) in which individuals construct and share symbols that in turn generate definitions of crime /deviance contingent upon social contexts. Crimes therefore are learned meanings, shared and defined differently.

Worth-based and efficacy-based esteem are each rooted primarily in *group-based* identities which become *role-based* identities that act as buffers or resources. Emerging in social interaction within the context of a complex society, subcultures are organized and differentiated in order to ensure persistence. In subcultures youths gets support from others to commit to an identity and in turn receive extrinsic and intrinsic rewards from the role identity. This commitment has two dimensions: a *quantitative* (ties to the social structure, commitment reflects the number of persons that one is tied to through an identity) and *qualitative* aspect (the more salient, stronger or the deeper the ties to others based on a particular identity, the higher the commitment to that identity; its relative *importance*). Commitment attaches significance or central meaning to affiliation, present and future.

An Overview of Criminological Canons

The bulk of criminological research on youth subcultures has discovered persisting, vigorous friendship involvements that provide vitality, sociability and support. But in their haste to rediscover well-established organizations and rich, complicated social relations within different cultures, studies of delinquency are quick to point out that the youth cultures fail to mesh with their surrounding social structures. Others have condemned them for unduly isolating youths from larger social structures. As will be discussed later, subcultures are derivative of larger economic and social orders especially the political economy of class structures. In critically evaluating youth subcultures, criminologists may have also advanced an updated anti-urban tradition, reminiscent of early writers who have pathologized youth cultures as sites of conflict. Youth cultures appeared as a direct effect of the need to reduce indirect costs of production and consumption of illegal services, thereby facilitating the rotation of capital, commodities and information.

But the concept of subcultures has been subject to endless and confusing debates regarding the necessarily grounded social and physical boundaries of these groupings, assigning many attributions ranging from subcultures as spatially defined units; as common ties or modes of relationships where a prevailing normative value system characterizes a sense of belongingness, cooperation or distinctiveness; and as a localized, autonomous social interaction. Network analysis arose in response to these a priori assumptions in suggesting that these social relations extend across wide areas that intersect, overlap or interact in various complicated ways. That is, the lowering of spatial barriers and the increased freedom to choose social relations have led to a proliferation of subcultures consisting of compatible and supportive networks of personal ties. Even in the most impersonal marketplace relations of advanced capitalist societies, the internet, youth cultures proliferate with identifiable patterns of relationships both locally and non-locally based, having their own organization, tied together only by a few interests Technological communications have changed the significance of space and locale for youth subcultures.

Normative Youth Cultures

Strain

Robert Merton (1957) underscores the significance of the social structure especially the discrepancies between objective social standards and conditions. Merton maintains that crime is a normal response to a given situation, the **strain** towards crime is remarkably similar to the pressure to conform. For Merton, deviance is a characteristic feature of social structure and not simply a property inherent in the individual. Deviance occurs as an outcome of imbalances in the social system; that is, whenever the social structure fails to maintain control over individual aspirations. Merton's social reality is an objective, independent and determining force, which for analytical purposes is dichotomized into "cultural" and "social" structures, or more specifically, *culturally defined goals and socially approved means,* respectively. The cultural structure is an organized set of socialized values that govern the behaviour of members of a society especially the pursuit of cultural norms such as the pursuit of possessive materialism, occupational prestige and consumerism. Culturally defined goals are legitimate objectives that frame aspirations, for example, success, especially when operationalized as the acquisition of wealth. The social structure consists of institutional norms and resources that define acceptable means for attaining cultural goals. But, institutionally prescribed means are not equally available, let alone accessible, to all interested candidates. Individuals vary in their location in the social structure; that is, they are not equally positioned to capitalize on such opportunities as work, training and education. Since the capitalist economy, for example, is based on inequality, the pursuit of profit is exclusionary—only some and certainly not all individuals can attain culturally defined success. The structure of society, therefore, fails to provide the means necessary (Merton 1957) to realize much celebrated cultural aspirations. According to Merton's central thesis, therefore, a discrepancy develops between the cultural goals and the legitimate means necessary to achieve goals. This breakdown between aspirations and their corresponding regulating norms produces a *"strain"* towards deviance. Regulatory norms break down as conformity becomes impossible. This strain leads to a search for different and often illicit means of achieving success. In explaining this stressful situation in which norms lose their power to regulate, Merton concentrates not on the individual actor but on the social order. This breakdown in cultural structure occurs whenever there is an acute disjuncture between cultural goals and the socially structured capacity of individuals to act by them. As the social structure prevents what the culture encourages, normlessness emerges and individuals feel compelled to act against their conscience. In this way, integration of society becomes tenuous and delinquency follows.

Disorganization

Talcott Parsons (1952) envisages social life as regulated by culture: common norms and values. Interactions are mediated by common *moral* standards or "norms" which structure action and maintain social order by constraining actors and regulating conflict. Through such key mechanisms as socialization, interactions are institutionally integrated (Parsons 1952) and subsequently internalized as bonds which in turn function to secure conformity. Disharmony occurs whenever an actor fails to fulfil expectations or is quite simply not exposed to role consensus. The sources of deviance include the following: a failure in the socialization process; strains arising out of difficulties of acting according to norms that then frustrate personality needs; and, strains arising whenever norms are ambiguous. Social functioning is contingent upon consensus; the dysfunctional nature of deviance is kept in check because of conscious and unconscious control mechanisms. Mechanisms of social control operate as "secondary defences" to combat deviance which, if left unchecked, would disrupt the much needed and well heeded social equilibrium and harmony. For Parsons, crime is a pathology, an incomplete articulation of relations between people or institutions in change, and an expression of a diseased and disorganized social body.

Elements of Social Affiliations

According to normative approaches, youth crime is the result of organized responses to elements of strain and disorganization. Specifically, delinquent youth subcultures are explained according to perspectives on control, social bond, containment, differential association, and neutralization.

Reaction Formations and Status Frustration

In general, the term "subculture" refers to an organized and recognized constellation of values that are different from and in opposition to prevailing dominant norms. In a fragmented and differentiated society, people contact and attend to the responses of others who share their distinct values. A collective wisdom emerges that serves to guide and validate perspectives and activities. The early subcultural approaches to deviance were reformulations of Merton's strain perspectives. Specifically, these perspectives reflect Merton's view that the larger society maintains generally accepted goals of success, wealth and education, and that the means for acquiring these goals are not distributed equally among social classes. With an emphasis on the origins and development of delinquency, subcultural approaches argued that lower class youths who lack access to appropriate means develop unique cultural values in supportive groups of similarly circumstanced others. Informed by Merton's contributions, Albert Cohen, in *Delinquent Boys* (1955), shifts deviance away from the character of the actor to the character of the acts. According to Cohen, "subcultural group formations" are the result of successful attempts to collectively overcome the problems of conformity to existing norms. His study commences with a review of how the dominant cultural order structures social existence. Within this normative orientation, human interaction is perceived to be governed by societal norms constructed by the people in authority. That is, middle class norms of well-respected individuals and groups symbolize conformity and reflect social consensus. Cohen charged that society encourages all classes to achieve status by internalizing middle-class success values. But, it is difficult for lower class youths to achieve success because they are ill-equipped to compete for opportunities. For example, the school system ensures the failure of lower class youths because it operates within a generalized middle class framework; middle class teachers reproduce middle class values by rewarding diligence, promptness, delays in gratification, industry, courtesy, respect for property, non violence, to name a few. Cohen contends that lower class youths are more likely to experience failure and humiliation because they are caught up in a game in which others are typically the "winners," and they are typically the "losers." Although they wish to be successful, these youths are ill-prepared to live up to the "middle-class measuring rods" of respectable status holders and thus experience "*status frustration*" (p.25). Common rejection, felt inferiority and economic disadvantage encourage them to band together and create new and more realistic standards for themselves. Likewise for Cohen, the relative deprivation of a youth's family impairs the much-needed socialization of middle class values resulting in a youth's inability to impress authorities and "measure up" to the standards of teachers and prospective employers. These youths learn to respond to rejection by adopting delinquent roles and by opposing middle class values. Unable to achieve middle class values, they retreat into the more comforting world of lower class peers who hang out at street corners, hustle, and drop out of school. Driven by a "status frustration," they return to their neighbourhoods and develop "delinquent subcultures" which enable them to compete more fairly with their peers and achieve status in their familiar worlds. To deal with the conflict inherent in this frustrating dilemma, the delinquent resorts to a defence mechanism—**reaction-formation**. Reaction-formation is a process of repudiating and inverting middle-class criteria by resorting to forms of irrational, malicious and unaccountable hostility to middle-class values. In contrast to traditional standards of acceptability, the delinquent subculture values non-utilitarian, short-term hedonism, the destruction of property, violence and the rejection of traditional taboos. Delinquent youths are careful to maintain group autonomy and resist the controlling pulls of their family, school and other authorities. Status is gained by succeeding in delinquent pursuits within highly structured solidarities like gangs, creating new means to achieve goals of peer defined success.

Illegitimate opportunities

Richard Cloward and Lloyd Ohlin who reason, in their study *Delinquency and Opportunity* (1959), that delinquency also depends on the nature of illegitimate opportunities that are not always evenly distributed. Essentially, these youths attribute their failure to "the system"; they respond to the latter's shortcomings by joining groups organized around specific activities and develop relationships that promote a group ideology that legitimates their respective deviance. They align themselves with like-minded others who also internalize contra-cultural perspectives to justify their deviance. More cohesive subcultural supports gradually replace their initial guilt, fear and shame. This criminal subculture incorporates both opportunity and learning structures that encourage the acquisition of values and skills associated with the performance of particular roles. Individuals learn appropriate perspectives and skills in order to discharge their roles for which they have been prepared. Both the opportunities of learning and applying one's skills are rational activities. Choice depends upon the peer group and the attendant collective definitions of the delinquent solution. The criminal gang emerges whenever there are high levels of integration among different age levels of offenders and equally high integration of conventional and deviant norms. In these cultural contexts youths have the opportunity to learn from older delinquents. Successful hustlers of drugs, sex, stolen merchandise, etc become role models to emulate. Knowledge and skills needed for success in criminal activities are communicated to neophytes who in turn learn to cooperate with mentors who teach them to regard the world with suspicion. If denied access to illegitimate or criminal opportunities, actors are forced into ritualism or retreatism. Not all disgruntled youths enjoy this integration with pre-existing criminal lifestyles nor are they equally located in the social structure of the criminal world. Where integration is low and role models remain absent, conflict emerges. Conflict results whenever youths lack access to both legitimate and illegitimate opportunities. These youth gangs, transient and fleeting, generate in deteriorated neighbourhoods. Appropriately, behaviour is more unpredictable and individualistic; crimes involve more violence and fewer financial rewards. Moreover, gang warfare is commonplace; violent acts such as assaults, arson and vandalism are frequently justified in terms of protecting one's turf and demonstrating gang loyalty. Simply, they manipulate violence to win status (ibid). For the conflict gang, the severe limitations in adjustments intensify their frustration. Lastly, the retreatist subcultures are double failures since they do not have access to either criminal or conventional means. They are unable and unwilling to gain success either through illegitimate opportunities; they have no where to turn and simply retreat. Typically the activity of this subculture revolves around a "consumption of drugs" or alcohol.

Control perspectives

Why do some youths decide to join deviant subcultures while others refuse such affiliation? Alternatively, one asks, why are there not more gangs? Why have we, as a society, not witnessed, let alone experienced rampant criminality? For these and many other related questions we defer to the contributions of criminology's "control theory." Consistent with the more social-structural aspects of deviance, control theory focuses on conformity rather than deviance. Again, conformity not deviance is problematic. Specifically, control theory asks: "Why do youths obey the rules of society?" "What causes conformity?" Once the causes of conformity have been determined, then the causes of deviance may be easily ascertained. Control theory states that all youths have the potential to violate rules and modern society offers many opportunities for illegal activity. According to control theory, youths are inclined to do both good and bad; they are naturally inclined to commit deviant acts and will do so under controlled conditions.

Those who refrain from deviance do so because they have a stake in conformity—an investment in obeying the rules of society. Control theory proposes that youths who are least attached to social institutions are most free to violate rules. Deviance emerges when *social bonds* are attenuated, that is fragile or ineffective. For Toby (1957), the concept of "stake in conformity" is a basic mechanism of control that regulates delinquent tendencies. Youths who do well in school risk being punished and jeopardize their future careers. Since they enjoy a relatively high stake in conformity they are more inclined to resist wayward proclivities. Hirschi (1969), in *Causes of Delinquency*, articulates a particular form of control theory, *"social bond"* theory, in which he cautions that all individuals can commit deviant acts, but most people refrain from deviance because of their strong bonds to society. The strength and direction of ties with conventional groups and institutions like the family, parents, friends, peers, schools, teachers and employers influence deviance. Youths bind themselves to society in four related ways: *attachment, commitment, involvement and belief.* Attachment refers to the sensitivity, affection and interest one exhibits towards the family, school, job and peers. The family as a basic mechanism of social control socializes and disciplines. For Hirschi, commitment also shapes social bonds. Commitment, as the amount of time and energy one invests towards the achievement of societal goals, incorporates conventional types of behaviour such as getting an education, holding a job, developing skills, building up a business, studying, and saving money. Youths who are committed are less likely to risk their social positions. Likewise, involvement in school, family and recreation insulate the youth from deviant temptations. Finally, the decision to conform or deviate is influenced by one's belief in the moral validity of rules. The deviant, in other words, does not subscribe to dominant values or moral obligations to conform and is therefore inclined to anti-social behaviour.

Containment

Walter Reckless (1967) proffers yet another version of control theory: *containment* theory. In general, containment theory claims that society produces a series of "pushes and pulls" towards deviance which are in turn counteracted by "internal and external containments" that help insulate the individual from criminality. Reckless asks how is it possible for a youth living in high crime, poverty area, to resist deviance? And, what personal properties insulate a person from deviance-producing influences? Reckless (1967) hypothesizes that external and internal pressures lead to deviance. External pressures include adverse living conditions that influence deviant behaviour such as relative deprivation, poverty, unemployment, minority status, limited opportunities, inequality, family conflicts, and limited access to opportunity structures. External pulls consists of deviant companions, membership in deviant subcultures and such influences as the mass media and pornography. The internal pressures that affect behaviour involve such personal factors as restlessness, discontent, hostility, rebellion, mental conflict, anxieties and the need for immediate gratification. However, besides the inner and outer forces that pressure individuals towards deviance, there are also inner and outer forces that protect and insulate against deviance, or more generally, "contain" deviant forces. Inner containments are strengths located within the individual that deter deviance, for example, a good self concept, ego strength, a well-developed super-ego, high frustration tolerance, high resistance to diversions, high sense of responsibility, goal orientation, the ability to find substituted satisfactions and tension-reducing capabilities. This inner containment is the product of internalization and develops throughout group socialization. On the other hand, outer containments consist of the normative constraints that societies and social groups use to control their members which include a sense of belongingness, consistent moral front, reinforcement of norms goals and values, effective supervision discipline and meaningful social roles. For Reckless, of the two influences, inner containment is more important primarily because youths spend much time away from their "containing" families and other supportive groups and therefore must then rely on their own inner strengths to control deviant pushes.

Differential Association, Reinforcement and Opportunities

Interestingly, peer associations have also been developed by studies of **differential associations**. A social learning approach maintains that deviance is a product of learning appropriate values; habits and knowledge are developed as a result of the experiences of individuals entering and adjusting to an environment. Social learning approach can be traced to Gabriel Tarde's (1843-1904) "laws of imitation." Accordingly, youths learn because of association with ideas that guide behaviour (Tarde [1903] 1962). In 1924 Edwin Sutherland, a prominent American criminologist, develops a social

69

learning theory known as differential association. Deviance is shaped by normal processes of social interaction and socialization. His theory maintains that criminal behaviour is learned in interaction within intimate personal groups in the process of communication. The learning includes: (a) techniques of committing the crime and (b) the specific direction of motives, drives, rationalizations and attitudes (Sutherland 1924). Differential association may vary in frequency, duration, priority and intensity. A youth becomes delinquent because of an excess of definitions favourable to the violation of law. This process of learning criminal behaviour by association with criminal and anti-criminal patterns involves all of the mechanisms associated with any other learning. Refining Sutherland's original theory, criminologists have suggested that differential association produces criminality not directly but rather through intervening mechanisms, differential reinforcement and *differential identification*, which stress the ways in which youths select models of behaviour. Youths pursue criminal behaviour to the extent that they identify themselves with real or imaginary persons from whose perspective criminal behaviour seems acceptable and this criminal behaviour is learned in non social situations that are reinforcing or rewarding (Glaser 1956; Burgess and Akers 1968; Akers 1985).

Maurice Cusson's (1983) explains delinquency according to a model of a *rational choice* or "differential anticipation." A fundamental hypothesis of this theorizing suggests that whenever youths wish to commit a crime, they select options that will have the greatest advantages at the least cost, that is, opportunities that yield the most benefits. Opportunities as determinants of choice (goals and methods) are resources

Neutralization Techniques

Neutralization, as developed by (Sykes and Matza 1957), maintains that most delinquents participate in the normative culture and hold conventional attitudes and techniques (crime-producing rationalizations) that are learned which enable youths to neutralize their values and drift back and forth between legitimate and illegitimate (subterranean) activities. Drift refers to the process by which an individual moves from one extreme of behaviour to another, sometimes in an unconventional, free or deviant manner and at other times with constraint and sobriety. Drift precedes delinquency and functions to loosen the mechanisms of control. Neutralization theory does not support the claim that criminals or delinquents reject middle-class values, rather they share accepted social values and participate in conventional pursuits is frame illegal behaviour within a set of conventional rationalizations, general impressions and judgments prevalent in the dominant culture. As noted in Chapter One, five techniques of neutralization (denial of responsibility, denial of injury, denial of a victim, condemnation of the condemners and appeals to higher loyalties) are justifications that minimize the influence of moral constraints.

In studying deviant phenomena, particularly in relation to delinquent formations, Matza (1964, 1969) rejects subcultural theories on the grounds that they characterized delinquents as holding to a system of values which were "an inversion of the values held by respectable society." Matza insists that these descriptions represented an over-antagonistic view of the relationship between delinquent values and those of the larger society. Matza asserts that delinquents are committed to values that are ultimately linked to those of the wider society. The youth is not involved in a rejection of conventional morality rather the adolescent neutralizes the normative bind of society's legal order.

The emphasis on the similarity of delinquent values and those of the larger society has led Matza to replace the notion of a "delinquent subculture" with the idea of a "subculture of delinquency" which exists in a subterranean fashion in normal society. If carefully examined, one discovers that many apparently delinquent values resemble closely those embodied in the leisure activities of the dominant society; that is, there is a similarity of larger societal values and delinquent ideologies.

Interpretive Approaches: Labelling Delinquency

In contrast to the above deterministic propositions, interpretive perspectives have explored the nature of the self-conscious individual who does not merely act but reflects on the meaning of action. Crime is an interpretation that is socially constructed. Howard Becker (1963:8) develops a principle element of the labelling perspective—crime and/or deviance as a creation of society, deviance is to be "discovered" in the "social reaction" of the community. He explains:

> [G]roups create deviance by making the rules whose infraction constitutes deviance, and by applying those rules to particular

71

people and labelling them as outsiders. From this point of view, deviance is not a quality of the act the person commits, but rather a consequence of the application by others of rules and sanctions to an "offender." The deviant is one to whom that label has successfully been applied; deviant behaviour is behaviour people so label. (Pp. 8-9, emphasis added)

Likewise, Kai Erikson (1966:11) indicates that:

Deviance is *not a property inherent* in certain forms of behaviour; it is a property conferred upon these forms by the audiences which directly or indirectly witness them. The critical variable in the study of deviance, then, is the social audience which *eventually determines* whether any episode of behaviour or any class of episodes is labelled deviant. (Emphasis added)

From the above excerpts, we discern that crime and deviance are politically and dynamically interactive processes. Definitions of crime and deviance are arrived at and constructed in negotiations between deviants and politically powerful audiences, thus directing attention to the understanding of welfare measures, rules of education, police practices and ideologies as vital components of an understanding of crime and deviance. Differences in the ability to define crime and deviance are inherently power differentials, the relative power of groups involved and their channels of publicity. Becker developed the concept of moral entrepreneur to refer to persons or groups who attempt to criminalize/deviantize certain acts and individuals by influencing law-makers and law-enforcers. Consequently, socially distant or marginal youth are treated in a way that exacerbates and exploits their vulnerability. Moral entrepreneurs affix stigmatizing labels to those who threaten the normative conceptions of societal "good." Stigmatization has extensive consequences for an individual's self concept. A label once affixed by powerful interests not only crystallizes identity but remains so sticky that it becomes difficult to remove. Specifically, labels generate new definitions of "self" for the particular person, his or her reference group and the larger societal audiences. Furthermore, when these individuals fail to shed the designation, they often "personalize" or internalize the labels by organizing their lifestyles around the assumptions associated with the labels. A "master status" emerges and overshadows all other aspects of identity.

Conflict Approaches

Informed by general theories of social conflict that directly implicate the dominant social and political processes structuring crime and deviance, contemporary conflict approaches scrutinized more closely those mechanisms that routinely reproduce extant inequalities. Conflict moved beyond viewing crime and deviance as a consequence of social definitions created and applied by those in power towards interrogating diverse political sites to determine in whose interest is crime/deviance created, maintained and punished. Deviance is not shaped by moral consensus but by the relative power of groups who use scarce resources to impose their moral preferences.

Thorsten Sellin (1938) concludes that cultural conflicts cause crime. For instance, the consequences of urbanization, especially social and cultural diversity, the attenuation of moral bonds, differentiation and inequality, the disintegration of the community and the social disorganization contribute to crime and deviance. Inter cultural clashes reduce social controls and generate stress that contributes to crime. George Vold (1958) delineates the "social" circumstances that frame crime; people in similar situations "group" together to secure their interests are in conflict whenever expectations or goals clash as they struggle to promote their interests and compete for resources which results in a continuous state of group or social conflict. Those in power translate their cultural norms into laws by differentially enacting laws, or as Vold (1958:209) describes:

> the whole political process of law making, law breaking and law enforcement becomes a direct reflection of deep-seated and fundamental conflicts between interest groups and then more general struggles for the control of police power of the state...those who produce legislative majorities win control over the police power and dominate the policies that decide who is likely to be involved in violation of the law.

In this context, crime or deviance can be understood as cultural conflict.

Ralf Dahrendorf's (1959) inquiries into conflicts over "authority in society" lead him to deduce that every society is based on a coercion of some of its members by others. He (ibid: 165) concludes:

[I]n every social organization some positions are entrusted with a right to exercise control over other positions in order to ensure effective coercion; it means, in other words, which there is a differential distribution of power and authority.

Comprised of a plurality of competing interest groups, Dahrendorf views society as organized into associations in which relationships comprise two groups: those who dominate and those who are subject to authority. Authority is the central source of conflict; classes are defined by relations of authority. In this context, people act in reference to their position in a pluralistic society wherein a range of authority-subject relationships directs action.

American criminologist Austin Turk (1969) applies Dahrendorf's insights to the processes, conditions and consequences of "criminalization." Turk enquires, for example, under what circumstances do those who violate norms become criminalized? Central to Turk's thesis is the argument that social order in modern societies is based on the relationship of conflict between *authorities* (the dominant decision-making category responsible for the enforcement of norms) and *subjects* (subordinates affected by the imposition of cultural and social definitions). Power is a critical dimension in the determination of authority-subject relations. The degree to which any individual or group acquires, controls and mobilizes power resources *will affect the outcome* of these relationships (1976a:280), criminality is the result of social conflicts between authorities and subjects. Conflict as an ongoing process is intrinsic to the creation, maintenance and extension of behavioural and relational patterns that maximize the life chances of individuals or groups (1966, 1976b:285, 1977). He suggests that the acquisition of a criminal status is largely due to the legal authority's definition of the person as criminal. Turk insists that the greater the cultural differences between authorities and subjects, the greater the probability of their conflict and subsequent criminalization. Figure 2.3 highlights the array of institutional influences on youths.

Critical Criminology: Delinquency as an Expression of Criminogenic Contexts

Ian Taylor, Paul Walton, and Jock Young (1973) advance a criminological perspective *The New Criminology* that incorporates basic elements that

Figure 2.3

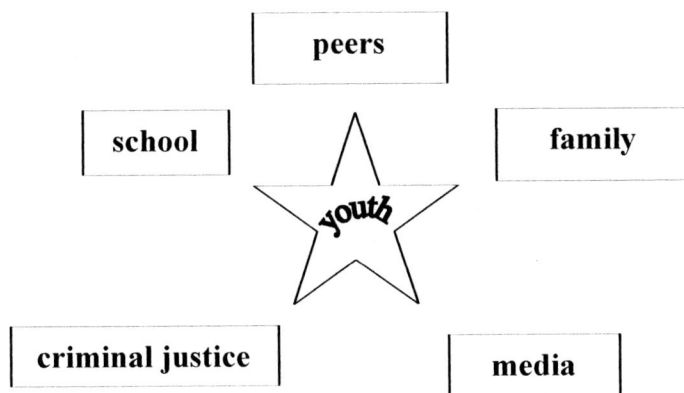

define Western societies: specific mode(s) of production and the resultant contradictions, that is, a political economic explanation of crime in which capitalism is singled out as the main criminogenic factor. The elements of this comprehensive theory include on the one hand, the political economy of crime, the social psychology of crime, social dynamics surrounding the actual events. On the other hand, a social psychology of social reactions to crime, a political economy of social reactions, the consequences of social reactions and the "criminalizing" or "deviantizing" process as a whole were articulated. The antagonistic contradictions between the individual and society cause crime notably structured inequalities of wealth, power, property and life chances—the bases of economic, political and social orders that constitute the culture of capitalism. Quinney (1974) directly assails capitalism as criminogenic, contending that the criminal law is used by the State and ruling classes to secure the survival of the capitalist system. Accordingly, those who own and control the means of production (the capitalist class), attempt to secure the existing order through various forms of domination, especially crime control. Quinney proposes four areas that require analysis: the development of capitalist political economy; systems of domination and repression; forms of accommodation and resistance; and lastly, the dialectic relationship of accommodation and resistance to the overall conditions of capitalist political economy, wherein one discovers the creation of both crimes of accommodation and crimes of domination. He accentuates the variety of complex processes and structures that enable the law to act as an instrument of the State and the ruling class in order to maintain and perpetuate the existing economic and social order. Crime control then, is simply a means for checking threats to the existing capitalist order. Many in this "new or critical criminological" tradition affirm that every comprehensive system of laws is essentially determined by class factors. More specifically, Schwendinger and Schwendinger (1977) endorse the following five claims: a) Legal relations secure the economic infrastructure that centres on the capitalist mode of production. The legal system is designed to guard the position of owners at the expense of workers. b) Legal relations maintain the family and school structure in order to secure a labour force. c) The class interests that underlie laws of the land are based on conditions that reproduce the class system. Laws, in other words, are designed to secure domination. d) The legal system may, at times, secure the interests of the working class—for example, protective or collective bargaining. e) Due to contradictions, all laws differ from the stated purposes of justice. The legal system not only highlights the ethos of individualism but also perpetuates a class system, protects the positions of privilege at the expense of the disadvantaged despite the appearance of "justice" in law and despite their articulated principles, laws inherently maintain the dominant hegemonies. Marxist criminology considers the criminal law and criminal justice system as vehicles for controlling the poor. The criminal justice system helps the powerful to: first, impose their morality and standards on all; second, protect their property and physical safety from the "have-nots"; and third, extend the definition of crime to encompass those who challenge the status quo. Moreover, it is argued that the poor are driven to crime because the rules imposed from above are irrelevant. Spitzer (1975) asks "why are problem populations criminalized"? He emphasizes that criminalization depends on the degree to which "problem populations" are perceived to be threatening; the size of the population; its degree of political organization; and, the effectiveness of alternate forms of social control. Criminals and deviants are selected from groups who create problems for those who rule. Criminalization occurs when any one of the five following features of capitalism challenge: a) capitalist modes of appropriating the product of human labour, for example, when the poor "steal" from the rich; b) social conditions under which capitalist production takes place, for instance, those who refuse or are unable to perform wage labour; c) patterns of distribution and consumption in capitalist society, i.e., those who use drugs for escape and transcendence rather than for sociability and adjustment; d) the process of socialization for productive and non-productive roles, e.g., youth who refuse to be schooled or those who deny the validity of "family life"; and, e) the ideology that supports the functioning of capitalist society—that is, proponents of alternate forms of social organization (Spitzer 1975:642). Problem populations are constructed from two sources: directly from the fundamental contradictions in the capitalist economy, and indirectly from the contradictions/disturbances in institutions of social control. An illustration of direct influences is the existence of surplus labour populations, populations that support capital accumulation by providing a pool of labour that may be conveniently manipulated and drawn into the wage labour market. Youths who drop out, or alternatively, students who develop insights critical of capitalism, are extremely vulnerable to the processes of criminalization. According to Spitzer (1975), there are two kinds of problem populations within capitalist economic orders: "social junk" and "social dynamite." Social junk populations are relatively harmless to society, but their control exacts a substantial cost. They do not participate fully in the capitalist marketplace. Examples include the differentially abled members of society for whom institutional support is provided—physically, mentally or emotionally challenged; alcohol/drug dependents; the elderly, and so on. The "social dynamite" category consists of those who have the potential to "call into question established relationships, especially relations of production and domination" (p.645). This group represents a political threat to the capitalist class and includes groups like the alienated, politicized youth, politically volatile associations and the Communist Party. Raymond Michalowski (1985) submits that the underlying elements of social organization, "particularly the production and distribution of economic, political and cultural services, largely shape the perception of what constitutes unacceptable social injury." It is the **social** construction of harm that gives form and character to the processes of law and injustice. He details four postulates about the nature of crime and its relationship to social order (pp. 14-17): first, social order precedes and shapes the nature of law and the definition of crime. Second, economic organizations shape and interact with other elements of social life in fundamental ways. Third, the study of crime should not be limited solely to those acts defined as criminal by the law, but should incorporate an analysis and comparison of officially designated crimes with other forms of socially harmful behaviour not designated as criminal. Fourth, criminal and other socially harmful behaviours emerge, for the most part, as individuals attempt to create meaningful lives as defined by their view of the world and the real and perceived alternatives for action that exist in a given economic, political and social context. Clearly, capitalist institutions protect the capitalist economy and define what constitutes crime. To repeat, government investigations of corporate crimes are deliberately negligible in order to divert attention from corporate misbehaviour and direct public opinion away from practices which are significantly more threatening than common crimes.

Assessing the Criminological Canons

Strain perspectives highlight a consensus a central in maintaining social order. Implicitly strain theory retreats to a fixed unitary, homogeneous image of human life caught between individual appetites and social necessities. Strain theory does not even hint at let alone suggest a modicum of political, economic or social restructuring of institutions to safeguard against the inevitability of crime. Merton's analyses fail to consider seriously the structural basis of capitalist societies that inherently promote the contradictions he so eloquently identifies. Why is wealth so celebrated as a successful goal? In contrast, why is poverty perceived as a threat? How do the virtues of economic affluence get extolled? The claim that youth crime is disproportionately more prevalent among lower classes is clearly a distorted class-biased model. By implication, poverty, therefore, causes people to commit crime. It fails to explain why people with full access to legitimate means commit crime rarely accounting for the behaviour of the more wealthy youths who cheat steal, embezzle, or defraud. In brief, the traditional literature on subcultures or oppositional cultures tends to support highly elitist claims that lower class youths tend to engage in delinquency. The deviance of so-called middle-class or upper-class youth is always ignored. Authorities seem to notice lower class youths more frequently because they "hang out" in public areas and lack the protection of property or privacy enjoyed by their equally deviant but largely ignored middle-class or upper-class counterparts. The latter group's deviance is hidden and therefore more privileged. Middle class youths display just as many cultural straits as irresponsibility, hedonism towards sex, drugs, thefts, gambling, drug abuse, violence, vandalism and theft, search for thrills, and immediate gratification.

Strain theory does not explain why people vary in their choice of deviance; why, for example, do youths resort to shoplifting rather than drug dealing? Admittedly, strain theory situates deviance as violating a conservative culture and not necessarily in psychological imbalances or the failings of an individual. Strain theory ignores the process by which people are designated as deviant by others. This process involves a conflict of values between those who have power to label and those who are so labelled. This approach is limited because it neither explains why individuals lose their identification with the larger culture nor why the majority of persons exposed to approximately similar strains do not deviate. Strain perspectives that are culturebound and class-bound do not challenge the legitimacy of prevailing moral standards. Because of its particular biases, strain theory overlooks the fact that people experience society differently and therefore will have varying reactions to the normative standards by which they are governed. Essentially, the assumptions inherent in the strain paradigm effectively obscure and frequently exclude structures and relations of power. At best, one discovers a glib and myopic acknowledgement that rules serve the "best interests of all." Also, the negotiative character of norms is completely discarded.

Major limitations of traditional subcultural explanations concerns the very concept of a subculture which suffers from gross simplification, too often becomes equated with the gang, refers to highly exaggerated structural formations, identifies formations as attributes of working class adolescent males, is limited to locality based factors that are fixed or static. Many self-maintaining subcultures, however, are fluid, loose and continually emerging webs of interaction loose, permeable and changing structures. Shifting membership, limited involvements, role discrepancies, norm ambiguities, incomplete rules, and change are just as much part of subcultures as stability or cohesively integrated structures. Subculture is not a neatly articulated response packaged according to shared values and constraints. But, a subculture emerges as a social construction caused through the characteristic interplay of self-definition, reaction and interaction, a consequence but a context of ongoing meaningful interpretations. Subcultural approaches do not adequately address why some youths who lack conventional commitments fail to deviate. Or alternatively, why do people committed to conventional values deviate.

Perspectives on social bond fail to implicate social control as a cause of deviance. These approaches reject the social structural sources (social, economic and cultural forces). Similarly, the notion of attachment is problematic in that it ignores the significance of attachments at different stages of one's life cycle. One cannot assume that all youths subscribe equally to the moral values of "the" dominant culture. Differential association is too simplistic. Furthermore, it falters in explaining why some youths develop associations; it fails to account how friends influence behaviour and teach us to deviate; and, it refuses to address the issue of why delinquent friends exist in the first place. If attachments lead to deviance, what then causes the deviance of friends? That is, what explains the sources of these deviance-inducing relationships? Finally, According to neutralization theory delinquents and non-delinquents support different values. Matza, however, did not indicate why youths continue to engage in delinquency over time nor does he suggest why they are drawn into it in the first place. Additionally, the rewards of delinquency are not specified. Furthermore, the evidence is weak concerning the invocation of these "justifications." Are they used before, during or after the commission of illegal acts? Neutralization implies that people who are committed to crime are more likely to resort to these accommodating techniques. The relationship between the practice of neutralizing excuses and the subsequent deviance exists only for those experienced individuals who had previously committed acts of deviance and not for those who have never deviated.

While the labelling perspective provides a theoretical framework from which social constructions of deviance are examined, concern with the application of labels during social reaction presents highly relativistic moral statements. For example, Gibbs (1966:12) alleges that this orientation fails to specify the conditions that must exist before an act or individual is labelled deviant. Specifically, labelling approaches fail to ask why youths commit the initial deviant act, and do not deal adequately with personal decision-making in the crime/deviance process (Akers 1968:463). Within this context, labelling assumes an exaggerated sense of equivalence, that is, once labelled similar consequences are felt by all transformed offenders. Furthermore, what is important yet often downplayed, is that much crime or deviance goes undetected and is never labelled. That which appears as criminal or deviant tends to be class specific due to visibility, vulnerability, and the lack of resources enjoyed by certain communities. Labelling approaches fail to consider the general deterrent effects of social control on deviance.

In a more general sense, the assumptions of labelling theory do not fully address more macro sociological concerns. For example, labelling theory examines how the deviant responds to the label applied, but fails to address the process by which the larger society has come to define him or her as deviant. The "deviant" in this instance is portrayed as a submissive, passive victim of a one-sided process. What needs to be developed is an interrelated typology of subjects, situations and societal sanctions, in order to predict the outcomes of the labels. Also, in its theoretical orientation, labelling theory does not examine the historical foundation upon which the labels were constructed. Again, labelling approaches neglect issues of social structure and class. By overemphasizing the causal aspects of labelling, the social reaction approach creates a somewhat insidious role inversion that promotes an "ideology of the underdog" (Gouldner 1968) within a liberal ethos. Many crimes go unreported, let alone detected. Thus, many crimes occur despite the label. Becker's (1963) argument implies that deviance does not exist until it is constituted or recognized, while simulta-neously allowing for the possibility of "secret" or unlabelled deviance. And yet, there are normative overtones to assumptions of the early labelling approaches that remain inconsistent with the theoretical foundations of interactionism. Assuming that rules are consistently applied by actors to define "crime" or "deviance," Becker unfortunately compromises various processes of interpretation. He "fills in" the process of interpretation by describing it as the "application of rules" instead of attempting to "catch the process as it occurs in the experience of the acting units which use it" (Blumer 1962:190). Likewise, Kitsuse (1964) notes that the critical feature of the criminal/deviant-defining process is not the behaviour of individuals who are defined as criminal or deviant, but rather the interpretations others make of their behaviour. He views the process of interpretation and defin-ing acts or individuals as "criminal" or "deviant" as extremely problematic. Unlike Becker, he asserts that the perspectives of those who define and interpret behaviour must be explicitly incorporated into a sociological defi-nition of crime and deviance. In this respect, his discussion on societal reactions strongly supports the interpretive approach in developing a methodology that asks, how do youths interpret their behaviours, and what are the consequences of those interpretations? Undoubtedly, this type of analysis would have confronted the politicality of social interaction, the process under which definitions are imposed on particular members of society and why social control agents are considered legitimate and credi-ble classifiers.

In reference to conflict theory Vold's model is useful for highlighting how criminalization reflects different degrees of political power but remains limited to situations in which individual acts flow from the collision of group loyalties. It fails to explain impulsive or irrational acts outside the context of, and unrelated to, any group interest. Lamentably, deviance or crime outside of intergroup clashes is not well addressed. According to Akers (1985:27), conflict theory "is less appropriate to the analysis of the behaviour of those involved in many types of common-law crimes, usual deviations, and vices." As Hagan (1991:130-131) re-iterates, group conflict theory fares best in explaining types of crime about which consensus is minimal. Similarly, some laws are based on a consensual model of society; that is, supported by societal consensus (Gibbons 1979:188). Concerning law, Carson and Wiles (1971) report that rules are not always expressions of powerful interests. Laws are often compromises different interest groups. Rock (1974) charges that conflict theory is far too simplistic, leading to a naive understanding of the following: the complexities of law; the constraints of law even upon law-makers and law enforcers; the accommodative aspects of law rather than just the overwhelming emphasis on the coercive dimensions; and the multi-dimensional, relational and dynamic character of law. Third, as Pfohl (1985:343) explains, pluralist conflict theory fails miserably in examining the historically based structural contexts within which power struggles occur. Fourth, as Taylor, Walton and Young (1973) describe, subordinates are too simplistically presented as cultural dopes all too compliant and passive. Turk, they insist, fails to explain how authority relations are linked to wider systems of social stratification. Similarly, Pfohl (1985:343) admonishes:

> Despite its analytic utility, Turk's theory is little more than a disruption of the way in which contemporary social life is hierarchically structured. Turk falsely equates the way things are with the way things naturally have to be. He fails to realize that social structures are historical creations.

Critical or radical approaches are dismissed, as Akers retorts (1980:138), because they fail to move beyond a polemic for a blueprint of the good society. Socialist societies have been unable to deliver on the promise of classlessness and economic equality. Although mainstream liberal and conservative criminologies are disturbed with the ideological tenor of radi-

82

cal criminology, they fail to see how their own assertions, hyperboles and prognostications are loaded with bias. For conservative and liberal criminologists alike, the most serious criticism directed at radical criminology concerns its lack of objectivity and scientific rigour. The new criminology has been dismissed as visionary, utopian (Nettler 1974), fantasy, empirically shallow, biased, scholastically bankrupt (Inciardi 1980:8), and virtually non-falsifiable (Erickson and Gibbs 1979). For Turk, the inherently dogmatic and partisan rhetoric of this perspective is politically rather than scientifically decided (Turk 1979). Radical criminology is frequently condemned as inauthentic and righteous. For Hagan (1977), these writings are used as a catalyst for a classless society. In addition, Hagan (1991:138) and Liska (1987:205) argue that the above conflict propositions are difficult, if not impossible to test. Beyond judging and discarding the methodology of radical criminology as invalid according to the orthodoxy of positivism, mainstream designs and natural science criteria, the substance of radical criminology has also been criticized by Marxist social commentators. Just as Klockars (1978:498) disputes the class bias of criminal justice systems, Greenburg (1975) equally questions the uni-dimensionality of radical criminology. Throughout the 1970s, radical criminology had paid considerable attention to the links between law and the state trying to move away from the instrumentalist Marxist position. Notwithstanding their obvious weaknesses, conflict and radical approaches offer a sound framework for grappling with macro and micro processes of inequalities. It is always difficult to ascertain which conceptual path(s) to follow unless we become familiar with past traditions and destinations. It is equally difficult to ask questions unless we can assess the analytic strengths and weaknesses of well respected texts.

Conclusions: Youth Crime as (Per)formative and Generative Alienation

Although a formal theory of crime, let alone a perspective on youth identity is relatively absent in the writings of Marx and Engels (Hirst 1972), there are several observations that warrant attention. For Marx, economic relations determine the manner in which state institutions structure order. Because of the prevailing inequalities, social control is manipulated. The ruling class (Tucker 1978:78), as a whole, can organize non-economic institutions as well, such as the law and the criminal justice, with coercive and persuasive devices. Law and its attendant ideological framework are tools of the bourgeoisie in perpetuating illusions of neutrality, fairness, and equality (Marx [1868] 1969). The promise of law is a persuasive bourgeois accommodation invented to disguise coercion. As will be argued in Chapter 4, the law tenaciously alludes to promises of freedom and equality in a limited mythological sense.

In his article *Capital Punishment*, Marx ([1853], 1956:230) reminds us that crime is produced by fundamental anti-social conditions. That is, instead of glorifying the hangman who executes many criminals, there is a "necessity for deeply reflecting upon an alteration of the system that breeds these crimes" (ibid). Beirne and Messerschmidt (1991:345) point out that Marx and Engels' sociological analysis of the links between crime and capitalism contained three roughly separate dimensions: criminalization as a violation of natural or human rights, crime and demoralization, and crime and primitive rebellion. In his empirical work, *The Condition of the Working Class in England in 1844*, Engels (1975) recognizes that the economic position of the working class is instrumental in generating crime. Since the proletariat is not allowed to pursue their aspirations and are constantly prevented from enjoying the benefits of the economic order, they strike out at the brutality of the bourgeoisie. Again, the conditions of capitalism (exploitation and pauperization) lead to demoralization that in turn leads to crime (Engels, [1845], 1975). Also, Marx and Engels reiterate that the abolition of private ownership would witness the disappearance of crimes.

In the *Productivity of Crime*, Marx noted that the most important function of crime in society is its contribution to temporary economic stability in an economic system that is inherently unstable. Marx (1969b:375-376) writes:

> A criminal produces crime...The criminal produces not only crimes, but also criminal law...the criminal moreover produces the whole of the police and of criminal justice, constables, judges...and all these different lines of business...The criminal produces an impression, partly moral and partly tragic,...and in this way *renders a "service" by arousing the moral and aesthetic feelings of the public.* (Emphasis added)

Of enormous relevance to the youth crime-culture nexus is Marx's concept of *alienation*. The culture of capitalism conditions the everyday life, from the mind, body to social relations. Admittedly, a person's psychology is inseparable from one's material well being. By acting upon their environments, actors engage in a dynamic process of changing their social realities. For Marx, people humans are social beings, developing consciousness of themselves through interactions especially labour. Marx indicates that it is through labour that people become conscious of their species-being. Labour, as a set of physical and mental activities, accommodates to social circumstances. Through an appreciation of one's work, however defined, one realizes his or her own nature. But as expected, labour cannot be appreciated by actors when they are themselves alienated from it. Labour has become simply a *means to an end*, an objectification of both physical and mental activities. In general, the essence of life is the capacity to labour (physically and/ or mentally) which gives expression to one's essence. When that capacity to labour, which makes the individual truly human, is bought, sold or taken away, the individual character is lost (Marx 1978:479). By becoming appendages of institutional machines, enslaved to meaningless roles ands rules, people are forced to become less human. This dehumanizing process is particularly evident under capitalism. Human labour is reduced to a relatively cheap commodity. During this process of exchange, labour loses its unique and humanistic quality and simply becomes a means to an end. For some, the end is profit, while for the honest worker the end is simply survival. Whenever labour is redefined and actualized as only "a means to an end," rather than "an end in itself," alienation emerges. Individualism (liberalism), accumulation/ ownership of private property (capitalism) and utility (modernity) are the sources much alienations. Combined or individually, possessiveness, instrumentalism and individualism, represent a destructive of forces which prevent people from expressing socially their creative abilities. Forces beyond one's control or even understanding frame the context of one's alienation. From the others and more importantly from one's inner selves (p.72). The product of one's work and the activity that produces it (p.74) are no longer part of the process of creating. This objectification of the self (alienation from the sources of life's meanings) and its social estrangement (alienation from fellow others) constitute the social conditions which prevent self-activity, self-expression and reflexivity. Within the dominant culture, the powerless are required to sell their labour power in return for wages. This system of labour displays four relations that are at the core of Marx's theory of alienation. Workers are alienated from their *productive activity*, that is, they play no part in deciding what to do and how to do it. Workers are alienated from the *product of this activity*—having no control over what is made and what happens to the product. Workers are alienated *from other human beings* as competition and indifference replace cooperation. And, workers are *alienated from the distinctive potential inherent in being a human being.*

The idea of self-constitution of the species through labour is to serve as the guide to appropriating the Phenomenology while demythologising it (Habermas 1968). By turning the construction of the manifestation of consciousness into an encoded representation of the self-production of the species, Marx discloses the mechanism of progress in the experience of reflection, a mechanism that was concealed in Hegel's philosophy. It is the development of the forces of production that provides the impetus to abolishing and surpassing a form of life that has been rigidified in positivity and become an abstraction. Reflection is linked to labour at the level of instrumental action. By reducing the self-positing of the absolute ego to the more tangible productive activity of the species, be eliminates reflection as such as a motive force of history, even though be retains the framework of the philosophy of reflection. The self-generative act of the human species is complete as soon as the social subject has emancipated itself from necessary labour and, so to speak, takes its place alongside scientised production. At that point labour time and the quantity of labour expended also become obsolete as a measure of the value of goods produced. The spell of materialism cast upon the process of humanisation by the shortage of available means and the compulsion to labour will be broken. Synthesis through labour mediates the social subject with external nature as its object. But this process of mediation is interlocked with synthesis through struggle, which, in each case, mediates two partial subjects of society that make each other into objects, in other words, two social classes. Knowledge, the synthesis of the material of experience and forms of the mind, is only one aspect of both processes of mediation. Reality is interpreted from a technical viewpoint in the former and from a practical viewpoint in the latter. Synthesis through labour brings about a theoretical-technical relation between subject and object; synthesis through struggle brings about a theoretical-practical relation between them. The institutionally secured suppression of the communication through which a society is divided into social classes amounts to fetishising the true social relations. Thus, according to Marx, the distinguishing feature of capitalism is that it has brought ideologies from the heights of mythological or religious legitimations of tangible domination and power down into the system of social labour. In liberal bourgeois society the legitimation of power is derived from the legitimation of the market, that is from the "justice" of the exchange of equivalents inherent in exchange relations. It is unmasked by the critique of commodity fetishism (ibid).

As noted earlier, the masses of people are educated in ways that encourage an acceptance of their own subordination. Moreover, the prevailing culture of capitalism hinders the development of consciousness. Marx advises, "your very ideas are but the outgrowth of your bourgeois production and bourgeois property" (Tucker 1978:487). The dominant culture is replete with illusions that enhance alienation. Alienation, a condition of the material environment, denies creativity and restricts choices. Hook (1933:41) enlightens:

> Marx realized that every culture is a structurally interrelated whole, and that any institutional activity, say religion or law, can be understood only in relation to a whole complex of other social activities.

As Marx (1956:304) expounds:

> The political, legal, philosophical, literary, and artistic developments rest on the economic base. It is not the case that the economic situation is the sole active cause and that everything else is merely a passive effect. There is, rather a reciprocity within a field of economic necessity which in the last instance asserts itself.

Marx's theory of alienation incorporates many valuable categories such as exploitation, degradation, and immiseration. Informed by Marx's theories of alienation, we ask what conditions prevent youths from "affirming," "confirming" or "actualizing" themselves. Youth alienation is an estrangement, a disharmony and a disagreement with the human essence. They become distant from their species-beings; instead, they occupy a space external to their original independence (Marx 1978:43). Alienation robs life of its actual content, renders one condition worthless and devoid of dignity, degraded and enslaved (Wood 1981:9). Alienation is a condition that emerges from the destruction of a person's individuality and transforms him or her into a thing (Fromm 1961:48). In this regard we discover in this chapter that ideologies transform youths into a subject – they as individuals adopt versions of the truth for themselves. On the other hand, sophisticated

87

ideological processes of domination succeed in creating processes of self subordination. Consent as will be discussed in chapter five is secured by the diffusion and popularization of dominant cultural views. The consent of the "youth" to their ongoing exclusion flows from the hegemonic practices of all institutions of the state and civil society as the following chapters illustrate. This consent is manifested through a generic loyalty to prevailing dominant values that are internalized and become part of their "common sense," values to be defended and exaggerated. *Can we hear? We listen well but do we hear. Hearing means that if we heard when others spoke, we would be challenged to change our practices, our discourses, our lives; hearing requires some contemplation, reflections, that is, giving something back.*

Figure 2.4

ideological structures of thought

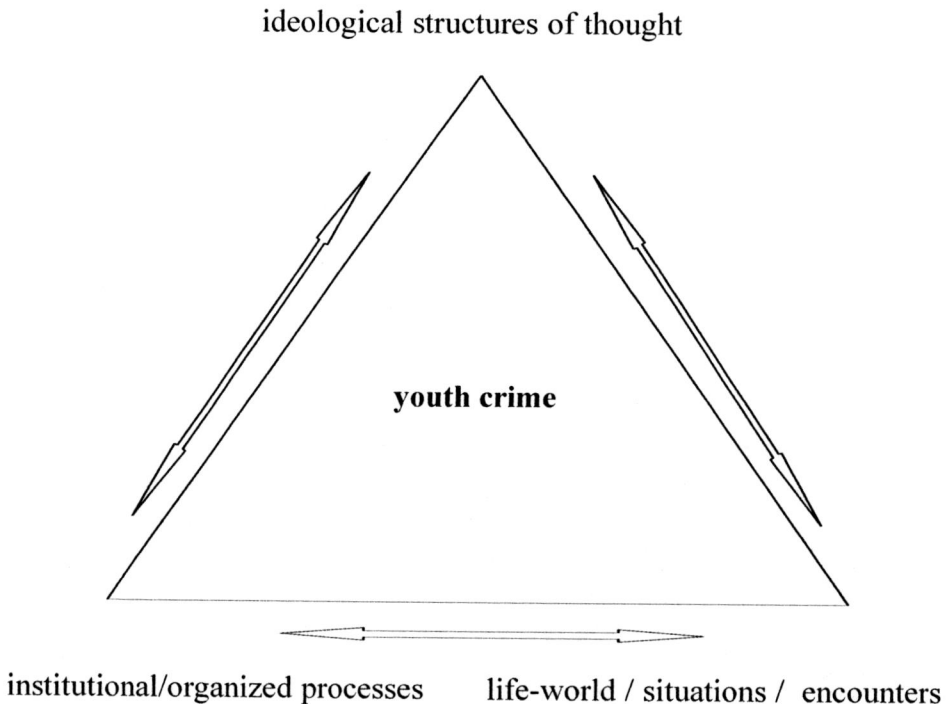

youth crime

institutional/organized processes   life-world / situations / encounters

Figure 2.5

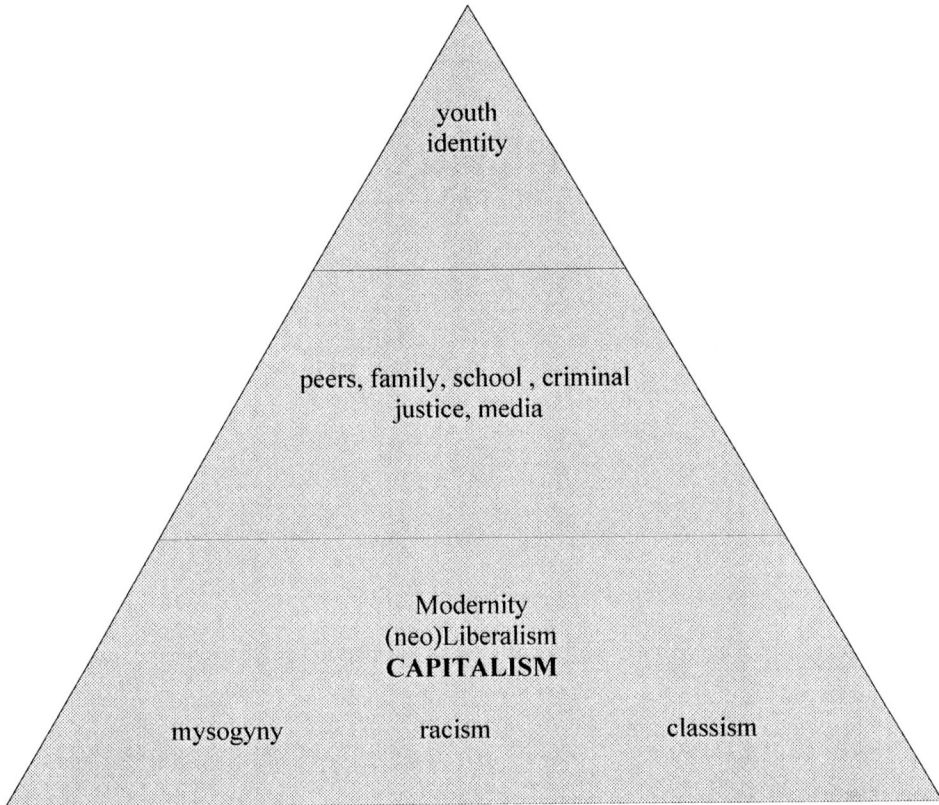

Chapter 3

"Cool" Cultures as Mediated Messages

"Propaganda begins when dialogue ends."
—Jacques Ellul (1964)

Introduction: Differential Impact of the Media on Youth

The culture-control nexus impacts on normative strategies that govern and manipulate subjective experiences of youths. Critical cultural approaches resist canonical narratives and open up praxis. Rather than blithely echo commonsensical assumptions that characterize the impact of the media on youth, this project in cultural criminology sets forth a series of hitherto ignored converging and conflicting challenges.

As the preceding chapter highlighted, culture is a social production that is inextricably tied to *political and economic concatenations of power.* Culture as an ideological superstructure is reflective and derivative of socio-economic structures that pervade social institutions. At the agentic level, culture is a social accomplishment rooted in history and expressed in action, forms of consciousness and forces of change. Culture, simply put, is the channel through which social relations are conducted. As a set of shared meanings, expectations and understanding, culture is manifested in symbolic communication: language, customs, myths, signs as well as material artefacts. Culture also incorporates the means and processes of production of symbolism and style (Griswald 1994:71; McNeely 1996).

91

Notably, *culture constructs consciousness.* Bennett (1982:51) observes that this dialectic involves a mutually interactive relationship between the subject (human agents) and the object (the conditions of their existence).

Culture consists of ideas that are selectively communicated, believed and legitimated quite often as knowledge. Oversimplified threats of danger as well as exaggerated claims of merit are manipulated in order to dismiss, counter or even create different beliefs. The morphology and content of the cultural messages assign primacy to materialism. This obsessive deference to materialism is overwhelmingly scripted in the media of communication configured according to seductive symbols which in turn becomes personalized and possessed. Loyalties to this pervasive value system are passionately defended and anchored generationally. All mainstream socializing institutions are implicated in reproducing this morality of individual possessiveness. These normative notions about the status quo are protected and become social catechisms that define the appropriateness of identity and behaviour.

People come to their respective understandings of reality through socialization wherein social interactions are internalized as experiences. The media plays a very important role in the socialization process because of its ability to provide images of experiences. Knowledge is unknowable except as mediated encounters which claim an experiential basis for understanding reality. Informed by Stuart Hall who has demonstrated that media portrayals legitimize order, build consent and delegitimate outsiders, we argue that mediated communications are supported by other institutions such as the criminal justice, education, work, family, etc. Rather than create, the media renews, amplifies and extends existing predispositions that constitute the dominant culture, (Gurevitch, Bennett, Curran, and Woollacott 1982:14). The ideological operation of the mass media in the West contributes to the reproduction of the capitalist system. The issue is not whether the media perpetuate dominant power relations but how youth and others experience the culture of the media differently (Giroux 1988, 1994). Cultural theorists (Hall 1980; Hall et al. 1978; Giroux 2001) reasons that there is a dialectics between "social being" and "social consciousness." Hall (1980) stresses the importance of how people make sense of media texts and the inscription dominant ideologies (narratives) according to "preferred," "oppositional" and "negotiated" readings of the media text.

The principle objective of this chapter, part of a larger ongoing study on youth, is to discuss the differential impact of the media on delinquency by comparing the perceptions of youths (school and street youth) of delinquency and their reaction to this perception. Accordingly, this research examines: a) media depictions of youth crime, b) images youth have of crime generally, c) youth interpretations of the media coverage of delinquency; d) variations in perceptions of the media coverage among different segments of the youth population; and, e) levels of youth resistance and accommodations to mediated messages of youth crime. Chapter five examines the different levels of accommodation / resistance youths use to negotiate various institutions of socializing control. Based on data collected from 2000-2005 on the use of the media by street and school youth, it is argued that youth cultures adopt prevailing cultural values regarding "coolness" to an extreme—a finding that contradicts extant youth research on resistance and suggests more critical directions for delinquency theorizing. Identity, social relations and discourses are juxtaposed against the role the media plays in the lives of young people, the dialectical interplay between culture and crime, the tensions and contradictions and the possibilities of its transcendence. In brief, this study examines how youth experience the media. By focussing on the tensive interplay between delinquency and the media, this study further highlights conceptually the inextricable relationship between discourse and subjectivity. By challenging the dominant ideologies of crime, this study makes a significant contribution to Canadian critical criminology by examining how the values of youth are constructed relationally in order to form the basis or "precondition of a politically engaged critique." Informed by a unique blend of interpretive sociology and critical theory, this research connects culture and crime in terms of inscribed social inequalities. The current study is an incremental conceptualization of my earlier studies on youth and culture (Visano 1987, 1988, 1990b, 1996a, 1998a).

Within the interpretive tradition in sociology, Weber's (1969) "verstehen," an empathic and interpretive understanding of the subjective meanings which actors attach to social action, is essential in contextualizing how actors take into account the actions of others and are guided by these subjective meanings. Theoretically, therefore, critical cultural criminology with its insights from both cultural studies and critical theory provides transformative possibilities by urging a relational view in which the component elements of social life are not individuals or institutions but combinations of economic, political, class, gender, age and legal relations. Contemporary criminology is advanced by examining the relationship youths have with the media and how the media, in turn, alters techniques of social presentation among youths. To what extent do the media impact on youth cultures by influencing the communicative processes and the net of social interaction thereby empowering them to expand or restrict their sites and targets of sociality (delinquency/ conformity)? For example, what informs the impressions and knowledge of youth regarding the crime? These are crucial questions, delineating important dimensions of the relationship between the crime and the wider society. Beyond this is the importance this research holds for the politics of "tough" deterrence which dominates current public policy. This research is important for predicting the effectiveness of neo liberal policies by determining whether youths even employ a calculus of costs and benefits in their decisions to engage in criminal activity. The issue is not that criminological theory has ignored media accounts of youth crime, but that it has ignored the extent to which the media exerts a basic influence over the social thoughts of youth. How then do the discourses and practices of the media create ideologically appropriate subjects for youths? How are these youths constructed in contradictions? How are their experiences articulated given the influences of hegemonic narratives in everyday lives and interpretations? What for youths conditions the constitution of connections between the culture and crime? What is the significance of media regulation and cultural integration especially along a time and space continuum? What do youths identify as the push pull factors in framing their master, hybrid or situational identities? Guided by Griswold's (1994) normative conceptualization of culture as a historically transmitted pattern of symbolic meanings, this study examines how the media and youth communicate, perpetuate, and develop knowledge. By exploring the mechanisms and systems of power which produce crime, this discussion will suggest that the experience of culture, as it is discursively embodied in the media, represents the paradox of assertion and recognition between "self" and "other." As Valverde (1990) advises, the reflexive relationship between identity and practical consciousness is organized through a specific articulation of images, objects and words.

Methodology

Epistemologically, the interpretive approaches directed this research project by providing a general proposal of guiding notions. Concepts such as identity and socialization assist in sensitizing researchers to move beyond concrete forms of empirical instances. This study incorporates quantitative and qualitative methods in data collection procedures which included: a) a preliminary study to investigate media sites of interest to youth (200 participants); b) detailed interviews of school and street youth (50 participants). Instruments included: i) demographic factors: age, education, race, class, ethnicity, gender, urban/ suburban; and, ii) personal factors: self esteem; peer group references; knowledge and reasoning; questions on how youth articulate their respective experiences; iii) interpersonal/ interactional contexts: networks of supportive relations; types of personal experiences; family/ peer dynamics; and, iv) organizational/ institutional factors: commitments to school, family, work, community, and peer groups. Content analyses of responses were utilized for ascertaining the language rules and vocabularies for encoding and decoding events and activities within a phenomenological approach. The instruments captured how one's interpretation of the media is conditioned by time, place and subjectivities. c) Site visits (12) were conducted in order to hold focus group sessions with youth in secondary schools and youth hostels in Metropolitan Toronto and the Greater Toronto Area (GTA): York, Peel, and Durham Regions. Institutional support had been secured from eight Metro Toronto secondary schools/ high schools, two GTA secondary schools, three elementary schools and five youth serving social service agencies. d) An ethnography of different media sites that were of interest to twenty youths involved an examination of school youth and street youth in their natural settings (including out of school surroundings or institutional settings to gather data in informal settings e.g. video games and internet media). These sources have become highly significant in creating, coding, reinforcing and shaping youth images and culture. We folded these sites into data collection and analysis at an early stage. The focus on the street (a comfortable venue for street youth) retained dimensions of the "naturalistic" talk and participation. The present study examined age related changes in youth's knowledge and reasoning about legal issues presumed to be important to them. Naturalistic observations in situationally relevant contexts enabled the discovery of meaning, action, identity, and status as organized around style—that is, the shared aesthetic of the subculture's members. The ethnography demonstrated that the interpretation of media is conditioned by time, place and subjectivity of the actor. This programmatic research approach based on primary strategies of qualitative and quantitative analyses in selected substantive areas was developed for in depth inquiry and a study of what youths actually know, or think they know about the crime. The second line of inquiry incorporated a set of specific questions pertaining to perceptions of the legal system and an understanding of its operation. These strategies were then combined into an interactive examination of the problem, proposing a somewhat different and compelling investigation of the relationship between law and society, with important theoretical and empirical implications for cultural, political, and criminological studies in general. Qualitative data (content and discourse analyses of the main themes and central meaning patterns also indicated that the differential reading of the media text is governed by mood, that is, a psychic vibration between the poles of boredom and anxiety. Both quantitative and qualitative approaches were employed to collect data on youths' impressions of reported youth crimes. Based on Ericson, Baranek, and Chan (1991), certain criteria of newsworthiness (e.g., simplification, dramatization, personalization, continuity) that are at work will be analyzed in terms of the basic requirements order, coherence, sequence. The following stages were used: a revelationary stage where delinquency is presented; (2) an interpretive stage where views of a privileged selection of "authorities" is given; and, (3) closure, where the coverage moves to recommendation, anticipated action/ reaction measures. The content analyses were useful in highlighting the diversity in responses of youth to media coverage of single events. The communication of words and images were studied. The contexts of linguistics—histories within configurations of temporal, geographic and social conditions as well as language events and discourse were described as instances of discourse. In dealing with each research phase we followed a standard, informative format: the theoretical specifications, observational and interview findings and testing of explanatory models. Diverse sampling strategies were used: snow ball, purposive, cross sectional and reputational (see Table 3.1). Participants over the age of 12 and under the age of 18 were selected (corresponding with the age specific contexts of the Youth Criminal Justice Act). e) Lastly, self-narratives were pursued. The narrative is often described as inherently particularizing but the particularities may be global and comparisons among narratives facilitate a form of general cross-situational knowledge. Narratives are useful for achieving different kinds of understanding or understandings of different issues (Calhoun 1995:4). Methodologically, narratives animate standpoint epistemologies by grappling with notions of the decentralized, extra social and extra language, that is, universal wisdom or essentialized differences. The

96

TABLE 3.1
SAMPLE: PURPOSIVE CROSS SECTIONAL (SELF IDENTIFIED)

	In school	Street kids	Gang not in school	Gang in school	Incarcerated probation	Totals
M	50	10	10	15	25	110
F	70	10	0	5	5	90
W	70	18	7	12	10	117
E-R	50	2	3	8	20	83
UMC	80	0	2	4	8	94
P/WC	40	20	8	16	22	106
12-15	54	2	0	4	0	60
16-19	66	18	10	16	30	140
Totals	120	20	10	20	30	**200**

Legend: M: males; F: females; W: white; ER: ethno racial; UMC: upper -middle-class; P/W: poor/ working-class.

key herein is the set of tensions/ contradictions that underpin self-narratives that point both to their situation in the larger historical reality and to the possibilities of transcendence. It is critical to be able to see the underlying pattern of causes and constraints, not merely the more contingent surface features of actual occurrences (p.9).The present study examined age related changes in youth's knowledge and reasoning about legal issues presumed to be important to them. They were voluntarily self-selected youth (12-17-year-olds inclusive). Second, this research investigated print and electronic journalism. Television news and newspaper crime coverage were major sources of data for uncovering how the media portrays youth and delinquency. Comparisons were also made with entertainment crime programmes. Content and discourse analyses of top-rated television programs, in which the main themes and protagonists are concerned with various dimensions of crime and law enforcement, were considered in order to obtain a general perspective on portrayals of the criminal justice system over time in the entertainment medium.

The above methodology is justifiable theoretically in enhancing the validity of the study. Rather than a preconceived and programmatic methodology, a flexible accommodation exists which is consistent with the demands of interpretive sociology. As a general methodology, qualitative sociology displays an "omnibus quality" by incorporating an array of well-reasoned exercises. These include variations of informal communicative strategies, direct participation, conversational or informal dialogue, and formal focused presentations. Interpretive sociology recognizes the importance of inner and outer perspectives in constituting their "central meaning patterns" (Rock 1979:198). This methodology follows the admonition of Hagan and McCarthy (1998), and Di Cristina (1995) that criminology move away from its heavy reliance on school surveys and selfreported criminality and work towards incorporating the more taxing "street criminology," which inspired early North American criminological research. A multi-perspectival approach is used in the study to incorporate various theoretical perspectives such as media culture, modernity, postmodernism, resistance, and various perspectives in the development and maintenance of identity. A multi-method approach was used in the study that employs naturalistic classroom observations and student interviews.

Conceptual Overview: Critical Cultural Criminology

Ideological criticism analyzes how cultural texts embody and enact particular values, beliefs and ideas, that is, how cultural practices produce particular knowledge. This ideological analysis draws upon the numerous insights and methods of different approaches—phenomenology, critical media analysis, literary studies, semiotics, constitutive criminology, narrative analysis, interpretive criminology, critical theory, and social constructionism to name but a few interdisciplinary modes of analysis. From Gramsci (1971), Goffman (1974), Althusser (1971), Hall (1977), Foucault (1979), Derrida (1981), Parenti (1992), Virilio (1994) to Eschholz and Bufkin (2001), analyses have attended to the location of culture within wider socio economic frames. The media plays an important rôle in the transmission of the dominant ideology. Consistent with both Bourdieu's (1977) notion of the relative autonomy of popular cultural capital and Habermas's (1981, 1998) assertion that the media consist of a variety of competing capitalist interests, this study proposes that the media culture industry constructs consensus by reproducing, manipulating and controlling any perceived challenges. Informed by the brilliant contributions of Gramsci, Bourdieu describes how cultural capital (cultural knowledge, behaviour, taste and opinions) become hegemonized thus "common sense" and naturalized forms of thinking. From Innis (1951) who documents the profound significance of the media throughout history, from Heidegger's (1977) claims that this new type of cultural system restructures the entire social world as an object of control to Habermas's (1962) discussion of how reasoning is now only formed by the mass media, this moves toward a Marxist culturalist research tradition (Hall et al. 1978). Accordingly, the mass media is a powerful influence that shapes public consciousness and reflects the ideas and values of those classes that own and control it. According to adherents of Marxist political economy, the mass media conceal the economic basis of class struggle; ideology becomes the route through which struggle is obliterated rather than the site of struggle (Gurevitch, Bennett, Curran, and Woollacott 1982:26). In other words, elements of the "culture industry" such as the media, education, arts, and entertainment, legitimate the interests of advanced capitalism. As Adorno and Horkheimer (1989:181) remark, the stronger the positions of the culture industry become, the more summarily it can deal with consumers' needs, producing them, controlling them, and disciplining them. The media rewards consumers and punitively impoverishes those actors and / or institutions actively engaged in interrogating the fundamental ethos of passivity, individuality and consumption. The subliminal seduction manipulated (Key 1981:40) by the corporate profit-oriented media (i.e., television, radio, newspapers, magazines and film, cultivate the dominant ideology) mould mindless ways of understanding; and homogenize everyday life experiences. The mass media plays a significant role in transforming the individual into a compliant consumer. There is little escape from images of "appropriateness" with which communities are relentlessly bombarded. These images become increasingly real as consumers develop relationships among themselves and the items they hear, read and see. Consumers are urged to buy the images, believe in the necessity of that which is produced by the media. In time, consumers emulate the images and engage in mindless and mimetic gestures of conformity as they become that which they purchase. In effect, the central political and economic role of mass culture in manipulating through propaganda and thought control destroys reason, literacy and imagination. A more critical approach assumes cultural products like the media reflect meanings that are grounded in the social structure in terms of hierarchical relations, interests, and the status quo (McNeely 1995). The media uphold and extend the societal status quo. As noted previously, Althusser's notion of interpellation allows Marxist media theorists to explain the political function of mass media texts. That is, as a preexisting structure, the text interpellates spectators, thereby constituting them as subjects. According to this view, the subject (viewer, listener, reader) is constituted by the text, and the power of the mass media reside in their ability to "position" the subject in such a way that their representations are taken to be reflections of everyday reality.

Substantive Sites

Televisual Thirsts

From popular and seemingly innocuous televised cartoons to more sober newscasts in mainstream media, certain versions of the truth are learned. All aspects of the dominant media project a complex set of "shared" knowledge, beliefs, and customs that in turn frame conventional thinking. Everyday media practices are replete with significant ceremonies, signs, symbols, cues and clues that pattern gestures, rituals, or performances that in turn stage degrees of cultural affiliations. Social membership or a binding way of life constitutes and is constituted by the interplay, therefore, between specific behavioural circumstances and powerful ideologies that structure society. For McLuhan (1964, 1967), the impact of television cannot be understood independent of its social system in which they are implemented and used. The TV is both a cultural producer and product, influencing that influences the world of meaning. Despite shallow claims of network executives who laud the entertaining basis of TV, the TV performs a number of transformative functions. The social, behavioural, and psychological functions of TV extend beyond leisure and entertainment. The TV is not only a source of social information; but rather lamentably, the TV has become the only credible and comfortable resource of knowledge and truth. Television is an incredible power resource especially since we are dealing not only with a captive audience but also with programmes that are deliberately addictive, reflecting romanticized notions of escape under the guise of entertainment.

Television requires little literacy but much faith. This "new religion" (Gerbner 1978:47; DeRooy 1994:40) cultivates images fitting the structure of social relations. This contrived TV reality shapes moods, dreams and fantasies. This alleged friend of the family assumes many roles. Not only does television entertain but also preaches through programs, newscasts and advertisements. Solemn sermons from distant corporate offices are miraculously delivered instantly in simple, attractive and of course colourful formats. Messages are stacked according to the requisite levels of compliance.

Television is the most popular media primarily because it provides both entertainment and information for all sectors of the population. Moreover, given both its accessibility and availability, television infiltrates the everyday lives of Canadians. Television has obvious advantages over newspapers in immediacy, motion, color, and convenience (Bagdikian 1997). The televisual immediacy and presentness invoke the illusion of reality. Stories are presented directly and live expressly for the viewer.

Television watching, for instance, is a favourite form of entertainment and pastime. The vast majority of Canadian households (97.5%) own at least one colour television set (Statistics Canada 1992). Canadians watch 21.6 hours per week on average (Statistics Canada 2004) and are subjected to over 25,000 commercials per year (De Rooy 1994:15). Many children spend one third of their waking hours in front of their television screens. Statistics Canada noted that the average child watches eighteen hours of TV a week, or a little more than 2.5 hours daily (Brown 1994:78). A third of all 0-6 year olds (36%) have a TV in their bedroom, more then one in four (27%) have a VCR or DVD, one in ten have a video game player, and 7% have a computer. Thirty percent of 0-3-year-olds have a TV in their room, and 43% of 4-6-year-olds do (http://www.sosparents.org/The%20Facts.htm). The average teen watches TV for just 14.1 hours per week (see Tables 3.2a and 3.2b). This means that just over 8% of their week is devoted to television. Parents and educators should take a step back and realize that teenagers are the group of Canadians that watch the least amount of TV! While the national average remained stable during that period, TV viewing time decreased by more than two hours among teens and by more than one hour among children. At the provincial level, New Brunswickers spent the most time watching television (24.1 hours per week), compared to Albertans who spend the least amount of time (19.4 hours) (http://www.statcan.ca/Daily/English/021202/d021202a.htm). Television was viewed the most in Quebec (23.8 hours per week); more than two hours more than the national average. The gap was greatest among those aged 35 and over. Quebec francophones spent the most time in front of the small screen (24.5 hours per week), while Quebec anglophones were, for the first time, those who watch television the least in Canada. Children and teens spent less time in front of the tube—two hours less per week than five years ago. Men aged 18 to 24 continued to be the group least interested in watching television, with only 12.6 hours per week. At the other extreme, women aged 60 and over watched television the most (nearly 36 hours per week). Overall, Canadians still spent a sizable portion of their time watching television, at 21.6 hours per week. The number of hours of television viewing has been relatively stable over the past four years (http://www.statcan.ca/Daily/English/021202/d021202ahtm, http://www.statcan.ca/Daily/English/031121/d031121a.htm).

According to Nielsen Media Research, 98% of U.S. households owned at least one TV set in 2003 (World Almanac Education Group 2004: 267). Another way to gauge the importance of TV is to note the ownership of TV sets per 1,000 residents. There are 938 television sets per 1,000 people in the United States; UK 950; Australia 731; Japan 731; Canada 691; Germany 637; France 632; Russia 538; Jamaica 374; Lebanon 357; Israel 330; Argentina 326; China 312; Thailand 300; Mexico 282; Cuba 251; Malaysia 202; Syria 172; Pakistan 150; Algeria 114; India 83 (World Almanac Education Group 2005:799).

The average household in the United States has a television turned on for almost eight hours a day, with the average viewing of four hours a day (McNeely 1995; Papazian 1988). The average American spends 7.5 hours each day watching television; the TV has become the greatest consumer of leisure time (USA Today 1994: 11A). In a year, the average child spends 900 hours in school and nearly 1,023 hours in front of a TV

TABLE 3.2A
AVERAGE HOURS PER WEEK OF TELEVISION VIEWING (2002)

	TOTAL POPULATION	CHILDREN 2 TO 11 YEARS	TEENS 12 TO 17 YEARS	18 YEARS AND OVER	
				Male	Female
Canada	**21.6**	**14.6**	**13.7**	**21.0**	**25.8**
Nfld & Labrador	22.7	**17.0**	13.7	22.1	26.6
Prince Edward Island	21.5	15.7	15.7	21.0	25.1
Nova Scotia	23.7	16.1	15.9	23.0	27.8
New Brunswick	23.3	16.3	13.4	21.8	28.4
Quebec	23.8	14.7	14.4	23.0	28.9
Quebec Anglophones	19.4	11.9	12.2	18.5	23.6
Que. Francophones	24.5	15.1	14.6	23.8	29.9
Ontario	20.6	14.5	13.8	20.0	24.5
Manitoba	21.6	15.0	13.9	20.9	26.3
Saskatchewan	21.2	16.0	12.3	20.8	25.4
Alberta	20.0	14.2	12.4	19.4	24.3
British Columbia	20.8	13.1	12.5	20.9	24.3

Notes: Data was collected over the Fall period (4 weeks of November). (Sources: Date modified: November 21, 2003 , Television viewing Fall 2002 Statistics Canada http://www.statcan.ca/Daily/English/031121/d031121a.htm) .

TABLE 3.2B
AVERAGE HOURS PER WEEK OF TELEVISION VIEWING, BY PROVINCE, AND AGE/SEX GROUPS (FALL 2002)

AGE	CAN	NL	PEI	NS	NB	QUE	ONT	MAN	SASK	ALTA	BC
Total	**21.6**	**22.7**	**21.5**	**23.7**	**23.3**	**23.8**	**20.6**	**21.6**	**21.2**	**20.0**	**20.8**
M											
18+	21.0	22.1	21.0	23.0	21.8	23.0	20.0	20.9	20.8	19.4	20.9
18-24	12.6	16.7	12.2	14.6	10.8	13.3	12.0	11.8	12.2	12.7	12.8
25-34	16.6	18.6	17.3	18.3	16.7	16.8	16.1	16.8	17.5	15.9	17.2
35-49	18.9	21.7	20.3	21.0	18.9	20.6	18.0	18.9	18.4	18.2	18.2
50-59	22.7	23.0	23.6	24.7	23.9	25.7	21.1	21.4	21.3	21.3	22.4
60+	31.9	28.0	27.6	32.4	33.1	35.7	30.4	32.5	31.0	29.6	31.1
F											
18+	25.8	26.6	25.1	27.8	28.4	28.9	24.5	26.3	25.4	24.3	24.3
18-24	16.3	20.0	16.5	16.4	17.2	17.0	16.1	16.2	16.2	17.2	13.7
25-34	21.7	25.7	24.8	24.5	24.9	22.8	20.7	25.0	22.5	22.6	19.9
35-49	22.7	26.0	22.3	26.3	26.5	25.1	21.3	22.3	22.2	21.3	21.1
50-59	27.5	26.3	26.0	28.7	29.8	31.6	26.5	27.3	24.3	25.0	23.9
60+	35.9	31.1	31.9	35.3	35.8	40.5	33.8	35.4	34.7	34.4	35.8
M+F											
12-17	13.7	13.7	15.7	15.9	13.4	14.4	13.8	13.9	12.3	12.4	12.5
2-11	14.6	17.0	15.7	16.1	16.3	14.7	14.5	15.0	16.0	14.2	13.1

Legend: F: women; M: men; M + F: men and women.
Sources: Date modified: November 21, 2003, *Television Viewing* (Fall 2002). Retrieved from Statistics Canada (http://www.statcan.ca/Daily/English/031121/d031121a.htm).

TABLE 3.2C
AVERAGE US TELEVISION VIEWING TIME (OCTOBER 2002)
(HOURS: MINUTES)

		TOTAL	Mon-Fri	Mon-Fri	Mon-SUN	SAT	Mon-Fri	SUN
Women	Age	per week	7-10 am	10am-4pm	8-11pm	7-1pm	11:30 pm-1am	1-7pm
	18+	35:17	5:11	5:11	9:42	0:54	1:37	1:09
	18-24	23:11	3:32	3:32	5:54	0:35	1:19	1:37
	25-54	33:16	4:25	4:25	9:16	0:55	1:39	1:34
	55+	44:01	7:16	7:16	12:04	1:01	1:40	1:55
Men	18+	21:31	1:40	3:38	9:10	0:50	1:37	1:68
	18-24	23:18	0:56	2:49	5:21	0:33	1:31	1:24
	25-54	30:25	1:29	2:56	8:55	0:51	1:36	1:56
	55+	39:39	2:25	5:26	11:29	0:57	1:35	2:19
Teens	12-77	21:00	0:50	1:53	5:54	0:49	0:52	1:16
Children	2-11	20:30	1:42	2:58	4:49	1:11	0:29	1:04
TOTALS		30:35	1:52	3:59	8:27		1:22	1:38

Source: Nielsen Media Research (hours: minutes per week). World Almanac Education Gro up (2004:268).

103

According to the American Academy of Pediatrics (AAP), kids in the United States watch about 4 hours of TV a day he average American child watches 3 to 5 hours of television every day. By high school graduation, most children have spent more time in front of the TV than in the classroom (http://www.kidshealth. org/ parent/positive/family /tv_affects_child.html). In fact, 65% of US teens have TV sets in their own rooms (http://www.pbs. org/wgbh/pages/frontline/teach/cool). By the time they complete grade 12, they will have spent between 3,000 and 4,000 hours more in front of the television than in the classroom (Canadian Teachers' Federation 1995). Two to five-year-olds watch, on average, about 28.5 hours of TV per week (kid media@airwaves.chi.il.us).

Advertisements and Commercial Propaganda

The twin products of television, information dissemination and entertainment, are shaped by commercial interests. The fundamental product of TV's fascination with crime in popular network programming is the audience which is manufactured by corporate interests. Irrespective of the media's own publicly stated commitments to inform, the media primarily strive to generate dividends attendant with increased circulation and enhanced revenues from advertisers. For Chomsky (1989), a careful scrutiny of the subtext reveals that illusions are necessary in order to maximize the profits of corporate interests, the main business propaganda industry (Chomsky 1997). The promotion of the message constitutes the raison d'être of the media. Commercials, per se, divert attention away from authentic reflexivity towards "cultivating" followers or "believers" through indoctrination. The spirit of capitalism is embodied in the altars of commercials that hold sacred the blessings of profits. TV commercials are omnipresent, extending from the proliferation of infomercials to the celebration of products. The television ostensibly sets the apolitical agenda, the mindless recipe for success and the formulae for fitness according to foreign criteria. Viewers are besieged with appropriate appetites and personalized products. All aspects of the human condition are inspected from personal hygiene on commercials to horrific atrocities on sensational talk shows. Personal privacy has been appropriated by corporate greed. The viewer's body has been refashioned while the mind remains idle. The viewer has been held captive; television annihilates the present lived moment by enabling viewers to enjoy experiences beyond time and space. These hostages view images on the screen, which are often new and improved images of themselves (sanitized, homogenized and, of course, colonized). Consciousness is constricted, advocacy muted and inequalities legitimized within these cultural codes. The media generally exploits and manipulates in the interests of power and self-preservation. The media conveys socially sanctioned messages about the consequences of unacceptable conduct. Although the estimates vary, urban North Americans are believed to be exposed to between 1,500 and 3,000 promotional messages each day (http://www.mediawatch.ca/industry/advertising).

The audience then is sold to advertisers through the market share process, upon which cost of air-time for commercials is calculated (DeRooy 1994:19). Since air time is expensive, advertisers are careful to present commercials that can only "capitalize" on their investment. Besides regular programs, viewers are drawn into commercials that are also designed to "attract and persuade" consumption (Schietz and Sprafkin 1978:69). As noted, commercial television and television commercials are in the commerce business—selling products that will generate profits. Distorted messages are communicated (Denisson and Tobey 1991) that manipulate the insecurities and curiosities of the individual, making the viewer feel incomplete without particular products. Clearly, advertising requires the communication of values—consumerism. Because of this insecurity, individuals see the product as a need to survive and succeed (Moog 1990). Commercials produce the wants that need to be satisfied. Commercials reinforce consumption and create new appetites, fetishes or needs measured as "the product." Industry figures reveal the extraordinary growth of the mass-consumption society. In 1950, as the postwar economy began to heat up American business spent $5.7 billion to advertise its goods and services; in 2003, expenditures again hit an all-time high, $245 billion. Nearly, 60% of all advertising dollars are spent on ads in newspapers or magazines or commercials on radio and television. While the Internet is a fast-growing medium, it still represents a fraction of all advertising dollars spent (World Almanac Education Group 2005:347). The biggest advertisers are the nation's largest manufacturers of automobiles, food, soft drinks, tobacco and beer (see Tables 3.3a and 3.3b for leading advertisers).

The television commercial is the most expensive and highly skilled artifact in North American society, using the most polished producers, actors, and technical reproduction and spending more for the creation and transmission of a series of thirty-second commercials than some school districts spend to educate children for a year. The artful construction of commercials has created thirty seconds as a basic attention unit, ideal for selling marginal goods but with negative psychological and intellectual consequences for the average American child, who, the statistics show, watches television for twice as many hours as he or she attends school. In general, there are 1,600 advertising messages aimed at consumers on any given day (Bagdikian 1997). American children watch 40,000 commercials each year.

TABLE 3.3A
ADVERTISING EXPENDITURES IN THE US (1776-2003)
($ MILLIONS)

YEAR	AMOUNT	YEAR	AMOUNT
1776	$0.2	1940	$2,110
1800	1	1950	5,700
1820	3	1960	11,960
1840	7	1970	19,550
1850	12	1980	54,780
1860	22	1985	94,750
1867	40	1990	128,640
1880	175	1995	160,930
1890	300	2000	243,680
1900	450	2001	231,300
1909	1,000	2002	236,875
1915	1,100	2003	245,477

Source: Advertising Age. These estimated figures refer to spending on placing advertising in all media; the costs of producing the advertising are not included (World Almanac Education Group 2005:347).

From the junk food and toy advertisements during Saturday morning cartoons to the appealing promos on the backs of cereal boxes, marketing messages inundate kids of all ages. And to them, everything looks ideal; like something they simply have to have. It all sounds so appealing; often, so much better than it really is. Under the age of 8 years, most children do not understand that commercials are for selling a product. Children 6 years and under are unable to distinguish program content from commercials, especially if their favorite animated characters are promoting a particular product (http://www.kidshealth.org/parent/positive/family/tv_affects_childhtml; http://www.pbs.org/wgbh/pages/frontline/teach/cool). Teens are exposed to an estimated 3,000 ads a day. Last year, US teens spent an estimated $105 billion and influenced their parents to spend an additional $48 billion (ibid). The commercial media caters to corporate manipulation of consumer appetites by fostering an unfettered exploration into the boundaries of seemingly random and spontaneous human desire. The revenues of media institutions are controlled by the needs of advertisers to produce audience-maximizing profits (Gurevitch, Bennett, Curran, and Woollacott 1982:18).

TABLE 3.3B
LEADING US ADVERTISERS, 1991-2003
ADVERTISING SPENDING
($MILLIONS)

Company 2003 Rank	1991	1995	2000	2002	2003
1. General Motors	$1,056.5	$1,499.0	$3,934.8	$3,652.2	**$3,429.9**
2. Procter & Gamble	1,166.4	1,507.4	2,363.5	2,673.4	**3,322.7**
3. Time Warner	311.3	543.0	1,770.1	2,922.8	**3,097.3**
4. Pfizer	NA	NA	2,265.3	2,566.2	**2,813.5**
S. DaimlerChrysler	414.8	954.7	1,984.0	2,031.8	**2,317.5**
6. Ford Motor	517.7	891.8	2;345.2	2,251.8	**2,233.8**
7. Walt Disney	257.3	777.8	1,757.5	1,083.0	**2,129.3**
8. Johnson & Johnson	371.1	601.3	1,601.2	1,799.0	**1,995.7**
9. Sony Corp	262.8	431.0	1,030.0	1,621.1	**1,811.4**
10. Toyota Motor	442.5	513.4	1273.9,	1,552.7	**1,682.7**
11. Verizon Comm	NA	NA	1,612.9	1,527.5	**1,674.2**
12. Sears, Roebuck	462.3	557.8	1,455.4	1,661.2	**1,633.6**
13. General Electric	NA	NA	1,310.1	579.0	**1,575.7**
14.GlaxoSmithKline	83.3	173.2	1,126.4	1,554.0	**1,553.7**
15. SBCCommunic.	NA	NA	1,786.0	1,091.6	**1,511.0**
16. McDonald's	87.4	586.4	1,273.9	1,335.7	**1,368.3**
17. Unilever	371.4	442.7	1,453.6	1,640.0	**1,332.1**
18. Altria Group	1,110.0	1,397.7	2,602.9	1,206.0	**1,311.0**
19. Nissan Motor	212.0	367.0	813	966.7	**1,300.0**
20. Merck & Co	129.5	199.0	9,83.9	1,158.4	**1,264.4**
21. Viacom	NA	NA	1,2209.0	1,259.8	**1,248.8**
22. L'Oreal	NA	NA	987.1	1,117.7	**1,239.4**
23. PepsiCo	542.0	730.2	2,100.7	1,113.9	**1,212.2**
24. Home Depot	NA	96.6	651.6	885.2	**1,149.2**
25. Microsoft Corp	NA	147.7	854.8	909.1	**1,147.2**
26. Honda Motor Co	242.5	388.8	1,035.0	1,192.0	**1,143.7**
27. Nestle	307.6	490.1	637.7	1,073.2	**1,112.7**
28. US Gov't	123.4	219.9	1,246.3	1,082.8	**1,102.3**
29. Target Corp	NA	NA	826.7	960.0	**1,083.0**
30. Sprint Corp	NA	213.9	1,227.3	863.0	**1,069.3**
31. AT&T Wireless	NA	NA	616.3	872.9	**1,034.9**

Source: World Almanac Education Group (2005:348).

Commercial television broadcasting's treatment of children and their needs continues to be a national disgrace. In 1951, when far fewer television channels existed, there were twenty-seven hours a week of children's programming. By the 1990s, with far more channels, there were only three or four hours a week on all networks. The role of children in modern commercial television is solely that of targets—targets for commercials that sell snacks, soft drinks, fashionable clothes, and toys. The idea of the child as future responsible citizen does not exist on commercial TV. That role seems to be left to public television, which in response to conservative critics and fiscal pressures has also become dependent upon corporate advertising (Bagdikian 1997).

The above overview demonstrates that culture is resourced by the power of the media that reinscribes through the "conditions of contingency and contradictoriness that attend upon the lives of those who are in the minority" (Bhabha 1994:2). In this context, culture embodies relations between differentially located subjects that constitute and are constituted by the dynamics of power. The media set (p.5) enunciative boundaries, ambulant, ambivalent articulation of the power relations from the material to the metaphoric within what Bourdieu calls symbolic capital—the processes of ideological intervention. Symbolic capital encapsulates speech, appearance, images, prestige, manners, etc., that are exploited by various organizations that seek to control the exchange of forms of capital. Such cultural ideas spill over from one contested site to another (Bourdieu 1977).

Crime News as Selective Views

Institutionalized behaviour, identity and thought have become "naturalized" such that crime becomes framed according to very familiar common-sense notions. But, how then is this sense of knowing something about youth crime acquired? Seldom interrogating the sources of knowledge the general public is encouraged to cite trite truths or glib gospels according to newspapers, television and radio accounts and learn to participate as crime experts, well-nourished by media illusions, deceptive bits and biased fragments. The public primarily gets its understanding of crime from the mainstream media.

Research suggests that 95% of Canadians learn about crime from the media, especially through entertainment television viewing, news programs or newspapers (Standing Committee 1997; Dowler 2003). Stated differently, Surette (1989:5) also notes that the media accounts for 95% of the information the public has about crime. Research further (Surette 1992; McNeely 1995) suggests that a majority of people receive much of their impressions and knowledge of the juvenile justice system through the media, again through the entertainment of television viewing. In fact, the most direct "contact" that most Canadians have with the juvenile justice system is through their respective "television experience." Specifically, 67% of Canadians watch TV news every day; 42% of Canadians read a newspaper every day; 90% of Canadians watch television news several times a week or more with only 6% who say they never watch (http://www.cmrcccrm.ca/english/reportcard2004/06.htm). What is even more interesting to note is that almost 60% of Canadians believe the news media get the facts straight and 48% of Canadians believe the news media help society solve problems (ibid). Television has become the authority (McNeely 1995; Saney 1986), a very powerful agent of socialization and source of knowledge and information. Similarly, the single largest news source for Americans is the television (Cook, Gomery, and Lichty 1992). On an average weeknight, ABC World News Tonight, CBS Evening News and NBC Nightly News are tuned in by approximately one-quarter of all the television-viewing homes in the United States (Howard 2002). About two-thirds of the American public follows current events regularly (Pew Research Center 2000).

The various media discipline by producing consent and by enjoying a virtual monopoly over information. The media have become more than just social mirrors; more accurately, they provide the only "windows" available through which largely eager constituencies hope to catch even a glimpse of events, individuals, or relations designated as deviant. Conceptually, crime exists in reference to well-established, even if poorly understood, impressions grounded in the canons of orthodox ideas and "common" experiences. Within all societies "coated" images and coded representations of knowledge, personified categories and empirically verifiable "facts" of crime are always circulated. These interpretations, respected as self-evident truths, succeed in disciplining understanding by compelling comfortable, if not convenient compliance. Specifically, the dominant culture creates ideologically appropriate subjects in crime discourses. Given the public "buy in," media practices control individual and collective insights by defining, moralizing, pathologizing and finally criminalizing differences.Underwriting the complex web of social, political, and economic connections, criminality becomes shaped within a media-asaturated environment and judged according mediated forms of presentation and representation. The reporting of crime is inseparable from its creation. The relationship between formal agents of social control (criminal justice system) and moral entrepreneurs (educational, religious, community, work, business, institutions who have routine media access succeed in manufacturing excitement, hysteria and crime) is not only calibrated to contain crime but more importantly, to create public outrage within a morality play that enhances the legitimacy of power. The latter assist in manipulating crime by providing the necessary moral rhetoric for justifying intrusions such as security and moral values.

The cast of CNN's American Morning TV show issued a warning to viewers: beware of Toronto CNN anchors discussed Toronto's Boxing Day shootout that killed 15-year-old Jane Creba and left 6 others in hospital (Westhead 2005:B1)."The murder rate in Toronto has doubled this year," Miles O'Brien CNN news anchor said. "There's a whole, you know, crime spree underway." The flurry of shootings on Yonge St. a day after Christmas that left a teenager dead marked the 52nd firearm-related death in Toronto this year, nearly twice as many as a year ago. The city's homicide toll stands at 78, close to the record 88 murders in 1991.The Boxing Day shootings remained front-page news yesterday for newspapers in Montreal, Calgary and Saskatoon, and received coverage in the large city U.S. papers such as the *Miami Herald*, the *Charlotte Observer* and the *Chicago Sun-Times*. In New York City alone, there have been 1,454 shootings (not all fatal) so far this year. In our city, politicians say they are working to provide solutions to the gun violence that has claimed 52 firearm homicides victims in Toronto in 2005.

In this section we will examine the role of an array of extraordinarily persuasive moral campaigns by media entrepreneurs, an industry of inter-related agencies obsessed with regulating differences and punishing defiance. The media conceal as much as they reveal about delinquency. Because of the pervasive influence of the media the general public is made to feel both content and competent in talking about crime generally and juvenile delinquency specifically. Without interrogating the sources of knowledge, this general public is encouraged to defer to television and radio accounts and learn to participate as crime experts well-nourished by media illusions, deceptive bits and biased fragments. Media crime talk satisfies basic consumption needs (O'Neill 1985:91-117). What, then, is the image of the delinquent in the public eye?

When a viewer sees a news anchor on the screen looking right at the camera, the viewer perceives the conversation to be intimate. Television is the only medium with this unique interpersonal interaction with the information provider. In addition to turning on the set, changing the channel and turning the volume up or down (Gunther 1995), viewers believe they have the power to become the medium by engaging in various interactive program formats that encourage viewer participation (phone-in, faxing, text messaging or e-mailing) as is common with CNN news programs. Interestingly, the public's perceived sincerity of television news is effective in influencing attitudes and behavior (Beniger 1987). In twenty two minutes, newscasts deliver snapshots of national and international news that not only frame current events for the public, but influence story selection at local affiliate stations, at radio outlets and in print media (Howard 2002). In addition to putting topics on the nation's agenda, the networks help set the range of debate on those issues by selecting sources who ostensibly represent the interests and opinions of the population (ibid).

Crime Experts as Engineers of Moral Panic?

Television newscasts, for example, are especially effective in capturing our attention and then hold us "captive" to "edited" accounts of "reality" slotted between commercials. The audience "gets close to the action," believing it knows immediately what is happening through the cultural intervention of a newscaster, impeccably attired to conjure up further images of integrity and professionalism. The audience is consumed in identifying with the messenger's so-called "objective" accounts, liturgical drama or self-evident truths. Ultimately, the audience is watching itself and the reproduction of dominant values without any discrimination of the misinformation. Through commercials, the economically powerful corporations hit hard in demonstrating that their consumerism will improve the quality of life for the audience. The audience buys the message and is programmed to believe that the purchase of more and more products enhances success, sociability, physical attractiveness, to name only a few benefits. Newscasters cannot simply be viewed as representing their own personal and organizational interests; rather they are also cultural workers reproducing dominant ideologies. Cultural managers share class interests and associations with state and business managers and other privileged sectors (Chomsky 1992:93). To serve the interests of the powerful, the media must present a

111

tolerably realistic picture of the world sacrificing professional integrity and honesty. But, the media are only one part of a larger doctrinal mirror; other parts include journals of opinion, the schools and universities, academic scholarship and so on.

This doctrinal system diverts the attention of the unwashed masses and reinforce basic social values: passivity, submissiveness to authority, the overriding virtue of greed and personal gain, lack of concern for others, fear of real or imagined enemies, etc (ibid., 95). The goal is to keep the bewildered masses even more bewildered, if not incarcerated. Therefore, it is unnecessary and culturally counter-productive for the "audience" to become bothered with what is happening in the world. In fact, if people see too much of a disturbing reality, they may think about changing their roles as spectators (Chomsky 1992; Chomsky 1997). Simply, the bewildered herd is supposed to follow the recipe orders and enjoy the fast food meals neatly prepared and seductively packaged by corporate interests. It is unnecessary for them to trouble themselves with what is actually happening in the world. In fact, it is undesirable! If they see too much reality, there is a fear that they may want to change it (ibid). This shared consciousness promotes laziness and silence. These homogenizing influences feed into components of a larger social machine (Meyrowitz 1992:230). News media especially offer disciplinary and normalizing discourses, intextually related to each other and to other disciplinary and normalizing institutions (Ericson, Baranek, and Chan 1992:235). As noted, the media succeed in fostering paranoia and a fortress mentality where the only comfort zone is in front of the television set in our homes. This market provision of security generates its own paranoid demand (Davis1992:224).

The popular media generally exploit and manipulate in the interests of power and self-preservation by conveying socially sanctioned messages about the consequences of unacceptable conduct. But this personal prison, incarcerated self or colonized will is fundamentally related to discursive practices. Structures of conformity are constituted through these disciplines. The media evade the most urgent and essential social issues. Narratives are designed to reproduce control, to confer object-like realities to deviance. Privilege channels thought within conformist boundaries (Chomsky 1989:vii). As a mode of discourse, the patho-centric script of delinquency objectifies challenges by invoking existing codes. Legal, scientific and professional discourses dominate the language of control. The script, the theme and opening sequences are pivotal "hooks" used to

112

entice the audience to tune in and stay tuned in. TV news is written for people who are not really listening so the words used must capture and hold the viewer's attention; therefore the story is generally written in a conversational or narrative style designed to highlight the most dramatic parts of the story. If there is a human-interest angle too, then so much the better and the story will be told purely from that point of view (Howard 2002).

Likewise, popular television programs promote conservative ideologies regarding the "survival of the slickest," laissez-faire vigilante-ism, seductive technological marvels, fantasies etc. As the distinguished analyst and former newscaster Peter Trueman (1980:169) points out, television news is a "stolid acceptance of the status quo." By mirroring the viewer, and establishing intimacy, television seeks to extend its control by extending its net or web of control widely. This cooptation of popular values diverts attention away from socio-political struggles inherent in an unequal society. Resistance and oppositional projects are simply dismissed as deviant and by that unprofitable.

Crime news "environments are not passive wrappings, but active processes which work over as completely, massaging the senses and imposing silent assumptions" (McLuhan 1964:69), mediated by barriers of language and social convention. In addition, media crime portrayals are uniformly uninformed, fragmentary and inaccurate, providing a distorted mirror reflection of crime within society and an equally distorted image of the community's response to such behaviour. For instance, Surette (1984:16) and Schissel (1997) join other authors (Baron and Hartnagel 1996; Sprott 1996) who have highlighted the role of the media in engineering "moral panics" and distorting the public's understanding of contemporary criminal activities, thereby reinforcing stereotypes. Research further demonstrates compellingly that this process of crime amplification supports only the self-serving interests of the criminal justice, political campaigns, media and the dominant culture. Messages driven by profit ratings, the bureaucratic and economic logic of news production, deadlines and financial pressures, result in an overreliance of readily available and easily legitimated information from official sources (Fishman 1980; Ericson, Baranek, and Chan 1991). For decades, criminologists have documented the effects of criminalization in creating youth crime waves, that is, illusions creating criminal identities. These news accounts are often intertwined with ideological visions of race, gender and class. Sociologically, panics solidify the disreputable identities of "certain" youths. Specifically, the media tend to cluster brief accounts of scattered crimes to create the illusion for example of the concentration of youth criminalities; all this despite, according to official statistics and academic research, the decline in the overall youth crime rate. Criminalizing youth has become popularized, dramatically expanding the sites and targets. Paradoxically, criminalization not only exacerbates social inequalities but also serves to empower those who have been routinely punished, as will be discussed later.

The media's labelling of youth counter-culture movements as "deviant" was the first step in a discursive process of social control (Cohen 1972). Describing the media's growing role in the intensifying anxiety about youth delinquency, Cohen (p.9) adds:

> A condition, episode, person or group of persons emerges to become defined as a threat to societal values and interests; its nature is presented in a stylised and stereotypical fashion...the moral barricades are manned...socially accredited experts pronounce their diagnoses and solutions; ways of coping are evolved or (more often) resorted to; the condition then disappears, submerges or deteriorates and becomes more visible.

Rather than concern itself with reasoned impartiality crime news seeks engineer accusations and hysteria. By manufacturing morality plays, the media reduce youth, for example, to a juridic and analgesic chatter of crime. This convenient obsession with crime news by the corporate media, the new social philosophers, engineers and theologians, alludes to customary meanings of morality. But, crime news is a problematic discourse that obstructs meaningful explanations. Typically, delinquency as an extreme expression of disturbance is celebrated opportunistically as a forum for public commentary and as a mechanism for solidifying the approbation of a consensually oriented society. Images of delinquency predominate as cultural markers designed to mirror a generic deference to the authority of law and the morality of traditional customs. A more prudent discussion of the presentation and brokerage of crime news, however, summons a critical analysis of the influences of culture, political economy and history. As argued throughout this chapter, the dominant order scripts crime as a commodity that is marketable and profitable for those who have a stake in conformity. Crime news, as an exercise of control, is linked to privilege.

Accordingly, we ask the following: who, for example, benefits from the reported incidence of delinquency? What do crime news produce and re-produce about existing hegemonic imperatives? What elements of the dominant culture define the appropriateness of conformity? To what extent are "stories" of delinquent youth contextualized culturally, mediated politically and articulated legally? What cultural capital is gained by these distorted tales, revered myths and absolutist monologues?

It is not simply that the mass media report in certain ways on youth criminal events, or provide fashionable fodder out of which criminal subcultures construct collective styles (Ferrell 1995) but rather the media play an essential role in shaping the intersections of culture and crime. That is, as Foucault describes, there is an insidious perversion wherein statements from one institution can be transcribed in the discourse of another. The media contribute to the connective narrative of capitalism and drive the engines of social reproduction, but do not, in themselves, provide a foundational frame for those molds of cultural identification and political affect that form around issues of law (bhabha 1994:6). Critical legal studies is mindful of these dialectics of struggle and linguistic control as several criminological theorists have called for the development and articulation of replacement discourses; that is, codes of speech more compatible with the stories and points of view of various disenfranchised collectives (Henry and Milovanovic 1991, 1996; Arrigo 1995). Interestingly, the mainstream print and electronic media disguise themselves as authoritative knowledge brokers, bringing together the collective conscience of a community (a normative moral consensus) by concentrating public attention on "their" definitions of disrepute, deviance or delinquency. Through processes of exclusion the media purport to explain a view that re-creates a "one-dimensional mind" (Marcuse 1964:10). By mythologizing, by publicizing a particular narrative of youth crime and by promoting moral recipes, the media mediate knowledge and indoctrinate values. Inevitably, electronic colonialism triumphs. The media not only seek to establish dependency relationships but also succeed in socializing thought by inculcating a set of foreign norms, values, and expectations (McPhail 1981:20). Sets of interrelated beliefs used for buttressing a particular social order are projected. Symbols are manipulated to control the definition of situations for readers who are perceived to be ill-informed and analytically lazy citizens. Knowledge is filtered through self-serving organizational lenses that demand deference from an all too willing public. The media as a vehicle of cultural incarceration not only seek to deliver messages but more importantly sustain dominant elitist values. The freedom of the press, for example, is nothing more than the freedom to monopolize. As Altheide (1976:173) comments events become news when transformed by the news perspective, and not because of their objective characteristics. The way news workers look at the world was shown to be influenced by commercialism, political influence, technology, and scheduling demands. Of interest to the media are stories that are unusual, that is, "eccentricities rather than in routine" (Martin 1947:57). In this regard, crime stories about "kiddies who kill" are especially attractive and easy to sell. The media focuses on the criminal act itself, its detection, followed by prosecution and conviction, thus creating morality tales. There is little discussion or analysis of the underlying causes of crime (social conditions, offender's background) or the inner workings of the criminal justice system). To reiterate, crime stories divert attention away from the real problems of capitalist society thereby orchestrating a panic and legitimating the introduction of greater social control measures during the crises of capitalism (Fishman 1980). This engineering requires that blame be individualized and that structural conditions be invisibilized within an ostensibly persuasive script replete with technical risk assessment talk, police crime jargon and popular moral appeal. Various crime industry voices (police, academic, and community) are incorporated to reflect the gravity of the crime news coverage.

Violence / Crime as Entertainment

Images of crime create a contagion, an infectious public appetite for even more sensational spectacles to be found in the pages of newspapers, the newscasts of culturally well tailored reporters or in the proliferation of popular radio phone-in, television talk-show programmes and televised tabloid newsmagazines. More than a quarter of all prime time shows have focused on themes of crime or criminal justice, which constitute the largest single subject matter on television today, across all types of programming. Despite some descriptions as "tabloid" television, these shows are evidently perceived in the manner in which they are presented and thus, although currently not dominant in prime time viewing slots, require serious consideration in terms of the "information" they present for public consumption and perception. The audience, as spectators or witnesses, are encouraged to focus attention on the personae of slick celebrities, commentators or crime "experts" who are all too mindful of the dazzle of their respective side-shows, advertisements and commercials. Note the following sample of prime (crime) time popular series (fiction), tabloid (reports), reality TV and talk show programs, respectively:

Law and Order, Law & Order: Criminal Intent, Law & Order: Special Victims Unit, law and Order Trial by Jury, CSI , CSI: Miami, CSI: NY, New Detectives, Crossing Jordan, Cold Case Files, Monk, Third Watch, Boston legal, Medical Investigation, etc.

Inside Edition, Inside Entertainment, Entertainment Tonight, The Insider, Celebrity Justice, 48 Hours; 20/20,; Dateline NBC; 60 Minutes; 60 Minutes Wednesday, Good Morning America, meet the Press, face the Nation, Studio 2, the fifth estate W-Five Canada AM, etc.

Court TV; America's Most Wanted, Unsolved Mysteries; People's Court; Divorce Court, Texas Justice, Cold Squad, The People's Court , Judge Hatchet, Judge Joe Brown , Judge Judy, Judge Mathis, Cops, American Justice, etc.

Larry King Live, The Daily Show With Jon Stewart, EXTRA, Dr Phil, At large With Geraldo Rivera; Maury, Oprah Winfrey; Montel Williams; Ellen DeGeneres Show, Dr. Phil,_Jerry Springer; Paula Zahn, Tavis Smiley, O'Reilley Factor, etc.

Crime stories have become the new circus, a public spectacle parading tragic events as advertised entertainment. In any typical week and in a random sampling of the above news-entertainment carnivals one discovers a cornucopia of delectable (seductive) images that will render viewers even more vulnerable targets of manipulation. Viewers in turn use the knowledge that they obtain from the media to construct an image of the world; these portrayals give viewers (and others participating in their production) clues about society and, thus, also act to "socialize" the public to a particular image of the prevalence of "certain" crimes.

Spectacles and Circuses

Crime spectacles distract, stupefy and paralyze public participation as with the sensational show trials and the crusades against crime, drugs and guns. Readers and viewers have become fixated in their fascination with the new clown, trapeze or animal acts in the form of bombastic, crude and shallow crime stories that plague both the electronic and printed media. Spectacles persist and become even more tantalizing with images of youth crime. Delinquency, according to this "television reality" is "programmed and staged" even if only to accommodate commercial requirements. Surette (1992:245246) argues, in every category-crimes, criminals, crime fighters, the investigation of crime, arrests, case processing, and case dispositions— the media present a world of crime and justice that is not found in reality. Items are presented as "real," and are often produced in a format and style associated with documentary or news reporting, about which questions of social presentation and accuracy can also be posed (Surette 1992; Altheide 1985). Television technology has further improved this voyeurism with instant, banal and simplistic social messages that delineate the good and the bad to captivated audiences. Note the media frenzy that accompanied the trials of Paul Bernardo, OJ Simpson, Robert Blake and not to mention Martha Stewart's release from prison. CNN and Fox News provided continuous commentary during the child molestation trial of Michael Jackson. The news media defends itself from the charge of fostering sensational violence by stating they are simply reflecting that which exists: real people are violated every day. This amusement is troublesome given its deliberate inculcation of distorted values. The fascination with crime, the appetite for violence and the delirium of the moment disguise the ongoing media deceit. This distorted carnival mirror (Reiman 1998) projects many different kinds of messages (O'Sullivan 1990) the negative effects of which viewers are less aware. Against this background, critical pedagogies strive to liberate social thought from the peculiar incubation of cultural controls. Juxtaposed against a reactionary morality, critical pedagogies encode and decode the production and consumption of discipline. Methods are available, however, in critical cultural theories that assist in deconstructing illusions and critically elaborating on the conditions and consequences of crime.

Newspapers and television news departments have finite news space, reporters, and budgets. The process of journalism—collecting, organizing, and disseminating information—happens in a series of priority-setting decisions about how to use those resources. In addition to the thoughtless and salacious nature of crime coverage, the mass media, the source of most public information about crime, do a very poor job of informing the public. Notice, for example, while reading the following captions one's own reaction or even the response of others to the assumptions implicit in the following headlines that appeared in newspapers and magazines.

NEWSPRINT HEADLINES

"Are violent teens suffering 'the rage of the unparented'? " *Globe and Mail*, December 18, 2004, F7

"How an awkward teen embraced a fiery hatred ." *Globe and Mail*, December 17, 2004, A1

"Russian teens sentenced for racist attack on girl, 5 ." *Globe and Mail*, December 9, 2004, A20

"Stabbing heightens fears of youth violence ." *Globe and Mail*, December 9, 2004, A17

"Tender youth, terrible crime, compelling case ." *Globe and Mail*, November 19, 2004, A16

"Teens brawl with sticks at Catholic high school ." *Globe and Mail*, December 17, 2004, A16

"Don't stand idly by, teens told Bully may quit if deprived of audience." *Toronto Star*, December 18, 2004

"15-year-old dies after being s tabbed in East York melee ." *Globe and Mail*, December 4, 2004, A24

"Teenagers plead not guilty to slaying of 12 -year-old boy." *Globe and Mail*, November 16, 2004, A11

"Violent youth crime rising : Stats reveal gangs and girls now figure more often in incidents." *Toronto Sun*, December 12, 2004

"Teenage girls cross over to realm of `adult serious.'" *Toronto Star*, December 3, 2004

"Police too late to save stabbed boy, 3 teens charged in 2003 slaying Boy, 12, killed; stepfather beaten." *Toronto Star*, December 3, 2004

"Charge 14-yr.-old in crime rampage." *NY Daily News*, December 8, 2004

"Try teen in rape case as juvenile, his lawye r urges." *LA Times*, December 11, 2004

"4 White youths held in Black teen's beating ." *LA Times*, December 8, 2004

"Md. teen charged in 10 robberies, 2 slayings; victims were Latino, Indian and African immigrants…" *The Washington Post*, November 11, 2004, B06

"Teen convicted of manslaughter." *Newsday*, December 4, 2004, A11

"Cops: Teens beat, stab boy at school." *Newsday*, December 4, 2004, A10

"2003 shooting, alleged killer arrai gned, the teen charged with murdering and robbing a visitor to a Brooklyn house party held without bail." *Newsday*, November 25, 2004, A20

119

What conclusions about delinquency are we as readers expected to draw? What images are manipulated? And how? Youth crime in Canada is dropping, the percentage of teen crimes that are deemed "violent" has remained relatively stable for the last 20 years and yet the media's obsession with news stories focusing on teen gangs and violence create remain unabated creating the impression that youth violence is actually increasing.

According to Surette (1984:16):

> Media images of crime and criminals are contained within numerous formats, including news reporting, documentaries, features, and entertainment programming. The images are often inaccurate and are uniformly fragmentary, providing a distorted mirror reflection of crime within society and an equally distorted image of the criminal justice system's response to such behaviour.

As McNeeley (1995) and Adler (1976) suggest, programs are not created in a vacuum, and it would be misleading to treat them in isolation from society. This constant "crime talk" manufactures perceptions of delinquency. In reference to youth crimes the media provides a catechism of self-evident truths, an essential part of an infallible dogma that demands reverence. As embodied moral statements, these caricatured fragments portray youth crime by acceding to convoluted logic, obfuscating symbols and mystifying rituals. Unqualified deference is extremely evident in the media coverage of "official statistics." To explain, historical and cultural features of the political economy are rendered invisible and seldom examined by the media and other socializing influences. Obediently, the public chatter is limited to news that entertains for the emotional moment; the quick fix that dazzles, pacifies or terrifies into inaction. Within the dominant culture, delinquency is a currency in popular discourse. This entertaining commodity fetish has no place for any serious analysis especially of fundamental social issues. To what then is public attention directed? What currency is exchanged in crime talk? These distorted views may stem largely from public ignorance or false consciousness, supported by the media. Admittedly, stories about youth crime rates sell newspapers (Cohen 1973:28-40); billions of dollars are earned in horrifying and titillating the general public.

Delinquency as a discourse is a major device for interpreting the culture of control, powerful panoptic prisons and ideological hegemony. In general, the media calculates the costs and the value of appropriate deception. Ideological manipulations as a legitimation exercise also make delinquency profitable. The related issue that makes certain crimes newsworthy and thus profitable is the entertainment value. Crime is always delivered to the audience in fragments whether in TV news or in newspapers. The subject of violence is everywhere, from talk radio to prime-time TV to rap videos to films. If that is so, how can it be that Americans are so misinformed about crime?

The Violence of Entertainment

Since the 1950s, researchers have conducted more than 3,000 studies to gauge the effects of representations of violence on audiences (Grossberg, Wartella, and Whitney 1998:300). Sixty percent of TV programming contains violence; an average hour of television portrays three to five violent acts according to the American Psychological Association (http://www.umext.maine.edu/onlinepubs/htmpubs/4100.htm;http://www.tr ivsion.ca/documents/Television%20Violence%20Study_March2002.pdf). Indeed, this ongoing susceptibility to the socialization of media-generated values is not surprising considering how much violence youths see on TV; the average American child will witness 200,000 violent acts on television by age 18 (http://www.kidshealth.org /parent/positive /family/tv_affects_ child.html). By the time the average American child is 14-years-old, she or he will have seen more than 8,000 murders and more than 100,000 other acts of violence on television (Mastronardi 2003). Dorfman, Woodruff, Chavez, and Wallack (1997) undertook a content analysis of 214 hours of local television news from California. They found that for 1,721 stories that violence dominated local television news coverage of youth; that over half of the stories on youth involved violence, while more than two thirds of the violence stories concerned youth.

Violence is a commodity sold to generate attention, secure funding especially for the juvenile justice system and its armies of consultants, and maximize a profit for the film industry. Again, images of violence are always manipulated. The popularity of adventure / action and horror films attest to this fixation. Note, for example, the incredible popularity of violent, vigilante, and macho-avenge films that pretend to portray a sense of popular justice. With a wide array of aggressive heroes and type-casts played by Segal, Schwarzenegger, Bronson, Eastwood, Norris, Stallone, Van Damme, Willis, etc., Hollywood recycles, promotes and delivers themes of violence repeatedly found in the following films and their sequels: Die Hard, Death Wish, Kill Bill, Terminator, Out for Justice, Lethal Weapon, Double Impact, Rambo, Reservoir Dogs, Rocky, True Lies, TimeCop, etc. Violence has no longer been restricted to mindless horror films like Friday the 13th, Doctor Giggles, Poltergeist, Nightmare on Elm Street, Texas Chain Saw Massacres, Child's Play, Halloween, or even to the drama / suspense films like Cape Fear, Natural Born Killers; Pulp Fiction or the 1991 Academy Award Winner Silence of the Lambs. Violence continues to be embedded in comedies like Home Alone, Hot Shots, which boasts that it contains the most killings of any movie. As will be noted later violence as entertainment has become ethnicized and racialized, as the following suggests: Casino, Bugsy, Analyze This, Analyze That, The Untouchables, Good Fellas, Bronx Tale, Raw Deal, Wannabes, The Godfather, Married to the Mob, Scarface, Carlito's Way, Donnie Brasco, Mobsters, The Firm as well as popular TV programs like the Sopranos. Violence as racialized killings, drive-by shootings and street fighting accompanied the premiering of such movies as Juice, Boyz 'n' the Hood, Jungle Fever, New Jack City, Ricochet, Fresh, and Trespass.

Violent video games are also very popular, raking in billions a year in the United States alone (Elmer-Dewitt 1993:42). On average, children play 1.5 hours daily on video machines (p.41). In 1993 Mortal Kombat, was the top grossing release; this "game" featured extreme brutal kick and punch violence. In Night Trap, five scantily clad women are stalked by blood thirsty vampires who like to drill holes in their victims' necks and hang them on meat hooks. The very popular Grand Theft Auto involves murder and prostitution. The player controls Tommy Vercetti, a paroled inmate who takes on robberies, assassinations and other assorted criminal missions for crime bosses. Throughout the game, a player is encouraged to beat up prostitutes and steal their money, as well as assault people on the street with a baseball bat. In Manhunt, the player controls James Earl Cash, a death row inmate, and has to survive in a bombed-out section of the city while gangs hunt him down. The player must sneak around and kill gang members. The player uses a variety of methods to kill, from suffocating his enemies with plastic bags, to jabbing shards of glass into their throats. In Max Payne, a story of a renegade cop the player has a slow-motion trick that slows down time while shooting. The replays show bullets going through people's heads. Especially since 1992 as fighting video games like Street Fighter, Mortal Kombat and Doom first hit the markets, digital media began to feature prominently in the public battles over children's media saturated lives. In the wake of the school shootings, such as the incident at Columbine High School in Littleton Colorado where 15 people died and several others were injured, renewed attention has focused on how the media affect behaviors. Specifically the claim has been made that teens, particularly males, learn violence from watching television and movies, visiting Internet sites, and playing certain types of video games (Eschholz and Bufkin 2001). A recent survey found that 92% of US kids ages 2 to 17 play video games, and their parents bought 225 million of them last year to the tune of $6.4 billion (see Table 3.4). In 2002 Grand Theft Auto 3, was the most popular video game in the United States selling 4.2 million copies since October 2001, at $50 each (http://www.sosparents.org/The%20 Facts.htm). Half of all 4-6-year-olds have played video games and one in four play several times a week or more (ibid). Children and teenagers still use the internet more than any other age group. By late 2001, according to a government statistics 65% of 10-13-year-olds and 75% of 14-17-year-olds had internet access despite income disparities (World Almanac Education Group 2005:802 803). In fact, 83% of American teens report going online last year (http://www.pbs.org/wgbh/pages/frontline/teach/cool).

TABLE 3.4
TOP-SELLING VIDEO GAMES (2002)

Platform	Title
1. Sony PlayStation 2	Grand Theft Auto: Vice City 2
2. Sony PlayStation 2	Grand Theft Auto 3
3. Sony PlayStation 2	Madden NFL 2003
4. Nintendo Game Boy Advance	Super Mario Advance 2
5. Sony PlayStation 2	Gran Turismo 3: A-Spec
6. Sony PlayStation 2	Medal Honor Frontline
7. Sony PlayStation 2	Spider-Man: The Movie
8. Sony PlayStation 2	Kingdom Hearts
9. Microsoft Xbox	Halo
10. Nintendo GameCube	Super Mario Sunshine
11. Sony PlayStation 2	Tony Hawks Pro Skater 4
12. Nintendo Game Boy Advance	Yu-Gi-Oh! Eternal
13. Nintendo Game Boy Advance	Dragonbali Z: Goku
14. Sony PlayStation 2	Lord of the Rings: Two Towers
15. Nintendo Game Boy Color	Yu-Gi-Oh! Dark Due

Source: The NPDFunworkSM TRSTS® Service, The NPDGroup Inc. Port Washington. NY; World Almanac Education Group (2004 :267).

The multi-billion dollar rage rock, gangsta rap, punk, grunge and hip-hop industries, whose effects are felt across the board from fashion to advertising to slang, are under scrutiny because of their commercial appeals. To illustrate in "Get Low," Lil Jon and the Eastside Boyz get low brow: "This bitch is fine. Now can I play with yo' pantyline?" Snoop Dogg, who adds: "You can't outrun the pimpin' bitch"; Eminem's countless references to "ho's" and "sluts." The current mainstream popularity of rap and rage rock musical genres is attributable to the violence against women, sexism and racism. The record industry, which is bankrolling and promoting material for the masses laced with the violence of negative gender, race and class depictions. Although media effects of video, TV and music violence have been debated for decades, the corporate boardroom is more concerned with capitalizing on the boredom of youth. But, the heavy consumption of violence in the media runs the risk of desensitizing viewers to the consequences of violence while enhancing notions of a danger (Mastronardi 2003; Huesmann, Moise-Titus, Podolski, and Eron 2003). Executives cash in on the violent deaths of hip-hop Gangsta rap stars like Tupac Shakur and Notorious B.I.G., as well as the satanic images, themes of rebellion and death of Marilyn Manson (Brian Warner). The misogyny of LL Cool J50 Cent (Curtis Jackson), Eminem , Snoop, Dr. Dre etc all in the name of profit especially for the record industries from Interscope Records to more mainstream outlets like MTV. For the mainstream, rap has become a misfit zoology absorbed with voyeurism and exhibitionism of a "foreign" culture. Violence in music has easily become an entertainingly eccentric journey into the erotic, erratic and exotic worlds that reinforces time-honoured racist and misogynist stereotypes blatantly perpetuated in the entertainment industry.

In summary, the above section argues that in the interest of profit the corporate media has succeeded in blurring the boundaries between entertainment and news. The news-entertainment nexus leads us to a discussion of the media and profits.

Defining News as Entertainment: Corporate Controls

The formula-driven violence in entertainment and news is the product of a complex manufacturing and marketing machine. Indeed, mergers, consolidation, conglomeratization and globalization fuel the for profit corporate machines. The concentration of ownership limits choice on the part of the consumer (see Appendices 3.1-3.5). Television, music and newspapers become part of large corporations; the people who run them are only loyal to the ethos of business or profit management. Profits define content. Concentration of media ownership is power without accountability (Huesmann, Moise-Titus, Podolski, and Eron 2003). The Canadian print and electronic media in news and entertainment (see Appendices 3.6-3.12) generally enjoy close ties with other influential business and political leaders. Consider for example, BCE's unloading some or all of a 68.5% stake in Bell Globemedia, holdings of which include The Globe and Mail newspaper and the CTV television network. Torstar and Ontario Teachers' Pension Plan Teachers' will each pick up a 20% stake in Bell Globemedia; Torstar and Bell Globemedia were linked through workopolis.com, the Internet careers advertising vehicle. And Torstar, parent of the Toronto Star, has spent the better part of a decade looking for a substantial way to get into the TV business. Through Bell Globemedia, Torstar now gets a financial stake in 15 specialty channels, including TSN, in addition to CTV. That will broaden Torstar's media interests beyond its current key holdings, which also include the CityMedia Group of newspapers, the Metroland community papers and Harlequin, publisher of women's fiction. As Torstar chief executive Robert Prichard told analysts: "It's very important to maintain the full independence, editorial and otherwise, of the Globe and Mail, as it is equally important to maintain the independent voice of each of our papers" (Kidd 2005).

Media class bias is also closely tied to the commercialization of the mass media, that is, to ratings and market share analyses thereby resulting in substantial pressure to avoid coverage of some actions, or to report on events in a way that would result in the loss of advertising dollars (Parenti 1986:42-52). The direction, scope, optics and interests of media corporate owners are shaped by advertising revenue, regulatory support and access to information (Howard 2002). Genuine news coverage and other media content are adversely affected by monopolistic corporate interests (Shah 2004). Stories end up biased or omitted so as not to offend their advertisers or owners. Economic and political influence and lack of accountability ensure the absence of diversity (ibid). In addition, governments have become sympathetic to dominant vertical corporations that have merged into ever larger and unrestrained social systems (Bagdikian 2000). Large media company owners are also entertainment companies and have vertical integration (i.e. own operations and businesses) across various industries and verticals, such as distribution networks, toys and clothing manufacture and/or retailing (Shah 2004). Vertical integration is also a part of a business strategy that serves to enhance market power, by allowing cross-promotion and cross-selling. Discussing the influence of interlocking businesses, Bagdikian (2000:65) concludes:

> Corporations have multimillion-dollar budgets to dissect and attack news reports they dislike. But with each passing year they have yet another power: They are not only hostile to independent journalists. They are their employers.

In our society where television is the main source of news, information and entertainment, Bay Street and Wall Street analysts/ leading investment houses determine how much and what kind of news and entertainment are to be provided. The forms of violence covered are related to the degree of commercial profit. Crime news as corporate views is also loaded with political bias. These cartels readily sacrifice representation for self interest. The most common source of news includes, for example, corporate representatives and economists whose stories reflect the networks' heavy coverage of business and financial stories. The economists were unlikely to provide perspectives that challenged the corporate spokespersons, since they generally came from major investment banks such as Goldman Sachs and Morgan Stanley, from conservative think tanks such as the Heritage Foundation, or from elite business schools such as those at Princeton and Stanford (Howard 2002). In 2001, the voices of Washington's elite politicians were the dominant sources of opinion on the network evening news. Moreover, the racial balance of all sources was firmly tilted toward the historically most powerful segment—white Americans. In reference to all the three major TV networks the distribution of races among US sources is as follows: 92% of racially categorized US sources were white, while 7% were black; Latinos were the next most quoted sources on all networks (0.6% on NBC, 0.5% on ABC and 0.7% on CBS) followed by Arab-Americans (0.6%, 0.5%, and 0.7% respectively) and Asian-Americans (0.2%, 0.3%, and 0.3% respectively) (Howard 2002). Women made up only 15% of total sources reflecting a tendency to quote men as the vast majority of authoritative voices (ibid). Even in coverage of gender-related policies (which made up 0.2% of coverage), women made up only 43% of the sources!

Cultural studies have long asserted that the media plays a very important role in the social construction of reality. There is consistent and convincing evidence that the media, as a principal means of socialization, cultivates views reflective and supportive of dominant beliefs and values (Altheide 1985; Roberts and Doob 1990; Ward 2003).

Summary of Research Findings

Incidence of Media Usage among Youth

TV is most popular media. TV music (MuchMusic /MTV), comedies and animations (Simpsons, South Park, King of the Hill) are the most frequently watched programs by youths, followed by sports and adult-themed talk shows. As teenagers grow older, they spend less time watching television and more time listening to music. They tend to be doing something else with music in the background. Music CDs and music videos (gangsta rap, hip-hop Heavy Metal, rage Rock grunge) were highest ranked followed by TV and Internet (surfing, gaming). Sports basketball, wrestling, blogging, car racing, hockey, baseball, playing and downloading music, e-mailing, surfing for fun, playing and downloading games, instant messaging (IM) and chat rooms. For older teens, the Internet has replaced television as the favored medium for escape. For most youths the media is defined as a "cool" tool especially in the areas of trends, music and fashion. The incidence of media usage among youth in our study is presented in Table 3.5.

For the 16 to 18 age group, the following are ranked in terms of time spent on the activity: music CDs, music videos, Internet and magazines. For the 12-15-year-old group almost as much time is spent listening to music as the entire number of hours spent in the classroom. Boys in this group tend to be doing something else with music constantly in the background. Ninety percent of girls turn more often to many types of media especially fashion magazines. Girls spend less time than boys watching TV and using the internet and are more interested in the print media (magazines and newspapers) than boys. Although boys are more likely than girls to watch television (sports), they spend more time down loading music, porn surfing and playing video games. Socio-economic class, as measured by family income, is also an indicator of media use. Children from high-income families spend the least amount of time with TV and more time on

TABLE 3.5
INCIDENCE OF MEDIA USAGE AMONG YOUTH

	12-15-YEAR-OLDS: % & (N)			16-18-YEAR-OLDS: % & (N)		
	Always	sometimes	never	always	sometimes	never
TV news	10(6)	30(18)	60(36)	30(42)	50(70)	20(28)
TV crime tabloids	10(6)	30(18)	60(36)	25(35)	40(56)	35(49)
TV Crime series	15(9)	65(39)	20(12)	35(49)	50(70)	15(21)
TV talk shows	5(3)	10(6)	85(51)	15(21)	30(42)	55(77)
TV animation	30(18)	60(36)	10(6)	20(28)	70(98)	10(14)
TV comedies	10(6)	85(51)	5(3)	30(42)	50(70)	20(28)
TV Sports	20(12)	60(36)	20(12)	25(35)	55(77)	20(28)
Internet	10(6)	45(27)	45(27)	30(42)	40(56)	30(42)
Messaging	30(18)	30(18)	40(24)	45(63)	50(70)	5(7)
Video games	30(18)	50(30)	20(12)	20(28)	60(85)	20(28)
Movies	15(9)	60(36)	25(15)	30(42)	45(63)	25(35)
Video/ DVD	10(6)	60(36)	30(18)	35(49)	40(56)	25(35)
MTV/Much Music	15(9)	30(18)	55(33)	30(42)	50(70)	20(28)
CD's	15(9)	55(33)	30(18)	45(63)	50(70)	5(7)
Radio	25(15)	45(27)	30(18)	35(49)	55(77)	5(7)
Magazines	20(12)	50(30)	30(18)	30(42)	40(56)	30(42)
Comics	15(9)	50(30)	35(21)	10(14)	25(35)	65(91)
Newspaper	10(6)	10(6)	80(48)	30(42)	40(56)	30(42)
N=200	60			140		

the net while children in lower income families spend the most amount of time watching TV and playing video games. In terms of ethno racial factors, Black students are much more likely than White students to watch four or more hours of television per day on weekdays. Young Black youths (12-15) watch more television than their white counterparts especially with family members whereas White boys spent more time with friends or alone on the net or watching TV.

Perceived Media–Identity Relations:
Self Concept, Skills, Reactions of Others

To understand the role of media in identity-construction, this study analyzed themes of discourse that are available in mediated texts and echoed throughout the culture, as well as various social, political, economic and other contexts that frame the youth's identity narratives and practices (Arnett 1991). Young people, especially students, invest considerable time studying fads, fashion and style as depicted in the media. Although media portrayals of youths are over sexualized, young people enjoy these depictions of youth in mediated messages of MTV and MuchMusic. In spite of the grim themes of the lyrics and the dark quality of the music, no one reported that listening to music videos made them unhappy or depressed. Quite the contrary, many youths report that they listened to them whenever they were upset and the lyrics calmed them. Messages of "making a fast buck" were seldom criticized. Magazines, most popular with young women, serve as vehicles for promoting and regulating stereotypically "feminine" modes. That is, young girls readily accept images of the thin "perfect" girl. Mediated body images and clothing appeal to a positive sense of "fashionable" identity. Four young teenage school girls report that their popularity was linked to their understanding of what they defined as the all cool and influential MuchMusic or MTV. Young boys criticize those who do not watch video music as real "losers." For these young teenagers (13-16-year-olds) TV music programs present positive role models—the "cool peeps" such as dancers, "celebs," entertainers always act with confidence, independence and intelligence. All youths in the study are very aware of the messages about gendered appearance: boys expected to wear loose clothing while girls would always display their bodies—tight fitting clothing exposing what one 14-year-old-girl proudly admits is "some sexy flesh." Older girls, ages 16-18, were less likely than younger girls ages 13-15 to think there are good role models for girls. In all the qualitative responses, one's self-esteem is linked to various advertised products; a sense of positive identity was associated with the latest clothing brands, fashion, music, games etc. In general, school youths are more likely see the media as not only providing positive role models but also instrumental in performing various educative (informative) functions especially in reference to drugs and gangs. Gang, incarcerated and street kids tend to emphasize the entertainment value and the fantasy making role of the media. Irrespective of the message, African-Canadian youth indicate a strong sense of satisfaction in seeing "their" people on television while Aboriginal, Latino and Asian children are critical of the reinforced stereotypes. Older teenagers who spend most time on computers and read newspapers are critical of the "sheep" mentality of younger teenagers arguing that the latter are unable to appreciate the aesthetic and creative value of music. Accordingly they report that the younger teenagers are far too vulnerable or too naïve to "figure things out" for themselves; moreover, they claim that drugs and alcohol exacerbate their psychological development.

Perceived Media–Institutions: Ideology Relations

For all youths, most media especially newsprint, television and radio enjoy close relationships with other institutions such as the family, school, religion, work, law and indirectly, the government. In the realm of entertainment, however, these affiliative relationships are less apparent for youths. For street youths, the media institutions contribute directly to abusive families, boredom in school, poor school performance, menial/ low paying jobs, precisely because of their messages that are irrelevant and meaningless. The newsprint, mainstream radio and TV are "disconnected" from them and succeed in pushing them out. For teenage boys, the attractive forces of the media, especially in unconventional music, video games and the internet, provide excitement, status and respect money where sex, drugs and violence are "cool." The media, for school youths, provide that which is unavailable elsewhere. As 15-year-old (Jeremy) commented:

> the media is cool "cause it's like my bud, my bro" you know. But you gotta find it. Most of the stuff out there is shit. It's a place to be. It's our time to do jack shit if we have to. The rap joins us. It tears

TABLE 3.6

TV NEWSCASTS

	IN SCHOOL	STREET KIDS	GANG NOT IN SCHOOL	GANG IN SCHOOL	INCARCERATED PROBATION
identity					
positive role models	L	L	M	H	M
informative	H	L	L	L	L
entertainment	L	L	L	L	L
"cool"/ fashionable	H	L	L	M	M
contributes to one's own delinquency	H	L	L	M	L
institutional					
Perception of peers as critical	similar	don't care	similar	similar	Similar
amplifies distortions	L	H	H	H	H
boring	L	H	H	M	H
contributes to crime of others	H	L	M	H	M
ideological					
contributes to status quo	L	H	H	M	M
inequalities	L	H	H	M	H
racism	L	H	H	H	H
sexism	H	L	L	M	L
individualism	L	H	H	M	H
materialism	L	H	H	H	H

Legend:
H High: over 67-100% of intra group agreement
M Medium: 34-66% of intra group agreement
L Low: 0-33% of intra group agreement N=200

TABLE 3.7
CRIME MOVIES AND CRIME TV SERIES

	IN SCHOOL	STREET KIDS	GANG NOT IN SCHOOL	GANG IN SCHOOL	INCARCERATED PROBATION
identity					
positive role models	L	L	H	H	H
informative	H	L	L	M	L
entertainment	H	L	L	H	M
"cool"/fashionable	H	L	L	M	L
contributes to one's own delinquency	H	L	L	M	M
institutional					
perception of peers as critical	similar	don't care	similar	similar	Similar
amplifies distortions	L	H	H	M	H
boring	L	H	L	L	L
contributes to crime of others	H	L	M	H	M
ideological					
contributes to status quo	L	H	H	H	H
inequalities	L	H	H	H	H
racism	L	H	H	H	M
sexism	H	L	L	M	L
individualism	L	H	H	M	H
materialism	L	H	H	H	H

Legend:
H High: over 67-100% of intra group agreement
M Medium: 34-66% of intra group agreement
L Low: 0-33% of intra group agreement N=200

down the bullshit out there. It's bad. It's cool shit. Everything else like is boring, really really cracked out.

In general, youths like the messages but these messages are differentially understood by street and school youths. For street youths, school youths enjoy the popularity of the media but do not understand the wider institutional contexts of music, poverty, illiteracy, limited options, unemployment, and so on. Further, street youths criticize the "games" or the "act" played by school youths who "talk tough" because of what they see in the media. Yet, school youths view media as problem solvers. Sixty percent of older school youths believed that the media addresses major social problems: crime, drugs; gangs, literacy, bullying, gender inequality, homophobia, etc. Street, incarcerated and gang youths view the widespread labelling of youth as trouble as problematic especially the negative depiction of "minority youth." They maintain that the mainstream media (television, newspapers and radio) overestimate youth crime and underestimate the values of peer loyalty. Street youths, however, are more inclined to see positive portrayals of ethnic minorities in music videos (gangsta rap). All youths assail the mainstream media for offering stereotypical and often negative representations of young people, thereby promoting discrimination, poor self-esteem, gender inequality and racism, etc. The mainstream media, for an overwhelming number of youths, is only concerned with creating conformity and deviantizing any diversity or difference. In other words, 70% of youths resent the regulatory or disciplining functions of mainstream media exempting of course MTV, BET or MuchMusic.

TABLE 3.8
CRIME COVERAGE IN NEWSPAPERS

	IN SCHOOL	STREET KIDS	GANG NOT IN SCHOOL	GANG IN SCHOOL	INCARCERATED PROBATION
identity					
positive role models	L	L	H	H	H
informative	H	L	L	M	L
entertainment	H	L	L	H	M
"cool"/fashionable	H	L	L	M	L
contributes to one's own delinquency	H	L	L	M	M
institutional					
perception of peers as critical	similar	don't care	similar	similar	Similar
amplifies distortions	L	H	H	M	H
boring	L	H	L	L	L
contributes to crime of others	H	L	M	H	M
ideological					
contributes to status quo	L	H	H	H	H
inequalities	L	H	H	H	H
racism	L	H	H	H	M
sexism	H	L	L	M	L
individualism	L	H	H	M	H
materialism	L	H	H	H	H
Legend:					

Legend:
H High: over 67-100% of intra group agreement
M Medium: 34-66% of intra group agreement
L Low: 0-33% of intra group agreement N=200

TABLE 3.9
MUSIC: GANGSTA RAP, RAGE ROCK, HEAVY METAL

	IN SCHOOL	STREET KIDS	GANG NOT IN SCHOOL	GANG IN SCHOOL	INCARCERATED PROBATION
identity					
positive role models	L	L	H	H	H
informative	H	L	L	M	L
entertainment	H	L	L	H	M
"cool"/fashionable	H	L	L	M	L
contributes to one's own delinquency	H	L	L	M	M
institutional					
perception of peers as critical	similar	don't care	similar	similar	Similar
amplifies distortions	L	H	H	M	H
boring	L	H	L	L	L
contributes to crime of others	H	L	M	H	M
ideological					
contributes to status quo	L	H	H	H	H
inequalities	L	H	H	H	H
racism	L	H	H	H	M
sexism	H	L	L	M	L
individualism	L	H	H	M	H
materialism	L	H	H	H	H

Legend:
H High: over 67-100% of intra group agreement
M Medium: 34-66% of intra group agreement
L Low: 0-33% of intra group agreement N=200

Focus: The Differential Impact of the Media on Youth Crime

The media construction of crime produces consequences for the development of selfhood and identity of youths. School youths are more likely to overestimate the impact of the media on criminality. For them, the participation of other youths, the creation of unsafe neighbourhoods, increasing drug use, gang formations, permissive sexual behaviour, bullying, aggressiveness and general anti-social behavior are far too overrated. And yet, school youths, more than the other groups, have an increased appetite for more and more violence in entertainment. The more economically privileged consider media violence as both entertaining and instructive. School youths are very impressionable and inclined to believe what is presented in the media (crime reporting). Notwithstanding their diverse interests and access to many media forms and ways of spending time, much of their time at school is spent comparing media originating stories, interpretations and

TABLE 3.10

VIDEO GAMES

	IN SCHOOL	STREET KIDS	GANG NOT IN SCHOOL	GANG IN SCHOOL	INCARCERATED PROBATION
identity					
positive role models	M	L	L	L	L
informative	L	L	L	L	L
entertainment	H	M	M	M	H
"cool"/fashionable	L	L	L	L	L
contributes to one's own delinquency	M	L	L	L	L
institutional					
perception of peers as critical	L	L	L	L	L
amplifies distortions	H	H	H	H	H
boring	L	L	L	L	L
contributes to crime of others	H	M	M	M	M
ideological					
contributes to status quo	L	H	L	H	H
inequalities	H	H	L	L	L
racism	L	L	H	H	H
sexism	M	L	L	L	L
individualism	H	H	H	H	H
materialism	L	H	L	L	M
Legend: **H** High: over 67-100% of intra group agreement **M** Medium: 34-66% of intra group agreement **L** Low: 0-33% of intra group agreement N=200					

fantasies. Although many will deny any personal direct impact they all noted that the messages of violence in gangsta rap, rage rock, grunge, the demonology of Marilyn Manson or Eminem, horror films, action video games influence how their peers behave, talk, walk and think. Seventy-five percent of school youths claim that their own sense of intelligence, family lives and educated friends buffered the effects of the media. School youth from the suburbs admitted trying to look like they're gangsta hip-hop kids. Gang and incarcerated youth are more analytical than school youths in reflecting on both the content and method of the message strong sense of group generation loyalty, a group-generation sense that is often accompanied by suspicion and hostility toward those who are not "in" this group. Interestingly those incarcerated youths who were least attached to mainstream were most attractive to mainstream music. Generally, the racial profiling by the media targets the Black youth cultures especially gang formations when covering specifically crime-related stories, once again, perpetuating the idea of this social segment being the most delinquent. This stratification is based on principles that value and reinforce racism, criminality and inequality. For gang members the media sanitizes and normalizes white middle class values ("white money") while highlighting the dangers of Black youths (criticizing the economic successes of Black entertainers). As Jerome (17-year-old) argues:

> what pisses me off is that gangsters are doin' business; they doin' business just like the big companies, what pisses me off even more is that they want a piece of our action. When it comes to money we're just as greedy for more. It's already in us to just do.

For gang members the media promotes norms of conformity. Gangs and school youths are most moved by the music and film entertainment media's "cool" messages about crime while propagating norms of conformity: unequal competition (context), rewards of materialism (goals) and the use of violence (means). Street kids are more marginalized, the least economically privileged, least institutionally attached, and least affected by media and yet are more enlightened about the impact of the media. Violence perpetuates violence and contributes directly to the delinquency of the weak as Rachel (a 17-year-old street prostitute) noted:

> Yeah the violence in the news, the violence in games, in rap—in all of this makes more violence. These kids at school and those wannabee tough believe it all. It doesn't help. It's like the news and all the other crap want to make criminals out of kids and kids—Black or White are too stupid to see it.

All youths note the significant role of media in shaping identity, relations and experiences of crime. The power and the contradictions of the media in shaping identity were most apparent and identifiable to the street youths. For school and gang youths the popular culture reinforces various ideals that could be incorporated. School youths however are inclined to see less benefit in the media promotion of racism and misogyny. Gang, incarcerated and street youths comment extensively on media contribution to violence, racism and crime fictions; in the words of 16-year-old Sammi, "they push perverted violence, you know violence for fun and not violence to get out this shit hole." The media contributes indirectly by creating conditions for

135

TABLE 3.11
PERCEIVED IMPACT OF MEDIA ON CRIME/DELINQUENCY

	IN SCHOOL	STREET KIDS	GANG NOT IN SCHOOL	GANG IN SCHOOL	INCARCERATED PROBATION
themselves					
immediate	M	L	H	M	M
long term	H	L	M	M	M
skills	H	L	L	M	L
interest	H	L	L	M	M
identity	M	L	L	M	M
others					
boys	H	H	M	M	H
girls	L	M	L	L	M
blacks	H	M	M	M	M
whites	M	L	M	M	M
siblings	H	L	H	H	H
peers	H	M	M	H	H
parents	L	H	M	M	M
society					
contributes to status quo	H	L	M	H	H
inequalities	L	H	H	H	H
racism	L	M	H	M	H
sexism	H	L	L	L	L
individualism	H	M	M	L	L
materialism	H	H	H	H	H

Legend:
H High: over 67-100% of intra group agreement
M Medium: 34-66% of intra group agreement
L Low: 0-33% of intra group agreement N=200

delinquency, by exaggerating the benefits of violent crime as entertainment as a means for accumulating wealth, as normative and as oppositional, as selective expressions of dominant culture. Media messages pathologize some crimes and the privilege others. In addition to class, gender, class and sexuality as mediating the impact of the media, the concept of "affiliation" characterizes the influence of the media. In other words, the location (relative distance) of one's own identity and social self vis à vis disciplining institutions and prevailing ideologies is significant. In general, White youths view media messages as counter hegemonic messages; majority of Black youths as hegemonic and a minority of Black youths perceive the messages as counter hegemonic. For street youths, the media shapes delinquency only in the realm of cultural moments of the spectacle or carnival. For many street kids, media crime is presented as an appearance (the visual) without substance and without reference to the political and economic realms. According to six street youths crime is a tool of the media designed to exaggerate defiance while disguising the deferential nature of media. That is, youths become immune to the horror of violence; gradually accept violence as problem solving. For all youths the media do not cause crime but influences the inculcation of a set of values that embraces violence as a way of life. Qualitative data from 65 interviews indicate that their differential reading of the media text is governed by mood, that is, a psychic vibration between the poles of boredom and anxiety. Boredom (Brienza 2000) figures prominently in their accounts. Boredom and anxiety inform,

PERCEPTIONS OF YOUTHS OF MEDIA CRIME MESSAGES AS HEGEMONIC	
School	Counter hegemonic
Gang at school	Counter hegemonic
Gang	Hegemonic and counter heg emonic
Street	Hegemonic (cooptation, homog enizing)

provoke and encourage reactions of withdrawal that throw participants into structural conditions of emotional hue. Crime talk, for youth, "fills in" the space with a creative response that is seen in their respective. Given the boredom or always "being busy doing something" as their connective cultural tissue, youths seldom question the singleness of media purposes, the constant sense of over saturation, actuarial decathlon, sludge of criminal detail and the media's vulgar determinism sustained by linguistic hegemony. Reading newspaper stories, on line chat groups or watching newscasts about similarly circumstanced others (squeegee kids, ravers, juvenile prostitutes or computer enthusiasts) socializes while "passing the time" into a public event. Because of this inability to grasp the nature of one's own possibilities, they are aptly prone to experience a crisis of meaning. The future orientation lacks the possible solidification of adulthood and exists within a space of uncertainty.

The above tables summarize the responses to the following questions: how do youth form and inform identities in relation to conflicting media narratives of their self and subjectivity? How do youth articulate their experiences in interpreting the media coverage of crime? On the basis of interviews with a representative sample of street and school youths, the following findings were significant: youths inhabit multiple worlds simultaneously, unlikely to be fixed culturally by a single categorical framework.

Older and more educated youths interpret the deforming gaze of the media, that is, the symbolic violence, in a manner that privileges their own icono-graphic discourses of rage, representation and resistance. Privileged youths note that the media coverage of crime and the attendant crackdown by the police were unnecessary but understandable given the aggressive "behav-iour" of youths, adopting the same rhetoric promoted by the state. Street youths objected to the media's reporting of a new breed of violence. To them their counter hegemonic praxis, in their appearances, music, recre-ation and consumption, as forms of resistance to the moral entrepreneurship of authorities (parents, police and school) is more significant issue. Canadian youths attribute much priority not to identity and difference but to the stead fast foci of current media attention B drugs, sports, sex, violence, etc. related to the general and particular distorted claims making. These findings suggest that youths are interpellated (constituted) as medi-ated subjects, subjects as legitimizing social relations by reifying and supporting hegemonic values.

Discussion

What Anthony Giddens calls the "double hermeneutic," the problem of interpretation across several lines of difference or what Dorothy Smith (1990) express as "the critique of socially organized practices of knowing" demonstrate that difference and identity affect an understanding of the world. Interpretations are constructed in contradictions of domination and submission. For example, excitement, as a means of articulating affective and instrumental relations, plays a key role in the formulation of opinions about crime news. Crime is often glamorized as activity that empowers, protects and marks territories. The consequences of illegal or unethical activity are not the images upon which young minds focus. Most youths interviewed are not aware of the dangers of the fixity and fetishism of the media's calcification of criminal identities. They are, for example, insulated from the historical contingencies and tragedies of media discourses. Instead, crime as a commodity is often fetishized in terms of impression management. Their interpretations negotiated rather than negated the valid-ity of news. According to Althusserian interpellationist theory, these comments suggest that youths are constituted as juridic subjects, subjects as legitimizing social relations by reifying and supporting hegemonic values.

Critical analysis of culture illustrates how youths have been socially, politically, economically as well as culturally and ideationally constructed to behave in self-negating ways. In the form of pleasure, the colonization of consciousness gets mobilized into self incurred domination. Reification occurs, a form of domination wherein subjective consciousness is constructed to facilitate the order of domination through the cultural production of consciousness (Lukács 1971). Unlike the alienation, which dissolves with changing conditions and relations, reification constitutes the normal mode of existence under cultural domination. It can be seen as a type of "positive domination" because it transmutes repression into a quick and easy need that could be satisfied with the purchase of uniforms from the Gap, an automobile, drugs etc. It is a form of unwitting self-negation because its processes remain concealed from conscious awareness (Gramsci's common sense). That which is assailed Buniformity is in fact rented or bought, retail or wholesale!

Bourdieu's argument that cultural domination is exercised through cultural capital is similar to Antonio Gramsci's theory of hegemony, which concerns the way the dominant classes exercise their cultural power through consensus rather than coercion. In cultural terms this can be seen in the way that repressed cultures often copy and replicate the modes and mores of the dominant culture. Anything worth respecting in the culture must first be legitimated if not validated by the encompassing dominant order. Gramsci examines how, for example, ideological power marks social relations and the capacity of the dominant class to rule not only by its control over the means of production but by its control of ideas. This insidious mode of oppression expresses the multiplicity of discourses that conveniently fetishizes economics generally or capital accumulation specifically. This new type of consciousness has become the dominant cultural mode of belonging and being, a mimetic mastery of what is defined as "criminal." For Fiske (1994), while popular texts appear to reinforce the status quo, to reproduce dominant cultural ideas, in fact many people respond creatively to the works of popular culture that they encounter, often reworking the meanings of these texts. Fiske introduces interesting arguments about the way in which people encounter the popular culture such as television programmes, films, music videos, magazines, newspaper articles, and the internet. In an original approach, Fiske argues that rather than just absorbing the ideological messages they carry, people react to the popular culture initially by evading the ideological message, and then by creating offensive forms of reaction to that message. In this phase, Fiske appears to be arguing, the meanings of the text are reconstituted at either the literal or imaginative level so as to be rendered wholly different. Due to the dominance of mass media forms such as popular music, fashion, television, the Internet, and video games in the lives of young people in industrialized societies today, it is fair to say that mass media forms constitute the primary cultural resource for youths (Mastronardi 2003:83). Moments of youthfulness does not emerge from the people in a self-conscious way as an expression of indigenous selves, but rather produced from a top down approach where culture is inculcated into public consciousness as something that has been materially invented. That is, a commodification of culture that no longer remains indigenous in this "mental production" prevails. This mass dissemination of public information about youth has regressed into ideology, into a "centrality of illusion" as one of many new forms by which reality is obscured (Rose 1978:14). The realization of mass society and the production of a mass consciousness has become possible through the development of new media technologies, cultural mythologies that serve as texts of meaning in a consumer oriented popular culture. For Adorno (1973:63) "it is part of the mechanism of domination to forbid recognition of the suffering it produces." For Marcuse (1972) the creation of this herd mentality, mechanisms of social constraint, the circle of mediocrity and the new cohesive forces of society are inherently in conflict with consciousness. The "society of the spectacle" distracts, stupefies and paralyzes the public conscience. Instead of political action, the public is captured by the text of spectator sports, advertising and other mass cultural forms Commodity and criminality are thus inextricably linked, encoded into the iconography of youth reifies a politics

Critical studies have long argued for the significance of the individual as "social," constituted by intersubjective relations with others in the complexity of multiple involvements. Habermas (1984) insists on the social construction of individual identity and pursued a theory of communicative action grounded in the universal presuppositions of language. For Habermas, socialized individuals are only sustained through group activity and language, thereby challenging the traditional philosophy of consciousness, the reliance on the presumed absolute identity of the individual as knower, embodied in the Cartesian epistemologies. Critical theory would take as its starting point "youth" not as any specific social group, but of a kind of thinking—necessarily done by and to the individuals—a thinking that incorporates the most categorical basic structure of the whole society, that which makes it whole, gives it its basic dynamism, and point to the possibilities of transcendence. Theoretically, critical cultural criminology incorporates both interpretive and normative perspectives on crime with insights about intrapsychic (internal) and intersubjective (interpersonal) meanings (Adorno 1973). Recently, constitutive criminology has pursued the discipline's transformative possibilities by urging a relational view in which the component elements of social life are not individuals or institutions but combinations of economic, political, class, gender, age and legal relations. As constitutive criminology implores, thinking about crime is a collective discursive production (Arrigo 1995:40). For Arrigo, Acontingencies, chance, randomness, contradictions and multiplicities are missing. Situated within such moments are these oppressed voices that remain silent, local knowledges that struggle for recognition, and political truths that have yet to be born. But given the transitional development of subjectivity, youths are susceptible to the dominant culture, that is, the popular culture and seldom question the false identity of the general and the particular. Furthermore, standards are based in the first place on consumers' needs are accepted with so little resistance. The need to challenge is suppressed by the control of the individual consciousness. The raison d'être of youth is the confirmation of a set of calculated mutations that serve all the more strongly to confirm the validity of the capitalist production, consumption and production of consumption which so confines them, body and soul as that they fall helpless victims to what is offered them. Within this unreflective and unimaginative theatre of illusion, possessive individualism, or more appropriately the idolisation of individuality, materialism, technological rationales, markets of pleasure, the anesthetized sense of identity, products of the culture industry are defended if not promoted. According to Adorno and Horkheimer (1979), functions of uniform, ideologically determined style, and the laughing throngs at the cinema, transform humans into barbaric monads. That is culture has always played its part in taming revolutionary and barbaric instincts by celebrating standardisation, stereotypes, mass production, the uniform logic of pleasure (excitement). Cultural commodification and reification in capitalist modernity has become a "melting down of all values in a giant crucible" (Adorno and Horkheimer 1979:xv). This absolute integration into the dominant order (ibid) has led to a new poverty of culture, which intentionally integrates its multiple manifestations. Homogeneity in assimilation has become normalized in the aggressive intensifications of consumerism and the distraction that accompanies it.

The media transform control by commodifying youths generally. The media industry impedes the development of autonomous, independent individuals who judge and decide consciously for themselves (Adorno and Horkheimer 1979). Culture collaborates with authority and cannot be understood "in terms of itself...an independent logic of culture." Adorno and Horkheimer (1989) acknowledge that ideology justifies the rubbish produced. Accordingly, the beauty of has been transformed into by-products or wastes of callous economic orders. Adorno and Horkheimer (1989:152) further affirm that "culture has always played its part in taming revolutionary and barbaric instincts." Accordingly, the media do not just manufacture illusions but are the tyrannical embodiments of social relations packaged symbolically.

The ideology of youth crime confines the body and soul and reproduces itself through the mass deception of the culture industry. Likewise, Habermas (1984) highlights the role of dogma in keeping individuals in a state of ignorance and repression. Socializing agencies controlled by dominant ideological discourses determine the subject, including thought, affect, enjoyment, meaning and identity. Legitimation or the cooptation of mass loyalty and support is also crucial for the continued existence of delinquency. The media shield and legitimize state supported conflicts. An important element of the media is the manner in which youths are implicated in manifestations of the corporate and state policies. This complicity is an important aspect of moral regulation. The media allude to insidious ways to control the individual without overt force of domination. The language of delinquency has always been a method used to silence opposition from youths. Our findings disagree with Weiss (2005:A19) who presumes that:

> we are more likely to live in an entertainment world of our own making...The entertainment industry is losing its clout: We're increasingly unwilling to accept someone else's packaging or schedule. We want our songs and our shows when we want them, and only the ones we're asking for, please. We want the news that suits our interests and political views. We want power...Our choices are more abundant than ever and, especially thanks to the Internet, easier to reach. But it's also easier than ever before to shut things out.

From all of the pop culture offerings in chat rooms, blogs, satellite radio, niche programming, Internet, TiVo, iTunes choices are more abundant than ever but these creations controlled by various industries. It is not a cultural sauntering, that is, a strolling through the world with our blinders off, as Washington's Center for Media and Public Affairs suggests (ibid). Rather, youths are products of mechanical reproduction that are brought and always deprecated (Benjamin 1968:211). This separation of instrumental functions from expressive symbols does not disguise the readiness of youth to consume.

Research by Acland (1995:10) propose that when studying the relationship between youth and the "news," we should be considering the "conjunction point for various discourses" such that race, gender, sexuality, class and age are at the very core of common understandings of the "crisis of youth." Despite this recommendation, however, there exist no data yet on young people's knowledge and perception of criminal justice, to my knowledge and confirmed by PetersonBadali and Koegl (2002).

Conclusions

The issue herein is not that the dominant culture has ignored youth, but rather the category of youth exerts a basic influence over social thoughts. Youth can only be understood in its undistorted essence when it becomes the universal category of society as a whole. But youth as commodity relations has assumed decisive importance both for the objective evolution and for the stance adopted towards it. Only then does the commodity become crucial for the subjugation of youth's consciousness to the forms in which this reification finds expression. Youth as progressively rationalized and mechanization of will is reinforced by the way in which awareness becomes less and less active, a negative of lived value. Youth identity is so complex and so full of metaphysical subtleties. This is the principle of youth fetishism, a selection of images which exist above it, and which simultaneously impose themselves as the tangible par excellence. The world of the commodity is identical to the estrangement of youth among themselves and in relation to their others. The spectacle is the moment when the commodity has attained the total occupation of social life and the fragmented individual becomes more fully separated from the productive forces operating as a whole. Spectacular consumption includes the recuperated repetition of the negative manifestations of the fragmented identity. The vulgar spectacle becomes implicated in an accommodating common culture. Interestingly, distance from the diversion of the spectacle is a requirement for authentic truth seeking. Otherwise, interpretations of delinquency are saturated with distorted images and illusions. Lamentably, the media as masters of the spectacle have succeeded with little effort and with much impunity to transform fiction into the new truth. But is this false reality, the source of knowledge, peculiar to youths? What is it about the phenomenon of youth that renders it so susceptible to manipulation? How is youth a fertile life stage for texts of delinquency to emerge? How is it possible to analyze the subtext of power in light of prevailing texts of delinquency (incidence of crime) and their contexts of law and popular culture? There are the "pulling" forces of more contemporary cultural features of variety and excitement—being cool. How do they learn about cool? Coolness is the ability to maximize gain and minimize effort while structuring relations in a way that favourably impresses others. Along with this cool orientation, these youths are encouraged to adopt a presentist attitude. Presentism is the lack of perseverance in the pursuit of long term projects (Cusson 1983:126,164), a form of immediate gratification. Youths learn to orient their lives to the quick fix of present pleasure. Herein lies the quintessential problematicBthe differential impact of the media! The media is part of a larger culture industry that is committed to a project of homogenization. Within the dominant culture, crime however distorted carry considerable currency in popular discourse. Parenthetically, this "crime as a commodity" fetish is crucial in signalling the cultural capital of crime thereby avoiding any serious analysis of inherent social justice issues. Crime is a cultural product. The violence-generating engines of the media contribute to the cultural characteristics of individualism, materialism and violence. Hypocrisy prevails in adult determined society that is fixated in being "forever young" (Danesi) while constantly criticizing if not punishing youth; condemning youth for unruly behaviour while celebrating violent predatory practices, military aggression and wholesale injustices. Indubitably, the glamorization of violence (crime as entertainment and entertainment as crime) and the perpetual self-gratification generate predispositions among adolescents and youths. A violent culture generates a self-fulfilling risk society.

The consciousness of desire and the desire for consciousness have become identical given their grounding in a morality of the material. Protecting the material is the legal domain.

144

Law represents a specific sphere of knowledge production, distribution and consumption that ensures the governmentalities of the cultural to such an extent that the lived has become the juridic. Equally, as we will note in the following chapter, the majesty of law like its mediocre media manipulates moments of youth crime.

Chapter 4

Criminal Law and Youth

Much law, but little justice.
        —Fuller, 1732 (Hyman 1993:272)
Justice is incidental to law and order.
        —J. Edgar Hoover (Green 1982:319)
We have accumulated a wealth of historical experience which
confirms our belief that the scales of justice are out of balance.
        —Angela Davis, 1971 (Baker 1992:157)

Introduction: Images and Statistics

Youth crime is a socially constructed and historically reproduced phenomenon whose form changes in response to socio-economic transformations. In other words, crime incorporates a set of economic, political, legal, and ideological practices through which a dominant group exercises hegemony. Conceptually, youth crime exists in reference to well-established, even if poorly understood, impressions grounded in the canons of "common" experiences. These interpretations, respected as self-evident truths, succeed in disciplining understanding and securing compliance. The Canadian state secures control over the nature of youth crimes according to powerful resources which proscribe criteria. Delinquency, as an expression of defiance, enables the differential exercise of state and corporate power. To know about delinquency is to think, talk, read, write and research the

147

politics of law. Given our concern with the totality of social relations, various social worlds and their material conditions this chapter asks the following basic questions: Who defines youth crime? What shapes delinquency? How are legal responses structured culturally?

As noted in previous chapters the dominant culture frames legal ideologies. In turn, the normative conception of order is shaped by certain versions of delinquency buttressed by images that shape the reaction of individuals and institutions. Images are socially reinforced and are internalized as common sense, claiming to inform empirically any understanding of trouble. A critical cultural calculus incorporates the manufacture of morality, images of danger, the politics of policing trouble, political economy of peace, functions of fiction, and the limitations of law. At the cultural level, images mask injustices, manufacture coercion and colonize consent. Likewise, delinquency is manipulated to legitimate and generate support for the status quo by bombarding the "public" with a plethora of threatening images. As an ideological text, youth crime images contribute to state formations by exaggerating threats to the body politic. Historically, youth crime has always been a commodity exploited conveniently by the state apparatus and fictive collective moralities. The dominant class continues to exercise control by stimulating seductive images that encourage deference to authority. Youth crime images exist within a framework of stupefying statistics, juridic jargon and technocratic talk to which we now turn.

The incarceration rate for youths in Canada reached an eight-year low in 2002/2003, according to a Statistics Canada (Huffman 2004:A8); that is, fewer youths are punished by incarceration. Currently, approximately 90% of young offenders are on supervised probation, 7% serving time in jail and 3% in custody awaiting a court appearance or sentencing (ibid). Specifically, on average 29,500 Canadian youths are in custody or on supervised probation. The total number of youths aged 12 to 17 in the correctional system decreased by 6% from 1993-1994 to 2002-2003. Youths held on remand (awaiting a court appearance or sentencing) increased by 21% over the same period, while those sentenced to custody decreased by 35% (ibid). The youth court caseload in Canada has been declining over the past decade, consistent with a decrease in charges laid by police. Youth courts heard 84,592 cases during the 2002-2003 fiscal year, 1% fewer than in 2001-2002, and 20% fewer than in 1991-1992. Steady declines in cases involving property crimes were primarily responsible for the overall drop in caseload. Judges heard 32,465 property crime cases in youth courts in 2002-2003, a drop of 47% from the 61,124 property cases heard in 1991-1992.The number of drug-related cases has tripled since 1991-1992, going from 1,920 to 5,907. In 2002-2003, 4,137 of these cases were for possession of drugs (Statistics Canada 2004a). Accused youth were found guilty in 6 out of 10 cases heard in youth courts in 2002-2003. *Criminal Code* traffic offences had the highest conviction rate (68%); drug-related crimes had the lowest (43%). About one-quarter of youth cases were withdrawn or dismissed. Transfers to adult court were rare, accounting for only 30 cases; 17 of these involved violent crimes. Youth court judges ordered a sentence of probation (alone or in combination with other sentences) more frequently than any other type of sentence in 2002-2003. Seven out of ten convicted youth cases received a probation order, averaging 375 days. The average length of these sentences has been getting longer; in 1991-1992, it was 316 days. The proportion of convicted youth cases receiving a sentence to secure custody increased gradually from 11% of convicted cases in 1991-1992 to 14% in 2002-2003 (ibid). However, the average length of these sentences got shorter over this period, declining from 95 days to 68 days. Judges were more likely to use sentences to custody for violent crimes than for other types of crime. In 2002-2003, 74% of convicted homicide cases resulted in a sentence of secure custody, while 16% resulted in open custody. Secure custody was ordered in 64% of attempted murder cases, while 14% of these cases resulted in a sentence of open custody. Robbery also frequently resulted in a custody sentence, with 25% of convicted cases receiving secure custody and 25% getting open (Statistics Canada 2004a).

Between 1991 and 2003, the total number of youth crime cases in Canada dropped by 20%. In that same period, the number of crimes against property committed by youth dropped a total of 47% to its lowest level in more than 25 years (Statistics Canada 2004b)! Violent youth crime was down by 2% in 2002. Of the 84,592 youth cases heard in youth court in 2002-03, just under 75% involved non-violent offences such as mischief and theft (ibid). And minor assaults accounted for more than half of the violent crimes committed by youth (Statistics Canada 2004c). The charge rate per 100,000 population in 2004 for homicide includes: total persons charged 1.9; youths charged 1.6; and adults 1.9; while rates for attempted murder were 1.9 for youths and 2.1 for adults per 100,000 (Statistics Canada 2005). The found guilty category in youth criminal court for homicide were: 16 in 1988; 24 in 1999; 16 in 2000; 8 in 2001; 19 in 2002

(Statistics Canada 2004d). In 2002, the federal government released a review of 111 studies on the effects of criminal justice sanctions on more than 442,000 offenders. It found that harsher punishments had no deterrent effect on repeat offences. In fact, it suggested that punishment caused a 3% increase in recidivism among all groups of offenders, including youth (Smith, Goggin, and Gaudreau 2002).

The media's tendency to focus on violent youth crime stories has contributed to a distortion of youth crime facts. An Ontario study found that 94% of youth crime stories in the media were about violent offences when less than 25% of Ontario's youth court cases actually involved violent crime. A similar American study conducted in 2000 found that crime news on network TV increased 83% from 1990 to 1998 and yet the crime rate dropped 20% during that period to its lowest level in 25 years. Yet, opinion polls reveal that two-thirds of Canadians believe crime to be on the rise (Department of Justice 2004).

In 2002, law enforcement agencies in the United States made an estimated 2.3 million arrests of persons under age 18, 19% fewer than the number of arrests in 1998 (Snyder 2004). The substantial growth in juvenile violent crime arrests that began in the late 1980s peaked in 1994. In 2002, for the eighth consecutive year, the rate of juvenile arrests for Violent Crime Index offenses—murder, forcible rape, robbery, and aggravated assault—*declined*. Specifically, between 1994 and 2002, the juvenile arrest rate for Violent Crime Index offenses fell 47%. As a result, the juvenile Violent Crime Index arrest rate in 2002 was at the lowest level since at least 1980. From its peak in 1993 to 2002, the juvenile arrest rate for murder fell 72%. Arrests of juveniles accounted for 17% of all arrests and 12% of all violent crimes cleared by arrest in 2002—specifically, 5% of murders, 12% of forcible rapes, 14% of robberies, and 12% of aggravated assaults. An estimated 16,200 murders were reported to law enforcement agencies in 2002 or 5.6 murders for every 100,000 U.S. residents. In the peak year of 1993, there were about 3,840 juvenile arrests for murder. Between 1993 and 2002, juvenile arrests for murder declined, with the number of arrests in 2002 (1,360) about one-third that in 1993 (3,840). That is, in 2002, juveniles were involved in 1 in 10 arrests for murder (or 10% of arrests for murder), 1 in 8 arrests for a drug abuse violation, 1 in 5 arrests for a weapons violation, and 1 in 4 arrests for robbery (Snyder 2004). In 2002, the juvenile arrest rate for forcible rape was near its lowest level for the 1980–2002 periods. The juvenile arrest rate for robbery declined during much of the 1980s, falling 30% between 1980 and 1988 (Office of Juvenile Justice and Delinquency Prevention 2004a). Between 1993 and 2002, there were substantial declines in juvenile arrests for murder (64%), motor vehicle theft (50%), and weapons law violations (47%) and major increases in juvenile arrests for drug abuse violations (59%) and (46%) for driving under the influence (Office of Juvenile Justice and Delinquency Prevention 2004b). Between 1992 and 2001 victimization rates at school and away from school declined. In 1993, 1995, 1997, 1999, 2001, and 2003 about 7 to 9% of students in grades 9 to 12 reported being threatened or injured with a weapon such as a gun, knife, or club on school property in the past 12 months. In 2003, about 6% of students carried a weapon such as a gun, knife, or club on school property in the past 30 days, a decline from 12% in 1993. Sixteen school-associated homicides were of school age children between July 1, 1999 and June 30, 2000. In 2003, 21% of students reported the presence of street gangs in their schools (Snyder 2004, Bureau of Justice Statistics 2004). Since 1973, 95 offenders younger than 18 (51%) have had their death sentences reversed, 17 (9%) have been executed, and 73 (39%) remain under sentence of death. Of the 73 offenders under sentence of death on December 31, 2000, for crimes committed at age 17 or younger, 55 were age 17 at the time of their offense and the remaining 18 were 16 (Streib 2001).

Crime statistics as coherent sets of "official" ideas, articulated in organizational exchanges do not just exist "out there" as objective things, but rather they are constructed and manipulated by authorities through various historical and cultural practices. How are rates of youth crime used to transform consciousness and regulate morality? How are these numbers linked to conventions of appropriateness to create the deferential subject, to inculcate both a sense of belongingness and distance? What is the role of authority relations in depersonalizing, alienating or "deindividuating" youth on the basis of these images?

Nature of Law: Recognition of Authority Relations

Law is always an authorized force, a force that justifies itself or is justified in applying itself, even if this justification may be judged from elsewhere to be unjust or unjustifiable. (Jacques Derrida 1990:925)

151

Authority signifies relations that constitute and are constituted by the dynamics of power. The ideological and institutional mechanisms of power create authority-subject relations. The imposition of authority, discipline or governmentalities, that is, regulation, requires recognition. Recognition is the capacity to connect the formal with the familiar. To present the representation of authority-subject relations as recognitions of familiar connections, common sense or normalized knowledge is invoked. This mutual recognition protects and maximizes the influence of the powerful while securing the compliance of the powerless.

Recognition, accomplished through ongoing processes of socialized identification that relinquishes the self to images of authority, is dependent upon regulation. It is not simply a matter of self denial or self sacrifice, but rather recognition of the self in the authority. Authority reconstitutes the self of the subject as coherent and less fragmented. This practice occurs precisely because as, Hannah Arendt (1906-1975) argues, genuine authority has vanished from the modern world. Moreover, we are no longer in a position to recognize real authority. Arendt claims that it is as though we are caught in distortions; a maze of abstractions, metaphors and figures of speech in which everything can be taken and mistaken for something else, because we have no reality to which we can unanimously appeal the coercion of instrumental reason. For Arendt, authority is a signifying form, always imaginary and hence subject to change through performative critical analysis (1958, 1961). According to Gadamer (1976, 1989), authority exercises dogmatic power in innumerable forms of domination; authority grows out of dogmatic acceptance, the concession of superiority in knowledge and insight. Authentic authority and tradition are legitimate sources of knowledge (Arendt 1958). However, as Max Weber (1969) elucidates, liberal democracies rely primarily on a legal system as authority, that is, a predictable, bureaucratic and rational form of regulation. Law as a bureaucratic and bureaucratizing organization guides not only the juridic quotidien but the everyday conduct in all fields. Legal technicians, as voices of objectivity, have legalized morality leaving behind only mirrors and windows through which knowledge is framed. The voices of these moral engineers resonate with evocative righteous convictions about the passionate and yet objective spirit of authority: discipline. In this regard Foucault's explorations into regulation as a political observatory (1979:281) clarify how legal discourse and practice create ideologically appropriate subject positions. The political economy as the fundamental authority enforces the law. Thus, Zatz (1987:85) and Balbus (1973) conclude that the legal system serves to represent the interests of a few, to institutionalize bias and to reinforce inequalities. Within this specific site of law, the state exercises a legal and legitimate monopoly over violence. At every stage of the justice system, from arrest, pre-trial hearing, conviction, sentencing, to classification and parole hearings, the less advantaged receive harsher penalties (Staples 1975; Koch and Clarke 1976; Carroll and Mondrick 1976; Lieber 1994). Donald Black plots the stratified nature of law along the horizontal and vertical matrices where "downward law is greater than upward law" (Black 1976:21), that is, upward crimes—crimes where the victim's status ranks above the offender's status—are treated as more serious than downward crimes, and punishment is more likely to have a downward than an upward direction.

Law is constructed in reference to well-established, albeit poorly understood, impressions that are grounded in liberal orthodox ideas that socialize "common" experiences in terms of mythologies of equality and its sibling freedom. The law is projected as neutral, innocent and too limited in responding to social injustices, thereby escaping complicitous connections (Fitzpatrick 1990:259). By providing "universalistic" protections, the law seeks to transcend material conditions; such liberal legal appeals to "equality" and "freedom" are powerful ideological tools.

Law is an "impositionalist" structure that remains immutable and often incorrigible to diverse interests. Law as a juridic "text" confines knowledge too narrowly. The lexicon of law, turgid case law, incomprehensible legalese and abstract principles conceal principles of justice. As noted previously, the criminal justice system perpetuates a pathology of trouble by problematizing youth by amplifying threats and popularizing criminal mythologies. To reiterate, law is not solely anchored in individual or institutional conditions but rather a consequence of complex configurations within the political economy and culture. Culture, mediated by the political economy, provides law with ideological drifts. Ideological drifts are the ongoing and changing impact(s) of legal ideas and symbols that promote sensitivity to new contexts while astutely ensuring the consistency of content. Artificial doctrinal distinctions (legal reform) conceal sustained (foundational) injustices. The law's indeterminacy, gaps and fragility, topics of everyday life for the legal establishment and its practitioners, maintain authority because of deeply rooted economic and cultural privileges. The indeterminacy of law enables variability of responses to the modern condition notably the adjustments to legitimacy crisis in substance and procedure. Any prudent analysis of law avoids facetious comments on the problematic authority of the legal code, and needs to examine how the implementation of the value of justice is exhibited and manipulated in the actual workings of the legal system in response to the political economy, the implications for the cultural system. Law as a rhetorical narrative of doctrines and policies demystifies the lived experiences and justifies itself morally in reference to rational discourse, as an expression of "all" in modern society. Law then becomes a systemic medium in the colonization of the lifeworld (Habermas 1983, 1984, 1987, 1998). Law enters the lifeworld to disrupt its communicative capacities so that disputes in the lifeworld (ideally dealt with through communicative action) become converted into monetary and bureaucratic matters. Law, as the institutionalized domain of moral-practical rationality, occupies a central place in this process of rationalization (ibid). This relational view of law, as economic, political and cultural, constitutes social relations.

Notwithstanding the language of law, agency is limited by structural contexts. As noted earlier, language as an integral part of culture—reflects, embodies and perpetuates the hegemonic relations of the society in which it is embedded. The imposition of a legal lexicon is a powerful instrument that supplies the taxonomies and vocabularies of utility. Language inculcates norms and socializes into conformity (Bourdieu 1991; Habermas 1975). Also, legal language is symbolic power designating status, cultural compliance and technical competence—the respected albeit artificial authority. Language channels privilege. As a mode of discourse, the pathocentric script of youth crime for example objectifies any challenge by invoking existing codes. Legal, scientific and professional discourses dominate the language of control. As professionals adhere to a privatized, mystifying and techno-bureaucratic language, a cornucopia of meaningless jargon and mythologies emerge. Communication is convoluted, meanings are degraded; debates remain limited; and, rituals that exalt public relations are rewarded. Moreover, specialized vocabularies conceal the real "services" rendered to the dangerous classes and justify further interventions. Law language objectifies, stultifies and disciplines expressions of self awareness. Language presupposes a context of rules which cannot be contradicted (Gellner1959:56). For Barthes (1973), language contributes to myth making; language politicizes myths by claiming reference to signifying signs; and, the clarity of language is misleading. Language is a performance that renders the more articulate as more legitimate and hence more knowledgeable. The subject is determined by language (Lacan 1977:298-300); the subject disappears in his or her discourse and becomes embodied in the spoken word of the othering authority. In order to reproduce meaning certain, "master signifiers" represent the subject for another signifier (Lacan 1977:316). Language is a situated and generic expression of authority, reproducing and not merely expressing meaning (de Saussure 1986).

Legal responses are cultural products that frame experiences, supply interpretations, legitimate decisions, provide histories and secure loyalties to rules. Within this mystifying calculus the "other" is produced, that is, a marginalized other is manufactured who, in turn, is easily transformed into a prospective alien, a parasitic suspect, accused or convict. This construction of the other is determined by dominant discourses, political, legal as well as cultural. But lamentably, the traditional text stylized in well respected formulae stress the primacy of a binary code; an encyclopaedic recipe in which identities, relations and activities are reduced to essentialist notions of *either* legal or illegal, guilt or innocence. This artificially bifurcated polarization misrepresents multi-layered identities or phenomena.

Canadian law abstracts and de-contextualizes individuals from their social relations by stressing the freedom and liberty of the individual in maximizing her or his life-chances. Ericson (1984) qualifies: "those who seek equality in social structure and social relations and, the justice this promises, should look more often to means other than the law" (p.3). Moreover, this lingering liberalism with its "libertarian principles" (Eberts 1985:12) tends to totalize and essentialize system dynamics, crisis tendencies, and conflict potentials while seldom attending to class dynamics and to the global political-economic processes that help shape ethnicity and inequality. An emphasis on the legal "individual" is at best a partial remedy. Social data are overwhelming in demonstrating that law, as a "disembodied spectacle" (O'Neill 1985), is unresponsive to current societal concerns, that is, divorced from its larger social foundations. Derived from classical notions of Locke and Hobbes, liberalism's "individualism" privatizes equality and freedom (Rawls 1996:155-6) and places great value on maximizing the citizens' freedom and self-determination, rights to choose and pursue self-interests freely. This distorted sense of social responsibility vitiates more moral, communal or collective projects of redistribution and recognition.

Additionally, law, as the backdrop of the criminal justice system, is influenced by the currents of culture, politics and economics. Irrespective of what different public roles are institutionalized on different occasions—the punitive officer (from the peace officer, prosecutor to the correctional officer), the supportive welfare worker (defense counsels, classifications officer, case worker, psychiatrists, the parole officer) or the neutral party (the judge, jury, bureaucrats), the "criminal" justice system is designed fundamentally to criminalize—to punish, to discipline and to correct. Within this "justice" system, occupational cultures and their concomitant ideologies, tasks, values, training, and organizational priorities vary. The legal culture consists of: a) a complex amalgam of the text (a corpus of substantive and procedural rules); b) the structure of the respective professions, the social organization of everyday work; c) patterns of relations with other elements "in the system"; and, d) ideology and consciousness. The activities of the criminal justice system reflect wider cultural characteristics (ideologies of modernity, capitalism and liberalism) that are also protected institutionally. On the one hand, the bureaucracies of the criminal justice system respond to trouble (crime) according to a culture of self-serving organizational interests which institutionalize inequality. On the other hand, the criminal justice system is an industry that is central to the well being of the social, political and economic orders. All institutions of this system, individually and collectively perform the ideological and repressive functions of the state. In turn, the criminal justice system provides jobs for tens of thousands of wage earners, extends lucrative contracts for consultants and rewards partisan political favours through series of appointments on numerous boards.

Interestingly, despite the obvious differences in temporal contexts these actors are engaged in micro-political (local) struggles shaped by more macro-cultural influences (global). Likewise, they are multiple subjects, enjoying a plurality of meanings that are displaced and re-constructed in concert with other hegemonic reproductions of discipline. Law, therefore, is depicted as expressions of political processes and consequences of politicized structures. Again, law is contextualized culturally, mediated politically and articulated historically. Culture as a calculus frames experience, supplies interpretations from which inferences are drawn, legitimates decisions, provides a history and secures a loyalty to rules. Law is cultural medium in which social identities are formed and re-formed, a privileged site that constructs, protects and represents certain interests, a mechanism that legitimates the creation and mobilization of social groups. Succinctly, the culture (media)—law (policing) nexus negotiates a normative guide that articulates the dominant culture. The notion of "culture as law" denotes the reconstruction of cultural enterprise as legal endeavor; through, for example, the public labeling of youth cultures as criminogenic.

From the above overview it is argued that crime does not belong exclusively to a juridic narrative. A constricted definition of law is equally meaningless and forecloses any possibility of social justice which presumably must implicate such dynamic features as history and political economy. Take for example the recent 2005 Boxing Day shooting spree in downtown Toronto. A 15-year-old girl lost her life and six others wounded during a brazen Yonge St. gun battle between two armed groups of about 15 youths. Within seconds, the answers to this violence focused primarily on deploying more officers on the streets and at the malls, urging judges to get tougher with gun-related crimes, more recreation programs, mentoring and job training for at-risk youths in crime-ridden or poverty-stricken neighbourhoods, forming a task force to deal with gangs and guns in high crime areas and Prime Minister Paul Martin's promise to ban handguns in Canada.

The Youth Criminal Justice Act (YCJA)

> *Professionals built the Titanic—amateurs the Ark.*
> —*Anon* (Hammonds and Morris 2004)

Youth crime laws have been subjected to considerable scrutiny. Although statistics show that the crime rates among youths has remained constant over the past few decades, there are widespread beliefs that youth crime is continually on the rise, that youth crime is becoming more serious in nature, and that "lenient" youth crime laws contribute to these trends. Stiffer penalties, if not necessarily meeting the needs of the young offender, meet the needs of a misinformed public constantly bombarded by police and media accounts of youth crime (Visano 2001). Public opinion surveys, media reports and police anecdotal accounts together show widespread negative attitudes toward the youth criminal justice system according to the Standing Committee on Justice and Legal Affairs (ibid). In response to a "public panic" and the concomitant pressures to "crackdown" on violent youth crime, former Justice Minister Allan Rock tabled amendments in 1994 (Bill C-37) to the Young Offenders Act (YOA). On May 12, 1998 Justice

Minister McLellan released the government's proposed strategy for youth justice renewal. According to the Minister, Canadians want a youth justice system that protects society and that helps youth avoid crime or turn their lives around if they do become involved in crime. On March 11, 1999, the Honourable Anne McLellan, Minister of Justice and Attorney General of Canada introduced the new Youth Criminal Justice Act (YCJA) in the House of Commons noting that:

> Canadians want a youth justice system that protects society and instills values such as accountability, responsibility and respect... They want governments to help prevent youth crime in the first place and make sure there are meaningful consequences when it occurs. The new Youth Criminal Justice Act is designed to help achieve these goals. (Visano 2001:3)

The new law replaces the Young Offenders Act and is a key element of the government's comprehensive strategy to renew Canada's youth justice system. On February 5, 2001 Minister McLellan, reintroduced the Youth Criminal Justice Act in the House of Commons. She commented (ibid., 4):

> The Government of Canada believes strongly in the guiding principles of the Youth Criminal Justice Act and is committed to passing it into law...The new Act is built on the values Canadians want in their youth justice system. They want a system that prevents crime by addressing the circumstances underlying a young person's offending behaviour, that rehabilitates young people who commit offences and safely reintegrates them into society, and that ensures that a young person is subject to meaningful consequences for his or her offences. Canadians know that this is the most effective way to achieve the long-term protection of society.

The Youth Criminal Justice Act (YCJA) replaces the Young Offenders Act (YOA) as the basis for Canada's youth justice system on April 1, 2003. The YCJA frames youth justice system and applies to young people between 12 and 17 years of age. The key objectives of the YCJA include: clear and coherent principles to guide decision-making in youth justice matters; increased use of measures outside the formal court process that are often more effective in addressing less serious youth crime; fairness in sentencing; including increased use of community-based sentences for non-violent youth crime; a more targeted approach to the use of custody for young people (Canada sends youth to custody at higher rates than any other Western country); an improvement in the system's ability to rehabilitate and reintegrate young offenders; clear distinction between serious violent offences and less serious offences; special measures for violent offenders that focus on intensive supervision and treatment (Department of Justice 2003). The YCJA was a key element of the Government of Canada's Youth Justice Renewal Initiative, launched in 1998. This Initiative went beyond the legislation and the traditional youth justice system to explore ways our society can address youth crime. The Youth Justice Renewal Fund was administered to achieve the broad goals of the Initiative, which are to: enable greater citizen and community participation in the youth justice system; increase public confidence in the youth justice system; improve public protection by reducing youth crime; increase the use of measures outside the formal court process; reduce the over-reliance on custody; increase the emphasis on rehabilitation and reintegration of young offenders; and, target measures for violent offenders (ibid). Provinces and territories, NGOs, and Aboriginal organizations can apply for funds from the Youth Justice Renewal Fund to support the Initiative and the implementation of the YCJA. Funds are available for training, developing or expanding partnerships, building capacity in communities to deliver community-based options, as well as to test projects designed to achieve the goals of the Initiative (ibid).

The following summarizes the major differences between the Youth Criminal Justice Act (YCJA) and the Young Offenders Act (YOA) in terms of their key elements: a) *Declaration of principle*: The YCJA provides a clear statement of goal and principles underlying the Act and youth justice system, including specific principles to guide the use of extrajudicial measures, the imposition of a sentence and custody. The YOA contained some of the same themes as the YCJA but was not supplemented by more specific principles at the various stages of the youth justice process. b) *Measures outside the court process*: The YCJA creates a presumption that measures other than court proceedings should be used for a first, non-violent offence. This Act encourages the involvement of families, victims and community members. The YOA allowed the use of measures other than court proceedings (alternative measures) but did not create a presumption that they should be used for minor offences. c) *Sentencing principles*: The YCJA includes specific principles, including need for proportionate sentences and importance of rehabilitation. The YOA included general principles that were inconsistent and competing. d) *Sentencing Options*: In the YCJA custody reserved for violent or repeat offences. All custody sentences are to be followed with a period of supervision in the community. New options are added to encourage the use of non-custody sentences and support reintegration. The Act also creates intensive custody and supervision as well as orders for serious violent offenders. The YOA had no restriction on use of custody, no requirement for community supervision following custody and did not provide for YCJA options like reprimand, intensive support and supervision or custody and supervision order for serious violent offenders. e) *Adult sentences*: In the YCJA the youth justice court is empowered to impose an adult sentence, eliminating transfers to adult court. The age limit for presumption of adult sentences for the most serious offences is lowered to 14 (however, provinces will have increased flexibility in regard to the age at which this presumption will apply within their jurisdiction).The most serious offences that carry a presumption of an adult sentence are extended to include pattern of serious, repeat, violent offences. The Crown can renounce the application of the presumption of adult sentence. In this case, the judge who finds the young person guilty has to impose a youth sentence. In the YOA there were lengthy transfer hearings prior to trial that took place in adult court without special procedural protections granted for youth. The age limit for the presumption of adult sentence was 16. Offences that carry a presumption of an adult sentence are murder, attempted murder, manslaughter and aggravated sexual offence only. The Crown could not renounce the application of the presumption of an adult sentence. f) *Publication*: The YCJA permits publication if an adult sentence is imposed; or if a youth sentence is imposed for an offence that carries a presumption of adult sentence, unless the judge decides publication is inappropriate. The publication is permitted only after the young person has been found guilty. The YOA permitted publication only if a youth was transferred to adult court to be sentenced as an adult. Publication was permitted before the youth was found guilty. g) *Victims*: The concerns of victims are recognized in principles of the YCJA. Victims have right to access youth court records and may be given access to other records. The Act encourages the participation of victims in formal and informal community-based measures and also establishes right of victims to information on extrajudicial measures taken. In the YOA there is no mention of victims in principles. Victims may have been given access to records but there was no recognition of victims' role in the process other than the right to produce a victim's impact statement. There was no right of victims to information on alternative measures. h) *Voluntary statements*: Under the YCJA voluntary statements to police can be admitted into evidence, despite minor, technical irregularities in complying with the statutory protections for young persons. Under the YOA any minor violation of statutory protections prevented a statement from being admitted into evidence. i) *Advisory groups (conferences)*: The YCJA allows advisory groups or "conferences" to advise police officer, judge or other decision-maker under the Act. They can advise on appropriate extra-judicial measures, conditions for release from pretrial detention, appropriate sentences and reintegration plans. Conferences may include parents of the young person, victim, community agencies or professionals. The YOA had no similar provision. j) *Custody and reintegration*: Under the YCJA all custody sentences comprise a portion served in custody and a portion served under supervision in the community. A plan for reintegration in the community must be prepared for each youth in custody. Reintegration leaves may be granted for up to 30 days. Under the YOA there were no requirements that there be supervised reintegration after custody, that is, no requirement to plan reintegration during custody (Visano 2001: 4; Department of Justice 2003).

From Street Clean Up Operations to Declarations of Wars

How is this law experienced? What is the focus and locus of the new youth crime law? Within the youth criminal justice system, law is presented as the ubiquitous framework that governs situational roles and identities. Law, as a codifying institution, provides not only well grounded criteria but strives to maintain a sense of continuity. The authority of law, however, is layered. Power is differentially dispersed among the various elements of the criminal justice "system" from the arresting police officer to the supervising probation officer. Despite their obvious differences and relative independence, officials within the criminal justice system are required to defer to law, that is to act prospectively and/or retrospectively according to legal codes to which they remain ultimately accountable. The youth criminal justice system continues to serve as a coercive apparatus of the state. Within this specific site, the state exercises a legal and legitimate monopoly over violence. At every stage of the justice system the law constructs and perpetuates a pathology by problematizing youth, popularizes criminal mythologies and promotes images, beliefs and common-sense notions about the nature of youth crime. Youths are transformed into criminalized categories.

Policing is situated in the complex web of relations of ruling. Crime, as a contested terrain, is shared unequally and enjoying different histories. The policing of youth is qualitatively different from the criminalization of adults especially since the former's formal social control reflects historical preferences that link explicitly youth to projects of moral regulation. For the police, youth crime has never been ambiguous nor problematic since the situated reality of youth is conflict—antagonistic expectations, differential interpretations and a lack of deference to police definitions. In addition, the policing of youths reflects wider socio-cultural conditioning, institutionally police sanctioned practices and informal occupationally derived subcultural attitudes regarding race, class, gender and sexuality. In reference to Black youths, Brake (1985:142) notes that "the ongoing problem of policing the blacks has become, for all practical purposes, synonymous with the wider problem of policing the crisis." Since arrest statistics are high in these so called "black" areas, crime in turn becomes a justification for aggressive surveillance and racist attitudes. Justice is traded for a White normative order; the concept of race determines the construction of the severity of the penalty. The combination of police work as "legitimation work" and the bureaucratic rationales regarding efficiency render youths even more vulnerable to control.

Interestingly the image of war is exploited to muster support, mobilize resources and justify cleanup operations. Morality plays are transformed into hostile declarations of power. This image of war sanitizes differences rather than sensitizes us to the complex social problems created by social inequalities. The "war on drugs," "war on gangs" and "clearing the streets" of street kids are inter-related vacuous and alarmist slogans designed to seduce and implicate an impressionable audience into supporting an insidious political agenda. The pragmatic interests of the powerful are buried in the language of fear and security, rehearsed routinely in public trials. In turn, public perceptions frame, inform and fan state intrusions. Images of the war indoctrinate thought through processes of propaganda but also succeed in distracting attention from the strain experienced by disadvantaged youths, the business of drugs and the politics of respectability. That is, war images divert attention away from fundamental social problems. The war on gangs and the war on drugs are constructed within a framework of sophisticated surveillance, characteristic of industrial and post industrial societies. From "squeegee kids" to the war on gangs, or the war on drugs exploit the credulities of the misinformed by locating the policing of youth as a moral crisis that legitimates state violence. The current "wars" subverts meaningful intervention; instead the foci have been on localized activities that include drug dealing, fire arms dealing, prostitution, loan sharking, fraud, extortion, theft, etc. This contrived war is an insidious convenience, an opportunistic accommodation especially to classist and racist ideologies. Fundamentally, the wars on youth crime are about expressions of state injustices and cultural controls. Youths "not belonging" are "out of place" according to the strictures of culture; their behaviour, real or imagined, warrants closure, containment and coercion given their crime contagion. Despite the Multiculturalism Act of 1988, the Charter of Rights and Freedoms and numerous Human Rights legislation, racial profiling is continues to be practiced with impunity. Liberalism's individualistic view of multicultural discourses have led to myopic, static, reified and fixed ethnic or cultural identities. The formation of racialized criminal identities and attendant definitions of diversity according to an arbitrary essentialism exist within legal pronouncements of the YCJA's preamble that states whereas Canada is a party to the United Nations Convention on the Rights of the Child and recognizes that young persons have rights and freedoms, including those stated in the Canadian Charter of Rights and Freedoms and the Canadian Bill of Rights, and have special guarantees of their rights and freedoms; and despite the Principle (iv) set out in YCJA that respects gender, ethnic, cultural and linguistic differences and respond to the needs of aboriginal young persons and of young persons with special requirements (Youth Criminal Justice Act 2002).

A more practical approach to understanding the policing of youth requires an analysis of police-youth relations. For example, at a town-hall meeting in the Jane and Finch neighbourhood, a Grade 10, 15-year-old Tameka Campbell student asked former Toronto Police Chief, Julian Fantino, why she and her friends should respect the police when they do not offer respect to members of the black community. Chief Fantino said her question was "totally undeserved." "I don't think it dignifies an answer," he said. Campbell replied, "I just want my question answered. I want them to treat us as they would treat Italians or Caucasians because we're not different" (Toronto Star 2003:A16).

163

Meanwhile, during the 2005 federal election campaign, Prime Minister indicated that he recognizes that gun violence in the country's largest city is a pressing issue. Toronto police Chief Bill Blair, speaking to reporters after a recent meeting at Queen's Park, says he wants to see the violence addressed by federal politicians during the campaign because "it's a very important issue to the people of Toronto" (Powell 2005:A1). Toronto Police Services Chief, Bill Blair noted, "We'll get the people responsible for taking that young girl's life," he vowed, adding police will also find those who help the "gangs that support what was going on down there. We're going to lock them up...It is a call to action for everyone." Speaking generally about what might be fuelling recent gang violence, Blair suggested it relates to "young emerging pretenders trying to establish street cred" by "carrying firearms and engaging in gunplay." Police identified Jane Glenn Creba, a Grade 10 student at Riverdale Collegiate, as the 15-year-old killed in crossfire during a dispute between two groups of about 15 young men near Yonge and Elm Streets on Boxing Day 2005. Toronto police immediately laid firearms charges against a 20-year-old and a teen immediately arrested after the shootings.

For the police the concept of youth has taken an exaggerated social significance. Intrusions in the name of policing are not only well sponsored but ideologically legitimated. In addition to cultural contradictions, the political economy of crime, the decriminalization of vices, or the inherent ethnocentric bias, efforts need to be directed towards incoherent law enforcement policies and limited public education crusades. Youth crime is attributable to the situational (interactional), institutional (organizational) and ideological (structural) conditions that contribute to inequalities. Witness for example what police and public reactions are evoked should we compare the revealed violence of ethno specific youth gang in Toronto like the Jane Finch Killaz, Piru Bloods, Gators, Vicelords, Mother Nature's Mistakes and Parkside Crips, Ghetto Girls, Lady Crew, Ruckus Crew Versace Crew, One love, A.K. Kannon and VVT gangs, Malvern Crew, Bloods, Crips, Snakeheads, Galloway Boys to the concealed violence of the Bay Street Boys, the Wall Street Boys, the IMF, World Bank, WTO. Youths, as subjects, are articulated as fractured, fragile and complexly constituted within a plurality of discourses which positions their identities. Violence originating within structures of dominance is attributable to a criminogenic culture founded on principles of injustice and inequality. Again, an enslaving materialism, coolness, and the survival of the slickest all guide and classify coherently the ways in which violence corrupts experiences, imagination and consciousness. The sanctity of the marketplace treats the gun trade, stolen goods, drugs, prostitution as commodities with a relative material value. These culturally defined goals frame aspirations, for example, success, especially when operationalized as the acquisition of wealth. But, institutionally prescribed means are not equally available, let alone accessible, to all interested candidates. Individuals vary in their location in the social structure; that is, they are not equally positioned to capitalize on such opportunities as work, training and education. Compounded with the class and colour that confer a master status of failure that stigmatizes them, violence and crime become easy alternatives. For youths with no other hope in a system that excludes them, the gang becomes their corporation, college, religion, family and life.

Youth/Child saving: Neoliberalism

Moreover, juvenile laws were historically designed to intervene and redirect youths in trouble within a framework of "child saving" or child protectionism. Youth crime legislation in Canada (Juvenile Delinquents Act of 1908, Young Offenders Act of 1984, and the current Youth Criminal Justice Act of 2002) was always philosophically grounded in the doctrine of parens patriae, which held that the state could intervene as a "kindly parent." To what extent has the juvenile justice system been governed by the overarching principle of the "best interests of the child"? The YCJA in practice is a punitive measure, contradicting the principles of "doing good." Like its predecessor, the JCJA has difficulties balancing "doing justice" and "doing good" approaches. Opting for "getting tough" is costly and with limited results. This money could be better spent on prevention and rehabilitation such as the development of a wider range of community alternatives and programs that include specialized care, intensive tracking, community centres, employment, and effective counselling. Note for instance how school violence is currently handled. The blame is fixed upon the youths and the pressure to "fix" the problem is typically placed on the police and the schools with very narrow solutions ranging from hiring more security personnel in schools, increased discipline, architectural designs, metal detectors, more teachers, relevant courses, zero tolerance, smaller classes, and so on. These responses tend to de-contextualize violence in the wider community. A zero tolerance policy will inflate statistics given the reporting of all violence, including minor cases.

165

Interestingly, the levels of analysis evident in the above changes to the YCJA remain confined to "manageable" remedies at the interpersonal and organizational. To illustrate, the following factors are continually recycled: family problems, including conflicts at home, abuse in its varying forms, or parents' involvement in criminal activity; school problems, including truancy, learning disabilities, failing grades, or conflict with teachers; a history of anti-social behaviour; drug or alcohol abuse; peer influences; membership in a gang. Youth crime or juvenile delinquency as measured by official numbers and articulated juridically has always been shaped by: political expedience in interpreting public sentiments, a flurry of proposals from an endless parade of self-serving consultants, bureaucratic pressures, powerful moral entrepreneurs, from the police to child welfare advocates. Consequently, juvenile offenders and their respective reactors have become the foci while the following remain untouched: fundamental issues of inequality, the equivocation of law, the institutions of authority like the family, the nature of the educational system, the sensational media, the lack of political will in seeking genuine remedies, unemployment and under-employment, unequal opportunities, the underfunding of pre-emptive social services interventions, the manufacture and proliferation of drugs as well as weapons, the over-representation of minorities, and the pervasive culture of violence. Despite its lofty pronouncements of neutrality, the spirit, content and applications of the YCJA will continue to be unresponsive to social injustices, thereby escaping its complicities with privilege. By providing "universalistic" protections, the YCJA seeks to transcend material conditions. Note the liberal legal appeal to rights evident in the Preamble (Youth Criminal Justice Act 2002): whereas members of society *share a responsibility* to address the developmental challenges and the needs of young persons and to guide them into adulthood; whereas communities, families, parents and others concerned with the development of young persons should, through multi-disciplinary approaches, take reasonable steps to prevent youth crime by addressing its underlying causes, to respond to the *needs of young persons*, and to provide guidance and support to those at risk of committing crimes; whereas information about youth justice, youth crime and the effectiveness of measures taken to address youth crime should be publicly available; and, whereas Canadian society should have a youth criminal justice system that commands respect, takes into account the interests of victims, fosters responsibility and ensures accountability through meaningful consequences and effective rehabilitation and reintegration, and that reserves its most serious intervention for the most serious crimes and reduces the over-reliance on incarceration for non-violent young persons (ibid., emphases added).

The YCJA is a dogmatic collection of liberal narratives that are inherently contradictory. Note the false oppositions regarding the responsibility of community to the offender and the responsibility of the offender to the community. The Act seeks to balance the interests of society with those of young persons; "doing good" and "doing justice"; conscience and convenience; accountability and due process. Witness, for example, the ambiguity, equivocation and doubletalk of the following sections in the Declaration of Principles which are intended to guide the policy and practices with respect to young persons. *Section 3.* (1) notes that the following principles apply in this Act: (*a*) the youth criminal justice system is intended to (i) prevent crime by *addressing the circumstances underlying* a young person's offending behaviour, (ii) *rehabilitate* young persons who commit offences and reintegrate them into society, and (iii) ensure that a young person is subject to meaningful consequences for his or her offence in order to promote the long-term protection of the public; (*b*) the criminal justice system for young persons must be separate from that of adults and emphasize the following: (i) rehabilitation and reintegration, (ii) fair and proportionate accountability that is consistent with the *greater dependency* of young persons and their reduced level of maturity, (iii) enhanced procedural protection to ensure that young persons are treated fairly and that their rights, including their right to privacy, are protected, (iv) timely intervention that reinforces the link between the offending behaviour and its consequences, and (v) the promptness and speed with which persons responsible for enforcing this Act must act, given young persons' perception of time; (*c*) within the limits of fair and proportionate accountability, the measures taken against young persons who commit offences should (i) reinforce respect for societal values, (ii) encourage the repair of harm done to victims and the community, (iii) *be meaningful for the individual young person given his or her needs and level of development* and, where appropriate, involve the parents, the extended family, the community and social or other agencies in the young person's rehabilitation and reintegration, and (iv) respect *gender, ethnic, cultural and linguistic differences* and respond to the needs of aboriginal young persons and of young persons with special requirements; and (*d*) special considerations apply in respect of proceedings against young persons and, in particular, (i) *young persons have rights and freedoms in their own right,* such as a right to be heard in the course of and to participate in the processes, other than the decision to prosecute, that lead to decisions that affect them, and young persons have special guarantees of their rights and freedoms (ibid., emphases added).

Neo liberalism in Canada is moving towards a more minimalist state involvement or protection within framework that enables market forces to operate according to its own logic. Throughout the 1990s neo-liberalism has succeeded in promoting a "responsibilization strategy." Responsibilization reflects both the diminishing ability of governments to provide full service and a process of downloading responsibility to the community. By linking responsibilization to community empowerment and governance, the community has become an effective appendage to criminal justice. By downloading responsibility, governments have restructured corrections according to a partnership. This re-alignment is shaped by the politics of financial exigencies and neo-liberal principles of private sector responsibility. This re-alignment enables certain elements of the community to engage in a discourse of criminalization. Responsibilization confers the "entitlements" of citizenship to those who are deemed responsible in carrying out their duties as citizens. In an age of rising deficits, a movement away from Keynesian economics and a growing disbelief in the welfare state, solutions are found in the interests of private capital. Neo-liberalism maintains that the private sector can do it not only more cheaply given extant cash-strapped public resources and but more efficiently in terms of "law-and-order." Cheaper is not necessarily better as it particularly applies to public safety and rehabilitation of youths. Neo-liberalism publicly parades the community as a decontextualized abstraction, that is, simply as an expression of state supreme practices while simultaneously adhering to the inviolability of possessive individualism.

The concept of a *community* has always been a seductive instrument of legal coercion. Throughout the last few decades The YCJA commodifies communities in a cultural marketplace. The inclusion of community voices introduces a localized discourse on the benefits of formal intervention. Canadians have witnessed a proliferation of programmes, strategies and policies ostensibly designed to encourage a greater degree of "community" participation. This notion of a community, as a juridic invention and a controlled social artefact, has invited a painstaking return to apparently local or parochial values as well as a more passionate rediscovery of viable alternatives to supplement extant more formal state controls. Indeed, the concept of a community has been appropriated ideologically by the state to legitimate decisions, preserve privilege and maintain authority relations. This shift towards community crime prevention, compensation, restitution, victimization and the simple return of the bad or the mad to the sacred community echo a lingering pastoral nostalgia, a return to more "basic" familiar values. The social control industry has been busily promoting a normatively oriented community argument in effort to capture the commonsense of different publics thereby ensuring greater degrees of cooperation, intelligence-gathering and support. Knowledge of law in the community is segmented and articulated within a variety of discourses that succeed in abstracting, mystifying and decontexualing social control. The reproduction of limited knowledge is an exclusionary practice; a way of experiencing how the world persists, preserves and universalizes inequality. The larger cultural text is a barrier to communication that has become institutionalized. Benign and often paternalistic provisions overwhelm and ought not to be confused with progress. Too many communities are all too familiar with the dubious benefits of state partnerships.

Given the twin pressures crime control and community downloading, the quintessential debate looms large regarding the capacity of YCJA to effect change. A number of issues remain unresolved despite the proliferation of different federal and provincial youth laws. To what extent does law shape and in turn is shaped by the nature of youth crime? Contrary to the fallacies of deterministic legal approaches which obfuscate and erroneously reduce crime to a legal public chatter, it is conceptually more fruitful to examine the "totality," the interconnectedness of events and activities, the intersections of history, culture and political economy.

An examination of the above principles of law and the discretionary practices of legal agents will unravel and challenge prevailing myths about juvenile justice. There is, for example, little evidence of organizational changes in the YCJA or its amendments designed to remove direct obstacles to equality. The law has failed miserably in extending the most fundamental features of subsistence and basic entitlements of citizenry to disenfranchised youths in health, education, employment, and social services. But, law is both remedial and coercive; a blessing for some and a curse for others. Law protects and punishes; imprisons and liberates. Does the law, therefore, appropriately reflect the dynamics, dialectics and diversity of Canada's youth? The YCJA cannot alone facilitate the resolution of social disputes; a system of restraints that is inimical to freedoms. Within its normative tone, the YCJA assumes a fundamental consensus, a taken-for-granted, a common-sense about the authority of institutions and the troubling character of youth.

Conclusion: Beyond the Text of Criminal Justice

Additionally, when discussing the behaviour of law, it is unnecessary and misleading to capitalize simply on the courts, police and administrative bodies which grind out rules every day. Laws frequently originate as trade-offs or compromises, with the written word poorly reflecting those social forces that have the upper hand. The legal system, in other words, need not mirror society itself. The interests that institutions associations and corporate entities enjoy depend on what power, direct and indirect, can be marshalled behind them. Analyses of historical origins and transformations of youth laws show not only the deliberate ambiguities of sanctions but also the conflicts waged by powerful organizations (police, welfare, child saving) to secure their respective interests). The YCJA advances interventionist strategies promoting welfare infrastructures; liberal welfare provisions continue to be directed towards disenfranchised populations. The state therefore, must be examined beyond instrumental notions of creating conditions favourable to capital accumulation to include efforts designed to harmonize and reduce potential trouble. The capitalist state fulfils two basic and often contradictory functions: accumulation and legitimization. The extended reproduction of a capitalist economy requires the increased intervention of the state in financing those services and facilitates which are too costly and unprofitable for private enterprise. This movement involves the expansion of state legitimation exercises in an imaginative and progressive manner in order to implicate the interests of the subordinate. Through state assistance the state represents itself as a neutral body, a benefactor of interests and a recipient of wholesale gratification. This regulation of consensus, although not directly related to capital accumulation, serves to maintain order. This pacification, in turn, creates a multiplicity of socio-political guarantors that foster public participation and encourage private or self-help initiatives. The impact of this brokerage role obfuscates conflicts and contests that result from asymmetrical relations and masquerades the political and ideological character of interventions. The logic of benign liberal welfare, supported by vocabularies of support and care, has transformed the social landscapes of social services. Undoubtedly, the state is allowed to expand its social terrain and simultaneously promote private arrangements. This discourse "in the name of individuals and of civil society" (Pasquino 1978:44) emerges as a simple and therefore a more seductive theme that disguises the need to "subject, intern or banish everything that opposed its advance along the royal road of accumulation and proletarianisation" (p.42). As Procacci (1991:51) details:

> We have rediscovered in the insane, the beggars, the paupers, the criminals, the women and children, the heretics...the multiplicity of social islands to be dealt with on a local level, of modes of behaviour to be combatted, encouraged or promoted.

In liberal society morality has been grafted on economics (Donzelot 1979). Relief measures, as expressive features of liberalism, implicate and integrate disenfranchised citizens in the existing order through a series of ad hoc, incoherent and short-term responses. The participation of this largely marginalized constituency in the activities of state appendages is a poor substitute for the redistribution and equalization of resources. Subsidized housing, education, health and a growing sensitivity towards affirmative action have not, however, prevented current privatization trends in these and other areas. Harmony or cohesion enables the state to relinquish or reclaim historically acquired benefits. Juvenile justice is embedded within many contexts—social, political, economic and legal. Despite its hyperbolic niceties, the frequently invoked local context conceals as much as it reveals. A circumspect appreciation of current strategies and initiatives demonstrates the inadequacies of prevailing juridic models. In brief, the juvenile justice as envisaged in Canadian society is a product of neo liberalism and the ethos of convenient accommodation. A constricted definition of law is also a meaningless exercise that forecloses any possibility of social justice which presumably must implicate such dynamic features as history and political economy. Lastly, why replicate and model the juvenile justice system after the adult criminal justice system which has remained ineffective in deterring violent crimes?

To repeat, the subject of youth is far too serious a matter to leave in the hands of self-proclaimed crime experts such as the police, lawyers, reporters or social workers. It is a subject matter that moves beyond the dubious celebration of sensational criminal investigations. Instead, the study of crime confronts directly the basis of social order. Since order is formative rather than normative, it is important to explore and explain the problematic nature of official meanings and action; rules and the manner in which youth criminalization is constructed and concretized; the consequences of these efforts to punish; the implications of power as criminogenic; and the legitimacy of authority. Juvenile justice is not a misfit zoology absorbed with voyeurism and exhibitionism nor is it an entertainingly eccentric media journey into the erotic, erratic and exotic worlds. Nor should the problems of youth crime belong exclusively to the confines of a juridic narratives and practices that ignore experience of youths and fail to consider youth crime as a socially and historically constructed phenomenon. That is, we need to move beyond the celebration of convenient chatter or the anaesthetizing gestures of conformity and interrogate ideologies that profitably reward the reproduction of youth social control. Law as a normative guide and an index of culture signifies the prominence of a certain social order; law constitutes the fabric that clothes, protects and privileges the body of the criminal justice. For de Certeau (1988), law writes on individual bodies, inscribing them with codes to produce normativity and thus allow them admittance into the social system. Law provides meaning and identity to the colonized and altered voice. Law is not formed based on coercion itself but on its capacity to present coercion as being in the service of freedom and harmony.

This chapter presented law as seductive and persuasive, and as actively productive of identity and cultural relations. Just as important as the legal surfaces and constitutional pastiche with simple rational rules of sequence and linear time is the role played by market forces in setting legal policies and practice. This chapter demonstrated that a focus on youth crime at the expense of the social and discursive construction of the gendered, classed and racialized subject limits the much needed understanding of the overlaps, intersections and collisions in relation to crime-culture debates. Specifically, the dialectics of agential and the social identities, struggles and changes permeate the intersections of emergent and innovative responses, forms of resistance, to which we now turn in the following chapter.

Chapter 5

Risk of Resistance and Crime as Conformity

No problem can be solved from the same level of consciousness that created it.
—*Albert Einstein* (Hammonds and Morris 2004)

Introduction: Resistance and Risk

The search for a comprehensive understanding of youth resistance has long eluded mainstream criminology. Informed by an inquiry into the relationship between ideologies and identity as mediated by institutions, this chapter explores resistance practices in terms of the interconnections and contradictions inherent in the culture and crime calculus. It is argued, first, that the normative emphasis on delinquency as resistance suffers from conceptual weaknesses regarding the interplay of ideology (modernity, liberalism and capitalism), institutions (media, schooling, criminal justice) and identity operationalized respectively as being, behaviour and beliefs respectively. Second, the parochial politicization of delinquency defers to the arrogance of ignorance by refusing to inquire into the conditions that constitute the ideology-institution identity nexus; the differential impact of ideologies on resistances; the differential impact of resistance on ideologies and the manner by which ideologies and institutions appropriate delinquency to attenuate any prospect for praxis. For Hardt and Negri (2000:275), the various approaches to resistance have done a great service

173

in insisting on just the political importance of cultural movements against narrowly economic perspectives that minimize their significance. These analyses, they argue are extremely limited themselves because, just like the perspectives they oppose, they perpetuate narrow understandings of the economic and the cultural. Most important, they fail to recognize *the profound economic power of the cultural movements,* or really the increasing indistinguishability of economic and cultural phenomena. On the one hand, capitalist relations were expanding to subsume all aspects of social production and reproduction, the entire realm of life; and on the other hand, cultural relations were redefining production processes and economic structures of value (Hardt and Negri 2000:275). Specifically, this chapter asks the following questions: To what extent do ideologies form and inform delinquencies in relation to conflicting narratives of resistance? How and why do youths talk up narratives of regulation and resistance? How does culture hegemonize resistance? How does delinquency function to mediate relations, representations and recognition?

The study of resistance provides a refreshingly bold and conceptually fertile set of insights into the competing and converging discourses that implicate political economy, history and materialist cultures. These perspectives encourage an appreciation of both the conditions and consequences of marginalizing the "other." Specifically, law, morality and capital weave banal and contrived binary fibres of identity ("good and evil," "pain and pleasure" and "suite and street crimes") into a cheap moral fabric of instrumental knowledge. It is further argued that resistance provides an insightful site, replete with generic implications and applications that directly confront issues of privilege and hegemonic knowledge claims.

The stereotypic designation of "resistance" refers to, challenges to dominant discourses of discipline. But, resistance is an elusive category of analysis, as it raises the question, "resistance to what?" A common, though troublesome, answer to that question is domination because it suggests that resistance and power are independent of and diametrically opposed to one another. If domination is truly carried out in this manner, however, it is difficult to imagine how social change would ever occur. That social structures and relationships do change (if only slowly and subtly—short of revolution) suggests that the field of power—where meanings are made and contested—entails a never ending negotiation of competing ideologies. For Foucault (1980), de Certeau (1988), Hardt and Negri (2000), there is no space outside power. Resistance is always already situated within a network of power relationships and thus resistive practices must make creative and adaptive use of the resources of the other (de Certeau 1988:37).In fact, resistance is actually prior to power (Hardt and Negri 2000). The form of domination of constituted power is always contextualized in the possibilities of resistance that it opens up and never reduced to the mask that power itself wears. The formal exercise of power, or potestas, is only ever set in motion in response to the creative energy it tries to contain (ibid). Power is thus expressed as a control that extends throughout the depths of the consciousnesses and bodies of the population—and at the same time across the entirety of social relations (ibid). For Foucault (1979) the micro physics of power is explained in some detail in terms of resisting the discipline offered by institutions. Power should again, be understood not within a conventional morality, or ethics, but as a set of relationships which determine the possibilities for living (de Certeau 1988:18). To understand the mechanisms of power, de Certeau (pp.34-38) distinguishes the strategic from the tactical—devices or strategies of power, and tactics of puissance. Strategies are institutional, spatial and ideological. Tactics are temporal and individual; they operate everyday through and in excess of ideology. There is a difference between strategies and tactics. Strategies require a subject (an enterprise) separated from an environment. They also require a "proper" place (institutionalised location) from which to generate relations with an exterior (their competitors or clients and so on). Strategies lie behind political and economic rationality. Tactics, on the other hand, have no "proper" localisation, and are not strongly separated from the other. Indeed, they often take place in the territory of the other. They are opportunistic, always on the watch and involve combining disparate elements to gain a momentary advantage. De Certeau (ibid) perceives ordinary people as developing "tactics" (an "art of the weak") that he contrasts with the "strategies" of the dominant elite, tactics for carrying out "raids" on the dominant culture. "Strategies" are used by total institutions such as the army, cities, supermarket chains to create and delimit their own place. Tactics are the response of the powerless.

Resistance is conceptualized as those symbolic and material practices that challenge cultural codes, rules, or norms, which through their everyday operation create, sustain, and naturalize the prevailing disciplinary structures in a particular space and time. Resistance is not necessarily defined broadly as universally contrary, but also is specific to particular times, places and social relationships thereby assigning significance of both praxis and theory, and action and principle.Resistance does not oppose domination from some space outside of power and history. It is, rather, a struggle over meanings that occurs within a discursive formation (Foucault 1979).

The writings of Antonio Gramsci (1971) are instrumental in understanding resistance by drawing attention to the possibility of creating a dissent in the cultural sphere. A Gramscian (1971:279-318) framework considers subversive and counter-hegemonic elements. For Gramsci hegemony (the ideological power structure in any given society, i.e., the status quo) and counter-hegemony are related to subversion. Domination is exercised as much through popular "consensus" achieved in civil society as through physical coercion (or threat of it) by the state apparatus, especially in advanced capitalist societies where education, the media, law, mass culture, etc. take on a new role (Boggs 1976). Hegemony, therefore, implies that all aspects of society and culture are tools of the current dominant order, either on a conscious or subconscious/subliminal level. Hegemony, like counter-hegemony, is an organic process; as an organic process there are occasional shifts that allow an opportunity for change and involve consciousness, action, history and language (ibid). True liberation required the creation of "a new 'integrated culture,'" a culture that would create a different world-view and thereby change the current hegemony. Counter-hegemony is the force behind true revolution and a counter-hegemonic structure is the only force capable of subverting the capacity of dominant elites to manipulate attitudes, values, and life-styles through media, education, culture, language (Gramsci 1971). Hegemonies have two powerful tools (of which the United States is an expert user), namely, reproduction and reification. Reproduction is simply the propagation of the hegemony; it is carried out through mass culture, folklore, language, the media—all the elements that are used by the dominant hegemony to control the subaltern group, the working class as well as any minority or sub group being dominated by hegemonic powers (ibid). A more insidious tool is reification, where the hegemony absorbs counter-hegemonic elements and presents them to the masses as their own. This process dilutes the original revolutionary strength; it dilutes and distorts a new world-view into something more like the old-world view (Boggs 1976; Gramsci 1971:279-318). The term reification, borrowed from Georg Lukács (Boggs 1976:68), is used interchangeably with rationalization, alienation, and commodification. The reason for relating reification with alienation is that the process takes away the identity of the subaltern group as a group. The process of reification is also closely related to Gramsci's (1971) passive revolution. Through the development of a counter hegemony (subversions), that is, the hegemony of the oppressed an alliance of different social groups is forged. During initial period of struggle a war of position rages in which the role of the party is to lead the "cultural-ideological" battle for moral, intellectual development. During military confrontations, the centralized combat party of professional revolutionaries assume primary importance in the war of "movement" (Boggs 1972). Revolution as a war of position is extremely relevant because it conceives change not as mere seizure of power but as the building of a new culture of counter-hegemony into a historical bloc which over time becomes the state (Adamson 1987). A war of "position" (led by the party) and of "manoeuvre" (Hall 1986) by the hegemonic party, as conceived in the works of Gramsci, must lead the nation as a whole and may have to sacrifice the short-term interests of its own social class in order to attain its broader goals (Garner and Garner 1981).

Clearly, resistance consists of expressions of subjectivity, autonomy and accountability. Gradually, the self becomes oriented towards un-learning the conventions of law and increasingly familiar with more progressive explanations of power and the consequences of non compliance (Hardt and Negri 2000). The answer rests with consciousness, knowing ourselves and our location (Gramsci 1971; Jouve 1991:8) requiring a deeper appreciation for the inseparable relationship between discourse and subjectivity (Arrigo 1995: 449-451). But dominant cultural values seek to manipulate subjectivity by focussing on convenience, self-serving rationales and instrumental common sense. The refusal of exploitation—or really resistance, sabotage, insubordination, rebellion, and revolution—constitutes the motor force of the reality we live, and at the same time is its living opposition (Hardt and Negri 2000:209). For Hardt and Negri, there are three key variables that will define this struggle: a) the guarantee of the network and its general control, in such a way that (positively) the network can always function and (negatively) it cannot function against those in power; b) those who distribute services in the network and the pretense that these services are remunerated equitably, so that the network can sustain and reproduce a capitalist economic system and at the same time produce the social and political segmentation that is proper to it; and, c) elements within the network itself; mechanisms by which differences among subjectivities are produced (p.320). These variables act in the realm between the common and the singular, between the axiomatic of command and the self-identification of the subject, and between the production of subjectivity by power and the autonomous resistance of the subjects themselves.

A regime of production, and above all a regime of the production of subjectivity, is being destroyed and another invented by the enormous accumulation of struggles (p.275). These new circuits of the production of subjectivity are realized within and against the final period of the disciplinary organization of society. The passage from the phase of perfecting the disciplinary regime to the successive phase of shifting the productive paradigm is now driven from below by dominated classes whose composition had already changed. Capital does not need to invent a new paradigm (even if it were capable of doing so) because the truly creative moment had already taken place; capital's problem is rather to dominate a new composition that has already been produced autonomously and defined within a new relationship to nature and labor, a relationship of autonomous production. Capital must always accomplish a negative mirroring and an inversion of the new quality of power; it must adjust itself so as to be able to command once again (p.276).

Resistances cannot be reduced to thought alone given that much of what passes for thinking is a product of strategies of domination. The positive problem is to find a way of asserting a qualitatively new social recomposition of the subordinated self in all its forms as an effective force. That is, the practical problems of struggle against the articulations of capitalist command, the problem of resisting and overthrowing the discipline of thought. Awareness of the unconscious, therefore, is an experience which is characterized by its spontaneity and suddenness. Resistance is founded in the identities of social subjects (p.44). In our disciplinary society individuals, productive practices and productive socialization seek to invade, colonize and organize consciousnesses institutionally. Admittedly, identities are neither autonomous nor self-determining, but differentially feed into and support hegemonies. Individual resistance alone runs the risk of misidentifying and thus masking the enemy. It is not a matter of whether there is resistance but rather how to determine the enemy against which to rebel. Indeed, often the inability to identify the enemy is what leads the will to resistance around in such paradoxical circles (p.211). Likewise defending the individual's resistance obscures and even negates the real alternatives and the potentials for liberation that exist within different regimes of relations. Accordingly, the primacy of the concept of truth can be a powerful and necessary form of resistance (p.155).

The conflictive relationship between the self and the social is also consistent with anarchism's interpretations of resistance which are informed by three basic qualities: a) an emphasis on individual responses to the "politics of truth"; b) a rejection of professionalism and departmental academicism; and c) a belief in the sanctity of private life. The root of the problem is society (Horowitz 1964:23).To better a civilization is a subtle form of corruption, of self delusion; abolition not improvement is needed (Malatesta 1949). Michael Bakunin's (1814-1876) sophisticated attacks on state authority and legal controls call for the destruction of the state and its replacement with the spontaneous and continuous action of the masses, the groups and the associations of people (Bakunin 1974: 58, 204). Anarchism seeks to abolish all forms of domination. The doctrines of anarchism are anti-egoistic especially since egoism is an expression of the institutionalized "social." Bakunin, an activist who spent eight years in prison in the dungeons of Tsarist Russia, influenced the writings of Fanon, Cleaver, Marcuse, and others. Fanon like Bakunin placed his revolutionary hopes not on the more advanced workers corrupted by middle class values but on the economically unprivileged labourers (Tifft 1979, Avrich 1987, Bakunin, 1974).Two such labourers Bartolomeo Vanzetti (1888-1927) and Nicola Sacco (1891-1927) were wrongfully arrested on charges of murder, tried, convicted and electrocuted in 1927. Vanzetti described:

> Yes they can crucify our bodies today as they are doing, but they cannot destroy our ideas...we were for the poor and against the exploitation and oppression of the man by the man. (Horowitz 1964:288-290)

Vanzetti adds: "Both Nick and I are anarchists...the radical of the radical, the black cats, the terrors of many, of all the bigots, exploiters, charlatans, fakers, and oppressors...I am and will be until the last instant an anarchist communist" (Avrich 1987:164). The anarchist belief in the destructive and dysfunctional influences of state authority has led to the insistence on the values of mutual aid, voluntary organizations and authentic communities (Pepinsky1978). Extant cultural constraints prevent the full realization of individual and collective potential. Specifically, institutions were never designed to respond to human needs and resistance against institutional power is long overdue. Taking marriage, as an example, Emma Goldman criticizes the instrumental discipline of institutions:

179

The institution of marriage makes a parasite of woman, an absolute dependent. It incapacitates her for life's struggle, annihilates her social consciousness, paralyzes her imagination, and imposes its gracious protection, which is in reality a snare, a travesty on human character. (Horowitz 1964:280)

For the anarchist, freedom is not an abstract philosophical concept, but the vital concrete possibility for every human being to bring to full development all the powers, capacities, and talents with which nature has endowed him, and turn them to social account. The less this natural development of man is influenced by ecclesiastical or political guardianship, the more efficient and harmonious will human personality become, the more will it become the measure of the intellectual culture of the society in which it has grown (Rocker1938:31).

Resistance as the struggle for change is always a challenge, a process that cannot be left to the so called "benevolent" gestures of authority agents. Briefly, problem solving is a collective accomplishment despite the denunciatory cacophony of authorities. Ameliorative action may be handled by applying existing practices, rules and policies (Lyman and Scott 1970). But, radically more compelling measures are required to secure even a modicum of social justice. Militancy must rediscover what has always been its proper form: not representational but constituent activity (Hardt and Negri 2000: 413); that is positive, constructive, and innovative especially in reference to the formation of cooperative apparatuses of production and community. This militancy makes resistance a project of love (ibid), identifying in the common condition of the multitude its enormous wealth, cooperation, simplicity, and also innocence.

This renewed emphasis on humanism encourages the development of a new consciousness, a change in the way we think. Resistance presents a vastly different understanding of the self-actualizing and self-governing individual. One method is peace making which promotes the evaluation of forms of intervention that will leave people interacting more or less empathically. Making peace in the face of such pervasive, deeply seated conflict promotes the survival value of the species in the long run, and of validating one another's suffering in the moment (Pepinsky and Quinney 1991; Sullivan and Tifft 1999).

Through love and compassion, moving well beyond the egocentric self, we can end suffering and live in peace personally and collectively. This love is not the naïve and hypocritical premises based on white privilege or bourgeois protection. Rather the programmes of action pursued by Gautama Buddha (circa 563-483 BC), Jesus Christ (circa 4 BC-AD 29), Elijah or Elias (9th century BC), Guru Nanak(1469), Lao-tzu (circa 570 490 BC), Muhammad (circa 570-632 AD), were *grounded in a wisdom that developed from the experiences with and exposure to violence.* This is an incredibly important and yet often dismissed theme. This love—the love lived by the Dalai Lama, Mahatma Gandhi, Martin Luther King Jr, Bob Marley and countless others—is an act of *developed consciousness in face of adversity.* There are also the powerful teachings of the First Nations guided by the wisdom of Mother Earth. The ending of suffering can be attained in a quieting of the mind and an opening of the heart, in being aware (Pepinsky and Quinney 1991: 3-4). This *privileged knowledge, feelings and memories shape the imagination,* the reconstructions of our existence and therefore the end of suffering which always begins with the mind. For Quinney (ibid., 10), the means must be no different than the end; peace must come out of peace. Without inner peace in each of us, without peace of mind and heart, there can be no social peace between people. In peace making we attend to the ultimate purpose of our existence: to heal the separation between all things and to live harmoniously in a state of unconditional love. Within this mutualist model of humanism, conflict is a weakening communion among its members, which implies a need for a restoration to full communion; inclusion rather than exclusion, re-admittance rather than isolation, reinterpretation rather than adjudication—a system guided more but the altruistic than the adversarial (Kirkpatrick 1986). Violence results from depersonalization, which can be induced in any number of ways, as by putting people in the bureaucratic position of doing things to others without responding to their experience and their feelings (Pepinsky and Quinney 1991). The eastern ethic of nonviolence and the Aboriginal ethos of non-interference incorporate various wealthy traditions and forms of peacemaking. The underlying assumption guiding this model is the conviction that human freedom is ultimately meaningful and fulfilling only in the community (Braswell, McCarthy, and McCarthy 1991). The connection of the inner peace to the outer peace is the connection between individuals who behave morally and a morally responsible society. This orientation reflects the Hegelian notion of value creation for the purpose of exploring a direction for a transpraxis, a humanistic transfiguration of man/woman and for movement toward the peacemaking community (Milovanovic 1997). Social movement revolves around the unfolding of an idea, a telos. This alternative form of subjectivity and social formation is consistent with Nietzsche's (1968), development of the higher being and the affirmation of new value positions. The essence of this movement lies in the imposition upon becoming the character of being—the will to power (Nietzsche 1968:330).

Lastly, social control shapes resistance, the defiance of normative and integrative efforts. In other words, subversion also functions symbolically as a rationale for control and becomes conveniently incorporated within a discourse that supports the intrusions of the more powerful. Lofland's (1996:305-344) research considers the impact of social control on resistance, differentiating between external, formal systems of social control (professional trouble shooters) and internalized, informal systems of social control (ongoing socialization). For Smelser (1962), formal social control as reactive mechanisms are mobilized after a threat, real or imagined. Berger (1990) adds that the nature of internalized, informal social controls is equally significant (externalization, objectivation, and internalization). Institutions are dependent on externalization and institutions also take on lives of their own, become objects of control. But de Certeau (1988) advises that it is myopic to view the public as shaped by the products imposed on it; it would be more appropriate to focus on the uses which people make of the commodities they are offered such as survival techniques. For de Certeau (1988) control is not passive, but rather an active utilization of products which is in itself a type of production.

Discipline and Distance: Youth Resistance

Of interest to us is the precise ways in which the concepts of authorship and authenticity get negotiated and defined within youth cultures. Moreover, this chapter examines the extent to which negotiated contexts influence the interpretive logic of youth that govern displays of resistance that define the interplay between culture and youth crime. More precisely, interactions originate between subjects through meaningful relationships with objects of their environments. In other words, actors and activities are "situated" within certain identifiable settings which contextualize relations and encounters. How then is authentic resistance possible in light of such hegemonic forces?

Studies on youth have analyzed form and content of subcultures as counter hegemonic responses to specific historical contradictions. Studies conducted at Center for Contemporary Cultural Studies at the University of Birmingham in England grounded the concept of resistance on a firm understanding of history, economics and class. Influenced by Antonio Gramsci, Stuart Hall and Tony Jefferson (1976), Paul Willis (1977), Dick Hebdige (1979) notices resistance in the multitude of subcultures that sprang up in postwar Britain. For Hebdige (1979), style is both tension and refusal, pregnant with significance, a movement toward a speech which offends the "silent majority." It is not merely appearance, but the way appearance, mannerisms, and attitudes are consciously deployed to create an identity. Style enables members of a subculture to challenge the hegemony of the dominant culture. In his later work, Hebdige (1988) sharpens his method, admitting that he had underestimated the power of commercial culture to appropriate, and indeed, to produce, counter-hegemonic styles. For Hebdige, youth subcultures shifted from "originality and opposition" working-class status to "commercial incorporation" bourgeois at the moment of incorporation, whereby styles lost their subcultural status and authenticity. Hebdige considers the media and commerce as "incorporating" subculture into the hegemony, swallowing them up and effectively dismantling them. Youth resistance is always mediated through a variety of channels such as the school, family, work, and the media (ibid). The typical members of a working-class youth culture in part contest and in part agree with the dominant definitions of who and what they are (ibid). Gramscian terms are especially useful in analyzing subcultures: conjuncture and specificity. Subcultures form in communal and symbolic engagements with the larger system of late industrial culture; they are organized around, but not wholly determined by, age and class, and are expressed in the creation of styles. These styles are produced within specific historical and cultural "conjunctures"; they are not to be read as simply resisting hegemony or as magical resolutions to social tensions, as earlier theorists had supposed.

For Hardt and Negri (2000: 273) the disciplinary regime clearly no longer succeeded in containing the needs and desires of young people. The prospect of getting a job that guarantees regular and stable work for eight hours a day, fifty weeks a year, for an entire working life, the prospect of entering the normalized regime of the social factory, which had been a dream for many of their parents, now appeared as a kind of death (pp.274-276). The mass refusal of the disciplinary regime, which took a variety of forms, was not only a negative expression but also a moment of creation. The various forms of social contestation and experimentation all centered on a refusal to value the kind of fixed program of material production typical of the disciplinary regime, its mass factories, and its nuclear family structure. The movements valued instead a more flexible dynamic of creativity and what might be considered more *immaterial* forms of production. From the standpoint of the traditional "political" segments of the US movements of the 1960s, various forms of cultural experimentation that blossomed with a vengeance during that period all appeared as a kind of distraction from the "real" political and economic struggles. What they failed to see was that the "merely cultural" experimentation had very profound political and economic effects. "Dropping out" was really a poor conception of what was going on throughout the 1960s and 1970s. The two essential operations were the refusal of the disciplinary regime and the experimentation with new forms of productivity. The refusal appeared in a wide variety of guises and proliferated in thousands of daily practices. Youths who refused the deadening repetition of the factory-society invented new forms of mobility and flexibility, new styles of living. Student movements forced a high social value to be accorded to knowledge and intellectual labor. The entire panoply of movements and the entire emerging counterculture highlighted the social value of cooperation and communication (ibid., 275). For Hardt and Negri, this massive transvaluation of the values of social production and production of new subjectivities opened the way for a powerful transformation of labor power.

Theoretically, the politics of recognition, that is, the relationship between identity and difference is the central issue confronting contemporary debates in youth resistance. Conditions, material and ideological, that foster the oppression, the silencing and ultimately the exclusion of youths must be met with a whole spectrum of political activity that ranges from acts of individual resistance to mass political mobilization that challenge the basic power relations

Case Studies of Resistance: the Street as a Site of Subversion

The "street" is a contested terrain and a discoursal practice, reflecting both local and universal institutions and processes. As both space and a place, the socially constructed street occurs as the effect produced by the operations that orient it, situate it, temporalize it, and make it function in a polyvalent unity of conflictual programs or contractual proximities (de Certeau 1988). When one takes into consideration vectors of direction, velocities, and time the street is transformed (ibid). The notion of spatial travel (spontaneous or sequential) is important in understanding the street as a place of practice (Hall, Coffey, and Williamson 1999; Robinson 2000). How does time articulate itself in this space (de Certeau 1988: 86)?

In his work, Lefebvre (1991b) suggests that just as everyday life has been colonised by capitalism, so too has its location—social space. Space is socially constructed and used to ensure the survival of capitalism. Because of its flexibility in constructing and reconstructing the relations of space and the global space economy, Lefebvre suggests that space is the ultimate locus and medium of struggle, and is therefore a crucial political issue: "There is a politics of space because space is political" (p.33). Unlike Cartesian co-ordinates, lines and planes or even Kantian ideas of space and time as a priori absolute categories, Lefebvre's emphasizes the production of space by historicising experience. In 1939, Lefebvre (1968:122, 133) had described geometric space as abstractive, and had likened it to clock time in its abstraction of the concrete, clearly drawing on the critique of geometric space in Heidegger's *Being and Time* and later works. We encounter space geometrically only when we pause to think about it, that is, when we conceptualise it. There is a difference between our conception of space—abstract, mental and geometric—and our perception of space – concrete, material and physical. The latter takes as its initial point of departure the body, which Lefebvre sees as the site of resistance within the discourse of Power in space (ibid 1976:89). Abstract, decorporalised space is an aspect of alienation. In order to make progress in understanding space, we need to grasp the concrete and the abstract together The construction, or production, of spaces therefore owes as much to the conceptual realms of material activities.

Indeed the street is a sociology of morality. Within this collective biography, morality is complexly articulated within a plurality of discourses that are never stable, static nor fixed. The relationship between discourse and social subjectivity is organized through a specific articulation of conflicting images. These images are naturalized as fantasies as well as horrors. The image of evil and the image of salvation embodied, respectively, are interchangeable. Metaphors of evil and good may appear exaggerated but they certainly contribute to an understanding of the process of moral regulation. Street is a formidable socio-cultural expression of the relationship between morality and mythology.

The street activates class divisions through class based codes of conduct, relocating that which has occupied the margins to the centre, and decentring and de-essentializing the subject. Street provides a long overdue method for clarifying contradictions and for delving into the forms and functions of struggles. The awareness of being different and seeing differences inspires manoeuvres that challenge moral authorities. From Wall Street to Times Square, from Trafalgar to Tiananmen Square, from Via Veneto to Rodeo Drive, from the burning of cars in suburban France to the looting on Bourbon Street, from the Vegas Strip to Red Square, from the street gutters to the sidewalk cafes, the street is a fractured frontier that is complexly articulated within a plurality of discourses that are never stable, static or fixed is objectified foundationally as existing "out there." In addition, the street is the historical and everyday cultural way (the "via") that directs fragmented and individualized identities to the cathedrals of capitalism where the authority of the predatory marketplace situates meanings and emotionally reflects the pleasures of the consumption. Today, the street highlights the liberal ethos of individualism, a condition and consequence of commodity exchanges as idealized and practised among street merchants or vendors. This contradictory and complementary geopolitical is a site of battle whenever it gives consciousness, new meanings and abolishes righteous moral claims of a variety of institutionalized disciplinary discourses. The street renders street lives inappropriate; various street experiences, from the hustlers' work on the street, the entrepreneurial spirit of squeegee kidz, the hanging out on street corners to the street battles in Quebec City, Seattle and Genova are regulated. Street closure, containment and coercion (police street crackdowns, street sweeps and curfews) occur whenever the capital function of constituting docile subjects is jeopardized. In addition to the regulation of desire, the street is a metaphor that is crucial to the construction of a moral panic. This moral regulation reproduces particular (proper, permitted, encouraged) forms of expressions, fixes (or tries to fix) particular signs, genres, repertoires, codes, as normal representations of "standard" experiences. In other words, culture mediates, provides rationality and articulates a language that magically defines conformity by imposing a familiar context and generates universal commitment. As a moral text, the street is informed by wider "structural" perspectives, that is, the cultural narratives of deterministic accounts which mysteriously remain consistent with a sense of agency. Let us examine street kids as an illustration of life on the street.

Life on the Street: Street Survivors

Besides the "pushing" influences of family and school "hassles," street boys and girls attribute their initial engagements on the street to the "pulling" forces of the street, notably its variety and excitement. The psychic lure of the downtown glitter of the "fast lanes" features prominent in their talk, especially for those who have learned to resent their many daily mundane rounds. Boys and girls characterized their first few hours on the street as a spirit of adventure (Visano 1998b). They speak of being intrigued with exploring this new world, and use a variety of images to portray themselves as special "survivors," "hunters," and "trappers," out in the "jungles" and "trenches" searching for "the action." Both these searches for prohibited pleasure-seeking activities and the existential state of uncertainty about what direction their lives are going to take, contribute to this stimulation. Expressions of freedom and adventure serve to further extricate them from their unpleasant and boring family and school experiences. Interestingly, these boys and girls project what Matza and Sykes (1970) conceptualize as a deterministic billiard ball conception of self. Accounts remain clearly within a normative framework that is particularly sensitive to the immediate context of their trouble. In addition, they offer melioristic impressions of the street which legitimate their decisions to leave home. According to more seasoned street kids, these early experiences as victims enable them to get a general conflict perspective, which they can readily invoke in legitimating violence against threatening others. Besides the family, school experiences are frequently singled out as a "pushing" influence. Although these kids note that school offers a measure of escape from abusive families, it too exacts a price. They resent the boredom of school. Whatever their motivations for being in school, they noted that the school occupies a meaningless place between the constraints of family life and the freedoms on the street (Visano 2001).These youths employ several coping strategies that reduce the meaningless of school. Their *resistance* ranges from apathy to direct forms of confrontation. Girls characterize themselves as a tired audience; they express a minimal level of participation in the classroom. Girls say they attend classes only to "pass the time." They daydream, come to school "wasted" on drugs or use school time to plan their evening activities. Boys, however, talk about disrupting classes, clowning around, selling drugs and committing truancy. Of the fifty youths interviewed, only fourteen kids, eight girls and six boys, spoke of the general value of formal education. Yet they too quickly disavowed that their schooling had any relevance. School youths fault their teachers for becoming directly implicated in their family lives, malign the rapport teachers develop with parents, and castigate teachers for informing parents of their poor progress at school. It is because they align themselves with parents in these ways that teachers are described by students as potentially troublesome. Essentially, teachers are disliked because their negative evaluations of school performance are part of the arsenal of reasons parents invoke in inflicting punishment against children. This socialization process which often discourages subjects from challenging parental power spills over to the school and is buttressed by teachers. To the chagrin of these children, teachers who were once quite encouraging seem to develop a growing disinterest in their students' well-being. According to these children, their teachers gradually accept the disparaging judgements of parents.

For all street youths, family problems such as physical and emotional abuse interfere with school performance. Their preoccupation with conflict-ridden family relationships often results in a decreasing interest in school work and greater recognition of the insignificance of education. They define their involvements at school as even less meaningful once they realize that these experiences fail to provide them with an immediate escape from family problems. Indeed, the alliance between teachers and parents adds to their problems at home and at school. Their accounts certainly do not mean that school failures are necessarily pivotal to the process of becoming a street kid. Rather, withdrawal from school occupies a degree of significance within their frame of reference for interpreting pre-entry conditions. Perceived family and school experiences are used to bring into focus a variety of legitimations designed to make good their claims that the street represents freedom. These reflective shreds and patches provide a common vision of what they understand to be factors "pushing" them out of conventional normative bonds. The street is conceptualized as an option which is immediately available and easily appreciated because of their limited future family and school hold for them.

"Hitting the Streets"

Street kids seldom arrive on the "street scene" unfamiliar with what awaits them. From their own limited weekend excursions and information shared with friends at school, they acquire favourable impressions of the excitement of the downtown streets. As the downtown becomes projected as an attractive alternative, the temptation to be on the street and to abandon family and school increases. In another study (Visano 1987), thirty-eight of the fifty kids contacted in face-to-face interviews report well over a dozen all-night, weekend excursions on the streets before actually deciding to move out permanently. Six girls said that during their stay at a group home they were exposed to various contacts who detailed the nature of sexual marketplaces, profitability of street activities and locations of hostels and missions (ibid).

These sketches however, provide a misleading, positive appraisal of street life. The language in which these accounts are cast understates the hardships they encounter during these early days on the street. The street as a problem is often glossed over and blithely ignored. Apart from exaggerated notions and few experiences, youths have little information or knowledge about how to survive on the street. Initially, newcomers face considerable hardship in trying to fit into the street environment. For the solo or solitary adventurers, this early period is marked by trial and error. Newcomers are not integrated into a meaningful web of friendship patterns on the street. They exist on the border of conventional and deviant worlds. They are "on," but not "of" the street.

Upon arrival, they do not participate in either the conventional society or in street subcultures. Their attitudes and behavioural patterns remain on the fringe. On the one hand, newcomers partially relinquish former cultural traditions. On the other hand, they have not won acceptance in the culture towards which they are beginning to drift. Although they have abandoned familiar associations, they have not carved out a place in their newly found street lifestyle.

During this initial phase on the street, newcomers become impoverished street transients. Their initial experiences assume a solitary quality. Despite the advantages of being free, newcomers soon realize that they are all alone "trying" to make it. In discussing their first few days on the street, they repeatedly single out difficulties "making it," in securing even the fundamental amenities of food and shelter.

In general, age is a liability for these newcomers. They fear the consequences of discovery, which usually include returning to the family home, a group home, or training school. Any reliance on welfare workers jeopardizes the likelihood of succeeding on the street, especially since agencies seek to reconcile youths with their families. They quickly learn that agencies are also compelled to notify the police if youths are under sixteen. What emerges is fear of exposure that presumably follows from divulging information to case workers.

Age also restricts employment possibilities. Initially, street neophytes try to avail themselves of employment prospects. They admit that most job searches are extremely frustrating because of continual rejections. They quickly discover that there are very few legitimate opportunities. Because of these early negative employment contacts, they become quickly discouraged, and abandon further job applications. In discussing their inability to secure employment however, they seldom focus attention on their limited skills. Instead, they provide lengthy explanations that negate work in general. Of the fifty children, ten boys and seven girls had part-time jobs in restaurants or as casual labourers while living at home or on the street (ibid).

Work is translated as a restriction on their mobility and subsequently, on their "fun" activities. Newcomers say that they did not leave their homes in order to embark on yet another constraining commitment. Securing a full-time legitimate job occupies little significance and is also cast as an irrelevant concern. Although in need of money, they refuse to be stuck in what they perceive to be meaningless or boring activities, like working in loading areas of warehouses, washing dishes or sweeping floors in restaurants. These jobs are described as time-consuming, poorly rewarding and, most important, in conflict with adventure. Moreover, neither their family nor school experiences prepare these poorly educated and unskilled youths to function in the legitimate workplace. Initially, newcomers live on meagre subsistence. They learn to rely on their wits to structure and seize upon any opportunity to survive. Living requires them to be constantly on the prowl and ready to score by rolling a drunk, boosting, smashing, grabbing anything of value, or simply panhandling.

Given the above, the term marginality accurately reflects the general conviction that these youths are somehow set apart from society and yet not fully part of street groupings. Their marginality is constituted on the street; a setting that is socially, economically and politically peripheral to the larger urban context.

For newcomers, social conceptions of age condition aspects of children's marginality. According to Hollingshead (1975:5), youths occupy a temporal period in life when the society refuses to regard them as children and yet denies them full adult status. Since newcomers are under sixteen years of age, provisions for accommodation and welfare services are not easily available to them. Marginality, the failure to be fully implicated in the street scene or in the wider conventional society, becomes their key to identify transformation. Since these boys and girls are not yet well integrated, they render themselves more susceptible to street socialization. Paradoxically then, the street kid faces the identity problem of developing an ongoing creation of self that is more compatible with this newly discovered environment.

The paradox of being "on" but not "of" the street does not in itself necessarily cause newcomers to seek out other street kids. But, newcomers do justify the development of their street relations accordingly. Early difficulties on the street, especially concerning securing food and shelter, contribute to a lowering of defenses and a greater susceptibility to involvements with more seasoned kids who are willing to offer support. Just as the street is perceived as a solution to prior family and school difficulties, street relations are seen as a solution to survival problems for newcomers. By focusing on these interactions, we see that becoming a street kid is a collective accomplishment emerging out of the various social relations that newcomers develop on the street. As a form of secondary socialization, becoming a street kid consists of both self-induction or enlistment and recruitment by others. The street therefore, is a social setting facilitating "seekership" (Prus 1984) and encouragement for these solitary wanderers.

The circumstances of being "on the street" are consistently invoked by all kids. They distinguish early days when they "just hit the streets" from later days when they sought street contacts. Early exposure to the streets is a significant prerequisite for initiating street connections that eventually introduce newcomers to the street as an attractive alternative to their former lives.

Establishing Street Connections and Transforming Identities

Street life is a complex amalgam of interactions which are influenced by many social, environmental and interpersonal factors. A kaleidoscope of street activities provides many significant contacts for newcomers once they learn the rules for gaining access. Specifically, the social organization of Main Street includes a variety of overlapping activities, fluid and fleeting relations, and numerous roles and rules. The structure of street relations is a contingency that shapes the newcomer's self-image as well as his/her understanding of situational difficulties. The street offers both limitations to, and possibilities for, survival.

In general, newcomers seek relations that offer them the possibility of solving some of their problems associated with being solitary street transients. Newcomers discover a number of street alignments by gravitating towards different hang-outs. During their frequent visits to arcades, parks, coffee-shops, hostels and street-corners, newcomers make contacts and come to the attention of more seasoned street kids. Newcomers gradually become enmeshed in pre existing social relations. They learn to sort out and discriminate groups for potential association. Some favour homophilic associations of generalized peer groups. A majority of street kids however, said that they prefer to interact with many different street contacts rather than simply drift towards a more specific congenial grouping (Visano 1987).

In discussions with street kids, the terminology of newcomer is confusing. On the one hand, there are newcomers to the street scene: neophyte street transients. On the other hand, there are street kids who are newcomers to street associations. In general, newcomers to the street are new group members. But new group members are not necessarily newcomers to the street scene. A few girls were new group members to a prostitution ring although they had been on the street for several months participating in various illicit street associations (ibid).

While "hanging out," goofing off and making the rounds, newcomers to a group gain an increasing familiarity with different income producing activities such as selling drugs, stealing merchandise, and selling sex. During these episodes of exposure, identities are revealed and receptivities of others tested. This early stage involves the learning of a newcomer's role, especially with its emphasis on naiveté and subservience. Recent arrivals organize their response around the preliminary reactions of strangers with whom they form loose, fleeting and casual street corner groups or "clusters" (West 1978). An important contingency involves the experience of being publicly accepted. During their interactions, newcomers pick up requisite jargon and listen attentively to the legends, successes and conflicts that seasoned street kids express. Because of their common situations, previously unacquainted street kids develop bonds. These relationships provide general assistance and support for neophytes. The latter become informed about shelter, food and detection of police. Considering their prior experiences and difficulties as solitary street transients, it is not surprising that the simple pleasures of a generalized street fellowship are enough to bind them.

It is in this context of fleeting peer acquaintances that newcomers begin to discover an array of inviting street associations. Hanging out contributes to the expansion of opportunities and contacts. Street1corner groupings constitute the most important means for recruitment to illicit activities. Hanging out at arcades enables neophytes to initiate contacts proactively, to make direct inquiries, and make themselves available for street relationships. Eventually, aspirants are invited to tag along and participate in unskilled tasks, the completion of which leads to acceptance. According to the data (Visano 1987), two fundamental issues concerning seekership emerge. First, these boys and girls do not see themselves as simply propelled in a "preordained" (Matza 1969:101) manner. They are involved in meaningful interactions with their street groups that they define as reasonable. Second, choices are made according to available evidence and attractive options. Newcomers drift into one of those reference groups for whom their limited street experience makes them eligible candidates. Fortuitous encounters are undoubtedly responsible for many initial introductions. The process of enlistment, or what Matza (ibid) refers to as the ordaining of self, is an accomplishment in which participants actively participate. In contrast to the views held by social workers that newcomers are forced into street life, all fifty subjects maintain that it was their own initiative to associate with seasoned hustlers.

Older seasoned kids typically go out of their way to help newcomers. In addition to sharing food and shelter, newcomers are invited to participate in various leisure pursuits. Admittedly, these relations are not different from general adolescent associations revolving around parties, alcohol, drugs and sex. There are however, several important features of this socialization process that are quite instructive in understanding apprenticeship. By spending many hours assessing newcomers to the street, testing their loyalties and determining their levels of naiveté, the seasoned street kid begins to act like a sponsor. Once the newcomer is accepted, the seasoned kid recommends the newcomer favourably to friends and serves as a source of knowledge about general situational uncertainties. Although a general mood of excitement characterizes these encounters, a dependency relationship emerges. In the company of these seasoned street kids, newcomers generally submit to this imbalance in exchange for scarce resources such as food and shelter, and for instructions in such areas as hustling skills.

Newcomers become caught up in reciprocal expectations that facilitate apprenticeship. Norms of reciprocity (Gouldner 1960) require these role incumbents to help those who have guided them. Specific expectations are defined by both parties as actual and perceived benefits to be gained. Together with determining how youths develop street relations during this initial stage, this case study includes an investigation of the motives of newcomers and seasoned street hustlers for reciprocal support.

The most common motives offered by street kids are: promises of money, companionship, and fun. Initially, interest binds actors in apprenticeship relationships. For sponsors, personal gain is operationalized according to the following benefits they receive. First, during early instructions newcomers are expected to do many undesirable jobs including: luring tricks into back-alleys or parks where seasoned boys or girls are waiting and ready to rob or score; acting as messengers running errands; serving as front people by obstructing shoppers and store clerks, or causing a distracting activity while experienced kids shoplift; and carrying drugs or weapons for older kids since their age and inexperience would result in a more lenient treatment if apprehended by the police. Second, newcomers act as look1outs and help reduce the probability of getting caught. Third, newcomers are regarded as potential sources of income for seasoned kids. These protégés may have certain strengths or marketable assets, such as youthfulness, attractiveness and naiveté. The revenue newcomers make is expected to be shared with their street buddies, often to defray the costs of rent, groceries, drugs or bail. Finally, seasoned street kids nurture these relations to ensure a smooth circulation of goods and services. Apprenticeship enables them to protect their established business interests against the potential competition of unbridled newcomers frequenting common job sites. Peer associations contribute to opportunities. Peers furnish the newcomer with a means of achieving certain ends. The street "does the opposite of what occurs in school or in the labour market: rather than blocking opportunities, it opens them up" (Cusson 1983:151). Youths select friends according to their affinities; a theme of "dangerous disaffiliations" characteristic of the early Chicago Schools.

Admittedly, newcomers are also motivated by self-interest. They arrive on the street in a state of confusion. On the one hand, they are impressed with the novelty of independence and the general wanderlust of the street scene. Yet, they suffer from a battered self-image and lack the confidence necessary for street survival. Getting into street relations is perceived as reconciling this dilemma. They are anxious to learn methods of survival while sustaining a sense of excitement.

The rewards of these associations are not simply limited to making money and securing a street education. Beyond interest-based motives, there are also friendship-oriented, sentimental ties. Once immediate situational difficulties are overcome, kids concentrate on the more emotionally rewarding aspects of being on the street, for instance, companionship, sociability, and recreation. For three fifths of street youths, their street companions are cited as their closest and only friends. Furthermore, twenty-one girls said they were sexually intimate with their "street buddies" (Visano 1987).

"The Street Hustle": Survival as Resistance

Newcomers avail themselves of opportunities for attaching themselves to the street. The management of contingencies is highly consequential for the development of a street identity. An omnipresent ideology of individualism pervades street relations. A newcomer learns that one always looks out for oneself. One is expected to take pride in independence. Street kids justify cooperative ventures only if loyalty is secured and immediate, personal advantage exists. Even in collective practices, cynicism prevails as children learn to expect very little from others.

Individualism is related to notions of survival. The theme of survival is consistently repeated in interactions on the street. Within this discourse, boys and girls continually talk about money and street wisdom. Beyond its relevance to survival, money is also viewed as a powerful and positive reward as well as an ongoing justification for action. Fast money assumes great significance. The immediate benefits associated with money such as partying, drugs, alcohol, and a lavish consumerism, are supplemented by its function in determining friendship patterns, status and respect.

Newcomers learn that to survive as street kids, they must be street smart. They must be prepared to take advantage of, or seize upon any opportunity that offers a fast buck. By being constantly on the prowl, they do not separate work from leisure. Newcomers are taught to acquire a constant interest in street opportunities and a curiosity about street knowledge especially information on criminal behaviour and street expectations. A smart hustler presents himself or herself to newcomers as a tough minded opportunist who lives by wits and avoids the humiliation of a regular job.

195

Learning to be street-smart requires coolness and toughness. Lyman and Scott (1970:145) defined coolness as

> the capacity to execute physical acts, including conversation, in a concerted smooth, self-controlled fashion in risky situations, or to maintain affective detachment during encounters involving considerable emotion.

Coolness on the street refers to their ability to maximize gain and minimize effort while structuring relations in a way that favourably impresses others. Along with this cool orientation, newcomers are encouraged to adopt a presentist attitude (Cusson 1983:126,164), a form of immediate gratification. Newcomers learn to orient their lives to the immediate pleasures of the present. This existential approach may be seen as a realistic strategy given children's uncertainties about their future.

It is, however, in his analysis of the concept of "presentism" that encouragingly bold theoretical contributions are made. "Presentism" is defined as the lack of perseverance in the pursuit of long term projects, a lack of persistence and the extremely limited temporal horizons of delinquents. According to Cusson (1983), this presentism is a major stimulus or determinant of delinquent activities. Two factors are isolated as the root of juvenile restlessness: lack of parental discipline and repeated failures. For Cusson, this immediate pleasure cannot go hand in hand with respect for one's obligations. He concludes that a presentist is neither a person of duty nor a person of his or her word. It is the delinquent's "Achilles' Heel" standing in the way of efficiency not only at work but also in the chosen field. Presentism pervades all the delinquent's interpersonal relations. Presentist opportunity and subcultural marginality occupy a central place in the lives of "troublesome" youths. Presentism, as an expression of the delinquent's identity and world vision, is a viable conceptual device for investigating the process of delinquency; he argues that "the more an adolescent commits crime, the less he is involved in establishing a career" (p. 125). Presentism, a procedure the individuals use to make sense of their delinquency, remains part of a larger, ongoing process of self indication or self validation. Presentism is one of many fundamental expressions used in building and maintaining symbolic worlds constituted by the skills of the actors, reactions of others and self identity.

Violence is also part of a newcomer's growing repertoire of cool techniques. Street kids consider fighting as a legitimate technique for resolving disputes on the street. A *game-oriented perspective* is a third salient feature of the socialization of newcomers. Games make apprenticeship more exciting and pleasurable, and are useful in sustaining the involvement of newcomers with more seasoned kids. For example, hustling provides both money and entertainment. A newcomer learns that survival is entrenched in this orientation. It is permissible to take the edge, or take advantage of other players, by altering the rules midway through a social encounter. In summary, the street offers newcomers a collective identity, a reference group from which to develop a valued identity. This new identity requires a display of appropriate perspectives. Specifically, a street perspective consists of the following values and rules of behaviour: an ethos of individualism, a theme of survival and a game perspective.

The view of street survival as a game serves to protect identity against possible spoilage. As Lofland (1969:13) suggested games can be used by actors to defend themselves against distrusted and suspicious others by allowing for tricks and masks. The game provides newcomers with many masks designed to secure favourable encounters. Newcomers learn to play games with social workers by offering them hard luck stories and with police by presenting themselves as victims exploited by adults.

In general, street survival is a comprehensive term for various street activities. By manipulating impressions, skilfully appraising and adjusting odds on events of chance, and by providing scarce or illicit services and goods, street kids enhance their own survival as they attempt to obtain money outside the conventional world of legitimate work. This income-generating behaviour includes a plethora of "con" games such as panhandling, welfare frauds, shoplifting, stealing, dealing in drugs and stolen goods, and prostitution. During the newcomer's introduction to the street there is little task specialization; on-the-street socialization exposes newcomers to a variety of enterprises. The problematic relationship between goals pursued and available opportunities, for example, are resolved at the level of subjective meanings, that is, in the social construction of action.

The metaphor of the survival may appear excessively dramatic but it certainly supplies a useful imagery of moral regulation. The metaphor is a figurative device that captures compellingly that which is not readily available with literal depictions. The street provides youths with many identities; the street person is the strange "other" who speaks a common language and yet is able to transcend time and space. Surviving essentializes street identity in terms of conflict. Moreover, from police violence to street muggings youths personalize crime as a parasitic life-form of survival, street survival requires sustenance—criminal hustles. Crime acts symbolically as a rationale for control and becomes conveniently incorporated within street discourses that support the intrusions of the more powerful. Power (from the police surveillance, welfare controls to seasoned street networks) exploits images of crime.

The following case study of youth prostitution highlights the acquisition of a general framework that cements disparate pragmatic accommodations to the street that further legitimate survival activities.

The Resistance of "Street Hooking"

Street prostitution is a social enterprise, the success of which depends on the willing participation of those others – the many so-called "respectables" who do not live off the street—the suburban tourists, urban voyeurs. Herein lies a contradiction! That is, prostitution viewed by the mainstream as a morally reprehensible service provides pleasure and protection to society's "insiders." Prostitution thrives as a result of the interaction of many on the street—the pimps, tricks ("johns"), police (who act like landlords constantly harassing street populations in an effort to develop an informant system and seek street information from street populations who are fertile sources of information), youth workers, etc. (Visano 1990a 1990b). Just as prostitutes take from their respective clients, they in turn give that which is forbidden in the dominant order—desire. Prostitution is also about the regulation of desire—both the desiring subject and object figure prominently. The expressions of sexual desire are manifested in contexts that are both attractive and repulsive. The body becomes a major symbolic site for shaping opinion and framing moral consciousness, a public consciousness that is calibrated to handle a steady flow of trouble. Trouble invites an elastic instrument of social control. Once exaggerated, this trouble legitimates further policing of desire even if it invites the illegal behaviour of the righteous. For example, the hunt for street hookers, for example, police crackdowns on johns and hustlers crystallize identities, establish boundaries, maintain a collective consciousness and restore the integrity of the prevailing value system. This hunt becomes a pretext to justify, expand and consolidate control by moral entrepreneurs and their persuasive campaigns. The concept of the "whore" enjoys many identities: she or he is the strange "other" who speaks a common language and yet is able to transcend time and space. To the trick, the prostitute is an abstraction always fictive, provisional and relational category in interpreting identities, relations, and events. Street prostitution debunks predictability in order to permit a critical entry into imaginary lifeworlds. The emergence of new individual identities or subject positions that abandon what in retrospect is the narrow scope of the modern individual with its claims to rationality and autonomy. The challenge for street hookers is captured in the following illogic of commodification: how can a client/trick hear, taste and touch the body of the prostitute given the inscription of evil identities? Who then is the real prostitute in this culture of capital?

On the one hand, the street sex trade is one of many street activities controlled by street girls and boys. The price, activities, location, levels of violence, etc On the other hand, capitalism supports and controls sex as a commodity. For Turner (1989:22) play and pleasure have to be restrained and subordinated to guilt in capitalist society in order to prevent any Airrational diversions from the centrality of productive labour. Interestingly, for Marcuse (1969), play and pleasure have a revolutionary potential which has been neglected by critical theory. Turner (1989:23) adds that capitalism comes to depend on "surplus repression" which goes beyond what might be regarded as the necessary constraints on individuals as members of society as such (Marcuse 1969). The main threat to these potentialities came from the commercialization and commodification of sex, which rendered sexuality profitable. Marcuse (ibid) adds that the so-called perverts replaced the proletariat as the principal agents of change within a capitalist society. The liberation of desire is implicitly the liberation of a particular desire (Turner 1989:23); prostitution reinforces rather than questions prevailing social relations. Prostitution, paradoxically, provides an illustration of the commercialization of sexual relationship and also of critical of power and dominance in sexuality. The commodification of sex lends support to the argument that modern society is a pornographic society, "a society so hypocritically and repressively constructed that it must inevitably produce an effusion of pornography as both its logical expression and its subversive, demotic antidote" (Carter 1979:86; Turner 1989: 23-25)—the expression of male desire over instrumental rationality. Thus, a consumer culture requires not the suppression of desire, but its manufacture, extension and detail (Turner 1989: 25). In this mass pleasure, the new consumerism is simply the old "bread and circus" approach to domination. The hegemonic control of capitalism over desires and needs is exhibited in the situation that capitalism can survive and tolerate individual deviance and social pluralism; the tolerance of capitalism is oppressive (p.26). The paradox of the hegemonic argument is that capitalism enjoys the hegemony of permissiveness which it does not actually require; capitalism achieves commodification of fantasies and pleasures. At the centre of prostitution is the set of political struggles: choice and regulation. Equally noteworthy are the various institutional arrangements for the commodification of bodies, herein prostitution is notoriously the most ancient of such arrangements. MacKinnon (1989: 234) argues that prostitution is the conversion of natural asset as a use-value into an exchange value, devoid of subjective commitment and affective attachment. This loss of a sensuous ownership of the body, therefore, could be one form of corporeal alienation. For Marx (MacKinnon 1989:17), the capitalism is the pimp (pp.17-18); Marx observed that the bourgeoisie are hypocritical in deploring prostitution because the "bourgeois marriage is in reality a system of wives in common." Marx adds: "Prostitution is only a specific expression of the general prostitution of the labourer" (Tong 1989:64). Foucault (1980:4) adds:

> The brothel and the mental hospital would be places of tolerance: the prostitute, the client and the pimp, together with the psychiatrist and his hysteric...see, to have surreptitiously transferred the pleasures that are unspoken into the order of things that are counted.

De Beauvoir's (Tong 1989:208) analysis of prostitution is complex. On the one hand, the prostitute is a paradigm for the Other, as object, as the exploited one. On the other hand, the prostitute, like the person who purchases the services is an exploiter. Prostitutes enjoy not only the money but also the narcissistic homage extended to their otherness. Prostitution as the affirmation of the authentic threatens the colonizing projects of the capitalist cultures. The image of the whore spills over into the consciousness of the oppressed. The disparagement of the prostitute as the whore exalts a number of mythologies of righteousness, desire and reason. The image of the whore is transcendent as an essential mode of resistance. As an object of consciousness the whore is both alluring and dangerous. The whore is not an atomized spectacle but remains fully emblematic of the success of capital. The political economy of production and consumption demand the commercialization of morality. As long as the whore is externalized as the enslaving Other, crass exploitation seems distant and apart from one's existential alienation. The self as a whore is fragmented, without a soul and ill connected thereby rendering incoherence to capital enterprises. Commodities and consumerism are perceived as prerequisites for the specialized selves. One then asks, who are the whores? Where did the stereotypic whore learn to practice with impunity that which is so readily rewarded? The whore is a ubiquitous characteristic of a duplicitous society that refuses to confront the governing logic of labour in a predatory culture. The concept of a street hooker is a fruitful theoretic tool that encapsulates the elasticity of insensitive commercial enterprises, the cornerstone of our economic order. Again, as one prostitute asked (Visano 1998b), "Who is the biggest whore of 'em all?"

Against a backdrop of *doubt and danger* we ask, for example, how do youths conceive of the reasons and motives for their actions? How are moral identities created? To what extent is resistance constituted and manipulated in terms of the convenience of arrogance and ignorance?

Resistance: "Crime as Conformity"

As discussed previously, youths seldom question the singleness of media purposes, the constant sense of over saturation, actuarial decathlon, sludge of criminal detail and the media's vulgar determinism sustained by linguistic hegemony. Crime is often glamorized as activity that empowers, protects and marks territories. The consequences of illegal or unethical activity are not the images upon which young minds focus. Crime is an expression of survival, individuality and independence and not necessarily an instance of resistance. Counter-hegemony is not necessarily organic but enjoys only occasional shifts in consciousness. As noted in chapter three, most youths interviewed were not aware of the dangers of the fixity and fetishism of the media's calcification of criminal identities. They, for example, remain insulated from the historical contingencies and tragedies of media discourses. Street kids, for example, remained insulated from the historical contingencies and tragedies of media discourses. Instead, crime as a commodity was often fetishized. Rather than negate the validity of news, youths negotiate their interpretations. Older and more educated youths interpret the deforming gaze of the media, that is, the symbolic violence, in a manner that privileges their own iconographic discourses of rage, representation and resistance. Privileged youths noted that the media coverage of Toronto's squeegee kids and the attendant crackdown by the police were unnecessary but understandable given their aggressive "panhandling" (the Safe Streets Act), adopting the same rhetoric promoted by the former Harris government. Currently youths object to the media's reporting of a new breed of gang and gun violence, the censoring of gangsta rappers like 50 Cent. And on the other hand, for political reasons grandstanding crusades like the one launched by Liberal MP Dan McTeague the junior foreign minister to prevent the platinum-plated gangsta rapper Curtis "50 Cent" Jackson from entering Canada whose music and recent, semi-autobiographical screen turn in *Get Rich* glorify gun violence and the thug lifestyle, and the CD artwork for 50's last album, *The Massacre*, contains several glamorous photo spreads that fetishized firearm possession more than any Smith & Wesson catalogue. Likewise, rap foe Valerie Smith tried to ban Eminem from entering Canada in 2000 and recently filed a complaint with the Ontario Human Rights Commission against HMV for selling "hate rap" (Rayner 2005).

The counter hegemonic praxis in their appearances, music, recreation and consumption are forms of resistance to the moral entrepreneurship of authorities (parents, police and school). Evident in many street youth cultures are manifestations of dominant liberal values taken to an extreme, notably possessive individualism, a gratifying consumerism and lingering need to do something because of a pervasive boredom. In time, they too will perfect these attributes! Note, for example, all major multi-billion dollar culture industries (music, fashion and advertising) are appropriating street images for commercial appeal.

The idea that youth constitutes a significant and distinct category is inevitably reinforced by the media. But as Giroux (1994) notes, young people are condemned to wander within and between multiple borders and spaces marked by excess, otherness and difference; popular conceptions of youth misrepresent youth as well as reconstruct the experience and meaning of youth. Youth resistance has become a commodity that manipulated by the dominant culture. One notices the underlying structure of capitalist ideology imposed on youth as well as the youth construction of mundane practices of youth; the agentic/ the situated self and determining structures (political economy, historical trends) intersecting. This mediated youth resistance can be understood by examining the reification of youth consciousness that finds expression in commodity relations. Rationalized and mechanized resistance has incorporated into fetishized images that simultaneously impose themselves as meaningful. Mindless conformity and crime are consequences of this estrangement to such an extent that youth cannot communicate in a language that is not appropriated and mediated. Commoditized criminality is conformity, the by-product of institutional and ideological interventions. As filmmaker Spike Lee noted:

> You have to have knowledge of self and knowledge of history. Because if you had that you would not use that terminology. You would not even be in that mindset. And we're in a time when young black boys and girls want to be pimps and strippers, because that is what they see…Gangsta rap is a modern-day minstrel show. You've got the gold, the Cristal (champagne), the cars, the rims, the video hos, and throwing $100 bills at the camera. (Large 2005)

Or data on 250 youths suggest that a demonstration of how meanings of resistance have been reworked, that is, typologies of accommodations rather than vacuous binaries of unity and closure that either, romanticize or demonize youth cultures, are theoretically more fruitful. A multi-perspectival approach is used in this study to incorporate various theoretical perspectives such as media culture, modernity, postmodernism, resistance, and various perspectives in the development and maintenance of identity. This multi-method approach also employs naturalistic classroom observations and student interviews.

Resistance = Identity + Institutions + Ideology

First, let us operationalize the salient concepts inherent in *ideologies* (cultural values, beliefs): a) modernity: instrumental, rational, institutional; b)liberalism: rights individualism, freedom; c) capitalism: possessiveness, property, materialism, inequality, adversarial, accumulation of capital propagates consumption, narcissism and material fetishes acquisition of money and wealth self interests. Within the set of *resisting ideological values* are the following: community, compassion, peace, connections, and equality. Within the set of *conforming ideological values* (liberalism, modernity, capitalism) are the following: aggression, violence, individualism,

203

FIGURE 4.1
FINDINGS:
TYPOLOGY/MATRIX OF RESISTANCE

IDENTITY (Being: subjectivity / consciousness)	INSTITUTIONS (Behaviour, means)	IDEOLOGIES (Beliefs, goals, aspirations)
FIRST ORDER RESISTANCE		
+/-	+/-	+/-
+	+	+
SECOND ORDER		
+	-	+
+	+	-
+	-	-
THIRD ORDER		
-	+	+
-	-	+
-	+	-
NON-RESISTANCE		
-	-	-

Legend: + resists/challenges/ subverts (does not fit)
  - accepts/accommodates (fits in)
  +/- rejects and replaces

consumption, inequalities, utility/instrumental, racism, misogyny, economic privilege, materialism, competition, and individuated freedoms.

Second, let us operationalize the salient concepts inherent in *institutions (means)* that correspond to the above ideologies of modernity, liberalism and capitalism respectively: a) organizations: bureaucratic and rules, exchange relations, specialization, mechanization (modernity), efficiency, impersonality, and hierarchies; b) contracts, law (common law, natural law), efficiency, (liberalism); c) market: self regulation, corporate capital, private property, private ownership. Within the set of *conforming institutional affiliations* are the following: *institutional* affiliations include ways, rules/ roles/ methods/ means (dominant division of labour, rational, specialized in school, work, law, family, and self-serving order. Within the set of *resisting institutional affiliations* are the following: anarchic, protests, spontaneous/direct action (inter subjective connections), connecting, peace as an anathema to prevailing institutions and ideologies.

204

Third, let us operationalize the salient concepts inherent in *identity*. *Identity* includes the self (being, subjectivity): consciousness, the material (physical), mental (intellectual, cognitive), emotional (feelings, passions) and spiritual selves as well as the unconscious selves (refer to chapter one). Within the set of *resisting identities* are: authentic, essence/ original position, race, gender, class sexuality, differentially challenged (mentally, emotionally and physically arrested/undeveloped), enlightened/transcends, intra psychic connections, producing selves or creating selves, much of which is drawn from the traditions of anarchic, peacemaking, First Nations and Eastern philosophies. Within the *set of conforming* are self-mentality, ego, mind, consumers, life-world, self-interest, ego gratification and the herd mentality.

From chapter one, it is clear that the self is not defined by socio-cultural values/ideologies (***beliefs***) nor just confined to organized/institutional practices (***behaviour***) but the self is also agentic (***being***),composed of the physical/material, emotional, intellectual and spiritual. Although the social impacts on the ideological (cultural goals, structural values, historical trends), the institutional (socialization, organizational values, means) and identity (consciousness, intention), resistance goes beyond the social which tends to define the material/physical and the intellectual to incorporate the emotional, the unconscious/the instinctual/ the unintentional and the spiritual. The following elements warrant consideration in assessing levels of resistance:

a) goals and means (immediate, intermediate, ultimate), c) behaviour and expectations;

d) precipitating and predisposing conditions; aggravating and mitigating factors;

e) time–space continuum (cultural, political and economic locations);

f) spontaneous versus planned; collective versus individual; moments and movements

g) overlapping levels of analyses: situational, organizational, systemic (micro, mecro, macro);

h) surface trends and foundational anchors;

i) private and public domains;

j) levels of recognition; and

k) target versus source.

205

How do youths try to make various resistances their own (self referential)? Alternatively, how do these practices enter the everyday world and assume oppositional perspectives? The symbolism and style of youth social inter-action—the culture of everyday life—in this way form a contested political terrain, embodying patterns of inequality, power, and privilege. In turn, these patterns are embedded with larger structures of mediated information and entertainment, cultural production and consumption, and legal and political authority. For example, to what extent is crime a cultural expres-sion of conformity and yet an instance of resistance? Crime is an expression of survival, individuality and independence may not necessarily constitute resistance. This counter-hegemony may only be an occasional shift in consciousness but not an organic transformation. That is, youth crimes are ideologically imbricated in the cultures within which they are embedded, defined, and implemented. The ethos of violence, a characteristic feature of the crime, is rewarded and manipulated in the larger social order. Youths as "criminals" define knowledge too narrowly. In so doing, youths are objec-tified according to a limited range of self-serving organizational criteria. The range of discourses used to construct youth criminality consists of ideological practices that typically articulate a narrative of danger, doubt and dependency as official and media formations of truth. A more thought-ful approach, however, suggests that crime is a consequence of relations of control. Crime is b) gradations of resistance (High, Medium, Low), ideo-logically conformist even though some activities are punished. Crime is denounced officially only in the sense of its institutional affiliations (ille-gitimate use of violence) but ideologically it is justified as success given its materialistic orientations. Both the consciousness (the self) and ideologies (beliefs) that accompany criminal activity are not necessarily subversive. This chapter argues that crime is not necessarily resistance but an accom-modation that ultimately promotes the interests of the dominant group. Crime promotes conformity; the emphasis on crime is a smoke screen that distracts attention from fundamental inequalities. The real danger is not crime, activities that fall well within the identity-institution / ideology conformity matrices, but that which is contrary to the values of capitalism, liberalism and modernity (individualism, materialism, aggression, violence, capital accumulation) such as a community of compassion. The dominant culture considers legally defined crimes as manageable and exploitable; the media and mechanisms of the criminal justice system are prepared to handle crimes given that they are not upset but rather feed into

FIGURE 4.2

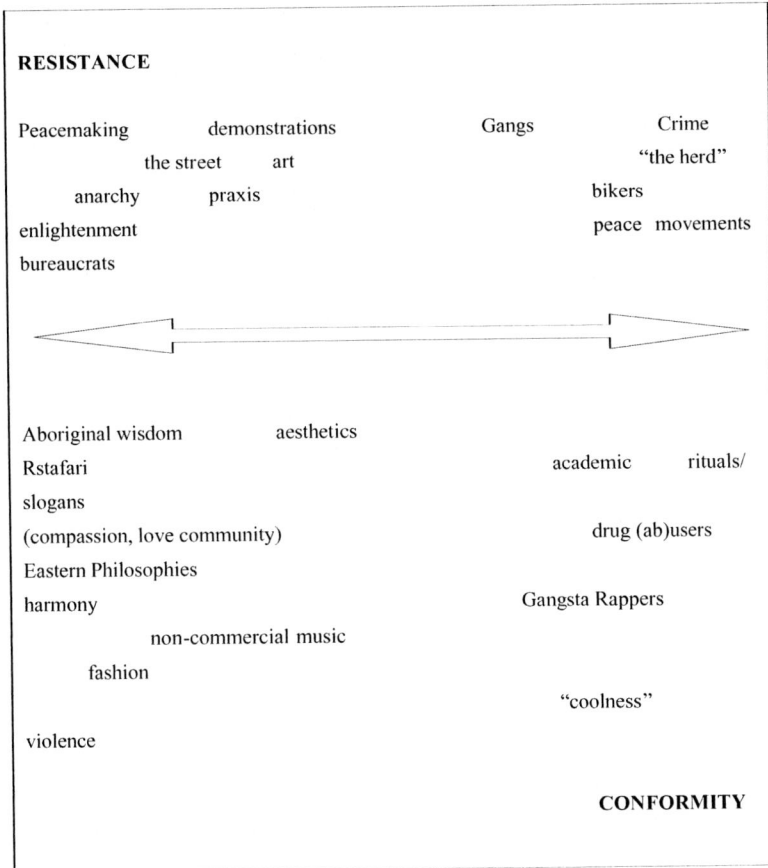

FIGURE 4.3

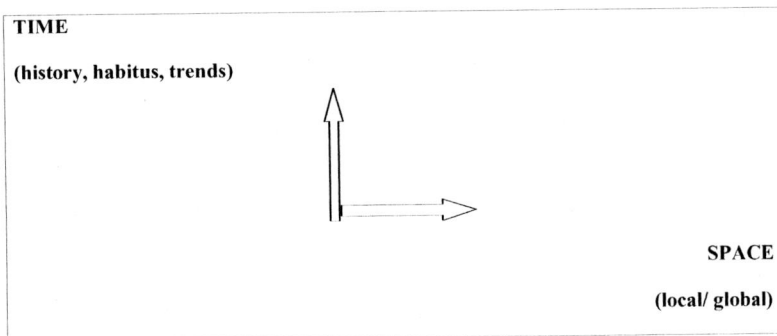

the status quo. The ongoing wars against crime, drugs and even "terrorism" generate incredible profits ideologically and financially. How then do we explain the differential treatment of corporate crime and street crime? Why are youths who violate custom or law penalized more severely? It is not a matter of a distorted and contradictory consciousness instead there is an unwillingness to connect crimes of the powerful with those of the powerless ignorance authorities discipline youth, to refuse to connect to the foundational frames of the social order. Going after the youth gangs is considered different from investigating the Bay Street or Wall Street "businesses." Why? Organized crime as depicted in the "Sopranos" is treated differently from how the White House is represented in the "West Wing" or the "Commander in Chief." Why?

In this study, the functions of crime are clarified. Youth crime serves to promote group solidarity and generate a common morality. Crime maintains boundaries that confine tolerable behaviour to a particular radius. The community draws a symbolic set of parentheses around a certain segment of that range and limits its own activities within that narrower zone. An individual who moves beyond the margins is called to account for that vagrancy. The community declares how much variability will be tolerated and defines the nature of the appropriate confrontations. Today, the media has replaced medieval public marketplace executions with information about the boundaries of acceptable conduct within communities.

Crime waves are moments of excitement, alarm and rashes of publicity where social control is calibrated to handle a steady flow of crime. Crime is a public spectacle that serves many functions. Chambliss and Mankoff (1976:8) outlined five functions of crime for society: a) Crime allows the capitalist class to create a false consciousness that advocates that the interests of the ruling class and the ruled are identical; b) Crime reduces the surplus labour by creating employment for criminals and non-criminals. Jobs are created, for example, for law enforcement agencies, welfare workers, and professors of criminality; c) Crime diverts attention of the working class population, shifting attention away from their own exploitation towards other members of their own class rather than towards the capitalist class or economic system; d) Crime increases the capitalist control over the proletariat. The working class is coerced into submission; and, e) Crime is a reality that exists only as it is created by those in society whose interests are served by its presence.

In Toronto, for example, gang rivalry perpetrated by young men who have grown up in community housing and embrace "gangsta" culture. It also underscores how the conflict between rival groups like the Blood, Ardwick Bloods, Jamestown Crips and Crips, long ago exported from Los Angeles, is firmly entrenched in Toronto, even if the offshoot groups have no direct affiliation with their American namesakes. In our study, former members boast chillingly about lethal reprisals and street supremacy as pivotal when trying to understand the gun violence. Toronto recorded a record number of fatal and non-fatal shootings in 2005 that were drug and gang related, much of it was isolated, involving either different factions feuding over turf and control of drug territory, some of it retaliation for rip-offs or revenge for what outsiders would consider trivial and profoundly absurd — bruised egos, perceived slights and disrespect.

In their study of 125 active and former members of criminal street gangs, aged 17 to 24, funded in part by the Solicitor General of Canada, Scot Wortley and Julian Tanner provide more liberal and mainstream interpretations that equally confirm the significance of dominant values. As Tanner notes:

> That they come from the most seriously disadvantaged home back-grounds that you could imagine. That there was a fair degree of desperation and defiance in what they had to say. They basically told us, and they've been telling us, that they will do anything to make money, anything to survive. (Rankin 2005a:A10)

Wortley adds:

> Rip-offs among individuals involved in any illegal economy, and that goes back to the days of Al Capone, have been a real concern. The one way you can prevent or cut down on rip-offs is establishing a reputation as somebody not to be messed with, that if you try to rip this person off, they're going to come after you, and they're going to kill or seriously hurt you...It's not like you can call the better business bureau... However, a lot of shootings don't meet the definition of gang violence, which can be rather vague at times. We tend to think of gang violence as one gangster against another gang-ster, or gangs duelling it out. Some of the violence is among people involved in the same gang, and often some of the violence is a

known gang member engaging in violence against somebody who is totally unconnected to gangs. There are these stand-offs where the slighted antagonist wants the individual to apologize or show respect, and that's not forthcoming and it escalates. We can look at it from the outside and say that's an absolutely ridiculous reason for violence to escalate, but within the gang culture it's kind of seen that if you don't retaliate, you're going to be viewed as a punk, you're going to be viewed as weak. (Rankin 2005a:A10)

Wortley echoes the hitherto well-established findings of mainstream criminology with the following:

One of the things was how distant and removed these youth felt from mainstream society. They really felt, at a very young age, that they just didn't have a stake in conformity, and how normative it was (to be in a gang). They would just kind of say, well, growing up in the neighbourhood, it was just kind of viewed as your option. It was just a natural progression. It wasn't like they sat down one day at a table and drew out a kind of life plan that said, 'I'll join the gang now...If you don't deal with the social environment that is creating young men who will engage in this type of violence, you're just going to have a problem that is going to increase or stay the same...It's almost like a job vacancy change. You have a housing project and you do a sweep, and you arrest all the gang members and you put them away. If you don't change the situation in that housing project, the next generation is just going to come up and fill the shoes. (Rankin 2005a:A10).

Clearly, bandana-wearing young men flashing guns and bragging about bullying neighbourhood snitches do not threaten the status quo. In fact, many social institutions from the media, the criminology industry (academics, researchers, policy analysts, consultants) to all agencies of the criminal justice system not only welcome but profit from its violence.

The popular media plays a significant role shaping what youths refer to as resistance. Instrumental interpretations have colonized youths who are herded into consuming slaves, who have made youths are far more susceptible to the dominant culture, that is, the popular culture and seldom question the false identity of the general and the particular. The fragmentation of self into the herd mentality prevails –uniform dress, talk and yet the emphasis on individuality that claims to challenge authority. In our study, unsurprisingly the loudest critics of the media were the street kids who also demonstrated a greater degree of commitment to resistance than the school kids or the gang members. School youth (city and suburban) learn the language, clichés but seldom act out their resistance, whereas street and gang youth talk less about subversion and act more spontaneously in expressing their resistance. In terms of race, class and gender we discovered considerable differences; minority youth and less economically advantaged youths not only talk about but praise those counter hegemonic activities that are responses to exclusionary projects of the dominant culture. Notwithstanding the differences among school youths regarding specific and more private acts of resistance, their reported behaviour reflect a substantial degree of cooptation and complacency. School youth exaggerate and boast about their rebellion in order to "fit in" the respective "cool" school cultures whereas the gang and street youths tend to minimize this behaviour. Acts of resistance are more "fashionable" for school youth whereas street and gang youths engage in what they considered as subversive activities (drugs, gangs, violence, hustling) which they felt were justified as survival activities, realistic life world responses. School youths note that the street is an authentic and open site of resistance given the absence of its institutional controls. They are inclined to compare the public street with the internet in the sense that surveillance may exist but users are not inhibited in articulating their subversion. For street youth the street is the only sources of spontaneous direct action against the status quo.

Youth crime validates the capitalist production, consumption and production of consumption which so confine them, body and soul as that they fall helpless victims to what is offered them. Possessive individualism, or more appropriately the idolisation of individuality, materialism, technological rationales, markets of pleasure, the anesthetized sense of identity are all products of the culture industry. Neo liberalism, capitalism and modernity produce youths as consumer products used not as tools for social change or for critiquing the status quo, but primarily for consumption and entertainment. Clearly, youth resistance is reflective and derivative of socioeconomic imperatives. But a genuine empowerment of youth will challenge the ethos of individualism, a theme of survival and a game perspective. As the discourse moves away from the talk of money, away from the contagious "affluenza" and towards a collective wisdom grounded in an enlightened pedagogy consistent with that that cannot be easily contaminated—an authentic ideology of youth emerges. Strength and curiosity are required to confront the contradictions and mediations of crime as related to the calculus of culture. As street youths articulate, the pseudo culture of empowerment of Much Music, MTV, and the record and fashion industries can never be considered forms of resistance. To understand resistance is to seek justice, peace, relational harmony, traditions inimical to such corporate entities. To resist as a youth is to become Simmel's stranger or wanderer, marginal to both dependency and responsibility, entering into a state of freedom to indulge not in the existential loneliness of J.D. Salinger's Holden Caulfield but rather to recover and respect their own ontological insecurities. This cognitive liberation advances a position that jeopardizes the convenience of ideological penetration. Admittedly, there is always some form of resistance given that there is no complete form of subordination or domination. Liberation outside the box whether expressed in Bob Marley's "One Love" message or the words of 15-year-old Chantel's words:

> Like, whatever. Just because society don't care does not mean I have to be like that. I've seen more than most in their lives. I tell ya they don't want us to care and don't want you to care. They say it is not normal You gotta shit on people to be liked. The uglier you are, the more respect you get. Doesn't have to be like that.

Similarly 17-year-old Ray suggests,

> so what? what do you expect? It is all about winnin', dissing, cheatin' and screwin' others. No wonder there's guns. Where is this coming from? These kids don't make guns. Look at the cops out here. They want us to be nasty. Everybody raps about respect, that's cool. The fightin' is about that. The killin' You either a fool or you cool. Get respect by being tough; fightin back. Get even by getting rich. The bread matters, a lot of gold, know what I saying. Just like the rest we want everything too. Threads, wheels, weed, tired of being poor. Can get the best lawyers who can really lie nice for you. For me resistance is having a hood family that'll do anything for you. Show me where that is any place else. We're one family.

Chapter 6

Conclusion:
"How Would They Know?"
From the Cycle of Coercion to
the Cycle of Compassion

Look at us, ok you know maybe we're not smart. That's cool. I don't pretend to be smart...Teachers supposed to be smart, supposed to know a couple of things about teaching. You think? Well, they don't know me and they're in my face. And they don't want to know me. So *how would they know* about me or my family? Man, you gotta sweat it a bit and try—they really really don't. No man, listen, *how would they know*? (Trevor, 17 years old)

Education: The Tyranny of Silence and the Cycle of Violence

Consistent with theme of relatedness, this study locates the youth crime-culture nexus within an array of institutional practices. Previous chapters dealt with the institutions of formal social control from the family and peers (chapters 1, 2 and 5), media (chapter 3), to law (chapter 4)—all from the prisms of youth. In this chapter we analyze the implications and applications of mainstream models that promote convenient and common sense assumptions about teaching youths. We endeavour to sketch a method for constructing a pedagogy that moves beyond the standard texts by linking state practices and cultural connections to a project of "unlearning" distancing ideologies. This effort requires a forthright excavation of intrinsic and commonsensical biases, specifically the foundation of experiences.

At the concrete level we analyze contradictions in the "schooling" of youth; the contemporary struggles for identity; and, the intersection of education and youth within specific and generic contexts. For example, by sketching the boundaries of cultural and state practices within a pursuit of knowledge framework, we can more fully appreciate how youths as categorized groups are deviantized and how both the ideology and the behaviour of the teachers institutionalize unlearning. This chapter encourages a critical appreciation of teaching with substantive applications of knowledge generation. Rather than examine, as is often customary for liberal teachers, the experiences of the learners alone this chapter directly confronts the practices of "teaching" that hide behind seemingly innocuous traditions of liberal conscience that in turn inform the rhetoric of pervasive institutional chatter. By evaluating critically the impact of teaching on youth we focus on the need to transform our understanding of the prospects and paradoxes of schools. It is generally accepted that schools prepare the students to become good citizens, generating and transmitting appropriate skills, knowledge, values and behaviours, but the issue of content therein depends upon the attitudes, values and belief systems of all participants. This approach, informed by progressive social orientations, that implicate the foundations of the wider culture, notably the centrality of coercion, represents a long overdue challenge to dominant cultural discourses by interrogating authority, control and power within the educational system. The meaningful participation of the most affected—youth guides this discussion; this participation must occur within wider interactive contexts and articulates discourses of power and privilege. According to John Dewey (1944:97): "[t]he conception of education as a social process and function has no definite meaning until we define the kind of society we have in mind." He clarifies (p.130):

> One has only to read any outgiving of the adherents of laisser-faire liberalism to see that it is the liberty of the entrepreneur in business undertakings which they prize and which they come close to identifying with the heart of all liberty.

The ideological nature of education prevails as he elucidates,

> Even when words remain the same, they mean something very different when they are uttered by a minority struggling against

214

repressive measures and when expressed by a group that has attained power and then uses ideas that were once weapons of emancipation as instruments for keeping the power and wealth they have obtained. (P.135)

But, the appropriation of resources by the state to legitimate programmes, re-socialize students and discredit discordance subverts any meaningful dialogue. Likewise, we are attempting to replace the cycles of violence with circles of life connections by suggesting that: how much youths know depends on what and how much teachers learn; how much teachers know depends on what and how much youths teach. It is important to explore how much teachers learn about students teaching them and what knowledge they have; that is, how teachers learn informs what they teach. This study ends by coming full circle to connect with ideas of the self, discussed above in the introduction.

Carceral Contexts of Culture: Conditioning the "Caged Herd"

What is the impact of culture on learning? How is teaching contextually determined? As noted in the previous chapter, the forces of capitalism, liberalism and modernity (economic, political and cultural) interact deeply in setting the contexts of teaching. Historically, education systems were conceived to 'transfer the culture of adult generations to younger generations', even more so in the case of secondary education than in primary education. Schooling functions to maintain solidarity and collective conformity to justify assimilation or more euphemistically social cohesion as a moral imperative. Based on their educational experiences, it is assumed that youth will assimilate the values and norms considered typical behaviour of concerned and altruistic citizens in a democratic society. An alternative educational goal of social efficiency emphasizes a school system that focuses on training workers and preparing youth to become capable contributors to the economic well being of the nation. Education is therefore perceived to be an investment in human capital required to maintain economic viability and relative position on a local and global level.

Contemporary teaching is ideologically grounded in evolving traditions of modernity, capitalism and liberalism. Modernity, liberalism, capitalism, and their respective foci on reason, rights and riches provide a synthetic unity to the foundations of the social. Modernity, as an ideology

215

with its emphasis on both the "rational" and the division of labour, has impacted on the self to such an extent that teaching has been reduced to a rational and technical calculation measuring "social value" (contractual considerations/ exchanges) that justifies distorted claims of efficiency by armies of specialized "professionals" (administrators, guidance advisors, consultants, teachers, government bureaucrats, trustees). In addition, modernist values and beliefs have exaggerated forms of social solidarity which now woefully displace and replace any vestiges of authentic collective consciousness that was previously identified as sacred – tradition. Modernity contributes to the fascination with utility or relevance of knowledge. Instrumental rationality especially its predatory practices of efficiency (school performance indicators), technical expertise and institutionalized discipline serve to attenuate considerably the promise and prospects of the enlightenment. Conditions are ripe for the creation of teaching as instrumental currency wherein crass opportunity prevails. As Einstein (1949:2) cautioned:

> This crippling of individuals I consider the worst evil of capitalism. Our whole educational system suffers from this evil. An exaggerated competitive attitude is inculcated into the student, who is trained to worship acquisitive success as a preparation for his future career…The education of the individual, in addition to promoting his own innate abilities, would attempt to develop in him a sense of responsibility for his fellow men in place of the glorification of power and success in our present society.

Equally, the roots of neo liberalism, founded on the marriage of classical liberalism and capitalism, maintains the sanctity of individualism. Possessive individualism, or more appropriately the idolisation of individuality is expressed through material consumption. Materialism is not simply the product of ongoing socialization but more importantly, an imperative of the economic order. Indeed, materialism, as a ubiquitous feature of our culture, speaks on our behalf; that is, our sense of self emerges from material dependence. It is used as a code, to guide and classify coherently the ways in which we display our experiences, imagination and consciousness. As a condition, materialism subjugates, enslaves and binds. An enslaving materialism inherent in the pursuit of private property has shaped all aspects of teaching structures and processes. As a society, we invest much

216

in carving out conformity as measured according to our possessions. The fixation on dollars not wise sense expedites a material self-enclosure that mediates mental, emotional and social expressions. These ideological features provide the the raison d'être of teaching as a capitalist production, consumption and production of consumption.

Celebrating standards set by opportunistic corporate criteria and agenda, school administrators and teachers have commodified education shamelessly and uncritically. Technological rationales, markets of pleasure and the anesthetized sense of the knowing self have left remarkably little room for imagination or reflection. The market demand for technical skills has transformed education; the basic logic for schooling, therefore, prepares students for a market mentality. Underneath this rubric of a market logic lies the imported needs of students to be extrinsically motivated to specialize. As the market ideology became dominant since the 1980's, schools have become more corporate, adopting a "market" model of governance. An actuarial logic of "the bottom line," guided by enrollment numbers and market place language, govern curriculum and planning. With the encouragement of government and the credulity of administrators, the private especially corporate interests use these sites to market their ideologies and promote narcissistically their product names on vending machines, names of buildings, to the obvious advertisements in hallways and washroom walls. Replete with convenient and inclusive rituals, illusions pacify and legitimate the articulation of the corporate marketplace.

The socio-economic trends, global and local, of this pernicious market economy (the influences of "neo liberalism" and its pervasive market mentality) have had a devastating impact on all social formations especially education. The education system operates according to such distorted claims: youths do have a significant culture of their own and therefore can offer no resistance; the adult culture is homogeneous irrespective of diversity; the adult culture as the stable dominant culture produces and structures knowledge; and, that schools are the main depositories of expertise in terms of transmitting this information (Galloway 1980).The dominant culture especially in reference to youths transforms the values of teaching and learning into more negotiable commodities, the value of which is conveniently determined by the privileged others. Knowledge is always ideologically situated, embedded within many contexts—social, political, economic and legal contexts. As Marx and Engels note: ([1947] 1960:7):

> As individuals express their life, so they are. What they are, therefore, coincides with their production, both with what they produce and with how they produce. The nature of individuals thus depends on the material conditions determining their production.

Prevailing cultural ideas influence elementary, secondary and post-secondary education by encouraging (rewarding) differences and a set of standards that guarantee the protection of privilege. For Bourdieu (1996), this represents the effort to transform economic and social capital into cultural capital through the process of education, which is often out of reach of people from minority groups and people from less affluent socio-economic backgrounds. Mass education is a process of class discipline. Commenting on this class bias, Livingstone (1998:51) notes, children of the affluent classes, who have acquired familiarity with bourgeois cultural forms at home (through exposure to their parents knowledge and manners, 'good' books, museums, etc.) are seen to possess the means of appropriating similarly oriented school knowledge relatively easily. Working class kids, in contrast, find their unfamiliarity with these cultural forms to be a major obstacle to successful school performance. Similarly, Corrigan (1979:20) admonishes:

> The education system does not allow sufficient mobility for working-class girls. They (the education system) have failed to realize the differential effects that home background has on different groups of pupils. Thus some kids come from homes which are bereft of books, with parents who fail to appreciate the importance of education for their girls' success in life; in short they come from educationally disadvantaged homes.

Not only is there an overwhelming class bias in all institutions of learning, there is a clear correlation between weak school performance and poverty (Cameron 1999). Forty percent of children in subsidized housing do poorly in school. In an economy where young people struggle to establish themselves economically, it is perhaps not surprising that one out of five of Canada's youngest citizens (1.4 million children) are growing up in *poverty* (Ross, Scott, and Smith 2000). Economic inequalities lie behind much of the failures in school (Brooks-Gunn et al. 1995; Brooks-Gunn et al. 1997). In brief, the school system discriminates against the poor, perpetuates a class system, and legitimizes inequality. In their research Lipman, Offord and Boyle have found strong and consistent relation between low family income and poor school performance (Toronto Star 1994b:A3). It is no wonder that the poor and culturally diverse are made to feel like strangers for whom schools are threatening places. Poverty is the underlying cause of illiteracy. No government has been able to make significant progress toward universal literacy (Hunter 1987).To their credit, teachers' organizations such as the British Columbia Teachers' Federation (BCTF) and the Canadian Teachers' Federation (CTF) speak to the issue of poverty and school performance. They warn that, unless we citizens address the economic inequality that lies behind much of the failure in school, our school remedial programs will have little effect (Canadian Teachers' Federation 1991:16).Given school "failures" the proportion of youth (15-19 years) who have never had employment increased substantially between 1989 and 1996. Youth who were born outside of Canada are less likely to have ever had paid work than Canadian-born youth. Paid employment provides experience in the labour market, opportunity for building skills and broadening networks, and helps to develop self-esteem as well as providing income (Canadian Council on Social Development 1998).

Youth consists of interrelated or overlapping relations—economic, class, political, legal, and social. A resource framework can be viewed as incorporating the following theoretical frames that have emerged to explain the relationship between poverty and educational outcomes. The "material resource" perspectives indicate that poor children suffer because their parents, communities and schools lack the financial resources that can aid learning and achievement. The "human capital" perspectives suggest that poor children suffer because of the poorer endowments and investments they receive from their parents (Becker 1993), or, by extension, the poorer human resources in the schools that they attend. The "social capital/network" perspectives suggest that impoverished parents and children lack supportive social relationships and networks within and outside of the family necessary for aspiring to and achieving success. And, the "cultural capital" perspectives maintains that that children of historically disadvantaged groups suffer because they lack the cultural environment at home that would allow them to connect to content in the classroom.

Specifically, low-income students *drop out* of school at more than twice the rate of other students (Ross, Scott, and Smith 2000:68). Older teens aged 16 to 19 years are normally expected to be either in school or in a job. However, they are 2.5 and 4.4 times more likely to be engaged in neither activity (in a sense, they are "idle") compared to teens from middle-income and higher-income families (ibid). Low-income students generally do move up in status (Cameron 1999). Twice as many poor children as any other economic category fall behind in educational achievement by the age of 15 (Canadian Child Welfare Association 1989:6). The *drop out rate* is twice as high for poor children than for any other group (ibid).

Youth unemployment has reached grave levels. Canada's youth (15 to 24 age group) are quickly becoming chronically unemployed. Rather than examine policies and practices of structured youth unemployment, both the state and the business communities have always attributed this unemployment to motivational causes, such as lacking any sense of initiative, industry, motivation or pathologized as too irresponsible, too lazy and too easily bored. Prospective employers tend to dismiss youths as inexperienced, unqualified and uncommitted to the normative work ethic. Special immediate and short-term programs have been created to focus on these youths but as of yet a commitment to long-term employment programs is missing. Instead, governments continue to increase tuition fees and cut back on social welfare expenditures providing little or no moral leadership for its youth beyond more idle chatter.

Homelessness, especially among youths is related to a large number of interrelated problems: drug and alcohol dependencies; sexual, emotional and physical abuse by relatives (Visano 1987), family stress, "dysfunctional" families, poor self-esteem, and the "lure" of the streets. Such pathological accounts are quite victim-oriented given that homelessness is a complex structural problem. Eighty-eight out of every 1000 children in the US are homeless. It is estimated that over 12,000 Canadian youths are homeless and the number is growing. Youths often leave homes where their guardians were substance abusers, physically or sexually abusive, or mentally ill. These youths have suffered from parental neglect, had problems at school or difficulty with communication. Other youths become homeless because their families suffer from financial crises. Together, they move into shelters and are then separated due to age restrictive shelter or child welfare policies. On any given night, approximately 33,000 Canadians are homeless, of which about 8,333 to 11,000 are youth (Covenant House 2005). For example, in Toronto, there are 12 shelters for youth, offering up to 522 beds. In 1979, there were only two youth shelters in the city, with 95 beds. In the past 25 years, there has been a 450%

increase in youth shelter beds. A good estimate suggests there are at least 10,000 different youth who are homeless at one point on any given year—and anywhere from 1,500 to 2,000 on a given nigh in Toronto alone (ibid). In fact, 64% of homeless youth (youth are under 25) are male, 91% of these men and 72% of females are between the ages of 19 and 25. Studies have shown that these youth generally leave home around the age of 15. Of the young men, 56% have grade 11 or less, 31% have grade 12 and 12% have university or college or technical school. For the young women, 60% have grade 11 or less, 33% have grade 12 and 6% have university, college or technical school. Of those who attended school and were assessed by counsellors, 25.6% were diagnosed with anger management problems, 19.1% with ADD, 15.2% with hyperactivity and 4.5% with dyslexia (ibid). In 2003 in Canada, there were a record 53,459 reports of runaway children (Covenant House 2005). Youth (16-24) have the highest unemployment rate of any group (National Anti-Poverty Organization 2004). Despite the fact that youth between the ages of 15-25 are the most impoverished in Canada, they represent only 15% of the social assistance caseload in Canada. Only 104,000 young adults between the ages of 20-24 received social assistance in 2001, compared to 191,000 in 1996. Among these youth, the average amount received from social assistance declined from $7,344 in 1993 to $4,620 in 2001 despite an increasing need. For youths under 20 years old, 20,000 received social assistance in 2001, compared to 59,000 in 1996. The average amount received from social assistance declined from $6,065 in 1995 to $5,206 in 2001. Young people aged 15-24 represent the majority of low paid workers with 56.9% of youth earning less than $10 per hour. In most provinces and territories, any wage below $10 per hour places the earner below the poverty line (National Anti-Poverty Organization 2004). Children and youth make up the single largest category of poor people. Almost half of those depending on the food banks for sustenance are under eighteen years of age. The child mortality rate is twice as high among families at the lowest income level as among those at the highest income level. Likewise, children from families receiving welfare benefits had one and a half times the rate of chronic health problems experienced by children from families who were not on welfare.

Globally, this tragedy has not abated especially since the eradication of poverty and underdevelopment are not overriding concerns to the more industrialized countries (George 1985:7). Nearly a billion people entered the 21st century unable to read a book or sign their names. Less than one percent of what the world spent every year on weapons was needed to put every child into school by the year 2000 and yet it didn't happen (Shah 2005). The lives of 1.7 million children were needlessly lost in 2005 because world governments have failed to reduce poverty levels (ibid). Seven million children die each year because of the debt crisis. Progress in reducing infant mortality was also considerably slower during the period of globalization (1980-1998) than over the previous two decades. Education and literacy: Progress in education also slowed during the period of globalization. The number of children in the world is 2.2 billion and the number living in poverty 1 billion (every second child)! For the 1.9 billion children from the developing world, there are: 640 million without adequate shelter (1 in 3); 400 million with no access to safe water (1 in 5); 270 million with no access to health services (1 in 7); children without any formal education worldwide: 121 million (Shah 2005).

Racism is integrally related to the process of designating deviance. In fact, racism is a resource for formulating and formatting practices of exclusion. This mechanism of racism constructs and commoditizes deviant discourses. The phenomenon of racism differentiates, marginalizes and negates identity. Contemporary reactions to racism are rooted deeply within seemingly innocuous traditions of liberal conscience that in turn inform the rhetoric of pervasive legal chatter. The culture of superiority conditions not only the armies of occupation, but also the offering to colonized peoples token opportunities in education. Education, as a critical socializing agent, reproduces the dominant culture of superiority. Unfortunately, schooling too often tends to be part of the problem of racist socializing and acculturation. Indeed, education becomes a significant social and political powerhouse facilitating the disenfranchisement of people of colour and other minority groups. Moreover, capitalism has always been interested in perpetuating racist mythologies in order to leverage its own privilege (Winks 1971; Oakes 1985).

Elementary and secondary schools are social systems that have a primary function to socialize and allocate students. As Das Gupta (2000: 195) details:

> Racism is one of the most hegemonic ideologies in the Canadian society. The ideologies rationalize the differentiation and subordination of people on the basis of superficial physical characteristics, such as skin colour, or in some feature, which can be defined as

222

group or community as "different from the norm." The negative labels...and racist stereotypes are themselves indicative of a culture that does not see African Canadians as individuals with their own identities and personalities. Instead, labels are imposed to create fixed images about entire communities based on their skin colour and physical appearance.

A main aspect of education that poses a problem for minority children is the formal government mandated curriculum. The curriculum created by white, middle-class males is a problem because it does not represent the experiences of the minorities. Whenever the curriculum mentions minorities, the dominant white culture is positioned as the criterion by which the needs of minority students are assessed. Whiteness continues to be *the* social identity and *the* dominant institution of society. Historically, school curricula highlight the significance of "white" contributions while dismissing the experiences of non whites as irrelevant or negligible. This distorted reality undermines the self-esteem of students who soon learn that they cannot participate equally nor are they allowed to claim any membership in the dominant culture. It remains difficult for children to learn in an abusive environment; a setting that negates their history and therefore their presence. As Kunjufu (1984:3) noted: "Our children need to know that slaves were beaten if found reading or learning how to write." Canadian accounts are written from a euro-centric perspective that solely highlights the contributions of Europeans. All others, that is, non Europeans are therefore left in the periphery. Their contributions are marginalized. In reference to the early years of schooling and socialization, Talbot (1984:82) wrote, black children

> do not recognize themselves as Africans but as Black Canadians, runaway slaves, West Indians, etc. The denial of their true origins in the education of black and white children, plus a long history of discrimination...has led many of them to try and escape this pain by denial of their roots and attempts to assimilate themselves into the dominant culture.

Labaree (1997) discusses the ways in which education has been plagued by the competing objectives of equality, efficiency and mobility and explores some of the issues surrounding how this influences operational forms such as structure, administration and curriculum in schools. This rivalry between educational objectives and functions provides some explanation as to the difficulty experienced by parents and children of from diverse ethno racial backgrounds, in their quest for a fair and equitable education.

Kenneth Clark (1965) reports in his book, *Dark Ghetto,* that by the age of four, children have a fairly well developed conception of race and racial difference. That conception of race and racial difference is patterned after the social practice existing in those white dominated societies. As

> [h]uman beings who are forced to live under ghetto conditions and whose daily experience tells them that almost nowhere in society are they respected and granted the ordinary dignity and courtesy accorded to others will, as a matter of course, begin to doubt their worth. (P.45)

As Walker (1982:5) admonished, many students go through the education system without being exposed to the history of Blacks in Canada. It "is not the events of the past, but the ignorance of the past...that has prevented the recognition of a...heroic Black community" (ibid). Segregated education, legalized in Ontario in 1849, allowed local municipalities to establish separate schools for "Negroes." The Separate Schools Act resulted in inferior teaching and learning, poorly funded and ill trained teachers for non whites. This segregation persisted until the closing of the last such school in 1965. As Baldwin cautioned, a child cannot be taught by someone who despises him or her (Excalibur, January 27, 1993:19). The following individuals have made considerable contributions to Canadian history and yet they remain virtually unknown, let alone studied, in Canadian schools: Josiah Henson (a soldier in the 1837 Rebellion who helped the capture of an American ship), Samuel Rinngold Ward (founder of the Provincial Freeman newspaper in 1853), Anderson Ruffin Abbott, William Hubbard (Acting Mayor of Toronto at the turn of the century), Abraham Shadd, the first Black to be elected to hold public office as a town councillor), John Ware, (pioneered the rodeo in 1882), Reverend Dr. Wilbur Howard, Mary Shadd Cary, and Rosemary Brown, to name only a few. In Canada, there were prominent black families like the Abbotts and Hubbards who entered politics successfully. For instance, supported by George Brown, W.P. Hubbard held office in the richest ward in Toronto and his son Frederick became the first Toronto Transit Commissioner in the 1930s (Henry et al. 2000).

Large numbers of textbooks used in classrooms remain culturally biased, both in their presentation of material and in their omission of material on the culture, history, or achievement of many of the national and cultural groups represented in schools. Books inculcate cultural values and self-identification. These visual stimuli hasten language skills and literacy and become the primary mode of learning and understanding. Traditionally, books have perpetuated myths about non whites, thus, encouraging children to believe, for example, that Black people are not only inferior, but also can look forward to a lifetime career on welfare (Council on Interracial Books for Children 1973). There is no better way to reach children than through their books. In these books, however, the omission of crucial images tells black children they have no respectable social place today or in the future (Sadker and Sadker 1977:130).

The monocultural curriculum fails to challenge the limited history, vision and expectations of the more privileged Anglo-centric emphasis and the devastating effects of oppression on minority children and their cultures. Moreover, schools simply deny the impact of racism on the attitudes and behaviour of learners and teachers (Molnor1989:72; Pollard 1989). According to a handout, a "Jamaican fact sheet," given to grade six students by a social studies teacher at Bloordale Elementary School in Toronto in October 1993, reported in the media in 1994, described the Jamaican Family Life as:

> Often a man and woman will marry after the child is born. Often the grandmother will raise the kids. Often a family is an unmarried woman with several kids who have different fathers. (Toronto Star 1994a:A6)

An inclusive curriculum, according to Dei (1996, 1998), is a curriculum with equity, justice, and representation; it requires pedagogies that respond to the social construction of difference in the school system and wider society. Similarly, he suggests the notion of "Afrocentricity" in replacement of the dominant Eurocentric dominance in the Inclusive curriculum in Canadian schools. Afrocentric discourse is a discourse of resistance, that is, a discursive space to rupture the culture of dominance in schools. Engaging Afrocentricity from other points of views is a constructive process that recognizes the limitations and partiality of all knowledges. Afrocentrcity is not a binary opposition between Eurocentrism and Afrocentricity; it is not a replacement of one hierarchy with another. Dei suggests that Afrocentricity is much deeper than a semantic understanding, it requires an understanding of the historical process and systematic nature of racism and devaluation of counter/oppositional thought in the West (Dei 1996, 1998). Afrocentric knowledge challenges the monopoly of Eurocentricity on knowledge.

In general, policies, teaching styles and curriculum content contribute to exclusionary and distorted practices. Schools have perpetuated further oppressive experiences for many non-whites in the classroom. Many teachers consider Black students disruptive, poorly motivated and academically weak (Carrington 1983:44; Gill, Mayor, and Blair 1992:31). While White students are encouraged to pursue academic interests, their Black counterparts are frequently streamed towards athletics. Because of the influence of teachers, coaches and the media, young Black students cling to unrealistic aspirations in professional sport (Gill, Mayor, and Blair 1992:46). Only 1.6% of Black athletes participating in collegiate football, baseball or basketball actually secure a professional contract (Edwards 1988:139). Moreover, only 40% of these hopefuls continue after four years of professional sport (ibid).

Moreover, Illich (1970:48) suggests that the *hidden curriculum* of schooling adds prejudice and guilt to the discrimination, which a society already practices against some of its members. Institutional racism and marginalization experienced by students of colour widely practised program of *streaming* children in schools. Both are important concepts to understand because of their connection with the underachievement of blacks in school. Claude Steele et al. (2003) articulate the notion of a "stereotype threat" to explain the consistency with which students of colour documented as academically gifted, failed to achieve high levels of academic performance. A stereotype threat is the fear of being seen through the looking glass of a negative stereotype, or, the apprehension of doing something that would confirm the validity of the negative stereotype. The practice of streaming in education is also well documented and controversial. It continues today even when significant research exists clearly indicating the dire and discriminatory consequences of its practice. Streaming, a blatant and systematic means of perpetrating discrimination in the education system, manifests itself in the consistent labelling of children from working class and poor families as slow learners, forcing them into secondary education cohorts that ultimately exclude them from accessing post-secondary education. Different forms of *streaming* students, that is, placing students in different levels of study based on scholastic abilities, have always been biased. The school system holds low teacher expectations and poor teacher-student interaction (Coelho 1988) for minority children. These low expectations are ultimately reflected in the attitudes of children of the lower tracks (Oakes 1985:141). Despite policy pronouncements, inequalities persist. Streaming places Black youths in the lowest achievement programs. Again, low expectation invites less intervention and attention from teachers. Consequently, youths and children are encouraged to equate colour with failure. Judy Katz (1978) points out that the *Commission on Mental Health* considers racism as the primary mental health problem in the United States. The destructive effects of racism severely cripple the growth and development of millions of our citizens, young and old alike. Lower track students have the most negative views of themselves academically and generally (p.143). Class based and culture biased tests further ensure an over-representation of non-white children in the lower streams. As Radwanski (1987:76) describes:

> While only 12% of students in the highest or advanced stream leave school before graduation, the dropout rate is 62% among students taking mainly General level courses and 79% among students at the basic level.

Throughout the 1980s and before the elimination of tracking system, in Toronto more than 20% of black children were registered in basic level courses compared to 14.2% of all white students (Share February 15, 1989). Furthermore, within the Toronto Board of Education, only 36% of black students in schools are enrolled in courses that would allow them to enter university (Tator 1987:9). Not surprisingly, the experience of Black parents is that their children are more likely to find themselves excluded from the Arts and Science stream and bound for community college or directly into the workforce. Blacks are tracked into the lower streams and undergo learning processes based on a biased curriculum. A White student is two times more likely to be assigned to a gifted class than a Black student. Black students are disproportionately being placed in lower academic groups while White students are placed into higher academic groups. Minority students are disadvantaged from the beginning and are set up to fail. Assignment of students to academic groups are based on test/grades and or

227

teacher reports which can make the difference between placement in a slow learners group in a regular academic program or placement in a more stigmatizing class (Meir, Stewart, and England 1989:33). Standardized tests have labeled a large number of minority students as intellectually subnormal and a distortional small number as gifted. Once placed in these programs it can be detrimental to the students' performance and it is no wonder that minorities fill the low academic or low tracking systems in school (ibid). Rist (1973) has demonstrated how teachers from very early, were classifying their students into different categories based on these factors (social class and race). Widely held class based stereotypes view students from "lower" social classes as failures, a stigma that follows them throughout their schooling. These assumptions turn into self-fulfilling expectations for individual children. In many classrooms, interaction patterns, rituals and codes replete with cues and clues exist to segregate students based on class and race. Simply, this segregation is often based on the belief that "students who are White are expected to learn, while students who are Black are not" (p.243). Those students whom the teacher believes meet the criteria essential for future academic success, are reinforced through positive treatment while the students who come into the class possessing attributes the teacher perceived as indicative of "failure" are reinforced through negative treatment. School segregation leads not only to minority students being concentrated in certain classrooms, but also to those school facing concentrations of poverty in their student populations. The students in these racially isolated, high-poverty schools are more likely to change schools during the year, have limited English proficiency, require Special Education services, and come from a single-parent family. In addressing the privileged nature of the schooling system, McLaren (1989:60) suggested that:

> Education, a middle-class pablum which, upon ingestion, socialized kids into uniform amorphous lumps. It was obvious my kids couldn't fit into the system, so the most obvious solution was to make the system more accommodating to "culturally and economically disadvantaged kids."

The school strives to affirm a student's identity that is consistent with the White dominant culture.

In the United States, a nationwide poll indicated that 85% of Blacks believe minorities have fewer opportunities because of bias and discrimination; six out of ten Blacks reported that they experienced racial discrimination whereas only one in ten Whites admits to having made a member of a racial or ethnic group uncomfortable. Sixty percent of the Blacks and ten percent of Whites say that Blacks should have special opportunities in education and employment (USA Today 1993:D1). Has much really changed since the classic May 17, 1954 US Supreme Court decision in Brown vs. Board of Education of Topeka that rendered school segregation illegal, thereby "legally" ending school discrimination (Brooks and Althouse 1993:19)? This case overturned the longstanding "separate but equal standard"; this standard maintained racial segregation since the 1890's. Stephen Lewis notes in his *Report on Racism in Ontario* (Rankin 2005b: A8):

> It is Black youth that is unemployed in excessive numbers, it is Black students who are being inappropriately streamed in schools, it is Black kids who are disproportionately dropping out, it is housing communities with large concentrations of Black residents where the sense of vulnerability and disadvantage is most acute, it is Black employees, professional and non-professional, on whom the doors of upward equity slam shut. Just as the soothing balm of "multiculturalism" cannot mask racism, so racism cannot mask its primary target...This reality of huge housing projects creating what many called "communities in distress" has to be dealt with. They're often under-serviced, and a persuasive case can be made for better transportation, for a Community College campus, for a thriving community centre, for some kind of outdoor recreational space. The list goes on. It all has relevance.

The cultural interests of all students are not equally reflected in schools but minority communities have also had limited organizational access in corporate decision-making bodies of their local schools. The politics of exclusion (silencing) is as Case (1977:20) describes:

> Africans have long been considered peripheral, marginal, peoples of Canada. Africans are inevitably looked upon as newcomers because schools and universities and other institutions within society do not

teach otherwise. The historical presence of these people has been successfully excluded from our collective consciousness.

For anti-racist educational practices and policies to be effective, it is necessary to move beyond the politics of exclusion towards an appreciation of the politics of difference. Typically, this requires that the monolithic notion of blackness, a form of "tribal sameness," must be challenged in light of "differences within and without" (Walcott 1994:15). It is also important to distinguish between the *official* and *unofficial* curriculum that teachers' attitudes, behaviour and relationship with students in the classroom have considerable influence on assessment practices. For instance the following expressions of racism are noteworthy because they constitute the unofficial curricula, which are not explicitly incorporated in handbooks, textbooks or manuals: a) the matter of what is emphasized casually in class, b) behaviour that is tolerated, promoted or punished, c) ideologies that are conveyed and, d) the types of relationships encouraged among students, parents and teachers. The manifestation of teacher attitudes, values and beliefs is inevitable, and, therefore directly influence the quality of the teacher-student relationship, the overall educational experience of children and learning outcomes. Despite official public rhetoric, students and parents have always had minimal control or limited ability in affecting meaningfully the learning climate in the classroom. Schooling for minority students may become very discouraging especially in perpetuating low self-esteem. When students are allocated into slower learning groups, silenced and punished because of their race, the school represents fear and frustration (Ogbu 1986:18). According to Claude Steele, Black students perform poorly on tests because of anxieties concomitant with negative stereotypes, which exacerbate test preparation (Steele 1998: 401).

Although the cultural and racial demographics of North America continue to change, public education still perpetuates a picture of world history that emphasizes Europe at the center of analysis. Many educators reduce all non-western societies to exotic and primitive and only teach about 'other' cultural or marginalized groups during a pre-determined and limited multicultural week or teaching unit. This reduction perpetuates cycles of inequality in educational institutions and the job market. Our world is diverse and not homogenous, but schools are missing opportunities to benefit society by examining questions of power and oppression:

> All students will benefit from learning to respect, understand, and values a society whose sense of social justice enables all of use to continue to advocate for the oppressed, whether or not we are members of such groups. (Dei 1996:2)

Educators Marx and Pennington (2003:92) in their research on white racism found:

> few educators have begun to address Whiteness and White racism with their teacher education students and the practicing teachers with whom they have worked through an anti-racism perspective.

Willinsky (1998) suggests that the current educational system in Canada is still deeply rooted in the colonial legacy. Teachers are still teaching from an experience that has been grossly influenced by the colonial past; educators seldom understand the subtle forms of imperial themes of difference and identity that continue to play themselves out in the lives of young people (p.6). Therefore, teachers owe students today an account of the historical divisions out of which we have fashioned ourselves as educated people (p.20), as racial, cultural and ethnic divisions are still evident in the education process. As a result, there needs to be a more critical approach to education. Students of colour are left feeling alienated, hopeless and invisible due to the reluctance of the school system to apply comprehensive anti-racist pedagogies. Inclusive education aims to have every student identify and connect with the school's educational and social environment by undertaking substantive structural and social transformations. An inclusive pedagogy (Dunlop 2003:65) replaces the extremely devastating homogenization of voices. This practice avoids the reproduction of a dominant hierarchical ordering and classification of individuals by race, class, gender and other hegemonic categories (Dei 1996:1). A racial meritocracy is evident whenever marginalized groups suffer from systemic exclusion from education and its opportunities (Bergerson 2003:54). Those in power have a responsibility to understand the everyday experience of the marginalized if there were to be a true commitment to ensuring structures and institutions best reflect the cultures of all students. Equally disturbing is the silence from student groups from the dominant culture who refuse to acknowledge the differential treatment of minority students (p.75). Anti-racism does not shy away from candid discussion of race and its intersections with other forms of difference become marginalized (Dei 1998).

Admittedly, education is essential for escaping poverty, developing skills, and for promoting change. And yet, in the mainstream classroom, the race and class of Canadian First Nations student are treated as liabilities and articulated in failures. For them, the White dominant pedagogies and curricula are not only irrelevant but have always been hostile expressions of colonial cultures replete with alien values and foreign languages. To pursue higher levels of education and/or training, Natives are compelled to leave their homes and families only to discover and experience institutional barriers that discourage educational attainment. Generally, the following are consequences of class and race inequalities in the schools: cultural biases in developmental/IQ testing; failure to deal with violence in the schools, pregnancy and poor school performance, drugs and school performance; effect of homelessness or multiple moves on school attendance; inadequate environmental stimulation; low expectation for success by child, parent, school, society; youth stresses; inadequate educational resources; "tracking" (grouping students by perceived ability); the core curriculum; before and after school programs, etc.

The State, Discipline and Governmentalities: Regulating Youth

Throughout history the image of youths as cultural terrorists (Leong 1992) has been dominant. Socializing institutions condemned the challenge, resistance and defiance of youth, preferring instead docile and deferential cultural dopes. There has also been a reluctance to consider these youths as products of the larger social order. The violence, sex, drugs consumption, escape are dismissed simply as counter hegemonic and destructive. Typically youths are marginalized; they are not persons in their own right; and, they are not allowed voice, let alone, representation. These stereotypic notions homogenize and blur diversities. Youths are to be simply senders and receivers, producers and consumers, rulers and ruled, made in the image of the interconnected authorities. The virulent and assertive school culture, informed by official reports, succeeds in transforming the youth as "the other," the foreigner and the stranger. An oppositional filter is constructed which invites attacks against the subject—youth. Distance, therefore, characterizes this construct; authority-youth relationships are mediated by notions of "difference" and "otherness."

Within the narration of distance there is a demand for manipulation and control, that is, discipline. For Foucault (1979: 206), discipline is

> a type of power, a modality for its exercise, comprising a whole set of instruments, techniques, procedures, levels of application, targets; it is a "physics" or an "anatomy" of power, a technology.

In its function, the power to punish is not essentially different from that of curing or educating (ibid).

Statutes like Vagrancy Laws, Poor Laws, Education Acts as well as more recent Mental Health Acts, were created to control this unproductive class of vagabonds, nomads or vagrants. The state seeks a banal accommodation to bureaucratic propaganda-image building, rather than the capacity to "learn." With reference to education, it is argued that the state secures control over the nature of our youth according to powerful resources, which proscribe state sponsored and self-serving criteria.

The Ontario secondary school program is designed to equip (some) students with the knowledge and skills that they need in order to lead satisfying and productive lives. According to the logic of official government policy, the program prepares students for further education and work, and helps them to become independent, productive and responsible members of society (Ministry of Education 1999). Moreover, this official rationale claims to prepare students effectively for the challenges that await them.

As with the Youth Criminal Justice Act (discussed in Chapter Four), the Multiculturalism Act, the Charter of Rights and Freedoms, Human Rights Acts, the Education Act too conceals as much as it reveals. Masking its racism, the Education Act is a calculable device designed to demystify by dignifying differences at least on paper. A circumspect appreciation of law demonstrates the inadequacies of the Education Act, the letter and spirit of which are derived from and relentlessly dwell on neo liberal principles of responsibility and freedom. Official education programs and practices, as enshrined in the Education Act, ministry policies, government and school board regulations, seek to manipulate by "de-politicizing" and "cooling-out." Let us carefully detail the policies and directives of the Education Act and highlight some suspicious claims.

Ontario's schools offer an education program that promotes a high standard of achievement, one in which provides all students with the learning opportunities and support they need, and that is relevant to society's needs and expectations. Those responsible for education *must also be accountable* to parents and to the Ontario community as a whole, for the ways in which they carry out their mandate (Ministry of Education 1999).

233

Education is a provincial government responsibility in Canada. In Ontario, principally the Education Act and its regulations govern education. The Education Act and its regulations set out duties and responsibilities of the Minister of Education, school boards, school board supervisory officers, principals, teachers, parents and students. Let us overview the institutionalized roles and instrumental rules that govern education as set by Ontario's Ministry of Education. Every student

a) can learn, every student can and should come to school ready to learn;

b) should learn in a school that is properly funded and in good repair;

c) should be able to read, write, do math and comprehend at a high level by the age of 12 as the *necessary foundation* for later educational and social choices;

d) should have significant exposure to music and the arts;

e) should enjoy regular physical activity, appreciate the benefits of a healthy lifestyle and *have access to a full range of extracurricular activities*;

f) should be safe and feel safe at school and in the schoolyard, every student should reach *the highest level of achievement* that his or her ability and willingness to work hard will permit;

g) should receive a good outcome from publicly funded education, whether it is an apprenticeship, job placement, or admission to a college or university; and,

h) should know how to think for him or herself, appreciate the rights and obligations of good citizenship and learn about character values. (Ministry of Education 2005c)

In terms of responsibilities, let us review the official pronouncements regarding the roles of various authorities. The Minister of Education represents the interests of the ministry at the provincial cabinet and assists in the development of education policy. With the assistance of the Ministry of Education, the Minister also administers the provincial statutes and regulations that concern education including those that set the length of the school year and allocate funds to school boards in a fair manner using the education-funding model (Ministry of Education 2005c). The *Minister* is also responsible for developing curriculum; setting policies and guidelines for school trustees, directors of education, principals and other school board officials; setting requirements for student diplomas and certificates; and preparing lists of approved textbooks and other learning materials. Ontario's school boards operate the province's publicly funded schools. The boards administer the funding they receive from the province for their schools. *School boards* are responsible for the following: determining the number, size and location of schools; building, equipping and furnishing schools; providi*ng education programs that meet the needs of the school community*, including needs for special education; prudent management of the funds allocated by the province to support all board activities, including education programs for elementary and secondary school students, and the building and maintaining of schools; preparing an annual budget; supervising the operation of schools and their teaching programs; developing policy for safe arrival programs for elementary schools; establishing a school council at each school; hiring teachers and other staff; helping teachers improve their teaching practices; teacher performance; *approving schools' textbook and learning materials* choices, based on the list of approved materials provided by the Ministry of Education; enforcing the student attendance provisions of the *Education Act*; and ensuring schools abide by the *Education Act* and its regulations. Principals are responsible for the quality of instruction at their school and for student discipline. One or more Vice Principals may also be assigned to the school to help the principal with his or her work. Each *principal* is responsible for determining the organization of the school and ensuring ongoing maintenance of the school buildings; administering the school's budget; student admission and placement; maintaining student records; ensuring report cards are sent to parents; developing a school safe arrival program with the help of the school council, *parents, and the community* (elementary schools); ensuring student supervision and school discipline; assigning teachers to classes and assisting and supervising them; making recommendations to the school board on the appointment, promotion, demotion and dismissal of teachers; and selecting textbooks and other learning materials from the approved Ministry of Education list, with the help of teachers (Ministry of Education 2005b).

Teachers are responsible for preparing lesson plans and teaching classes; encouraging students in their studies and evaluating student work and progress; supervising students behaviour and maintaining classroom discipline; demonstrating *good citizenship and respect for all groups of*

235

people; and acting as teacher-advisers for students in grades 7-11, for example, helping students complete their annual education plans and monitoring their school performance and progress toward their career goals (ibid). *Students* are responsible for attending classes, taking examinations, exercising self-discipline, and behaving courteously toward both their teachers and their fellow students (ibid). *Parents are responsible for ensuring their children attend school.* Attendance is compulsory between the ages of 6 and 16 (ibid). *School Councils* advise principals and, where appropriate, school boards on issues affecting the education programs and the operation of individual schools. Their membership reflects both the school and the community, and must include parents and guardians of students, the principal, a teacher, a student representative (secondary school councils), a non-teaching school staff member, as well as members from the community at large. Parents and guardians must make up the majority of council members. School Councils may advise the principal or the school board on: school year calendars; codes of student behaviour; curriculum priorities; programs and strategies to improve school performance on provincial and school boards tests; safe arrival programs (elementary schools); communications to parents and communications to the community; community use of the school, and community programs and services provided at the school through school-community partnerships; school board policies that will affect the school; and selection of principals (ibid). In 1996 Ontario government established the Education Quality and Accountability Office (EQAO) to evaluate the quality and effectiveness of elementary and secondary school education. The EQAO is responsible for developing and administering tests to evaluate the achievement of Ontario elementary and secondary school students, reporting test results to the Minister and to the public; and providing recommendations to improve test results.

Code of Conduct

In addition to the general legal rights and responsibilities, the Education Act speaks loudly to issues of resistance in school. The Education Act states that a school is a place that *promotes responsibility, respect, civility and academic excellence in a safe learning and teaching environment.* All students, parents, teachers and staff have the right to be safe, and feel safe, in their school community. With this right comes the responsibility to be law-abiding citizens and to be accountable for actions that put at risk the

236

safety of others or oneself. The Ontario Code of Conduct sets clear provincial standards of behaviour. It specifies the mandatory consequences for student actions that do not comply with these standards. The Provincial standards of behaviour apply not only to students, but also to all individuals involved in the publicly funded school system—parents or guardians, volunteers, teachers and other staff members—whether they are on school property, on school buses or at school-authorized events or activities. The Guiding Principles include the following: a) All participants involved in the publicly funded school system—students, parents or guardians, volunteers, teachers and other staff members—are included in this Code of Conduct whether they are on school property, on school buses or at school-authorized events or activities. b) All members of the school *community are to be treated with respect and dignity, especially persons in positions of authority.* c) Responsible citizenship involves appropriate participation in the civic life of the school community. Active and engaged citizens are aware of their rights, but more importantly, they accept responsibility for protecting their rights and the rights of others. d) Members of the school community are expected to use non-violent means to resolve conflict. Physically aggressive behaviour is not a responsible way to interact with others. e) The possession, use or threatened use of any object to injure another person endangers the safety of oneself and others. In addition, f) Alcohol and illegal drugs are addictive and present a health hazard. Ontario *schools will work cooperatively with police*, drug and alcohol agencies to promote prevention strategies and, where necessary, respond to school members who are in possession of, or under the influence of, alcohol or illegal drugs.

Principals under the direction of their school board, take a leadership role in the daily operation of a school. They provide this leadership by demonstrating care and commitment to academic excellence and a safe teaching and learning environment; *holding everyone, under their authority, accountable* for their behaviour and actions; communicating regularly and meaningfully with all members of their school community.

Teachers and school staff under the leadership of their principals maintain order in the school and are expected to hold everyone to the highest standard of respectful and responsible behaviour. As role models, staff uphold these high standards when they: help students work to their full potential and develop their self-worth; communicate regularly and meaningfully with parents; maintain consistent standards of behaviour for all students; demonstrate respect for all students, staff and parents; prepare students for the full responsibilities of citizenship.

237

According to these policies and regulations students are to be treated with *respect and dignity*. In return, they must demonstrate respect for themselves, for others and for the responsibilities of citizenship through acceptable behaviour. Respect and responsibility are demonstrated when a student: comes to school prepared, on time and ready to learn; shows respect for themselves, for others and for those in authority; refrains from bringing anything to school that may compromise the safety of others; follows the established rules and takes responsibility for his or her own action. Parents play an important role in the education of their children and have a responsibility to support the efforts of school staff in maintaining a safe and respectful learning environment for all students. Parents fulfill this responsibility when they: show an active interest in their child's school work and progress; communicate regularly with the school; help their child be neat, appropriately dressed and prepared for school; ensure that their child attends school regularly and on time; promptly report to the school their child's absence or late arrival; become familiar with the Code of Conduct and school rules; encourage and assist their child in following the rules of behaviour; assist school staff in dealing with disciplinary issues. Police and community members are essential partners in making our schools and communities safer. Community members need to support and respect the rules of their local schools. Police investigate incidents in accordance with the protocol developed with the local school board. These protocols are based on a provincial model developed by the Ministry of the Solicitor General and the Ministry of Education. The Minister can establish additional policies and guidelines about conduct in schools and is authorized to establish policies and guidelines about such matters as disciplining pupils and promoting their safety. These powers are set out in section 301 of the *Education Act*. The specific standards of behaviour include respect, civility and responsible citizenship. Standards were set for safe learning and safe teaching in Ontario schools by the *Safe Schools Act, 2000* (section 301 of the Education Act). The *Safe Schools Act* prohibits specific behaviours in every school in Ontario and, if no mitigating factors exist, requires mandatory suspensions or expulsions from school and from all school-related activities, including sports and clubs (Ministry of Education 2005c). Accordingly, all school members must: *respect* and comply with all applicable federal, provincial and municipal laws; demonstrate honesty and integrity; respect differences in people, their ideas and opinions; treat one another with dignity and respect at all times, and especially when there is disagreement; respect and treat others fairly, regardless of their race, ancestry, place of origin, colour, ethnic origin, citizenship, religion, gender, sexual orientation, age or disability; respect the rights of others; show proper care and regard for school property and the property of others; take appropriate measures to help those in need; respect persons who are in a position of authority; respect the need of others to work in an environment of learning and teaching. In terms of physical safety, *all school members must* not be in possession of any weapon, including but not limited to firearms; not use any object to threaten or intimidate another person; not cause injury to any person with an object. All *school members must* not be in possession of, or under the influence of, or provide others with, alcohol or illegal drugs. *All school members must* not inflict or encourage others to inflict bodily harm on another person; rather they are to seek staff assistance, if necessary, to resolve conflict peacefully. Mandatory consequences include the involvement of the police, as indicated by the police/school protocol, and the student will be immediately suspended and proceed to an expulsion hearing for the following: possession of a weapon, including, but not limited to firearms; trafficking in drugs or weapons; robbery; use of a weapon to cause bodily harm, or to threaten serious harm; physical assault causing bodily harm requiring professional medical treatment; sexual assault; providing alcohol to minors. Immediate suspension will be the minimum penalty faced by a student for: uttering a threat to inflict serious bodily harm, possession of illegal drugs, acts of vandalism causing extensive damage to school property or property located on school premises. In these instances, police will be involved, as required, and conditions to return to school will be specified in accordance with school board policies. A student will be immediately suspended for swearing at a teacher, or other person in authority; being in possession of alcohol; being under the influence of alcohol. In 2004, there were 686,763 students, 40,961.28 secondary school teachers and 870 (Ministry of Education 2005c). For 2003-04, 152,626 students were suspended or 7.2% of all students attending Ontario schools; 229,394 total suspensions were issued, accounting for multiple suspensions for individual students (Ministry of Education, 2005a). In 2000-01, the year before the Safe Schools Act, 113,778 students were suspended and 106 students were expelled. Suspensions and expulsions spiked in the first two years of the Safe Schools Act 82,411 or 54% were secondary students (12% of all secondary students). 1,909 students were expelled 1,548 were secondary students (ibid). Recently, legislation that will, if passed, require young people to keep learning—in a classroom, apprenticeship or workplace training program—until at least age 18, instead of being allowed to drop out at age 16 (Office of the Premier 2005). Teens who drop out before turning 18 or graduating won't be able to get or keep a driver's licence under what critics are calling "punitive" and "hare-brained" legislation proposed yesterday by Education Minister Gerard Kennedy. The idea, borrowed from several US states, is the final piece of the government's plan to keep more teens in school. It would raise the age for mandatory school attendance to 18 from 16. Ontario, where 45,000 students quit school early every year, would be the first province to restrict access to driver's licences. The law also provides for fines of up to $1,000 for students who are regularly absent from school and would fine parents the same amount, up from $200 under current legislation. Employers who have students working during school hours could also be fined $1,000 (Ferguson 2005).

The state enjoys a long history of inflicting violence against youth. The United States is a world leader in executing juveniles, according to Human Rights Watch. More young persons are on death row in the United States than any other country. Although 112 UN countries prohibit the killing of offenders less than 18 years of age at the time of arrest, the US, Iran and Iraq lead the world. In the US, 40 juveniles await executions at the end of 1994. Moreover, these executions are on the rise in the United States. For instance, four out of the nine adolescents executed in the US in the past 15 years were put to death during the last 6 months of 1993 alone. Since the 1970s, 137 death sentences have been handed out for juveniles (Toronto Star 1995:E9). Closer to home, in Ontario police officers have been assigned to schools as part of community policing projects designed to prevent crime and humanize the police forces. One does not witness this magnanimous concern for crime prevention, the policing of such sites as the boardrooms of multinational corporations, financial institutions, stock exchanges, etc. Why is there no "zero tolerance policy" for corporate criminals, systemic racism, and institutionalized misogyny? How is it that the great majority of people, especially youths, suffer structured inequalities? Despite all the talk of diversity, youths are seen as special colonial subjects. This thinking is reproduced routinely in the experiences of youth. In reference to class inequalities, discipline limits discourse and encourages practices which "bend the minds" and "break the bodies" of those judged to be recalcitrant. This is clearly apparent with the impoverishment of youth and children.

Throughout the 1990s media revelations continue to contradict the role of religion in ensuring the silence of children and youths violated by their religious authorities. For instance, how does one make sense of the behaviour of various state departments including education in dealing with the abusive conduct of Christian lay brothers at Mount Cashel in Newfoundland; the twenty-eight Christian clergy charged with hundreds of counts of sexual abuse at Alfred (20 former staff members) and Uxbridge in Ontario (Toronto Star 1992:A3) and in Goleta, California? As Nietzsche (1966) noted, this type of bad conscience is a key stage in the emergence of this modern subject—a slave morality.

Cultures of Escape: Fugitive Youths

Admittedly, as Giroux (1988) admonishes, knowledge "never speaks for itself, but rather is constantly mediated through the ideological and cultural experiences that students bring to the classroom" (p.100). The social environment of the school is a key factor influencing the healthy development of young people. The school culture, the student sense of school membership, mental health, academic performance, and behavioural problems are all implicated. Likewise, at the local level, the occupational culture of teachers, the disciplines and bureaucratic administrations influence teaching and learning. Thus, in addition to the politics and risks associated with the teaching and learning processes, we must also recognize that schooling occurs within wider contexts, an analysis of which requires a balancing of pedagogical ideals and formidable institutional constraints. Bureaucracies claim professional, political and financial monopolies over the social imagination of all stakeholder groups by setting rigid standards of what is valuable and what is feasible. This monopoly is at the root of the modernization of poverty (Illich 1970:4).Within our increasingly technological and skills-oriented culture, critical thinking is currently undermined as irrelevant. With ever-increasing fortitude, greater importance is being attributed to skills, technology, and capital. Empty epithets such as "high-tech," "world class," and "state-of-the art and internationally renowned typically refer to technological advancements. Recently, the proliferation of euphemisms conceals more than it reveals about the panoptic gaze of privileged values (McMahon 1998). Moreover, as Dei argues, schools are not only agencies for cultural, political, and economic reproduction, but are also sites of contestation between groups differentially situated in terms of power relations (Dei 1996:21). Willis (1977:65) adds:

> the school is the agency of face to face control *par excellence.* The stern look of the inquiring teacher; the relentless pursuit of the truth set up as a value even above good behaviour; the common weapon of ridicule; the techniques learned over time whereby particular troublemakers can always be reduced to tears; the stereotyped deputy head, body poised, head lowered, finger jabbing the culprit; the head unexpectedly bearing down on a group in the corridor— these are all tactics for exposing and destroying, or freezing.

The culture of a school plays a critical role to play in many aspects of student life and learning. In a study conducted of 22 Ontario high schools that explored the perceptions of 2,400 grade 9 students regarding school cultures, sense of school membership, mental health, academic performance and behavioural problems, DeWit, McKee, Fjeld and Karioja (2003) found that only one in every three students was in agreement or strong agreement that teachers and students trust one another. About one-third of students felt that teachers give special privileges or treatment to kids who get good grades. Less than half of the students believed that other students at the school were academically oriented. Many students were strongly dissatisfied with the level of disorder at their school: over half of those surveyed felt that alcohol and drug use, truancy, and verbal abuse were serious problems. Only one in every five students reported feeling close to their teachers.

Moreover, only one-third of all students reported that other students took their opinions seriously or that they were included in school activities. Only a fifth of students had been involved in extra-curricular activities at school in the four weeks leading up to the survey.

Between the first survey, at the beginning of Grade 9, and the last, at the beginning of Grade 10, the percentage of students reporting warm, trusting, and respectful relations among students and between students and teachers at their school declined by 10 and 20% respectively. Most notable was a 20% decline in the overall percentage of students (between the first and last surveys) who agreed with statements that teachers emphasize understanding and mastery of subject matter when evaluating student performance. Moreover, a corresponding increase in numbers reported that teachers' emphases on competition and relative ability translated into preferential treatment (good grades, or praise or care). Depression, anxiety and in-school problems were common (ibid). The organizational responses, for example, to anti bullying included the increased use of hall monitors. Schools seldom deal with issues like respect and self-esteem. Students may feel excluded because their clothes do not carry a fashionable label, because they get tired of being called dumb in a hundred subtle ways, because they can not find the money for books and field trips, because they have been reduced to silence because the school and its curriculum do not reflect their life experience (ibid). In many cases, self-esteem has been so battered that students become bullies, ignore the teachers, refuse to go to school, etc. Unfortunately, students generally blame themselves for their failure, and the school system blames them as well. Schools do not care to know their students especially since students are reminded that they have low IQs, that they are culturally deprived, or that they are slow learners. Students learn to feel stupid in school, and they accept that as meaning they *are* stupid. School failure, for the most part, is not due to lack of intelligence or motivation on the part of low-income students. It is due, rather, to an inability of the child to grasp the school's dominant culture (language and power structure, for example), and the inability of the school to meet the needs of children who are different from the middle-class norm. Intelligence is social; it takes two to fail (Cameron 1999).

Dropping out

In the United States in 1990, 33% of all Black high school students went on to college; they also have the highest registered *truancy* records and also a very disturbing high school dropout rate of 7.7%, which is twice that of their White peers (Scott 1992:43). According to Wilson Head (1975:98), a substantial number (20% of Black youth) felt that discrimination prevents them from reaching their goals. The hostile environment black students experience results in alienation, divorcing them from even the modicum benefits of schooling. In other words, they are not encouraged to participate in any meaningful way. Recently, Canada has tied with Iceland for one of the world's worst school truancy rates, according to a new report by Douglas Willms from the Organization for Economic Cooperation and Development, who says kids who skip classes regularly may have a bad influence on other students, and are more likely to become drop-outs (OECD 2003). He also says the Canadian truancy rate is a sign that something is wrong with the education system, such as such as poor student-teacher relations and the disciplinary climate in the classroom.

Truancy (unexcused absence) rates across Canada, for English-speaking 16-year-old students who are absent six days or more per school year are as follows: Yukon 68%; Newfoundland/Labrador 60%; NWT/Nunavut 59%; Quebec 54%; Manitoba 52%; British Columbia 52%; Saskatchewan 50%; Alberta 48%; New Brunswick 48%; Nova Scotia 45%; Prince Edward Island 44%; and, Ontario 44% (Macyshon 2003).

Youths experience excessive amount of stress and difficulties in responding to a large number of obstacles/ barriers in schools. Forty percent of youths in our study of 250 youths commented on their inability to secure needed services, from counselling to relevant education. They noted that they have and have had minimal organizational access, that is, they are not are represented meaningfully nor do they participate in the planning, development, delivery and administration of any services. Access is a central dynamic that influences the interplay between the student and the school. Access refers to the level of involvement, setting directions for change, ongoing consultations, shared ownership of the agenda that to date have been exclusively controlled by institutions of schooling. That is, youths explain that they have little or no access at the interpersonal or inter-actional, organizational or institutional, and structural or systemic levels. The following attributions highlight what youths identify as obstacles that contribute to school truancy:

a) *Ignorance* and *arrogance*

Youths report that administrators and their staff make little effort in trying to understand them, let alone appreciate any cultural differences. Cultural barriers were correlated with informational barriers. Serious knowledge gaps exist in the information base of schools regarding cultural and racial characteristics of their students. School curricula must give priority to the educational value of the knowledge contained (Galloway 1980). The world outside exists *within* the walls of the school building also, and, is similarly represented in the structural, institutional and administrative management of the education system. There is ample evidence supporting the premise that race, class and culture affect the learning outcomes and school experiences of youths and their parents. The array of relationships in the school setting: teacher-student, parent-teacher, administration-teacher, student-administration, parent/student-administration are all impacted by cultural and racial diversity. Each stakeholder brings their own life-experiences to the table of discourse and interaction. Youths perceive as a general reluctance among teachers and administrators to know what students want. Students, current and former expanded on the ill founded or distorted sense of entitlement that prevails among teachers.

—"They don't listen to us. They have all the answers." (#78, 14 years old male)

—"School's a bunch of crap. Teach you nothing maybe some sports, what else? If I wanna learn about life I'd rather be doin' time it's is better." (#35, 15-year-old female)

—"I missed school for a week cause my mom was sick I had to take care of her. They suspended me I never went back." (#65, 17year male old drop out)

—"School is a bore Man I agree with the black guys there is nothing to do. Like a jail can't wait to break out." (#21, 16 old male)

—"I drove to school in my uncle's car. The VP called me in and asked me if I stole the car. What that about?" (#187, 17-year-old male)

—"I regularly attend classes but many of us don't belong. They don't know and pretend to. The school is an ignorant place." (#176, 18-year-old male)

—"They're fools why give them any thought." (#182, 17-year-old male)

b) A dysfunctional accountability and a displacement of responsibility: *cowardice*

—"Nobody takes responsibility. They're a bunch of cowards. They call the cops. They don't call the parents." (#132, 15-year-old male)

—"Call the cops on us for anything stupid so I m on welfare that makes me a punk I guess in their eyes." (#29, 14-year-old female)

—"Out of place here. The principal treats us like criminals or clowns." (#98, 14-year-old male)

—"The teachers are bad but the principals and the main office even worst." (#193, 14-year-old female)

—"They really (*write this down*), they really don't care." (# 34 13-

year-old male)

—"They cowards and afraid of the students." (#182, 17-years-old male)

c) From comments that youths make, they appear to detect a sense of lethargy that invites what youth refer to as the *laziness of administrators and teachers. Instead of working with parents or the community to* improve communication, students comment on the lack of interest in anything that requires any extra curricular effort on the part of school officials. They note that very few staff members devote any energy to understand youths in trouble.

—"Lazy they "pass the buck." (#176, 18-year-old male)

—"You name it. From the teachers to the cops. What do they know about us? What kind of example are they. School ends and they're the first to run out of the." (#35 15-year-old female)

d) Despite all the rhetoric noted in school policies and governmental regulations regarding the rights of students, youths commented on the *hypocrisy* of school officials. For youths, teachers talk much about the need for human rights, cultural sensitivities, peace and democracy, while at the same time showing little concern for the rights and cultural peculiarities of their own students.

—"They pull together only to protect themselves. They not here for us." (#21, 16 old male)

—"Cover their asses." (#65, 17year old male drop out)

—"They have problems in communicating with students because we see through their lies." (#182, 17-year-old male)

—"Same shit year after year." (#99, 14-year-old female)

—"We are not gangbangers Listen to us for a change." (#170, 15-year-old male)

—"Treat us with respect if not we give nothin' back." (#54, 15-year-old male)

—"School I learned to deal and score more there than in the joint." (#21, 16-year-old male)

e) A number of youths report that school officials tend to be too ego centric, an orientation that impacts on the self confidence and self image of many youths. Self-interest shapes the availability of services ostensibly designed to serve youths.

> —"They don't care. I'm not stupid. I'm not interested in sports and that's all these white teachers talked to me about. They talk about what they want. Whatever interests them and not us." (#65, 17-year-old male drop out)
>
> —"Asked the guidance folks for a hand—doing bad in school. All that he wanted to talk about was how I can help him." (#182, 17-year-old male)
>
> —"I had a part time job at a garage and the teacher just wanted me to fix his car. When I refused told me I should grow up." (#176, 18-year-old male)
>
> —"Cause my grades were poor I thought it cool to check out the teacher for help. Told me she had no time. What are they paid for? Just interested in doin' little and getting paid." (#21, 16-year-old male)

Students are unlikely to experience academic or behavioural problems if exposed to a school culture in which students and teachers respect, trust, and support one another and welcome a greater degree of student participation in school decision-making matters (DeWit, McKee, Fjeld, and Karioja 2003). Self-confidence figures prominently in the accounts of youths. These accounts incorporate lessons often learned after some school tragedy. The Columbine high school rampage was perceived to be the result of poor self-esteem, misunderstanding, felt isolation and the effects of bullying. Traditional school programs that limit their focus to changing negative student attitudes and behaviour neglect the overlapping spheres of influence such as family, peer group, work and community. Programs are needed that aim to reduce or modify aspects of the social environment of the school that are hazardous to the health and well-being of young people.

But teaching youths is a complex process that defies simplistic steps catalogued clearly and packaged uniformly as inventories of routines. Regrettably, to date the orthodoxy of crime research has ignored the accounts of youths regarding their school experiences. Instead, extant published studies relegate youth concerns about schooling to a few ritualis-

247

tic fleeting paragraphs, homogenized within a dubious profiling of their failed efforts. Traditional texts are analgesic, forever anesthetizing into complacency.

From Mirrors to Windows: Prospects of Power and the Promises of Pedagogy

> *I keep picturing all these little kids playing some game in this big field of rye and all. Thousands of little kids, and nobody's around— nobody big I mean, except me. And I'm standing on the edge of some crazy cliff. What I have to do, I have to catch everybody if they start to go over the cliff. I mean if they're running and they don't look where they're going I have to come out from somewhere and catch them...I'd just be the catcher in the rye and all.* (Salinger 1951:173)

The search for a comprehensive understanding of the teaching-learning dynamic has long eluded teachers, students and administrators. Despite the proliferation of studies in education, the strategic and tactical considerations of interactional, institutional and ideological are woefully misunderstood or ignored. Just as the epistemological and ontological bases of knowledge generation and transmission are pivotal to learning, any commitment to teaching must assign priority to the dynamic interplay of content ("the what"—curriculum), methods ("the how"—style) and ethics ("the who"—moral leadership). The following discussion will argue that the prospects of power (self discovery, enlightenment) are essentially related to promises of pedagogy (community development, social development). Instead of just reaching out to youths, conditions must be appropriate for youths to reach in the teaching-learning dialectics. The primacy of interpersonal relationships *is* guided by a redemptive truth and not by instrumentally based rational models. Transformation is required not only in the direction of teaching but also in the attitudes towards learning. Just as thinking and doing are inseparable so too are teaching and learning, processes that involve commitment.

The Essence of Teaching and Learning

Context and content constitute an analytic framework for understanding how learning is taught and how teaching is learned. Context *and* content shape the dynamics of the teacher—learner relations. Moreover, context refers to those forms, structural and experiential, that condition the content of teaching and learning. Both social contexts (affiliations, resources and skills) and personal contexts (ideology, motivations and self-concept) mediate the message—the subject matter of learning.

Teaching is process of "reaching in" and "reaching out" wherein the personal and social converge rather than diverge as opposing interests. In addressing the question of agency or, alternatively, the role of the teacher and learner in constituting social relations and forms consciousness, teaching is evolutionary and built from the bottom up, rather than imposed by authorities alone. The emphasis is on a commitment to "being" "believing" and "becoming" aware, thereby moving well beyond the mindless "doing" of routines. First, "reaching in," the intrapsychic dimension of the knowledge-identity nexus, focuses on self-consciousness as an active meaning creation activity that connects the past selves in the present to transcendent possibilities. This self-awareness moves beyond the prevailing Western rational, scientific and linear models to more intuitive acts of knowing secured in the "power of self-definition" (Giroux 1983, 2001). As Nietzsche ([1887] 1973) observed, of all the knowledge that we seek, self-knowledge is the most difficult to achieve primarily because one's own set of ontological assumptions, intellectual traditions and knowledge escape scrutiny. Since an understanding of the world is filtered through one's understanding of self, introspection or inner conversation enables the self to think through relations, actions, symbols, meanings and other socio-cultural components (Brunner 1999). Effective informed teaching is contingent upon self-awareness, an inner search for freedom, equality and dignity. As hooks (1990:157) states, "one of the deepest expressions of our internalization of the colonizers' mentality has been self censorship." By recognizing the protective benefits of privilege and the limitations of material existence, teachers become better suited to identify their communities, their way of life, their labour, and, more importantly, their ways of thinking. Fear, however, vitiates the actions of the privileged and arrests the development of "social" empathy that is so necessary in coming to terms with one's own position vis-à-vis the experiences of the learners.

Second, "reaching out," the intersubjective pedagogic self-other interactions is a recognition of the ongoing and transbehavioural and constructions that occur between the inner and outer perspectives. The ability of teachers to know themselves *and* to understand others through sympathetic introspection require collaborative exchanges based on mutual recognition that exists in all forms of social and cultural interactions. An emphasis on inclusion, readmittance and reinterpretation communicates connectiveness. In Giroux's (1988) words, knowledge "never speaks for itself, but rather is constantly mediated through the ideological and cultural experiences" (p.100). Learning through reciprocal involvement reflects a pedagogy that is "engaged" (hooks 1994). As bell hooks (1990:8) elaborates:

> Critical pedagogy (expressed in writing, teaching, and habits of being) is fundamentally linked to a concern with creating strategies that will enable colonized folks to decolonize their minds and actions, thereby promoting the insurrection of subjugated knowledge.

In contrast to the competing neo-conservative view of skills training, critical pedagogy maintains that education *is* practical, in that it provides practical knowledge for living life dynamically, critically, and creatively. Moreover, a more critical and emancipatory education provides us with roots—an historical consciousness. Ideally, there should be a partnership between technical skill and knowledge. Education must be enabling and empowering in terms of permitting flexible thinking. In this sense critical thinking is "a lived activity, not an academic pastime" (Brookfield 1987:14). This activity is emancipatory, dialectical, and reflective. Critical pedagogy challenges normative patterns of teaching and learning and urges "a social praxis," that is, a process that helps "free human beings from the oppression that strangles them in their objective reality" (Freire 1985:125). Towards this end, difference has played an important role in making visible how power is inscribed differently in and between zones of culture (Giroux and Simon 1989). It is argued, first, the teaching – learning practices, as resistance, interrogate the interplay of ideology (modernity, liberalism and capitalism), institutions (media, schooling) and identity operationalized empirically as being, behaviour and beliefs, respectively. Teaching as resistance defies the normative and integrative efforts ostensibly designed to "conform" actors, groups or communities. Praxis is an ideologically informed action-based orientation to knowledge or truth claims.

Praxis essentially meets the methodological demands of progressive teaching by encouraging the teacher to grasp a first hand knowledge about the subjects at hand. This close proximity to, or familiarity with, different social realities enables the teacher to capture more fully the experiences of the learning students. This experiential and intellectual integration refers to the relational, positional and provisional functions of interpretation. This integration serves to validate and repudiate multiple discourses and their expressions of reality construction in divergent social arrangements. In this regard, we can speak of standpoint epistemologies—attitudinal knowledges with their corresponding ideologies—myths, symbols, metaphors (Arrigo 1998). Praxis, a theory-informed practical commitment to social change, unites ideas and action. Praxis, as an ideologically progressive pedagogy, incorporates political confrontations and reflexivity. For far too long teaching continues to serve as an ideological state apparatus and more currently an instrument of industry. Praxis essentially meets the methodological demands of progressive teaching by encouraging the teacher as researcher to grasp a first hand knowledge about the social world in question. This close proximity to the social reality enables the teacher to develop conceptual categories from the emergent empirical experiences. Praxis elicits information and draws inferences from objectively presented and subjectively interpreted behaviour. The intent, therefore, is to capture the experience of students in their symbolic and behavioural worlds by appreciating their "everyday" worlds.

Experience is important only if it is authentic. Students respect teaching if their experience of socially sensitive material is based on a variety of flexible approaches. Teaching reflects much of what students and teachers have learned ideologically in different contexts. Student engagement results from a sense of bold imagination and uncompromising integrity; open, clear and direct communication; and active listening on the part of the teacher. Teaching therefore invites the process of experiencing the connections between oneself and the "other."

Authenticity as the Passion of Compassion

To be a teacher is to become one. The idea of being as becoming is the essence of teaching. This authenticity is a commitment to resistance, and as Trotman (1993) clarifies, an authenticity that moves beyond western thinking to begin the work of constructing alternate social realities. The authentic social construction of a different reality (James 1963a, 1963b) requires the creation and transformation of hegemonic dominance.

251

Authentic voices are seldom heard, voices which move people to social action. This search for the conscious voice will be determined by the social conditions in which it is generated (James 1963a, 1963b; Trotman 1993). Authenticity encourages an awareness of the other; it does not refer to social paralysis. There is a connection between the self as subject and the other; the location of the self in society. Authenticity considers the self as a knowing being, a powerful self that possesses a clear understanding of one's place in the world (ibid). A more omnibus approach to the study of crime seeks to understand structures of inequality, social trends, cultural contradictions and progressive transformations. Peter McLaren, in *Predatory Culture and the Politics of Education*, (1995:7) observes:

> What is especially significant about these new predatory times is that the US citizens have become **wardens of their own souls** through the global logic of consumer sovereignty and the thrilling self indulgence that marks the ecocidal desire to endlessly consume...The "post modern" form of democracy asserts that consumers vote with their dollars in a free market where consumer demands determine products...The predatory culture naturalized by and entrenched in primitive accumulation has exceeded even its wildest fantasies of acquisition and has dropped its facade of civility and *window-dressing compassion*. (Emphasis added)

Teaching is an act of connecting. Connections are spontaneous, exciting and passionate moments, moments better left not rationalizing. It is better left unknown with only a desire to explore further, a passion that can take flight once the limits of language and the righteousness of reason are recognized and overcome. The pedagogic passions inherent in moments of connections are better left unspoken and articulated by the senses. Estrangement occurs once the feeling of uniqueness vanishes from this experienced connection. Teaching everyday is replete with living moments (temporal spaces) that require fulfillment in order to be liberated. As noted earlier, the forces of instrumental reason contaminate desire by rewarding conformity and by punishing passion as resistance. Logic and calculated generalizations serve to herd experiences and meanings. Teaching and learning to embrace in a normative society, to empower, to "sense" and "experience," in other words, to respect the authentic indubitably risk rendering the teacher vulnerable, confused and subject to painful criticism (Rosen 2004).

252

For students, the teacher's sense of self worth is linked to the ability to experience the above connection that is only possible with trust. To ensure trust teachers ought not to detach themselves from the consequences of their work. It behooves us not only to provide significant lesson plans and report the grades but also to be sensitive to the way learning can expand. An extraordinary burden is ultimately placed on these trusting relationships especially in situations where the student urges the teacher to move beyond normative authoritarian roles. To establish trust one cannot avoid stirring up painful or sensitive personal and political issues. It is incumbent upon teachers to prove that they could be trusted. There is no reason for students to believe trust claims at face value. Youths know all too well that there are "in" but not necessarily "of" the school despite hyperbolic government announcements regarding the significance of student input. As a student, one is never able to shake off one's marginality nor is it advisable to do so. In the interests of connections, it is advisable that the teacher too reveal her or his marginal and curious roles that are sensitive to the suspicions of one's students, a practice that is even more crucial where there is considerable distance between the teacher and the student.

Consciousness is an antecedent to understanding—knowing our location and ourselves. Critical self-consciousness is not an illusion but a chain of connections; it is created in "social" relationships, which link levels of awareness. An awareness of being different and seeing differences inspires maneuvers that remove cultural closures and facilitate intersubjectivities. Although understanding seems to be in short supply, teachers need to journey beyond a reflexive celebration of state based criteria towards a more critical appraisal of the general implications regarding the limited knowledge of youth. A prudent response to this pressing agenda warrants a detailed audit of accountability of one's own knowledge. Critical pedagogy and praxis transform the taken-for-granted meta-narrative in favour of developing awareness that one's own interpretive framework (consciousness) is part of a hegemonic force.

In schools the privilege of the teacher is not only normalized but this supremacy has become commonsensical. A shift is only possible once teachers come to terms with their respective privileges by "undoing" themselves and by acknowledging the sources of their own ignorance and arrogance. Teachers who render more knowable, more visible and more public the advantages that they have enjoyed (the secret paths), the ease and convenience with which they work (the networks of affiliation) and the structured benefits (power) are in essence listening, acknowledging their indifference to differences, redefining their centres and connecting with other forms of consciousness. Traditional teaching suffers from selective amnesia and listens only to discriminating soft sounds, and adopts a "stir and mix" approach to student interests. Some tough choices are required in order to understand youths, if indeed understanding is in demand. Privilege is an abusive site that refuses to address its own limitations and recognize the authenticity of other experiences. Routinely learned principles embedded in well revered texts contradict lived experiences. For Gramsci, the transformation of the dominant cultural hegemony is both an inevitable process and a prerequisite for the creation of an organic consciousness. Cultural praxis is a mode of resistance that assigns priority to a moral epistemology that foster intellectual and moral reform and transcend the reality of corporate and state domination in the spheres of knowledge generation. Teachers, for instance, are urged to become organic and public intellectuals in developing a counter hegemony that forges authentic alliances of different social groups from care takers to youth workers. Some tough choices are required in order to understand youths.

The cultural identities in the school (student, teacher, administrator, board member, and parent) reflect contrived common historical experiences and share shallow cultural codes, which seemingly provide a nostalgic and stable familiarity. The organic intellectual is someone who is positioned to have experienced and is experiencing, the particular consequences of living from a certain social position; and has articulated a set of problems associated with one's life and other people's lives. Thus, one develops familiar connections to effect change in the oppressive structures of dominance. It is critical, to locate oneself historically, to make salient, for the student, for the community of learners, those experiences and ways of understanding that inform one's own knowledge and one's responsibility to share that knowledge. Enlightenment comes through a process of self-reflection; self reflection ideally reveals distorted self-knowledge and institutional domination that inhibit dialogue. As bell hooks (1989:107) states:

> Politicisation of the self can have its starting point in an exploration of the personal wherein what is first revolutionised is the way we think about the self. To begin revisioning, we must acknowledge the need to examine the self from a new, critical standpoint. Such a perspective, while it would assist on the self as a site for politicisa-

254

tion, would equally insist that simply describing one's experience of exploitation or oppression is not to become politicised. It is not sufficient to know the personal but to know to speak it in a different way. Knowing the personal might mean naming spaces of ignorance, gaps in knowledge, ones that render us unable to link the personal with the political.

She further argues that the process should also include education for critical consciousness, which teaches about the power structures of domination and how they function. She confirms that it is an understanding of the latter that enables us to imagine new possibilities, strategies for change and transformation (hooks 1989:108).

As noted above, the coterminous forces of context and content are not only integral to teaching controversy but also characterize current theoretical developments in critical pedagogy. Teaching is a social enterprise that tells us just as much about the "teaching" individual or organization as about the phenomena being taught. To ignore the lived realities of teachers and learners alike is a perniciously anti-intellectual act that refuses to understand the significance of *context* and *content* as constituting an analytic framework for articulating identity, subjectivity and social interactions. *Context conditions the content* of teaching and learning. The set of structural and experiential forms constitute both social contexts (affiliations, resources and skills) and personal contexts (ideology, motivations and self-concept) which in turn mediate the message—the subject matter of learning. The coterminous forces of context and content are not only integral to teaching but also anchor the often-ignored engagements with life experiences. The self is always located in living experiences that are deeply ingrained discourses of power. Accordingly, experiences, as ontological categories, ground the basis of knowledge. It is the everyday life experiences that account for social ontologies, for expressions of knowledge and for how we are mired in the mystifications of materialistic projects that measure progress. Admittedly, a study of everyday life foregrounds human "becoming," transformations (Debord 1967; de Certeau 1988) and the generation of emancipatory principles by exposing the inherent problems of alienation. Also, schooling, as everyday life practices "is defined by contradictions" (Lefebvre 1968:13, 14). Everyday life is unknown or unfamiliar (Debord 1967; Lefebvre 1968, 1976, 1991; de Certeau 1988) whenever thinking is absent.

255

Empowerment of Teachers and Learners

Learning is a complex and multi-faceted concept, a medium in which individuals and groups create and mobilize rights and obligations. Traditionally the notion of a student was founded on duties, participation, community and autonomy, which provided the foundations for engagement. From the early classical time, throughout the Middle Ages and in modernity, dialogue played a decisive role in learning to communicate ideas. This empowerment was always related to a rootedness in one's community. Learning, as empowering oneself, is as Giroux and McLaren (Rezai-Rashti 1995: 19) describe:

> [It is] the process whereby students acquire the means to critically appropriate knowledge existing outside of their immediate experience in order to broaden their understanding of themselves, the world, and the possibilities for transforming the taken-for-granted assumptions about the way we live.

Learners are not empowered because they have been "given voice." Giving voice suggests that those who have been silenced have been enabled with the right to speak (Troyna 1994:8). Empowerment of the learner is not simply the consequence of a teacher's willingness to share power (knowledge, skills and ability), that is, a matter of harmonizing power. Rather, empowerment is change that results from an authentic commitment to *challenge that which has been conferred* on one's being, beliefs and behaviour—one's self. Empowerment privileges learning. Learning uses one's experiences to increase awareness and develop a meaningful framework for understanding the actions and words of individuals, institutions and structures. Learning for all, students and teachers alike, provides opportunities to understand form and content of teaching. "Form" is organic in nature rather than the constructed artifice of content. Content is an accomplishment, an imposed text. Learning invites a critical understanding of both reality and appearance, the distinct realms of phenomena and noumena. Phenomena or *appearances* constitute our experience. Noumena, *things themselves as they are,* constitute concrete reality, that is, as objects they exit independently of one's awareness. Learning and teaching are self-related moral enterprises that connect duties and responsibilities as organic practices. Integrity guides these empowering (learning) and sharing (teach-

256

ing) activities by implicating a) a recovery of the liberated self, b) a respect for justice, and c) a resistance to predatory socializations. According to Ellsworth (1992), there is an illusion of equality while in fact leaving the authoritarian nature of the teacher/student relationship untouched.

The cognitive processes of learning is a matter of inter and intra connectedness, that which emerges from within and with others in consultation and collaboration. Empowerment emanates from all those senses (seeing, touching, hearing, tasting, smelling) and sensations (emotions, affect) that facilitate cognition. Modernity strives to arrest or engineer senses and sensations to such an extent that today many people hear only what they see despite problems with their vision. They hear what they see despite problems with communication and language comprehension. Ideologies impair these activities by encouraging people to hear only that which is presented, leaving their critical faculties calcified in suitable representations. Society's hegemonic culture is one that values discipline, conformity and respect for authority. These values, which are perpetuated by longstanding traditional educational practices, pose formidable challenges for critically responsive pedagogical alternatives. Specifically, unlike critical pedagogy's emphasis on "the teacher as learner," traditional pedagogy subscribes dangerously to roles that over-identify and whole-heartedly accept "the teaching as authority" mind set. The following provide ways of thinking about knowing how to learn and teach. A *social development model*, requiring effort and resources directs attention to the following: early childhood education and support programs for parents; violence, poor housing, lack of recreational opportunities, health and mental health needs; employment programs that break the cycle of poverty; positive long-term and creative ways of regaining control over our own communities; and, the treatment of young people. The following changes could easily be implemented. For instance, all social institutions need to: promote an understanding of youth issues; increase the flow of information by encouraging proactive consultation and the full utilization of community resources; integrated collaboration and resource sharing of health, education, employment, social assistance of youths; publicize widely and sensitize culturally the activities of the respective government programs; invite a wider participation in the programme planning of all youth serving institutions; develop meaningful mentoring roles in all schools. At the situational/ interactional level youth confidence must be restored and relations repaired in order to pull together as a collectivity and create a sense of belongingness. Instead of constantly changing youth legislation and school regulations, priority should be given to character building for both learners and teachers, the improvement of communication and the redirection of consultation (initiatives from below / bottom up). It is not simply a matter of "moving over" and making room for youths and their communities but a response from within the communities that challenge fundamental system inequalities. Moving outside the box authenticates advocacy and community involvement by abandoning the common practice of selecting voices that are institutionally convenient. At the institutional or organizational levels, vigilance is required on the part of the affected communities in reclaiming that which belongs to them. The community concept provides more than ideological legitimacy. Often manipulated by sophisticated cadres of well intentioned state bureaucrats committed to public relations campaigns, the community concept is used to discipline "outside" participation, pre-empt criticism and discourage much needed critical dialogue. Instead, communities need to stamp out those many institutions which promote discrimination and poor self-esteem, gender inequality and racism, violence, materialism and individualism. At the structural / systemic levels, inequities based on ideologies that reward capital and reinforce hypocrisy must be confronted with moral courage and conviction. Education cannot be considered in isolation from other signifying practices.Take for example, environmental conditions that shape student feelings and attitudes, which in turn exert a direct impact on their academic performance, mental health, and behavioural tendencies. As environments, schools are encouraged to provide students with access to resources and activities that hold potential for promoting positive recognition, for improving communication, for strengthening learning goals that place more emphasis on mastery and understanding of subject matter and less emphasis on competition and relative ability in the evaluation of student performance. In the school environment, youths must be understood in their own language, a style of intrinsic tension, which is dialectical in form and content. Environmental relatedness, the convergence of diverse perspectives and different temporal/spatial sites contributes enormously to understanding and transforming the cycle of violence. Ultimately, the self is the lens through which students interpret change and contradictions in education policy and schooling practices. As Mannheim explained, education must play a central role in shaping a society free of its old, deforming conflicts, themes spelt out in his *Man and Society in an Age of Reconstruction* (1940).

Conclusions: a Text without a Context is a Pretext

This book explores the contradictory inner dynamics that leads to the development of youth actions and strategies. To understand the nature of trends and conflicts it is necessary to understand the inner tendencies and characteristics of youth. Contradictions are the inner dynamics that help to promote youth risks and uncertainties. What, then, are the inner dynamics that encourage both youth resistance as well as authority reactions against youths? Contradictions, paradoxes and ironies relate to processes or events that comprise opposites, that is, endogenous processes of change that operate in opposition to the events themselves thereby resulting in much conflict. Obviously, what might be in the individual's youth's interest may not be in the interest of controlling institutions. Likewise, what youths expect and what they discover in reality are equally inconsistent, leading to conflicting social and individual interpretations about knowledge. What youths, adults and authorities know about youth is related to beliefs and values, grounded in experiences. Knowledge is shaped by experience however defined.

EXPERIENCE ⟵⎯⎯⎯⎯⟶ **KNOWLEDGE**

From this study we discovered that youths *"know what they do not know"* whereas adults generally *"do not know what they know."* Adults "define" (retrospective reconstructions of control) experience whereas "experience" (captured in prospective moments of spontaneity unfettered by roles and rules) defines youths. Moodie's (an 18-year-old former gang member) comments reveal many insights about crime from which many authorities and experts may learn much:

> I dunno. I know the heat pretends to know. Teachers think they know. Nobody tells the truth that they know shit. Here, we tell you straight up—we just dunno. Just like with all these shootings everybody's an expert and they this and that. A lot of dancing with fancy words about poverty, this and that. Look in the papers and talk shows you got this cop, that politician, that professor, that social worker, this parent they all think they know. You know lazy people talk a lot. Liars talk a lot. No real action only hassles. Listen bro'

259

anybody bother to ask us? Instead of harassing us all the time- all the time, the cops aint interested in knowing. Bunch of cowboys who just want to crack heads. They know shit. Anybody bother to chill with us. No, 'cause they lie to themselves pretending to know. Whatever! We dunno but we still no more than these fools. Can't they do what you doing—just hanging out. That's how you get to know.

Likewise, 17-year-old Patti responds:

Check it out. When a White kid gets hurt, man there's big drama. The Oscars. When a poor kid gets killed it's not news. So what. When a Black kid needs help she's told to get lost. When a rich kid. A White kid wants something, they get everything. It's first class all the way.We had shootings for a long time. Get real. Remember the Viet Nam and Chinese gangs? My old man used to talk about the Italians killing each other, you should know that. Now people are going nuts. When you asked me what do they know. Here it is. Kids know what they see. They can't rat. Can't talk much about much – you know, the drugs and violence. "Grown ups" don't get it. Know nothin' period! They believe the crap they hear from the newspapers and from the cops. They'll only get it if they listen to people who know – like us. Cops talk to cops. Teachers talk top teachers. Reporters talk to reporters. They just don't want to know.

By rendering themselves, open youths approach their experiences more honestly. A belief system (youth or dominant adult/ cultural) may not be able to incorporate the main (especially imposed) dimensions of reality into its ontology. Beliefs need to be flexible enough to adapt to change in order to comprehend, if not survive, different "real" events and processes. However, beliefs tend to gravitate to those ideas considered more useful. As noted in chapter one, early socialization strives to make the dominant values, beliefs, and norms of society "the" internalized roles and norms (Croteau and Hoynes 2000:14). *Forces of socialization shape forms of youth identities. Culture conditions the constitution of connections.* Discourse and intercourse create ideologically appropriate subjects to the extent that the subject is constructed in contradictions. Youth, as a commodity, assumes decisive importance both for the objective evolution and for the cultural stance adopted towards it. This commodity become crucial for the subjugation of consciousness to forms in which this reification finds expression. Youth as progressively rationalized as the mechanization of will is reinforced by the way, in which awareness becomes less and less active and becomes a negative of lived value. This principle of youth fetishism, for example, selects images, which impose a world of commodities, which estrange youth among themselves and in relation to their others for them to become caricatures of dominant culture: individualism, possessiveness, materialism, consumption and narcissism. This notion of youth as a fixed trait or confined state fails to appreciate the complexities and metaphysical subtleties of subjectivities. The fragmenting subject who creates different cultural spaces of the immediate and the mediated displaces youth alienation. Culture herein is both a shock absorber and a multiplier effect especially in terms of iconography.

Nevertheless, youth as a concept distinguishes itself by not presuming continuity; its uniqueness and diversity are not solely the constructions of dominant cultural processes. Adults define youth as a stage of development, a state of *"becoming,"* "adults in the making" and refuse to consider youth as a state of *"being."* Adults supply those values for which they created a demand. Youth crime is one such adult imposition. The influence of affluence is a social construction engineered by institutions over which youths have absolutely no control. What youths know about crime, notably unsophisticated crimes, is quite limited compared to the well-resourced world of wealthy adults engaged in crimes (suite or street). For youths, confusion, uncertainty and change define their essence and for youths adults are righteously entrenched in such institutions as work, family, education, law, etc. For youths, however, their state of being involves a series of searching activities—seeking "emotional" firsts in their impulsive recreations of desires. Having less to lose than their boring and "rational" adult counterparts youths are risk takers, real and imagined. In this study we noticed that the younger the youth, the more careless and the more honest they represent themselves. For adults, youths lose track of their selves (a sense of time and space) therefore requiring disciplined direction. Adults see youths through the eyes of other adults perpetuating two solitudes their own and that of the fictive other (youth) characterized by contradictions in expectations. On the one hand, youths for adults are expected to be dependent and on the other hand, youths are expected to be their reproduced images. In this study, we advanced the thesis that the (adult dominant) culture controls youth; the less cultural controls on youths, the greater degree of imposed criminalization. Likewise, for youths the greater degree of cultural controls leads to greater degrees of resistance. Cultural values mediate the control of youths. Cultural traditions thrive on their own conditions of idea reproduction that maintain an imperative force in securing continuity especially in response to market utilities. In this regard, what Paul Riceour (1981) calls the "hermeneutics of suspicion" is helpful in questioning ordered interpersonal relations. By marketing individualism as an ontological constitution that manifests itself in the empirical world, subjectivity becomes inextricably interwoven with cultural practices. Today, the agentic (free agency) is equated with the liberated forces of the market. Procedures of free choice therein legitimate the methods of capitalism which in turn depoliticize ethical discourse and repoliticize self-interested forms of rational action. These self-interested forms of action are ubiquitous in our current world (Habermas 1987).

This study problematizes these ontological affirmations by redirecting attention to the importance of provisional and relational understandings of youths. Youths occupy spaces *in between* culture and crime. What adults think about youth is less important to youths than what youths construct for themselves. Admittedly, cultural controls subvert consciousness to further the interests of prevailing ideologies that strive to blur the distinctions between crime and youth. Structures of dominance get mediated by the discursive practices within youth cultures through indexing the everyday youth confrontations with contradictions. It is demonstrated throughout this study that the nature of crime shapes and is shaped by the quality of culture. This study demonstrated how youths challenge and rework their identity within processes of resistance production, discursive displays of experience and history that influence narratives of selfhood. Youths form and inform identities in relation to conflicting social narratives of the self and subjectivity. This study began with doubt as it questioned ideological constructions vis-à-vis the politics of identity, the politics of experience and the politics of knowledge. Dialectics of knowledge and experience suggest that youths are not sedated depositories of sedimented knowledge but rather are knowledge producers, translating the empirical world of experience into consciousness. By thematizing processes of reflexivity, we argue that individual and collective experiences constitute knowledge that is not necessarily dictated by an a priori socializing linearity. The dialectics of discovery recovers a consciousness that interrogates the ways culture controls

youths. Existential exigencies such as affiliative proxemics ensure continu-
ities and ruptures in the distal and proxal destinal path to a social and
cathartic imaginary. How people define themselves in relation to everyday
life a focus not on difference but on difference producing practices allow us
to pursue the unfolding of talk and thought.

The concepts of youth crime and culture constitute a fertile terrain
for exploring tensions of the above noted agency-structure foci. Agency and
structure continuously change in relation to each other. The connective
tissue of agency and structure construct differences in degrees of emphasis.
The problem with this is not the fact of imported ideas (structures) but the
absence of the critical wherewithal (agency) regarding how materialism
defines identity. "Structured agency" incorporates the idea of created
values (intrinsic to being, emotions, unconscious, instincts) and imposed
values (subcultural, institutional); indigenous and imported. Values are
socially constructed as individually experienced (habituated institutions) in
meaningful interactions usually with similarly circumstanced others.
Agency and structure correspond to freedom (notion of a liberated
consciousness) and citizenship (notion of herd entitlements). Agency exists
within historical and material conditions. "Being-in-the-world" rather than
agency-subject is more meaningful to us in terms of their use in certain
contexts, which are defined by social norms. However, all of these norms
are radically contingent. This truth of "being in the world," the self-revela-
tion in the material conditions involves a more fundamental kind of truth,
the disclosure of being in which the being of beings is unconcealed
(Heidegger 1975, 1977a, 1988). The total understanding of being results
from an explication of the implicit knowledge of being that inheres in all
human behavior. This study redefines normative strategies which govern
and manipulate the subjective and the agentic experiences of fragmentary
excavations shaping moments of determinism. Existence and essence, as
mediated by conditions of being (culture and history) suture constructed
differentiations and ruptures in self disclosure. For youths, crime as
consumption is on the one hand their freedom "to" overcome strains in
moral recognition and a freedom "of" institutionalized reactions to redefine the normal. The contingency of connection and the ethic of
self-cultivation dismantle cultural ontologies responsible for constructing
youth crime. The dominant ideological structures that have produced and
continue to produce the conditions of modernity, liberalism and capitalism
construct youth identities within the interplay of institutional dynamics. By

clarifying the contradictions of conventional approaches, we open up possibilities of resistance and change. In so doing we engage in processes of mutual recognition that acknowledge the self in structure and the structure in the self. The Hegelian notion that consciousness is an antecedent to understanding and liberation suggests that the self-conscious individual transforms consciousness. Kant (1996) advocates the idea that we should become autonomous individuals who freely investigate the world in and around us without appeal to external authorities (whether they be human or divine).We should live freely by subjecting ourselves to laws of our own creation. And, we are beings whose immeasurable value and dignity lie in our innate capacity to feel free and to enjoy freedom of thought and action. But, peers influence the agency of youths. Typically, institutions impose values on the more vulnerable. To adults, the concept of youth resistance is subject to institutional manipulations. Adults view youth resistance as both dangerous (the subject of the criminal justice system) and profitable (a commodity of the entertainment media). For youths, resistance is commonplace from moments of subversion to a lifeworld of opposition. Accordingly, disaffiliated street youths are freer, tend to resist more consistently and refuse to see themselves through the lenses of institutions. This study further demonstrates that ideologies institutionalize identity. Institutions mediate the relations between ideologies and identities. Youth values herein are never divorced from structure (relations of production).

Youth crime as a "text" defines knowledge narrowly. In so doing, crime is objectified according to a limited range of self-serving organizational criteria. The range of discourses used to construct this delinquency consists of ideological intercourses. What is articulated as knowledge of crime is problematic given official and media formations of truth. Both law talk and media images exclude the authentic representation of youth, the diverse experiences and political struggles. This argument is based on the conceptualization of delinquency as inseparable from the structural components of youth. A more coherent framework is warranted in approaching delinquency as a consequence of power imbalances. When studying delinquency it is imperative to shift one's own deeply entrenched beliefs and engage in intellectual cynicism regarding organizational practices that constitute the text. Only by going behind and beyond that which is uniformly masqueraded as truths, only by going beyond what Marx referred to as "fetishism of the commodity," and only by going behind the illusions of the media and the narcissism of the familiar codes of crime, can we hope to grapple with what "we" really know. That said, cultural criminology should not only be simply thought of as in any way oppositional to the more mainstream criminological enterprise, rather it should be seen as a means of reinvigorating the study of youth crime. The "bending or breaking the boundaries of criminology" does not undermine contemporary criminology as much as it expands it and enlivens it (Ferrell and Sanders, 1995: 17). The disciplinary boundaries of criminology are constantly being transversed. In recent years, attention has been turned to the criminologies of everyday life. On the one side, this may be the conservative routine activities. On the other, an emerging cultural criminology looks at the criminalisation and transgressions of the everyday in terms of the excitement and seductions involved. Presdee has suggested that one of the great strengths of the 'cultural approach' is that it tackles the subject of crime and criminality from a variety of new perspectives and academic disciplines. In effect, its remit is to keep 'turning the kaleidoscope' on the way that we think about crime, and importantly, the legal and societal responses to crime:

> Cultural criminology uses the "evidence" of everyday existence, wherever it is found and in whatever form it can be found; the debris of everyday life is its "data." It uses cultural artifacts whenever and wherever they present themselves, examining the cultural "trail" they leave behind. Life histories, images, music and dance, all have a story to tell in the unraveling of crime. Such stories tell us more about the nature of crime than a report full of statistics. (Presdee 2000:15)

Presdee (2000:30) draws our attention to the pleasures of voyeurism:

> to be involved in some way in the act of transgression as a voyeur is pleasure enough. To watch, to be there yet absent, is enough…A global multimedia industry enables us to consume many of these forbidden pleasures in the privacy of our own homes…others do our crime for us and the multimedia deliver the pleasures to us via the Internet and a growing "reality" television.

Various intersections of youth, culture and crime have defined the evolution of public controversies. Critical cultural criminology examines the foundations of everyday injustices. For instance, critical cultural criminology analyzes the symbiotic relationships of crime and culture in hitherto ignored cases as the forceful relocation of Aboriginal youths to the residential school system within the framework of race and assimilation. Miller (1996) notes how the travesty of aboriginal experience in residential schools, which continued for over one hundred years, is a telling example of how schooling can be used to engineer and perpetuate a social order in keeping with the agenda of the dominant culture. Or even the injustices felt by a million children, more than 15 percent of all Canadian kids, who are growing up poor in a country that consistently posts budget surpluses, says the group, a coalition of 90 anti-poverty organizations across Canada (Globe and Mail November 23, 2004:A16).

An inquiry into youth crime and culture demonstrates that an *anaesthetized soul* has not only accepted the ravages of injustices as commonplace but continues to promote violence as a personal, institutional and ideological solution. Contemporary tailor-made approaches and more generic strategies focus on quick, cheap, ready made band-aids like stiffer penalties, increased budgets for police services, the creation of "gun interdiction unit," anti-gang programs, ineffective laws regarding gun control, community policing, etc. Complementing the law and order appeal is a set of programmes that tend to include education for offenders, increased use of youth outreach workers, community groups, mentoring projects, etc. For the past thirty years these "same old" recycled remedies have been recommended in numerous and costly government inquiries with limited results. For instance, many youth crimes are often drug related and yet the latter social problem is poorly appreciated in terms of a health issue or as a business activity supported by well-established networks of criminal syndicates (Visano 1996c, 1999). The following excerpts represent contrasting mainstream responses to youth crime.

There isn't any question that looking at the "root causes" of crime, and funding programs designed to prevent people from turning to violence, are worthy endeavours. But there also isn't any question that once someone belongs to a gang, or is willing to murder, carjack, rape, or steal, root causes are pretty much points rendered moot. Once the crime has been committed, the fact that the perpetrator may come from a bad neighbourhood or have been the victim of racism or be young, no longer matters...I think, more than anything else, the shootings demonstrate that Canada's justice

266

system is too soft on violent crime and brutes out there know it…The Youth Criminal Justice Act needs changing, too—tougher sentencing for lesser offences, and eliminating "alternative" sentencing (such as attendance in community programs) for offenders. (Adamson 2005:A16)

Ten years ago, Mike Harris slashed Ontario's welfare rates by 22 per cent, thereby cutting by almost one-quarter the incomes of Ontario's most vulnerable families.

The young kids in those vulnerable families are now teenagers. Recently, there's been an upsurge in violent crime by gangs of teenagers…There's ample research to show that conditions of poverty, economic disparity and social marginalization…Today's poor live amid general affluence, giving them a dangerous sense of exclusion from the mainstream…We still don't seem to grasp the connection between slashing social supports and social breakdown, including violent crime…Economics teaches us there's no such thing as a free lunch. Recent experience in Toronto should remind us there's no such thing as a free tax cut. (McQuaig 2006:A16)

The above comments ignore the role of culture and in a grossly misleading manner attribute crime to poverty. The criminogenic conditions of capitalism (disparities in a society that respects only private wealth), however obtained, are woefully ignored. Wealth, more than poverty contributes to a culture that exploits crime. The poor, the unemployed are always singled out without directly confronting social, political and economic values that exacerbate crime. Instead, we could be asking the following: How does one explain the popularity of firearms? How does one account for the ease with which those in power and those subjected to that power use violence as a solution? Power does not share key resources that ensure its own destruction. Power shares only attractive appearances and misguided representations of privilege. Therein are the cultural contexts of youth crime.

What about the devaluation of life? "Being young and poor in neighbourhoods like this one has become a crime" as Elubia Velasquez comments on the abduction, assassination and disappearance of thousands of youths in Guatemala (Thompson 2006:A8). Take for example the treat-

267

ment of one youth—*Andre Burnett* Toronto's 54th homicide victim in 2005. In one incident Case Holder, Burnett's mother claims that the police were looking for a neighbour who had sold cocaine to an undercover officer, but ended up arresting one of Andre's half-brothers. During the nighttime raid, police searched the house with guns drawn, while young Andre was in bed. "My house was like five hurricanes passed through it," she says. "They didn't even apologize," she says, "and later they arrested the guy who they wanted." The charges against her son were eventually dismissed. The raid left her youngest child, Andre with an indelible and quite justified impression of police and white people. On July 10, 2003, in another police operation aimed at flushing out a wanted gunman in a nearby park Andre Burnett was shot once in the back by police, who alleged he had fired first. Police found a 9 mm handgun at the scene, but, following a thorough search of the area by the province's civilian Special Investigations Unit, no forensic evidence was found to indicate the gun had been fired that night—no residue, no shell and no bullet could be found. The SIU found the shooting to be justified, and cleared the two officers who opened fire of any wrongdoing. Burnett, badly wounded by the police bullet, found himself charged with attempting to kill the two officers. Following the police shooting, Burnett spent most of his recovery in jail until the most serious charges against him were suddenly dropped after one of the two police officers he was accused of trying to kill, on the eve of Burnett's trial, changed his story. In a last-minute deal, Burnett pleaded guilty to possessing the handgun, and walked out of court a free man. Ten days later Mr Burnett was gunned down near his old home. There is no indication Burnett was in a gang nor have the police indicated what they think might be a motive for his killing (Rankin 2005b:A8).

Youth crime is related to the culture of success, aggressive competition, and the unrelenting emphasis on individualism over all else. The antidote to competition is not simply out of compassion and charity, but empathy and an authentic sense of community. Empathy premised on a commonality of experience is an identification of oneself in someone else (Kielburger and Kielburger 2004). All too often, Gordon (2005) argues, people build fortresses around themselves because, as infants, they never acquired the interpersonal skills needed to navigate this increasingly complex world. Dropping out, aggression, self-absorption, indifference, intolerance and isolation become celebrated solutions. Gordon advocates helping children develop empathy, beginning in kindergarten and lasting throughout their years in elementary school. By empathy, she means the ability to identify with the feelings and perspectives of others and to respond in an appropriate way, in pedagogies of hope. Individual empathy, the gateway to collaboration, especially with the more vulnerable has surrendered to a cultural apathy.

In response to the question, "What do they know?" a concern raised constantly by both youths and authorities, the following is also asked: "What do they want to know?," "Why do they want to know?" "Who really cares?" These answers are located in respective subtexts of violence and the intersections of inequalities that have long characterized and continue to characterize the nature of "our" society.

> The conscience of an awakened activist cannot be satisfied with a focus on local problems, if only because he [she] sees that local problems are all interconnected with world problems. (Martin Luther King Jr. 1967b:50)

> The ultimate measure of a man [woman] is not where he [she] stands in moments of comfort and convenience, but where he [she] stands at times of challenge and controversy. (Martin Luther King Jr. 1963:20)

Appendices

NEWS—ENTERTAINMENT CORPORATE MEDIA CONCENTRATION: A PARATIAL OVERVIEW

APPENDIX 3.1. TIME WARNER

Revenues	*$42 Billion* largest media company in the world
Books/ Publish	The second largest book -publishing business in the world. Holdings include: Little, Brown and Company, Warner, Time Inc, Oxmoor, + 6 other major publishing houses
Mag/ News Print	Time, Fortune, Sports Illustrated People, Money, Life, Entertainment Weekly, Popular Science, MAD + dozens of others, + 77 IPC Group Limited magazine
TV	CNN, CNN International, 212 countries, with a daily audience of 1 billion, TBS, TNT , Court TV WB TV Network, Cinemax, HBO pay channels and available in over 35 countries. + 7 others. The largest cable system in the United States, controlling 22 of the largest 100 markets; Time Warner Cable, C NN, HBO, Headline News + 2 pay cable channels
TV Stations	Tribune Co's 16 U.S. television stations, which reach 25 percent of U.S. TV households
Film & TV Prod. & Distrib. + Studios	Warner Bros. , New Line Cinema, Castle Rock, Cinemax, Fine Line Features, Turner, Hanna - Barbera Cartoons + 6 others,+1,000 screens outside of USA
Radio Stations	
Music	Warner Music Group, one of the largest global music businesses with nearly 60 percent of revenues from ou tside the United States. The Atlantic Group, + 15 others, Rhino
Sports	Atlanta Braves, Atlanta Hawks Atlanta Thrashers, Turner Sports W C Wrestling Goodwill Games
Online	Netscape, AOL Instant , ICQ, Winamp + 9 others
Parks	Six Flags theme park chain
Other	Retail stores, incl uding over 150 Warner Bros. stores and Turner Retail Group, interests in Atari & Hasbro

APPENDIX 3.2. DISNEY

Revenues	30.87 Billion
Books/ Publishers	Fairchild Pub. Hyperion Miramax Books ESPN Books, Theia, ABC Daytime Press, Disney Publishing, Cal Publishing Inc., Michael di Caupa Books, Disney Global Children's Books + 3, other major publishing houses
Magazines/ Newsprint	Fairchild Publications, Chilton Publications, Automotive Industries Biography, Discover, Institutional Investor + 13 others, 5 newspapers
TV Broadcasting	ABC, ABC television and radio networks, + 20 others, Disney Channel, ESPN, ESPNews; Lifetime, A & E, + shares in others. International: 13
TV Stations	Ten US major city television stations
Film & TV Product. & Distribution, Studios	More than 11 including Hollywood, Caravan, Walt Disney, Miramax, Buena Vista, Touchs tone three wholly owned production facilities in Japan, Australia, Canada
Radio Stations	Capital City ABC Radio Networks, ESPN, Disney, 27 radio stations, a radio network with 420 affiliates, 61 US-radio stations major cities
Music	Buena Vista Music Group, Lyric Street Hollywood Mammoth, Walt Disney Records
Sports	Anaheim Mighty, Anaheim Angels ESPN International dominates televised sport, broadcasting on a 24-hour basis in 21 languages to over 165 countries
Online	ABC Internet Group ABC.com, NFL.com + 9 others
Theme Parks	Disney Disneyland, Disney-MGM Studios, Epcot, EuroDisney, Disneyland Japan, Disney Cruise Line
Other Businesses	2000 Disney character dolls, Consumer Products more than 550 Disney retail stores worldwide, Walt Disney Theatrical Productions, 17 resort hotels, Sid R. Bass Financial; partial interest - crude petroleum and natural gas production

APPENDICES

APPENDIX 3.3. VIACOM

Revenues	$22.53 Billion
Books/ Publishers	Simon & Schuster, Scribner; Macmillan, Free Press, MTVAtria, Pocket + 4 other major publishing houses
Magazines/ Newsprint	
TV Broadcasting	CBS, UPN, MTV Network (MTV: 250 million homes) and Nickelodeon in 70 countries, MTV2, Showtime, Nickelodeon, Spike TV, CMT, TNN, BET + 9 others
Television Stations	Infinity owns and operates over 180 stations, 17 CBS 18 UPN & 13 US stations
Film & TV Production / Distribution/ Studios	Paramount Pictures, Famous Players, MTV Films, , United, Spelling, King World, Big Ticket +7 others . Nickelodeon a world leader in children's television, reachi ng 90 million TV households in 70 countries other than the United States --where it can be seen in 68 million households and com pletely dominates children's tv.
Radio	185 radio stations through Infinity Broadcasting
Music	The Atlantic Group, Warner Bros. Rhino Records, Elektra, Columbia House Entertainment
Theme Parks	5 Paramount Pictures and Paramount Theme Parks
Other Businesses	the U.S Star Trek franchise, Blockbuster Video and Music stores, the world's largest video rental stores50 percent stake in United Cinemas International, one of the world's three largest theater companies

APPENDIX 3.4. NEWS/FOX

Revenues	$12 Billion
Books/ Publishers	HarperCollins General Book Group, William Morrow & Co., + 3 other major publishing houses
Magazines/ Newsprint	25 magazines, TV Guide, 132 newspapers including the London Times New York Post, The Times
TV Broadcasting	Fox, Fox News Channel; Twentieth Century Fox Television , Sky, STAR TV FOX Broadcasting Company, FOX News Channel
Television Stations	22 Fox affili ated stations co vering over 40% of US -TV households
Film & TV Production / Distribution/ Studios	20th Century Fox Films Television Blue Sky Studios, Fox, Searchlight Pictures, Fox Kids Worldwide
Sports	LA Dodgers, Partial ow ner of: NY Knicks & Rangers, LA Lakers & Kings, Dodger Stadium, Staples Center & Madison Square Gardens
Other Businesses	Manages the assets of Hughes Electronics, Satellite services, DirecTV's parent Fox Television Stations owns and operates 35 full pow er stations

APPENDIX 3.5. GENERAL ELECTRIC

Revenues	*$152.36 Billion*
TV Broadcasting	NBC network, NBC Universal CNBC Bravo USA, CNBC, MSNBC as well as shares in some 20 other
TV Stations	11 television, 14 NBC stations, 14 Telemundo Stations
Film & TV Production / Distribution/	Universal Pictures
Theme Parks	Universal Parks & Resorts
Other Businesses	Paxson Communications (30%), General Electric Businesses, Aircraft Engines, Commercial Finance, Consumer Products, Industrial Systems, Insurance, Medical Systems, Plastics, Power Systems, Specialty Materials, Transportation Systems

Sources for Appendices 3.1- 3.5: Visano (2005); Anup Shaw, Bagdikian, 1997, 2001 FRONTLINE, pbsonline, McChesney, http://www.cjr.org/tools /owners/timewarner.asp; http://www.pbs.org/wgbh/pages/frontline/shows /cool/giants/; http://www.pbs.org/wgbh/pages/frontline/shows/cool/giants/ aoltimewarner.html).

CANADIAN NEWS—ENTERTAINMENT MEDIA CONCENTRATION: A PARTIAL OVERVIEW

APPENDIX 3.6. CANWEST

2004 Revenue	*$1.75 Billion*
TV	Television stations in 8 provinces reaching 88 % of English-speaking Canadians, Global Global Television Network + 11 stations, COOL TV Xtreme Sports PRIME TV Prime TV and five television stations not affiliated with the Glo bal chain interests in Network TEN, which stations in the 5 capital cities of Australia, 45% of the ordinary shares of Canwest Granada Media Holdings Ltd, which owns and operates TV3 Ireland
News print, magazines	Largest owner of newspapers, 40% of our print media, *National Post,* over 100 community newspapers, more than 200 publications, including 14 major dailies, 14 English language dailies (10 daily metropolitan newspapers), Southam Publications + 35 newspapers
Internet	Internet sites
Radio	Solid Gold FM, The Rock FM, The Edge FM, Channel Z FM, five other stations. In New Zealand, the Company owns a 70% interest in CanWest MediaWorks (NZ), five national networks are Radio Pacific AM (amplitude modulation) (a talkback format) targeted at the older dem ographic
Other	Holdings constitute over 30% of a Canadian media market

APPENDIX 3.7. ROGERS

2004 Revenue	*$4.5 Billion USD*
TV	Country's largest cable TV , two television stations in Ont , interests in Sportsnet, Canada's Shopping Channel. Toronto's CFMT
News print, magazines	*Maclean's Chatelaine,* and *Canadian Business* , 70 magazines, trade, professional publications and directories
Internet	high-speed Internet
Radio	43 radio stations
Other	Rogers Cable, Rogers Wireless, Rogers Media, Toronto Blue Jays, Rogers Centre (SkyDome) video stores. Rogers Communications Inc. (TSX: RCI; NYSE: RG) is a diversified Canadian communications and media company. Its three primary businesses include Rogers Wireless, Canada's largest wireless voice and data communications services provider and the country's only carrier operating on the world standard GSM/GPRS technology platform; Rogers Cable, Canada's largest cable television provider offering cable television, high -speed Internet access and video retailing; and Rogers Media, Canada's premier collection of category leading media assets with businesses in radio, television broadcasting, televised shopping, publishing and sport entertainment

APPENDIX 3.8. BCE

2004 Revenue	*$16 Billion USD*
TV	CTV, TSN, RDS, Discovery, Newsnet, The Comedy Network, Outdoor Life Network, Talk TV, ROB TV , CTV Travel. CTV, interests in ESPN Classic Canada, Through Bell Globemedia, we hold interests in some of Canada's leading media organizations including CTV, TQS, a French -language network operating in Quebec. Animal Planet, Discovery Civilization Channel , CKY NHL Network, CFCF, Montreal's largest English -language television station
News print, magazines	Globe and Mail
Internet	Sympatico-Lycos, Globe Interactive, Internet access, data, satellite television and other services to residential and business customers through some 27 million customer connections.
Radio	
Other	Incumbent telephone company in Ontario and Quebec Bell Canada Enterprises is Canada's largest communications company. Bell Mobility p Bell ExpressVu

APPENDIX 3.9. QUEBECOR

2004 Revenue	
TV	TVA TV network; Power Corporation, owns virtually all the French broadsheets in Quebec
News print, magazines	The *Sun* tabloids Sun newspaper chain, with 16 dailies across the country, *Le Journal de Montreal*, *Le Journal de Quebec*
Internet	Canoe.ca Internet news provider
Radio	
Other	Quebecor World, is the world's largest commercial printer

APPENDIX 3.10. SHAW

2004 Revenue	
TV	Owns 49 radio and television stations
News print, magazines	
Internet	Shaw High-Speed Internet
Radio	
Other	A television production & distribution company. Moffatt Communications

APPENDIX 3.11. TORSTAR

2003 Revenue	1.4 billion
TV	Torstar Media Group Television, a 24 -hour direct-response television business operating the SHOP TV Canada channel, which reaches approximately 1.4 million cabled households in the Greater Toronto Area. It also includes Transi t Television Network, a US-based operation that delivers broadcast -quality information to passengers on buses, rail and other modes of mass transit screens mounted in the vehicles
News print, magazines	*Over 100 newspapers, The Toronto Star* , Canada's largest newspaper, as well as the daily papers in Hamilton, Kitchener Harlequin Enterprises, a leading global publisher of women's fiction. CityMedia Group, publishers of daily and community newspapers in Southwestern Ontario; Metroland Printing, Publishing & D istributing, publishers of more than 60 community newspapers in Southern Ontario CityMedia Group owns three leading dailies (The Hamilton Spectator, The Record and the Guelph Mercury) and 11 weekly or monthly publications. Metroland publishes 63 community newspapers, and jointly owns Metro, Toronto's leading free daily commuter newspaper, and Sing Tao, Canada's largest Chinese daily newspaper Metroland Printing, Publishing & Distributing is the largest and most successful publisher of weekly community newsp apers in Canada
Internet	thestar.com, waymoresports.com , workopolis.com, 50 % of toronto.com from Sympatico Inc. 50% of toronto.com
Radio	
Other	Six printing plants

Sources: Visano (2005)

http://www.mala.bc.ca/~soules/mTheory/vol3/cashman/monopoly.htm
http://www.cjr.org/tools/owners/canwest.asp
http://www.misc-iecm.mcgill.ca/publications/goldbloom.pdf.
http://www.pogge.ca/archives/000064.shtml
http://www.modern-communism.ca/mc42702.htm
http://www.torstar.com/NASApp/cs/ContentServer?pagename=torstar/Ren
der&c=Page&cid=1014656039217
http://www.torstar.com/images/torstar/pdf/annual_report_2003.pdf
http://www.rogers.com/english/investorrelations/index.html
http://biz.yahoo.com/bw/050112/125807_1.html

References

Acland, C. 1995. *Youth, Murder, Spectacle: The Cultural Politics of Youth in Crisis*. Boulder: Westview.

Adamson, R. 2006. "Thugs Know They Won't Be Severely Punished." January 1, *Toronto Star*, A16.

Adamson, W. 1987. "Gramsci and the Politics of Civil Society." *Praxis-International* 7(3-4):320-339.

Adler, R. 1976. *Television as a Cultural Force*. New York: Facts on File.

Adorno, T. 1973. *Negative Dialectics*. New York: Continuum.

Adorno, T.W. and M. Horkheimer, 1979[1944]. *Dialectic of Enlightenment*. Translated by J. Cumming London: Verso.

_____. 1989. "Selections from 'The Culture Industry: Enlightenment as Mass Deception.'" In R. Gottlieb (ed.) *An Anthology of Western Marxism*. New York: Oxford University Press.

Akers, R. 1968. "Problems in the Sociology of Deviance." *Social Forces* 46(June):455-465.

_____. 1980. "Further Critical Thoughts on Marxist Criminology: Comments on Turk, Toby and Klockars." In J. Inciardi (ed.). *Radical Criminology*. Beverly Hills: Sage.

Akers, R. 1985. *Deviant Behaviour: A Social Learning Approach*. Belmont, California, Wadsworth.

Altheide, D. 1976. *Creating Reality*. Bevery Hills: Sage.

_____. 1985. *Media Power*. Beverly Hills: Sage.

Althusser, L. 1971. *Lenin and Philosophy and Other Essays*. Translated by B. Brewster. London: New Left Books.

Arendt, H. 1958. *The Human Condition*. Chicago: University of Chicago Press.

_____. 1961 *Between Past and Future*. London: Faber and Faber.

_____. 1994. "Some Questions of Moral Philosophy." *Social Research* 61(4):73964.

Arnett, Jeffrey. 1991. "Adolescents and Heavy Metal Music: From the Mouths of Metalheads." *Youth and Society* 23:76-98.

Arrigo, B. 1994." Legal Discourse and the Disordered Criminal Defendant: Contributions from Psychoanalytic Semiotics and Chaos Theory." *Legal Studies Forum* 18(1):93112.

_____. 1995. "The Peripheral Core of Law and Criminology: On Postmodern Social Theory and Conceptual Integration." *Justice Quarterly* 12(3):447472.

_____. 1998. "Marxist Criminology and Lacanian Psychoanalysis: Outline for a General Constitutive Theory of Crime." In J.I. Ross (ed.). *Cutting the Edge: Current Perspectives in Radical/Criminology and Criminal Justice.* Westport Conn: Praeger.

Avrich, P. 1987. *Anarchist Portraits.* Princeton: Princeton University Press.

Bagdikian B.H. 1997. *Media Monopoly.* Boston: Beacon Press.

_____. 2000. *Media Monopoly.* Boston: Beacon Press.

Baker, D. 1992. *Power Quotes.* Detroit: Visible Ink.

Bakunin, M. 1974. *Selected Writings.* New York: Grove Press.

Balbus, I. 1973. *The Dialectics of Legal Repression: Black Rebels before the American Criminal Courts.* New York: Russell Sage.

Bandura, A. 1986. *Social Foundations of Thought and Action.* Englewood Cliffs: Prentice-Hall.

Barak, G. 1994. *Media, Process, and the Social Construction of Crime: Studies in Newsmaking Criminology.* New York: Garland Press.

Barker, M. and J. Petley. 2001. *Communication and Society.* London, Routledge.

Baron, S. and T. Hartnagel. 1996. "Lock 'em up': Attitudes toward Punishing Young Offenders." *Canadian Journal of Criminology* 38(2):191212.

Barrett-Coppin, C. 2003. Sociology of Education-Advanced Perspectives, "Negotiation as a Form of Empowerment'" AK/SOCI 4620 6.0 York University.

Barthes, R. 1987 [1973]. Mythologies. New York: Hill and Wang.

_____. 1975. *Le Plaisir du Texte.* New York: Hill and Wang.

Baudrillard, J. 1983. *Simulations.* New York: Semiotext(e).

_____. 1993. *The Transparency of Evil.* Paris: Verso.

Bauman Z. 1993. *Postmodern Ethics.* Oxford: Blackwell.

_____. 1995. *Life in Fragments: Essays in Postmodern Morality.* Cambridge: Blackwell.

Becker, H. 1963. *Outsiders: Studies in the Sociology of Deviance.* New York: Free Press.

Becker, G.S. 1993. *Human Capital: a Theoretical and Empirical Analysis, with Special Reference to Education.* Chicago: The University of Chicago Press.

Beirne, P. and J. Messerschmidt. 1991. *Criminology.* New York: Harcourt, Brace and Jovanovich.

Beniger, J.R. 1987. "Personalization of Mass Media and the Growth of PseudoCommunity." *Communications Research* June:352-371.

Benjamin, W. 1968. *Illuminations.* New York: Schocken.

Bennett, T. 1982: "Theories of the Media, Theories of Society." In M. Gurevitch et al. (eds.). *Culture, Society and the Media.* London: Methuen.

Berger. P. 1990. *The Capitalist Spirit: Toward a Religious Ethic of Wealth Creation.* Oakland, Ca: Institute for Contemporary Studies.

Bergerson, A. 2003. "Critical Race Theory and White Racism: Is There Room for White Scholars in Fighting Racism in Education." *Qualitative Studies in Education* 16(1):51-63.

Bhabha, H. 1992. "A Good Judge of Character: Men, Metaphors and the Common Culture." In T. Morrison (ed.). *Race-ing Justice, En-gendering Power.* New York: Pantheon.

_____. 1994. *The Location of Culture.* New York: Routledge.

Black, D. 1976. *The Behaviour of Law.* New York: Academic.

Blumer, H. 1962. "Society as Symbolic Interactionism." In A.M. Rose (ed.). *Human Behaviour and Social Processes.* New York: Houghton-Mifflin.

Bocock, R. 1986. *Hegemony.* London: Tavistock.

Boden, M. 1977. *Artificial Intelligence and Natural Man.* New York: Basic Books.

Boggs, C. 1972. "Gramsci's Prison Notebooks: Part 2." *Socialist Revolution* 2(Nov- Dec)6:29-56.

_____. 1976. *Gramsci's Marxism.* London: Pluto Press.

Bourdieu, P. 1977. *Outline of a Theory of Practice.* Cambridge: University Press.

_____. 1990. *Reproduction in Education, Society and Culture.* London: Sage Publications.

_____. 1991. *Language and Symbolic Power.* Cambridge, MA: Harvard University Press.

_____. 1989. *Distinctions: A Social Critique of the Judgement of Taste.* London: Routledge.

_____. 1993. *The Field of Cultural Production.* New York: Columbia University Press.

_____. 1996. *The Logic of Practice.* Stanford: Stanford University Press.

Brake, M. 1980. *The Sociology of Youth Culture and Youth Subcultures.* London: Routledge and Kegan Paul.

_____. 1985. *Comparative Youth Culture.* New York: Routledge and Kegan Paul.

Braswell, M.C., R. Belinda, R. McCarthy, and B.J. McCarthy .1991. *Justice, Crime and Ethics.* Cincinnati: Anderson.

Brienza, P. 2000. "The Phenomenology of Youth." Department of Sociology, York University, doctoral programme. Unpublished paper.

Brookfield, S.D. 1995. *Becoming a Critically Reflective Teacher.* San Francisco, CA: Jossey-Bass.

_____.1987. *Developing Critical Thinkers: Challenging Adults to Explore Alternative Ways of Thinking and Acting.* San Francisco: Jossey-Bass.

Brooks, D. and R. Althouse. 1993. *Racism in College Athletes.* Morgantown: Fitness Information Technology.

Brooks-Gunn, J., B. Brown, G.J. Duncan, and K.A. Moore. 1995. "Child Development in the Context of Family and Community Resources," In *Integrating Federal Statistics on Children: Report on a Workshop.* National Research Council, Institute of Medicine. Washington D.C.: National Academy Press.

Brooks-Gunn, J., G.J. Duncan, and J.L. Aber. 1997. *Neighborhood Poverty: Context and Consequences for Development.* New York: Russell Sage Foundation.

Brown, L. 1994. "Taming the TV Monster." *Starweek Magazine* (October):78.

Brunner D. 1999. "Performance, Reflexivity, and Critical Teaching." *The Journal of Critical Pedagogy* III(1)(November):23-41.

Bureau of Justice Statistics. 2004. "Young Offenders." Washington, DC: Department of Justice. Available at (www.ojp.usdoj.gov/bjs/).

Burgess, R. and R. Akers. 1968. "Differential Association-Reinforcement Theory of Criminal Behaviour." *Social Problems* 14(Fall):128-147.

Butler, J. 1991. "Contingent Foundations: Feminism and the Question of 'Postmodernism.'" In J. Butler and J. Scott (eds.). *Feminists Theorize the Political.* New York: Routledge.

Calhoun, C. 1995. *Critical Social Theory.* Oxford: Blackwell.

Cameron S. 1999. *Taking Another Look at Class.* Ottawa: Canadian Centre for Policy Alternatives.

Canadian Child Welfare Association. 1989. *A Choice of Futures: Canada's Commitment to its Children.* Ottawa: Canadian Child Welfare Association.

Canadian Council on Social Development. 1998. *Youth at Work in Canada: A Research Report.* Ottawa: Canadian Council on Social Development.

Canadian Teachers' Federation. 1991. *Children, Schools and Poverty.* No. 16 Ottawa: Canadian Teachers' Federation.

_____. 1995. "Young Offenders and Youth Violence." *National Issues in Education.* Issue Sheet no. 10. Ottawa: Canadian Teachers' Federation. (ab167@freenet.carleton.ca).

Carlsnaes, W. 1981. *The Concept of Ideology and Political Analysis: A Critical Examination of its Usage by Marx, Lenin and Mannheim.* Westport: Connecticut: Greenwood Press.

Carrington, B. 1983. "Sport as a Side-Track: An Analysis of West Indian Involvement in Extra-Curricular Sport." *Race, Class and Education*, pp. 40-62.

Carroll, L and M. Mondrick. 1976. "Racial Bias in the Decision to Grant Parole" *Law and Society Review* 2(1)Fall:93-109.

Carson, W.G. and P. Wiles. 1971. *Crime and Delinquency in Britain.* London: Martin Robertson.

Carter, G.E. 1979. *Report to the Civic Authorities of Metropolitan Toronto and its Citizens.* Toronto: City Clerk's Office.

Case, F. 1977. *Racism and National Consciousness.* Toronto: Ploughshare Press.

Chambliss, W. and M. Mankoff. 1976. *Whose Law, What Order: A Conflict Approach to Criminality.* New York: John Wiley and Sons.

Chomsky, N. 1980. *Rules and Representations.* New York: Columbia University Press.

_____.1989. *Necessary Illusions.* Toronto: CBC Enterprises.

_____. 1997 [1991]. *Media Control: The Spectacular Achievements of Propaganda* New York: Seven Stories Press.

_____. 1992. *What Uncle Sam Really Wants.* Berkeley: Odonian Press.

_____.1997. "What Makes Mainstream Media Mainstream: From a talk at Z Media Institute." *Z Magazine,* June. Available at (http://www.zmag.org/zmag/articles/chomoct97.htm).

Churchill, L. 1971. "Ethnomethodology and Measurement." *Social Forces* 50(2)(December):182-191.

Clark, K. 1965. *Dark Ghetto.* New York: Harper Row.

Cloward, R. and L. Ohlin. 1959. *Delinquency and Opportunity: A Theory of Delinquent Gangs.* Glencoe Illinois: Free Press.

Coelho, E. 1989. *Caribbean Students in Canadian Schools.* Toronto: Carib-Can Publishers.

Cohen, A. 1955. *Delinquent Boys: The Culture of the Gang.* New York: Free Press.

Cohen, S. 1990 [1972]. *Folk Devils and Moral Panics.* Oxford: Basil Blackwell.

_____.1973. *The Manufacture of News.* London: Anchor.

_____. 1985. *Visions of Social Control.* Cambridge: Polity.

Cohen, S. and J. Young. 1981. *The Manufacture of News–Social Problems, Deviance and the Mass Media.* Beverley Hills: Sage.

Collins Hills, P. 2000. *Black Feminist Thought: Knowledge, Consciousness, and the Politics of Empowerment.* New York: Routledge.

Cook, P.S., D. Gomery, and L.W. Lichty. 1992. *The Future of News; Television-Newspapers-Wire Services-Newsmagazines.* Washington, DC: The Woodrow Wilson Press.

Cooley, C.H. 1956 [1902]. *Human Nature and the Social Order.* New York: Charles Scribner's Sons.

Corbett, L. 1989. "Kohut and Jung: A Comparison of Theory and Therapy." In W. Douglas Detrick and Susan B. Detrick (eds.). *Self Psychology: Comparisons and Contrasts.* Hillsdale, NJ: The Analytic Press.

Corrigan, P. 1979. *Schooling the Smash Street Kids.* London: Macmillan.

_____.1990. "Social Forms: Human Capacities." *Essays in Authority and Difference.* Routledge: London.

Council on Interracial Books for Children. 1973. *Guidelines for Selecting Bias-Free Textbooks and Storybooks.* New York: Council on Interracial Books for Children.

Counihan, C. 1986. "Antonio Gramsci and Social Science." *Dialectical Anthropology* 11(1):3-9.

Covenant House. 2005. "Facts and Stats about Youth Homelessness." Toronto. Available at (http://www.covenanthouse.on.ca/web/facts_and_stats.html).

Croteau, D. and W. Hoynes. 2000. *Media/Society: Industries, Images, and Audiences*. Thousand Oaks, Ca: Pine Forge Press.

Curran, J. 1996. *Cultural Studies and Communication*. London: Arnold.

Cusson, M. 1983. *Why Delinquency?* Toronto: University of Toronto Press.

Dahrendorf, R. 1959. *Class and Class Conflict in Industrial Society*. Stanford: Stanford University Press.

Das Gupta, T. 2000. *Racism & Paid Work*. Toronto: Garamond Press.

Davis, A. 1989. *Women, Culture, Politics*. New York: Vintage Books.

Davis, C. 2004. "Can the Dead Speak to Us? De Man, Levinas and Agamben Culture." *Theory & Critique* 45(1):77–89.

Davis, M. 1992. *City of Quartz*. New York: Vintage.

Debord, Guy. 1967. *The Society of the Spectacle*. New York: Zone.

de Certeau, M. 1988. *The Practice of Everyday Life*. Berkeley, CA: University of California Press.

Dei, G. 1996. *Anti-Racism Education—Theory and Practice*. Halifax: Fernwood Publishing.

_____. 1998. "Why Write Back? The Role of Afrocentric Discourse in Social Change." *Canadian Journal of Education* 23(2):200-208.

_____. 2003. "Communicating Across the Tracks: Challenges for Anti-Racist Educators in Ontario Today." *Orbit* 33(3). Toronto: Ontario Institute for Studies in Education.

Denisson, D. and L. Tobey. 1991. *The Advertising Handbook*. Bellington, Washington: International Self-Counsel Press.

Department of Justice. 1999. *Youth Justice Statistics*. April. Department of Justice, Ottawa: Supply and Services.

Department of Justice. 2003. *Backgrounder Youth Criminal Justice Act*. Department of Justice. Ottawa: Supply and Services. Last Updated: 2004-02-03. Available at (www.canada.justice.gc.ca/youth).

Department of Justice. 2004. *Myths and Realities about Youth Justice*. Department of Justice. Ottawa: Supply and Services. Available at (http://www.justice.gc.ca/en/ps/yj/information/mythreal.html).

de Rooy, E. 1994. "Sexism in Television Commercials: A Comparative Content Analysis and Probe into Subjects Perceptions." Ph.D. dissertation, Department of Psychology, York University.

Derrida, J. 1972. "Structure, Sign and Play in the Discourse of the Human Sciences." In R. Macksey and A. Donato (eds.). *The Structuralist Controversy*. Baltimore: Johns Hopkins University Press.

_____. 1974. "White Mythology: Metaphor in the Text of Philosophy." *New Literary History* 6(1).

_____. 1981 [1967]. *Of Grammatology.* Baltimore: Johns Hopkins University Press.

_____. 1978. *Writing and Difference.* Chicago: University of Chicago Press.

_____. 1981. *Positions.* Chicago: University of Chicago Press.

_____. 1990. "Force of Law. The Mystical Foundation of Authority." *Cordozo Law Review*, pp. 919-1045.

de Saussure, F. 1986. *Course in General Linguistics.* Chicago: Open Court.

Dewey, John. 1944. *Democracy and Education.* New York: The London Press.

DeWit D., C. McKee, J. Fjeld, and K. Karioja. 2003. *The Critical Role of School Culture in Student Success.* Toronto: Centre for Addiction and Mental Health.

DiCristina, B. 1995. *Method in Criminology: A PhilosophicalPrimer.* New York: Harrow and Heston.

Donzelot, J. 1979. *The Policing of Families.* New York: Pantheon.

Doob, A.N. and J.B. Sprott. 1998. "Is the 'Quality' of Youth Violence Becoming More Serious?" *Canadian Journal of Criminology* 40(2):185-194.

Dorfman, L. and L.K. Woodruff. 1997. "Youth and Violence on Local Television News in California." *American Journal of Public Health* 87(8):1311-1316.

Dowler K. 2003. "Media Consumption and Public Attitudes toward Crime and Justice: the Relationship between Fear of Crime, Punitive Attitudes, and Perceived Police Effectiveness." *Journal of Criminal Justice and Popular Culture* 10(2):109-126.

Dunlop, R. 2003. "Beyond Dualism: Toward a Dialogic Negotiation of Differences." *Canadian Journal of Education* 24(1): 57-69.

Eberts, M. 1985. "Sex and Equality Rights." In A. Bayefsky and M. Eberts (eds.). *Equality Rights and the Canadian Charter of Rights and Freedoms* Toronto: Carswell.

Edwards, H. 1988. "The Single-Minded Pursuit of Sports, Fame and Fortune: An Institutionalized Triple Tragedy in Black Society." *Ebony* 8(August):139-140.

Education Act, 1990. Chapter E.2, Revised Statutes of Ontario, 1990 (RSO), as Amended. Toronto: Queen's Park.

Einstein, A. 1949. "Why Socialism?" *Monthly Review* 1(1) (May):5-8.

Ellsworth, E. 1992. "Why Doesn't This Feel Empowering? Working through the Repressive Myths of Critical Pedagogy." In L. Carmen and J. Gore (eds.). *Feminisms and Critical Pedagogy.* New York: Routledge.

Ellul, J. 1964. *The Technological Society.* New York: Vintage.

Elmer-Dewitt, P. 1993. "The Amazing Video Game Boom." *Time*, September 27, p.41.

Engels, F. [1845] 1975. "The Condition of the Working Class in England." In K. Marx and F. Engels. *Collected Works Vol. 4.* New York: International Publishing.

Erickson, M. and J. Gibbs. 1979. "Community Tolerance and Measures of Delinquency." *Journal of Research in Crime and Delinquency* 17:55-79.

Ericson, R. 1984. *The Constitution of Legal Inequality.* Ottawa: Carlton University.

Ericson, R., P. Baranek, and J. Chan. 1987. *Visualizing Deviance.* Toronto: University of Toronto Press.

Ericson, R.V., P.M. Baranek, and J.B.L. Chan. 1991. *Representing Order: Crime, Law, and Justice in the News Media.* University of Toronto Press.

_____. "Representing Order." In H. Holmes and D. Taras (eds.). *Seeing Ourselves, Media Power and Policy in Canada.* Toronto: Harcourt, Brace, Jovanovich.

Erikson, E. 1963. *Childhood and Society.* New York: Norton and Co.

_____. 1968. *Identity, Youth, and Crisis.* New York: Norton.

Erikson, K. 1964 [1962]. "Notes on the Sociology of Deviance." In H. Becker (ed.). *The Other Side.* New York: Free Press.

Erikson, K. 1965. "A Comment on Disguised Observations in Sociology." *Social Problems* 12(4):366-373.

Erikson, K. 1966 [1964]. *Wayward Puritans.* New York: Wiley and Sons.

Eschholz1, S. and J. Bufkin. 2001. "Crime in the Movies: Investigating the Efficacy of Measures of Both Sex and Gender for Predicting Victimization and Offending in Film." *Sociological Forum* 16(4)(December):655-676.

Excalibur. 2004. "Albert Einstein, Why Socialism." October 13, p.2. York University, Toronto.

Fanon, F. 1967 [1982]. *Black Skin, White Masks*. New York: Grove.

Ferguson, R. 2005. "Aims to Keep Teens in School Until 18 Critics Call Proposed Law 'Hare-Brained.'" *Toronto Star*, December 14. Available at (http://www.thestar.com/NASApp/cs/ContentServer?pagename=thestar/Layout/Article_Type1&c=Article&cid=1134515413544&call_pageid=970599119419).

Ferrell, J. 1995. "Anarchy against the Discipline." *Journal of Criminal Justice and Popular Culture* 3:86-91.

_____.1995. "Culture, Crime, and Cultural Criminology." *Journal of Criminal Justice and Popular Culture* 3(2):2542.

Ferrell, J., and C.S. Sanders. 1995. *Cultural Criminology*. Boston: Northeastern University Press.

Fishman, M. 1980. *Manufacturing the News*. Austin: University of Texas Press.

Fiske, J. 1994. *Media Matters: Everyday Culture and Political Change*. Minneapolis: University of Minnesota Press.

Fitzpatrick, P. 1990. "Racism and the Innocence of Law." In D. Goldberg (ed.). *Anatomy of Racism*. Minneapolis: University of Minnesota.

Flax, J. 1998. *The American Dream in Black and White: The Clarence Thomas Hearings*. Ithaca: Cornell University Press.

Foucault, M. 1970. *The Order of Things*. New York: Vintage.

_____. 1979 [1977]. *Discipline and Power*. New York: Pantheon.

_____. 1980a. *Power and Knowledge: Selected Interviews and Other Writings 1972-1977*. New York: Vintage.

_____. 1980b. *The History of Sexuality. Vol. I*. New York: Vintage.

Freire, Paolo. 1985. *The Politics of Education: Culture, Power and Liberation*. Granby, Mass: Bergin and Garvey.

Freud, S. 1930. *Civilization and Its Discontents*. New York: Norton and Company.

_____. 1985. *Explorations in the Self*. New York: Academic Press.

Fromm, E. 1941. *Escape from Freedom*. New York: Farrar and Rhinehart.

_____. 1961. *Marx's Concept of Man*. New York: Fredrick Ungar.

Gadamer, H.G. 1976. *Philosophical Hermeneutics*. Edited and translated by David E. Linge. Berkeley: University of California Press.

_____. 1989 [1975]. *Truth and Method*. New York: Crossroad.

Galloway, P. 1980. *What's Wrong with High School English?...it's sexist, un-Canadian, outdated*. Toronto: OISE Press.

Garfinkel, H. 1967. *Studies in Ethnomethodology.* Englewood Cliffs: Prentice-Hall.

Garner, L. and R. Garner. 1981. "Problems of the Hegemonic Party: The PCI and the Structural Limits of Reform." *Science and Society* 45(Fall)3:257-273.

Gellner, E. 1959. *Words and Things.* London: Routledge and Kegan.

George, S. 1985. *Feeding the Few: Corporate Control of Food.* Toronto: Institute for Policy Studies.

Gerbner, G. 1972. "Violence and Television Drama: Trends and Symbolic Functions." In G.A. Comstock and E.A. Rubinstein (eds.). *Content and Control Television and Social Behavior, Vol. 1.* Washington, DC: U.S. Government Printing Office.

Gerbner, G. and L. Gross. 1976. "Living With Television: The Violence Profile." *Journal of Communication* 26(Spring)2:173-99.

Gerbner, G. 1978. "The Dynamics of Cultural Resistance." In G. Tuchman, A.K. Daniels and J. Benet (eds.). *Hearth and Home: Images of Women in the Mass Media.* New York: OUP.

Gergen, K.J. 1991. *The Saturated Self: Dilemmas of Identity in Contemporary Life.* New York: Basic Books.

Gergen, K.J. 1994. *Realities and Relationships.* Cambridge, MA: Harvard University Press.

Gibbons, D. 1979. *The Criminological Enterprise: Theories and Perspectives.* Englewood Cliffs: Prentice-Hall.

Gibbs, J. 1966. "Conceptions of Deviant Behaviour—The Old and the New." *Pacific Sociological Review* 9(Spring):9-14.

Giddens, A. [1991] 1992. *Modernity and Self-Identity.* Stanford: Stanford University Press.

Gill, D., B. Mayor, and M. Blair. 1992. *Racism and Education: Structures and Strategies* London: Sage.

Gilroy, P. 1987. *There Ain't No Black in the Unions Jack The Cultural Politics of Race and Nation.* London: Unwin Publishers.

Giroux, H.A. 1981. *Ideology Culture and the Process of Schooling.* Philadelphia: Temple University Press.

_____. *Theory and Resistance: A Pedagogy for the Opposition.* South Hadley, MA: Bergin and Garvey.

_____. 1988. *Schooling and the Struggle for Public Life.* Minneapolis: University of Minnesota Press.

_____. 1994. *Disturbing Pleasures: Learning Popular Culture.* New York: Routledge.

_____. 1998. *Surfing: Racism, the Media, and the Destruction of Today's Youth.* New York: St. Martin's Press.

_____. 2000. *Stealing Innocence: Youth, Corporate Power, and the Politics of Culture.* New York: St. Martin's Press.

_____. 2001. *Public Spaces, Private Lives: Beyond the Culture of Cynicism.* New York: Rowman and Littlefield.

Giroux, H. and Roger Simon. 1989. "Schooling, Popular Culture and a Pedagogy of Possibility." In Henry Giroux and Roger Simon (eds.). *Popular Culture Schooling and Everyday Life.* Granby, Mass: Bergin & Garvey.

Giugni, M., D. McAdam, and C. Tilly. 1999. *How Social Movements Matter.* Minneapolis, MN: University of Minnesota Press.

Glaser, D. 1956. "Criminality Theories and Behavioural Images." *American Journal of Sociology* 61(March):433-444.

Globe and Mail. 2004. "Level of Child Poverty on Rise Again, Study Finds." November 23, A16.

Goffman, E. 1959. *Presentation of Self in Everyday Life.* New York: Anchor.

_____. 1963. *Stigma.* Englewood Cliffs: Prentice-Hall.

_____. 1963a. *Behaviour in Public Places.* Glencoe, Illinois: Free Press.

_____. 1974. *Frame Analysis.* Cambridge, MA: Harvard University Press.

Gouldner, A. 1960. "The Norm of Reciprocity." *American Journal Review* 25 (April):161-178.

_____. 1968. "The Sociology as Partisan: Sociology and the Welfare State." *American Sociologist* 3(May):103-116.

Gordon, M. 2005. *Roots of Empathy: Changing the World Child by Child.* Toronto: Thomas Allen Publishers.

Gramsci, A. 1971. *Prison Notebooks: Selections.* New York: International Publishers.

_____. 1988. *Antonio Gramsci: Selected Writings 1916-1935.* New York: Schocker.

Green, J. 1982. *The Pan Dictionary of Contemporary Quotations.* London: Pan Books.

Greenberg, D. 1981. *Crime and Capitalism.* Palo Alto, California: Mayfield.

Griswold, W. 1994. *Cultures and Societies in a Changing World.* Thousand Oaks: Pine Forge Press.

Grossberg, L., W. Wartella, and C. Whitney. 1998. *Media Making: Mass Media in a Popular Culture.* Thousand Oaks, CA: Sage.

Gunther, M. 1995. "News You Can Choose." *American Journalism Review* Nov., pp.35-39.

Gurevitch, M., T. Bennett, J. Curran, and J.Woollacott. 1982. *Culture, Society and the Media.* London: Methuen.

Habermas, J. 1989 [1962]. *The Structural Transformation of the Public Sphere: An Inquiry into a Category of Bourgeois Society.* London: Polity.

_____. [1968] 1987. *Knowledge & Human Interest.* Polity Press.

_____. 1974. *Theory and Practice.* London: Heinemann Educational Books.

_____. 1975. *Legitimization Crisis.* Boston: Beacon.

_____. 1983. "Modernity-An Incomplete Project." In I. Foster (ed.). *Anti-Aesthetic Essays on Post-modern Culture.* Seattle: Bay Press.

_____. 1987 [1984]. *The Theory of Communication Action: Reason and Realization of Society.* Boston: Heinemann Educational Books.

_____. 1998. *The Inclusion of the Other. Studies in Political Theory.* Cambridge: MIT Press.

Hagan, J. 1977. "Criminal Justice in Rural and Urban Communities: A Study of Bureaucratization of Justice." *Social Forces* 55 (3):597-612.

Hagan, J. 1991. *Disreputable Pleasures.* Toronto: McGraw Hill.

Hagan, J. and B. McCarthy. 1998. *Mean Streets: Youth Crime and Homelessness* Cambridge: CUP.

Hall, S. 1980. "Encoding/decoding." *Culture, Media, Language.* Centre for Contemporary Cultural Studies. London: Hutchinson.

_____. 1981. "The Whites of their Eyes: Racist Ideologies and the Media." In G. Bridges and R. Brunt (eds.). *Silver Linings: Some Strategies for the Eighties.* London: Lawrence and Withart.

_____. 1986. "Gramsci's Relevance for the Study of Race and Ethnicity." *Journal of Communication Inquiry* 10(Summer)2:5-27.

_____. 1988. "Toad in the Garden: Thatcherian Among the Theorist." In C. Nelson and L. Grossberg (eds.). *Marxism and the Interpretation of Culture.* Urbana: University of Illinois.

_____. 1992. "Cultural Studies and it Theoretical Legacies." In L. Grossberg, C. Nelson, and P. Treichler (eds). *Cultural Studies*. New York: Routledge.

Hall, S. and T. Jefferson. 1976. *Resistance through Ritual: Working Class Youth Subcultures in Post-War Britain*. London: Hutchinson.

Hall, S., B. Lumley, and G. McLennan. 1977. "Politics and Ideology: Gramsci." *Working Papers in Cultural Studies* 10:45-76.

Hall, S., C. Critcher, T. Jefferson, J. Clark, and B. Roberts. 1978. *Policing the Crisis*. London: Macmillan.

Hall, T., A. Coffey, and H. Williamson. 1999. "Self, Space and Place: Youth Identities and Citizenship." *British Journal of Sociology of Education* 20(4):501-513.

Hammonds, B. and W. Morris. 2004. "Leading and Learning for the 21st Century." *Quality Learning* 20(October):1-3.

Haraway, D.J. 1991. *Simians, Cyborgs, and Women: the Reinvention of Nature*. New York: Routledge.

Halliday, M.A.K. 1978. *Language as Social Semiotic: the Social Interpretation of Language and Meaning*. London: Arnold.

Hardt, M. and A. Negri. 2000. *Empire*. Cambridge, MA: Harvard University Press.

Hebdige, D. 1979. *Subculture: The Meaning of Style*. London: Routledge.

_____. 1987. "The Impossible Object: Towards a Sociology of the Sublime." *New Formations* 1:47-76.

_____. 1988. *Hiding in the Light, On Images and Things*. London: Routledge.

Head, W. 1975. *The Black Presence in the Canadian Mosaic*. Toronto: Human Rights Commission.

Hegel, G.W.F. 1967. *The Phenomenology of Mind*. New York: Harper and Row.

Heidegger, M. 1975 [1954]. *The Basic Problems of Phenomenology*. Bloomington IN: Indiana University Press.

_____. 1977a. *Basic Writings*. London: Routledge and Kegan Paul.

_____. 1977b. *The Question Concerning Technology*. New York: Harper and Row.

_____. 1988 [1927]. *Being and Time*. Oxford: Basil Blackwell.

Henry, F., C. Tator, W. Mattis, and T. Rees. 2000. *The Colour of Democracy Racism in Canadian Society*. Toronto: Harcourt.

Henry, S. and D. Milovanovic. 1991. "Constitutive Criminology: The

Maturation of Critical Theory." *Criminology* 29(2):293-315.

_____. 1996. *Constitutive Criminology: Beyond Postmodernism.* London: Sage.

Hirschi, T. 1969. *Causes of Delinquency.* Berkeley: University of California Press.

Hirst, P. 1972. "Marx and Engels on Law, Crime and Morality." *Economy and Society* 1:28-56.

Holnzer, B. 1968. *Reality Construction in Society.* Cambridge: Schenknan.

Hollingshead, A.B. 1975. *Elmtown's Youth and Elmtown Revisited.* New York: John Wiley and Son.

Horkheimer, M. and T. Adorno. 1989. *Dialectic of Enlightenment.* Palo Alto, CA: Stanford University Press.

Hook, S. 1933. *Towards the Understanding of Karl Marx: A Revolutionary Interpretation.* Ann Arbor: University of Michigan.

hooks, b. 1981. *Ain't I a Woman.* Boston: South End Press.

_____. 1984. *Feminist Theory: From Margin to Center.* Boston: South End Press.

_____. 1989. *Talking Back: Thinking Feminist, Thinking Black.* Boston: South End.

_____. 1990. *Yearning: Race, Gender, and Cultural Politics.* Boston: South End.

_____. 1994. *Teaching to Transgress: Education as the Practice of Freedom.* New York: Routledge.

Horowitz, I. 1964. "A Postscript to the Anarchists." *The Anarchists.* New York: Dell.

Howard, I. 2002. "Power Sources: On Party, Gender, Race and Class. TV News Looks to the Most Powerful Groups." *Extra!*, May/June. Available at (http://www.fair.org/extra/0205/power_sources.html).

Huesmann, L., J. Moise-Titus, C.L. Podolski, and L.D. Eron. 2003. "Longitudinal Relations between Children's Exposure to TV Violence and Their Aggressive and Violent Behavior in Young Adulthood: 1977-1992." *Developmental Psychology* 39(2):201-221.

Huffman, T. 2004. "Fewer Youths Behind Bars." *Toronto Star,* October 14, 2004, A8.

Hunt, A. 1993. *Explorations in Law and Society: Toward a Constitutive Theory of Law.* New York: Routledge.

Hunter, C. St. J. 1987. "Myths & Realities of Literacy/Illiteracy." *Convergence* 20(1):23-35.

Husserl, E. 1962. *The Ideas.* New York: Collier.

_____. 1970. *The Idea of Phenomenology.* Hague: Martinus Nijhoff.

Illich, I. 1970. *Deschooling Society.* New York: Harper and Row.

Inciardi, J. 980. *Radical Criminology.* Beverly Hills: Sage.

Innis, H. 1951. *The Bias of Communication.* Toronto: University of Toronto Press.

Irigaray, L. 1985. *This Sex Is Not One.* Ithaca: Cornell University Press.

Jackson. T.J. 1985. "The Concept of Cultural Hegemony: Problems and Possibilities." *The American Historical Review* 90(June):567-593.

Jakubowski, L. and L. Visano. 2002. *Teaching Controversy.* Halifax: Fernwood.

James, C.E. 1997. "Contradictory Tensions in the Experiences of African Canadian in a Faculty of Education with an Access Program." *Canadian Journal of Education* 22(2):158-174.

James, C.L.R. 1963a. *The Black Jacobins.* New York: Vintage.

James, C.L.R. 1963b. *Beyond A Boundary.* London: Hutchinson.

James W. 1981 [1890]. *The Principles of Psychology.* Cambridge, MA: Harvard University Press.

Jouve, N.W. 1991. *White Woman Speaks With Forked Tongue: Criticism as Autobiography.* London: Routledge.

Jung, C. G. 1945. "The Relations between the Ego and the Unconscious." In H. Read, M. Fordham, and G. Adler (eds.). *The Collected Works of C.G. Jung.* Princeton, NJ: Princeton University Press.

_____. 1966. [1917]. "Two Essays on Analytical Psychology." In H. Read, M. Fordham, and G. Adler (eds.). *The Collected Works of C. G. Jung.* Vol. 7. Princeton, NJ: Princeton University Press.

_____. 1968. "Aion: Researches into the Phenomenology of the Self." In H. Read, M. Fordham, and G. Adler (eds.). *The Collected Works of C.G. Jung.* Vol. 9ii. Princeton, NJ: Princeton University Press.

_____. 1969. "The Structure and Dynamics of the Psyche." In H. Read, M. Fordham, and G. Adler (eds.). *The Collected Works of C. G. Jung.* Vol. 8. Princeton, NJ: Princeton University Press.

_____. 1971. "Psychological Types." In H. Read, M. Fordham, and G. Adler (eds.). *The Collected Works of C.G. Jung.* Vol. 6. Princeton, NJ: Princeton University Press.

Kant, I. 1996. *Critique of Pure Reason*. Indianapolis: Hackett.

_____. 1998. *Immanuel Kant: Critique of Pure Reason*. Cambridge: Cambridge University Press.

_____. 1998. *Groundwork of the Metaphysics of Morals*. New York: Cambridge University Press.

Katz, J. 1978. *White Awareness*. Norman, OK: University of Oklahoma Press.

Key, W.B. 1981. *Subliminal Seduction*. New York: Signet.

Kidd, K. 2005. "How Canada's Media Landscape has Shifted." *Toronto Star,* December 3. Available at (http://www.thestar.com/NASA pp/cs/ContentServer?pagename=thestar/Layout/Article_Type1&c= Article&cid=1133566817806&call_pageid=970599119419).

Kielburger, C. and M. Kielburger. 2004. *Me to We: Turning Self-Help on Its Head.* Toronto: John Wiley & Sons.

King, M.L. Jr. 1963. *The Strength to Love*. New York: Harper and Row.

_____. 1964. *Why We Can't Wait*. New York: Harper and Row.

_____. 1967a. *Where Do We Go From Here?* New York: Harper and Row.

_____. 1967b. *The Trumpet of Conscience*. New York: Harper and Row.

Kirkpatrick, F.G. 1986. *Community: A Trinity of Models*. Washington, DC: Georgetown University Press.

Kitsuse, J. 1964. "Societal Reaction to Deviant Behaviour: Problems of Theory and Method." In H. Becker (ed.). *The Other Side*. New York: Free Press.

Klockars, C. 1978. "The Contemporary Crises of Marxist Criminology." *Criminology* 16(3):477-515.

Koch, G. and S. Clarke. 1976. "The Influence of Income and Other Factors on Whether Criminal Defendants Go to Prison." *Law and Society Review* 2(1)Fall:57-93.

Kohut, H. 1977. *The Restoration of the Self.* New York: International Universities Press.

Kristeva, J. 1982. *Powers of Horror: An Essay on Abjection*. New York: Columbia University Press.

_____. 1991. *Strangers to Ourselves*. New York: Columbia University Press.

Kunjufu, J. 1984. *Developing Positive Self Images and Discipline in Black Children*. Chicago: African American Images.

Labaree, D.F. 1997. "Public Goods, Private Goods: The American Struggle over Education Goals." *American Educational Research Journal* 34(1):39-81.

Lacan, J. 1968. *The Language of the Self: The Function of Language in Psychoanalysis*. Baltimore: The Johns Hopkins University Press.

Lacan, J. 1977. *Ecrits: A Selection*. New York: Norton.

_____. 1988. *The Seminar of Jacques Lacan. Book II: The Ego in Freud's Theory and in the Technique of Psychoanalysis (1954-1955)*. New York: Norton.

Laclau, E. and C. Mouffe. 1985. *Hegemony and Socialist Strategy: Towards a Radical Democratic*. New York: New Left Books.

Large, M. 2005. "Lee Takes Aim at Rap, NCAA, Rice" *Macon Telegraph*. Posted on February 5, 2005 at (http://www.macon.com/mld/telegraph/10822497.htm).

Leahy, D.G. 1994. *Novitas Mundi: Perception of the History of Being*. Albany, NY: State University of New York Press.

Lefebvre, H. 1968. *Dialectical Materialism*. London: Jonathan Cape.

_____. 1971. *Everyday Life in the Modern World*. Harmondsworth, UK: Allen Lane.

_____. 1976. *The Survival of Capitalism*. London: Allison and Busby.

_____. 1991a. *Critique of Everyday Life*. London: Verso.

_____. 1991b. *The Production of Space*. Oxford: Blackwell.

Lemke, J.L. 1988. "Text Structure and Text Semantics." In E. Steiner and R. Veltman (eds.). *Pragmatics, Discourse and Text*. London: Pinter.

Leong, L. 1992. "Cultural Resistance: The Cultural Terrorism of British Male Working-Class Youth." *Current Perspectives in Social Theory* 12:29-58.

Levinas, E. 1961. *Totality and Infinity: An Essay on Exteriority*. Pittsburgh: Duquesne University Press.

_____. 1985. *Ethics and Infinity: Conversations with Philippe Nemo*. Pittsburgh: Duquesne University Press.

_____. 1997. *Otherwise than Being, or Beyond Essence*. Boston: Kluwer.

Lieber, M. 1994. "A Comparison of Juvenile Court Outcomes for Native Americans, African Americans, and Whites." *Justice Quarterly* 11(June):257-279.

Liska, A. 1987. *Perspectives on Deviance*. Englewood Cliffs: Prentice-Hall.

Livingstone, D.W. 1998. *The Education-Jobs Gap: Underemployment or Economic Democracy*. Boulder, CO: Westview Press.

Lofland, J. 1969. *Deviance and Identity*. Englewood Cliffs: Prentice-Hall.

_____. 1996. *Social Movement Organizations: Guide to Research on Insurgent Realities*. Aldine De Gruyter.

_____. 1985. *Protest.* New Brunswick, NJ: Transaction.

Lukács, G. 1971 [1923]. *History and Class Consciousness.* London: Merlin Press.

Lyman, S. and M. Scott. 1970a. *Revolt of the Students.* Columbus: Charles E. Merrill.

_____. 1970b. *The Sociology of the Absurd.* New York: Appleton-Century-Crofts.

Lyotard, J.F. 1984. *The Postmodern Condition: A Report on Knowledge.* Manchester: Manchester University Press.

_____. 1991. *The Inhuman: Reflections on Time.* Cambridge: Polity Press.

MacKinnon, C. 1989. *Toward A Feminist Theory of the State.* Cambridge: Harvard University Press.

Macyshon, J. 2003. "One in Four Canadian Students Misses Class Regularly." CTV, Oct 15. Available at (http://www.ctv.ca/servlet/ArticleNews/story/CTVNews/1066180234014_61589434©Copyright2002-2006BellGlobemediaInc).

Malatesta, E. 1949 [1907]. *Anarchy.* London: Freedom Press.

Mannheim, K. 1936. *Ideology and Utopia.* London: Routledge & Kegan Paul.

_____. 1940. *Man and Society in an Age of Reconstruction.* London: Routledge & Kegan Paul.

Manning, P. 1991. "Strands in the Postmodern Rope: Ethnographic Themes." In N. Denzin (ed.). *12 Studies in Symbolic Interactionism.* Greenwich, CT: JAI.

Marcuse, H. 1969 [1955]. *Eros and Civilization.* Boston: Beacon.

_____. 1972 [1964]. *One Dimensional Man.* Boston: Beacon.

Martin, K. 1947. *The Press the Public Wants.* London: Hogarth.

Marx, K. 1930 [1847]. *The Poverty of Philosophy.* New York: International.

_____. 1956. *Selected Writings in Sociology and Social Philosophy.* London: Watts and Company.

_____. 1964 [1844]. *The Economic and Philosophic Manuscripts of 1844.* New York: International Publishers.

_____. 1965 [1848]. *The Communist Manifesto.* Chicago: Gateway.

_____. 1969 [1848]. *Selected Works. Vol. I.* Moscow: Progress Publishing.

_____. 1969a [1857]. *Capital. Volumes I, II, III. A Critique of Political Economy.* Moscow: Progress Publishers.

_____. 1969b. [1852]. "The Eighteenth Brumaire of Louis Bonaparte." In K. Marx and F. Engels. *Selected Works. Vol. I* Moscow: Progress Publishing.

_____. 1969c. "The Productivity of Crime." In K.Marx. *Theories of Surplus Value. Vol. I.* Moscow: Foreign Languages Publishing.

_____. 1978. *The Marx-Engels Reader.* R. Tucker (ed.). New York: W.W. Morton.

Marx, K. and F. Engels. 1960 [1947]. *The German Ideology.* New York: International.

_____. 1962. *Selected Works.* Moscow: Foreign Language Press.

Marx, S. and J. Pennington. 2003. "Pedagogies of Critical Race Theory: Experimentations with White Preservice Teachers." *Qualitative Studies in Education* 16(1):91-110.

Mastronardi, M. 2003. "Adolescence and Media." *Journal of Language and Social Psychology* 22(1):83-93.

Matza, D. 1964. *Delinquency and Drift.* New York: J. Wiley.

_____. 1969. *Becoming Deviant.* Englewood Cliffs: Prentice-Hall.

Matza, D. and G. Sykes. 1961. "Juvenile Delinquency and Subterranean Values." *American Sociological Review* 26(October):712-719.

Matza, D. and G. Sykes. 1970. "Techniques of Delinquency." In M. Wolfgang, M. Savitz, and N. Johnston (eds.). *Sociology of Crime and Delinquency.* New York: J. Wiley.

McChesney, R. 1997. "The Global Media Giants: We are the World Fair." *Extra!* November/December. Available at (http://www.fair.org/index.php?page=1406).

McLaren, P. 1989. *Life in Schools.* Toronto: Irwin.

McLaren. P. 1995. "Predatory Culture and the Politics of Education." *Cultural Studies Times* 1(3):1-17.

McLuhan, H.M. 1964. *Understanding Media: The Extensions of Man.* New York: Mentor.

McLuhan, H. Marshall, with Q. Fiore, and J. Angel. 1967. *The Medium is the Message: An Inventory of Effects.* New York: Bantam.

McMahon S. 1998. *Women, Crime and Culture.* Toronto: Canadian Scholars' Press.

McQuaig, L. 2006. "There is a Deadly Cost to Cutting Social Programs." January 1, *Toronto Star,* A16.

McNeely, C. 1995. "Perceptions of the Criminal Justice System: Television Imagery and Public Knowledge in the United States." *Journal of Criminal Justice and Popular Culture* 3(1):120.

McNeely, C. 1996. "Understanding Culture in a Changing World: A Sociological Perspective." *Journal of Criminal Justice and Popular Culture* 4(1):2-11.

298

McPhail, T. 1981. *Electronic Colonialism.* Beverly Hills: Sage Library of Social Research.

Mead, G. 1934. *Mind, Self and Society.* Chicago: University of Chicago Press.

Meir, K., J. Stewart, and R. England. 1989. *Race, Class and Education: The Politics of Second-Generation Discrimination.* Madison Wisconsin: University of Wisconsin Press.

Mensah, J. 2002. *Black Canadians History, Experience, Social Conditions.* Halifax: Fernwood Publishing.

Merleau-Ponty, M.1964. *The Primacy of Perception.* Evanston Ill.: Northwestern University Press.

Merrignton, J. 1968. "Theory and Practice in Gramsci's Marxism." *Sociologist Register,* pp.145-176.

Merton, R.K. 1957. *Social Theory and Social Structure.* New York: Free Press.

Meyrowitz, J. 1985. *No Sense of Place: The Impact of Electronic Media on Social Behavior.* New York: Oxford University Press.

_____. 1992. "Television: The Shared Arena." In H. Holmes and D. Taras (eds.). *Seeing Ourselves, Media Power and Policy in Canada.* Toronto: Harcourt, Brace Jovanovich.

_____. 1993. "Images of Media: Hidden Ferment—and Harmony—In the Field." *Journal of Communication* 43(3):55-66.

Michalowski, R. 1985. *Order, Law and Crime.* New York: Random House.

Miller, J.R. 1996. *Shingwauk's Vision: A History of Native Residential Schools.* Toronto: University of Toronto Press.

Miller, H. 1945. "The Soul of Anaesthesia." In H. Mille. *The Air-Conditioned Nightmare.* New York: New Directions Publishing Corporation.

Milovanovic, D. 1997. *Chaos, Crime, and Social Justice.* Westport, CT: Greenwood Press.

Minh-Ha, T.T. 1992. *Framer Framed.* New York: Routledge.

Ministry of Education. 1999. *The Ontario Secondary Schools Grades 9 to 12 Program and Diploma Requirements.* Ministry of Education and Training. Toronto: Queen's Printer.

_____. 2001. *Code of Conduct.* Ministry of Education and Training. Toronto: Queen's Printer.

_____. 2005a. Minister's Office News Release. "McGuinty Government Releases Data on School Discipline Launches Public Review of

Safe Schools Act, Consultations Across The Province Underway." Toronto, November 23. Queen's Park.

_____. 2005b. "Who's Responsible For Your Child's Education? Fact Sheet." Ministry of Education. Toronto: Queen's Printer.

_____. 2005c. "Safer Schools...Safer Communities, Safe Schools Action Team." November. Discussion Guide. Policy and Program Branch. Toronto: Queen's Printer.

Molnar, A. 1989. "Racism in America: A Continuing Dilemma." *Educational Leadership* October:71-72.

Moog, C. 1990. *Are They Selling Her Lips: Advertising and Identity.* New York: William Morrow.

Mouffe, C. 1988. "Hegemony and New Political Subjects: Toward a New Concept of Democracy." In C. Nelson and L. Grossberg (eds.). *Marxism and the Interpretation of Culture.* Urbana: University of Illinois.

National Anti-Poverty Organization. 2004. *Introduction to Youth Poverty.* Report Ottawa: National Anti-Poverty Organization.

Nettler, G. 1974. *Explaining Crime.* New York: McGraw-Hill.

Nietzsche, F. 1966 [1886]. *Beyond Good and Evil.* New York: Random House.

_____. 1967 [1872]. *The Birth of Tragedy.* New York: Random House.

_____. 1968. [1901]. *The Will to Power.* New York: Random House.

_____. 1973 [1887]. *On the Genealogy of Morals.* New York: Vintage Books.

_____. 1986. [1878]. *Human All Too Human: A Book for Free Spirits.* Cambridge: Cambridge University Press.

Nordentoft, K. 1978. *Kierkegaard's Psychology.* Pittsburgh, PA: Duquesne University Press.

Oakes, J. 1985. *Keeping Track.* New Haven: Yale University Press.

OECD. 2003. *Student Engagement at School: Results from PISA (Program for International Student Assessment).* Paris: Organization for Economic Cooperation and Development.

Office of Juvenile Justice and Delinquency Prevention. 2004. *OJJDP Statistical Briefing Book.* August 1. Available at (http://ojjdp. ncjrs.org/ojstatbb/crime/qa05302.asp?qaDate=20040801).

Office of Juvenile Justice and Delinquency Prevention. 2004a. *OJJDP Bulletin.* "Juvenile Arrests 2002." Available at (http://www.ncjrs. org/html/ojjdp/204608/contents.html).

Office of Juvenile Justice and Delinquency Prevention. 2004b. OJJDP Bulletin. Available at (http://www.ojp.usdoj.gov/bjs/cvictgen.htm).

Office of the Premier. 2005. *Student Success Teachers, Special Projects and Class Size Limits Improving High School Graduation Rates.* October 17. Toronto: Queen's Printer.

Ogbu, J.U. 1986. *The Consequences of the American Caste System.* Hillsdale, New Jersey: Erlbaum.

O'Neill, J. 1972. *Sociology as a Skin Trade.* London: Heinemann.

_____. *Five Bodies.* Ithaca: Cornell University Press.

O'Sullivan, C. 1990. *Television.* San Diego: Greenhaven Press.

Papazian, E. 1988. *TV Dimensions '88.* New York: Media Dynamics.

Parenti, M. 1986. *The Politics of the Mass Media.* New York: St. Martins Press.

_____. 1992. *Make Believe Media: The Politics of Entertainment.* New York: St. Martin's Press.

Parsons, T. 1952. *The Social System.* New York: Free Press.

Pasquino, P. 1978. "Theatrum Politicum: The Genealogy of Capital" Police and the State of Prosperity." *Ideology and Consciousness* 4(Autumn):41-54.

Pepinsky, H.E. 1978. "Communist Anarchism as an Alternative to the Rule of Criminal Law." *Contemporary Crises* 2:315-327.

_____. 1988. "Violence as Unresponsiveness: Toward a New Conception of Crime." *Justice Quarterly* 5(4):539-63.

Pepinsky, H.E. and R. Quinney. 1991. *Criminology as Peacemaking.* Bloomington, IN: Indiana University Press.

Peterson-Badali, M. and C.J. Koegl. 2002. "Juvenile Offenders' Experiences of Incarceration: The Role of Correctional Staff in Peer-on-Peer Violence." *Journal of Criminal Justice* 30:41-49.

Pew Research Center. 2000. *Pew Project 2000 Findings and Analysis.* Washington, DC: The Pew Research Center for the People and the Press.

Pfohl, S. 1994 [1985]. *Images of Deviance and Social Control: A Sociological History.* Boston: McGraw-Hill.

Plato. 1920. *Gorgias.* Translated by B. Jowett. Oxford: OUP.

_____. 1901. *The Republic.* Translated by B. Jowett. New York: P.F. Collier and Son.

Pollard, D. 1989. "Reducing the Impact of Racism on Students." *Educational Leadership* October:73-75.

Polletta, F. 2001. *Passionate Politics: Emotions and Social Movements.* Chicago: University of Chicago Press.

Powell, B. 2005. "We're Going to Lock Them Up: Police." *Toronto Star,* December 29, A1.

Pozzolini, A. 1968. *Antonio Gramsci: An Introduction to His Thoughts.* London: Pluto.

Presdee, M. 2000. *Cultural Criminology and the Carnival of Crime.* London: Routledge.

Procacci, G. 1978. "Social Economy and the Government of Poverty." *Ideology and Consciousness* 4(Autumn):29-55.

Prus, R. 1984. "Anthropological and Sociological Approaches to Deviance: An Ethnographic Prospect." Paper presented at Deviance in a Cross-Cultural Context Conference, University of Waterloo.

Quinney, R. 1974. *Critique of Legal Order: Crime Control in Capitalist Society.* Boston: Little, Brown.

Radwanski, G. 1987. *Ontario Study of the Relevance of Education and the Issue of Drop-Outs.* Ontario: Ministry of Education.

Rankin, J. 2005a. "The Voices of Toronto Gangs." *Toronto Star,* November 27, 2005, A10.

Rankin, J. 2005b. "A Loving Mother's Son." *Toronto Star,* December 31, A22.

Rawls, J. 1996. *Political Liberalism.* New York: Columbia University Press.

Rayner, B. 2005. "Stop Giving Hip Hop a Bad Rap." Available at (http://www.thestar.com/NASApp/cs/ContentServer?pagename=th estar/Layout/Article_Type1&c=Article&pubid=968163964505&ci d=1132786213093&call_page=TS_News&call_pageid=96833218 8492&call_pagepath=News/News).

Reckless, W. 1967. *The Crime Problem.* New York: Appleton Century-Crafts.

Rée, J. and J. Chamberlain. 1998. *Kierkegaard: A Critical Reader.* Oxford: Blackwell.

Reiman, J. 1998. *The Rich Get Richer and the Poor Get Prison: Ideology, Class and Criminal Justice.* Boston: Allyn and Bacon.

Rezai-Rashti G. 1995. "Connecting Racism and Sexism: The Dilemma of Working with Minority Female Students". In R. Ng, P. Staton, and J. Scane (eds.). *Anti-racism, Feminism and Critical Approaches to Education.* Westport, CT: Greenwood Publishers.

Ricoeur, P. 1981. *Hermeneutics and the Human Sciences.* Cambridge: University of Cambridge Press.

Rist, R.C. 1973. *The Urban School: A Factory for Failure; A Study of Education in American Society.* Cambridge, Massachusetts: MIT Press.

Roberts, J.V. and A. Doob. 1990. "News Media Influences on Public Views of Sentencing." *Law and Human Behavior* 14(5):451468.

Robinson, C. 2000. "Creating Space, Creating Self: Street Frequenting Youth in the City and Suburbs." *Journal of Youth Studies* 3(4):429-443.

Rock, P. 1973. "Phenomenalism and Essentialism in the Sociology of Deviance." *Sociology* 7:17-29.

_____. 1979. *The Making of Symbolic Interactionism.* London: Macmillan.

Rocker, R. 1938. *Anarchosyndicalism.* London: Secker & Warburg.

Rogers, C.R. 1959. "A Theory of Therapy, Personality and Interpersonal Relationships, as Developed in the Client-Centered Framework." In S. Koch (ed.). *Psychology: A Study of Science.* New York: McGraw Hill.

_____. 1961. *On Becoming a Person.* Boston: Houghton Mifflin.

_____. 1965. "A Humanistic Conception of Man." In R.E. Farson (ed.). *Science and Human Affairs.* Palo Alto, CA: Science and Behavior Books.

_____. 1977. *Carl Rogers on Personal Power.* New York: Delacorte Press.

Rosch, E. 1997. "Mindfulness, Meditation, and the Private(?) Self." In U. Neisser and D.A. Jopling (eds.). *The Conceptual Self in Context.* New York: Cambridge University Press.

Rose, G. 1978. *The Melancholy Science: An Introduction to the Thought of Theodor W. Adorno.* New York: Macmillan.

Rosen, S. 2004. Personal Communication, October. Toronto: York University.

Ross, D.P., K.J. Scott, and P.J. Smith. 2000. *The Canadian Fact Book on Poverty.* Ottawa: Canadian Council on Social Development.

Sadker, D. and M. Sadker. 1977. *Now upon a Time: A Contemporary View of Children's Literature.* New York: Harper and Row.

Said, E. 1979. *Orientalism.* New York: Vintage.

Salinger, J.D. 1951. *The Catcher in the Rye.* Boston: Little, Brown and Company.

Saney, P. 1986. *Crime and Culture in America.* Westport, CT: Greenwood Press.

Sartre, J.P. 1962 [1936]. *Transcendence of the Ego.* New York: Noonday Press.

_____. 1956 [1943]. *Being & Nothingness: A Phenomenological Essay on Ontology.* New York: New York Philosophical Library.

_____. 1956 [1946]. "Existentialism Is A Humanism." In W. Kaufmann (ed.). *Existentialism from Dostoevsky to Sartre.* New York: Meridian Books.

_____. 1948 [1946]. *Anti-Semite and Jew.* New York: Schocken.

_____.1960. *Critique of Dialectical Reason.* London: New Left Books.

_____. 1968 [1958]. *Search for a Method.* New York: Random House.

Schietz, S. and J.N. Sprafkin. 1978. "Spot Messages Within Saturday Morning Television Programs." In G. Tuchman, A. Daniels, and J. Benet (eds.). *Hearth and Home: Images of Women in the Mass Media.* New York: OUP.

Schissel, B. 1997. *Blaming Children: Youth Crime, Moral Panics and the Politics of Hate.* Halifax: Fernwood.

Schutz, A. 1964. *Collected Papers II: Studies in Social Theory.* The Hague: Martinus Nijhoff.

_____. 1974. *The Structures of the Life-World.* London: Heinemann.

Schwendinger, H. and J. Schwendinger 1977. "Social Class and the Definition of Crime." *Crime and Social Justice* 7(Summer):4-13.

Scott G.S. 1992. "The Hidden Hurdle." *Time,* March 16, p.42-45.

Scott, M.B. and S.M. Lyman. 1968. "Accounts." *American Sociological Review* 33:46-62.

Shah, A. 2004. "Corporate Influence in the Media: Media Conglomerates, Mergers, Concentration of Ownership." April 15, 2004. Available at (http://www.globalissues.org/HumanRights/Media/Corporations/Owners.asp).

_____. 2005. "Causes of Poverty Facts and Stats." June 11, 2005. Available at (http://www.globalissues.org/TradeRelated/Poverty.asp).

Share. 1989. February 15, Toronto, p6.

Sellin, T. 1938. *Culture, Conflict and Crime.* New York: Social Science Research Council.

Simmel, G, 1969 [1950]. "Types of Social Relationships by Degrees of Reciprocal Knowledge of Their Participants." In K. Wolff (ed.). *The Sociology of George Simmel.* New York: Free Press.

_____. 1969a [1950]."The Isolated Individual and the Dyad." In K. Wolff (ed.). *The Sociology of George Simmel.* New York: Free Press.

Skinner, R.F. 1956. "The Control of Human Behavior" (with Carl R. Rogers). *Science* 124:1057-1066.

Smelser, P. 1962. *Theory of Collective Behavior*. London: Routledge and Kegan Paul.

Smith, D. 1987. *The Everyday World as Problematic: A Feminist Sociology*. Toronto: University of Toronto Press.

_____. 1990. *The Conceptual Practices of Power*. Toronto: University of Toronto Press.

Smith, P., C. Goggin, and P. Gaudreau. 2002. *The Effects of Prison Sentences and Intermediate Sanctions on Recidivism: General Effects and Individual Differences*. (User Report 2001-2002). Ottawa: Solicitor General Canada.

Snyder, H.N. 2004. *Juvenile Arrests 2002*. US Department of Justice Office of Justice Programs *Office of Juvenile Justice and Delinquency Prevention*. Washington, DC: US Government Printing Office.

Solomos, J. 1988. *Black Youth, Racism and the State—The Politics of Ideology and Polity*. Cambridge UK: CUP.

Spitzer, S. 1975. "Towards a Marxian Theory of Deviance." *Social Problems* 22(June)5:638-651.

Spivak, G.C. 1985. "The Rani of Sirmur." In F. Barker et al.(eds.). *Europe and Its Others*. Colchester: University of Essex.

Sprott, J. 1996. "Understanding Public Views of Youth Crime and the Youth Justice System." *Canadian Journal of Criminology* 38(3):271290.

Staples, R. 1975. "White Racism, Black Crime, and American Justice: An Application of the Colonial Model to Explain Crime and Race." *Phylon* 36(1)March:14-23.

Standing Committee. 1997. *Report*. April 22, Minutes of Proceedings. The Thirteenth Report to the House, Ottawa: Supply and Services.

Statistics Canada. 1991. "Juristat: Police Personnel and Expenditures in Canada." *Juristat Service Bulletin* 12:2. Centre for Justice Statistics. Ottawa: Supply and Services.

Statistics Canada. 1992. *Report Ottawa*: Supply and Services.

Statistics Canada. 2001. *Children and Youth in Canada*. Canadian Centre for Justice Statistics Profile Series, Ottawa: Supply and Services.

Statistics Canada. 2003. "Television Viewing," Fall 2002. *The Daily*, November 21, 2003. Ottawa: Statistics Canada. Available at (http://www.statcan.ca/Daily/English/031121/d031121a.htm).

Statistics Canada. 2004. Ottawa: Supply and Services.

Statistics Canada. 2004a. Youth Court Statistics." *The Daily*, March 12, 2004. Ottawa: Supply and Services.

Statistics Canada. 2004b. *Youth Court Statistics,* March 2002. Ottawa: Supply and Services.

Statistics Canada. 2004c. *Youth Court Statistics,* March 2002. Ottawa: Supply and Services.

Statistics Canada. 2004d. 11-25.CANSIM, table 252-0030 and Catalogue no. 85-002-X. *Cases in Youth Criminal Court.* Ottawa: Supply and Services.

Statistics Canada. 2005. *Persons Charged by Type of Offence, by Province and Territory.* Ottawa: Supply and Services. Available at (http://www40.statcan.ca/l01/cst01/legal17a.htm).

Steele, C. 1998. *Stereotype Threat and the Test Performance of Academically Successful African Americans.* Washington, DC: Brookings Institution Press.

Steele, C. et al. 2003. "Stereotype Threat and African-American Student Achievement." In *Young, Gifted and Black-Promoting High Achievement among African-American Students.* Boston: Beacon Press.

Streib, V. 2001. "Death Sentences and Executions for Juvenile Crimes, January 1, 1973–December 31, 2000." *Juvenile Death Penalty Today.* Ada, OH: Ohio Northern University.

Sullivan, D. and L. Tifft. 1999. "A Criminology as Peacemaking: A Peace-Oriented Perspective on Crime, Punishment, and Justice that Takes into Account the Needs of All." *The Justice Professional* 1(1-2):5-34.

Surette, R. 1984. *Justice and the Media.* Springfield: Charles C. Thomas.

_____. 1989. "Media Trials." *Journal of Criminal Justice* 17:293-308.

_____. 1990. *The Media and Criminal Justice Policy: Recent Research and Social Effects.* Springfield, IL: Charles C. Thomas.

_____. 1992. *Media, Crime, and Criminal Justice: Images and Realities.* Pacific Groves CA: Brooks/Cole.

_____. 1998. *Media, Crime, and Criminal Justice: Images and Realities,* 2d ed. New York: Wadsworth Publishing.

Sutherland, E. 1924. *Criminology.* Philadelphia: J.B. Lippincott.

Sykes, G. and P. Matza. 1957. "Techniques of Neutralization: A Theory of Delinquency." *American Sociological Review* 22(5):664-670.

Talbot, C. 1984. *Growing Up Black in Canada.* Toronto: Williams-Wallace.

Tarde, G. [1903] 1962. *The Laws of Emitation.* Gloucester MA: Peter Smith.

Tator, C. 1987. "Anti-Racist Education." *Currents* 4(4):8-11.

Taylor, C. 1989. *Sources of the Self.* Cambridge, MA: Harvard University Press.

Taylor, I. 1981. "Crime Waves in Post-War Britain." *Contemporary Crises* 5(1):43-62.

Taylor, I., P. Walton, and J. Young. 1973. *The New Criminology.* London: Routledge and Kegan Paul.

Thompson, G. 2006. "Even in Peace, Nation Ravaged by Killings." *Toronto Star*, January 1, p.A8.

Thornton, S. 1995. *Club Cultures.* Hanover, NH: Wesleyan University Press.

Tihanov, G. 1995. "Reification and Dialogue: Aspects of the Theory of Culture." In *Lukács and Bakhtin.* Bakhtin Centre Papers, Bakhtin Centre. Sheffield: UK.

_____. 2000. *The Master and the Slave: Lukács, Bakhtin, and the Ideas of Their Time.* Oxford: Clarendon.

Tifft, L. 1979. "The Coming Redefinition of Crime: An Anarchist Perspective." *Social Problems* 26:392-402.

Toby, J. 1957. "The Differential Impact of Family Disorganization." *American Sociological Review* 22(October):505-512.

Tong, R. 1989. *Feminist Thought: A Comprehensive Introduction.* San Francisco: Westview.

Touraine, A. 2001. *Beyond Neoliberalism.* Cambridge: Polity Press.

Trotman, A. 1993. "African-Caribbean Perspectives of Worldview: C.L.R. James Explores the Authentic Voice." Ph.D. dissertation, Department of Sociology, York University.

Troyna, B. 1994. "Blind Faith: Empowerment and Educational Research." Paper for International Sociology of Education Conference. University of Sheffield.

Trueman, P. 1980. *Smoke and Mirrors.* Toronto: McClelland and Stewart.

Tucker, R.1978. *The Marx-Engels Reader.* New York: W.W. Norton and Company.

Turk, A. 1966. "Conflict and Criminality." *American Sociological Review* 31(June):338-352.

_____. 1967. "On the Parsonian Approach to Theory Construction." *Sociological Quarterly* 8:37-50.

_____. 1969. *Criminality and Legal Order.* Chicago: Rand McNally and Company.

_____. 1976. "Law as a Weapon in Social Conflict." *Social Problems* 23(February)3:276-291.

_____. 1976b. "Law, Conflict and Order: From Theorizing Towards Theories." *Canadian Review of Sociology and Anthropology* 13(August)3:282-294.

_____. 1977. "Class, Conflict and Criminalization." *Sociological Focus* 10:209-220.

_____. 1979. "Analysing Official Deviance: For Non-Partisan Conflict Analyses in Criminology." *Criminology* 16:459-476.

Turner, B. 1989. *The Body and Society.* New York: Basil Blackwell.

Valverde, M. 1990. "The Rhetoric of Reform: Tropes and the Moral Subject." *International Journal of the Sociology of Law* 18:61-73.

Virilio P. 1994. *The Vision Machine.* Bloomington: Indiana University Press.

Visano, A.F. 2005. "Report on Corporate Investments." Mimeo. Toronto: Strategic Capital.

Visano, L.A. 1987. *This Idle Trade.* Concord: VitaSana Books.

_____. 1988. "Generic and Generative Dimensions of Interactionism." *International Journal of Comparative Sociology* 29(3):230-244.

_____. 1990a. "Crime as a Commodity: Police Use of Informers." *Journal of Human Justice* 2(1):105-114.

_____. 1990b. "The Socialization of Street Kids." *Sociological Studies of Child Development* 3:139-161.

_____. 1991. "The Impact of Age on Paid Sexual Encounters." *Journal of Homosexuality* 20(3/4):207-236.

_____. 1992. "Becoming A Hustler." In T. Fleming (ed.). *Youth Injustice.* Toronto: Canadian Scholars' Press.

_____. 1996a. "Delinquency as Mediated Texts." In G. O'Bireck. *Youth Deviance.* Toronto: Nelson.

_____. 1996b."Youth and Children as Mediated Texts: A Critical Ethnography into Cultures of Compliance and Rituals of Resistance." Paper presented at the Annual Meeting of the Qualitative Analysis Conference, May 30, McMaster University.

_____. 1996c. "War on Drugs: From the Politics of Punishment to the Prospects of Peacekeeping." *Addictions: An International Research Journal* 1(Fall):81-95.

_____. 1998a. *Crime and Culture: Refining the Traditions*. Canadian Scholars' Press. Toronto.

_____. 1998b. "Whores and Heroes: Prostituting the Self as a Mediated Commodity". In S. McMahon (ed.). *Women, Crime and Culture*. Toronto: Canadian Scholars' Press.

_____. 1999. "Racism and the War on Drugs." Paper presented at The Second International Conference on Drug War Prisoners, March 20, Toronto.

_____. 2001. "A Programme of Action: Concrete Proposals to address the Implementation of the new Youth Criminal Justice Act." Consultation paper, National Youth Justice Roundtable, Ottawa: Department of Justice.

Vold, G.B. 1958. *Theoretical Criminology*. New York: OUP.

Walcott, R. 1994. "The Need for a Politics of Difference." *Orbit* 25: 2.

Walker, J. 1980. *Racial Discrimination in Canada: The Black Experience*. No. 41. Ottawa: Canadian Historical Association.

_____. 1982. *A History of Blacks in Canada*. Quebec: Government Printing House.

_____. 1990. *Race and the Historian: Some Lessons from Canadian Public Policy*. Toronto: Osgoode Hall.

Wacquant L. 1998. "Negative Social Capital: State Breakdown and Social Destitution in America's Urban Core." *The Netherlands Journal of the Built Environment* 13:25-4.

Ward L.M. 2003. "Understanding the Role of Entertainment Media in the Sexual Socialization of American Youth: A Review of Empirical Research." *Developmental Review* 23:347-388.

Weber, M. 1969 [1947]. *The Theory of Social and Economic Organization*. New York: Free Press.

Weiss J. 2005. "Are we seeing the end of serendipity?" *Toronto Star*, December 29, A19.

West, W.G. 1978. "The Short-Term Careers of Serious Thieves." *Canadian Journal of Criminology* 20(2):169-190.

Westhead, R. 2005. "Beware Toronto, CNN Tells Viewers." *Toronto Star*, December 29, B1.

Willinsky, J. 1998. *Learning to Divide the World: Education at Empire's End*. Minneapolis: University of Minnesota Press.

Willis, P. 1980 [1977]. *Learning to Labour* Farnborough: Gower.

_____. 1990. *Common Culture: Symbolic Work at Play in the Everyday Cultures of the Young.* Buckingham: Open University Press.

Winks, R. 1971. *The Blacks in Canada.* Montreal: McGill-Queen's University Press.

Wiseman, M.B. 1989. *The Ecstasies of Roland Barthes.* London: Routledge.

Wittgenstein, L. 1980. *Culture and Value.* Chicago: The University of Chicago Press.

World Almanac Education Group. 2004. *The World Almanac and Book of Facts.* New York: World Almanac Books.

_____. 2005. *The World Almanac and Book of Facts.* New York: World Almanac Books.

Wolff, R. 1989. "Gramsci, Marxism and Philosophy." *Rethinking Marxism* 2(2):41-54.

Wood, A. 1981. *Karl Marx.* Boston: Routledge and Kegan Paul.

Wright L. 2003. "The Worse it Gets, The Better it Sells Makes a Killing by Belittling Women Dominates Pop Culture Worldwide." *Toronto Star,* October 26. Available at (http://www.thestar.com/NASApp/cs/ContentServer?pagename=thestar/Layout/Article_Type1&call_pag eid=971358637177&c=Article&cid=1067121007380).

Youth Criminal Justice Act. 2002. "An Act in Respect of Criminal Justice for Young Persons and to Amend and Repeal Other Acts Royal Assent, February 19, 2002. Statutes of Canada 2002, c.1. The Consolidated Statutes and Regulations of Canada. Department of Justice Canada.

Zatz, M. 1987. "The Changing Forms of Racial and Ethnic Biases in Sentencing." *Journal of Research in Crime and Delinquency* 24(1):69-92.

Untitled Newsprint

Toronto Star. 1992. December 12, A3.
Toronto Star. 1994a. January 25, A6.
Toronto Star. 1994b. August 15, A3.
Toronto Star. 1995. March 26, E9.
Toronto Star. 2003. January 9, A16.
USA Today. 1993. January 14, D1.
USA Today. 1994. August 19, 11A.

Internet Sources

The American Academy of Child and Adolescent Psychiatry Children.
http://www.aacap.org/

The Center for Successful Parenting
http://www.sosparents.org/The%20Facts.htm

kidmedia@airwaves.chi.il.us

Kathleen McLaughlin-Hoppe Kid TV/Music: The Evolution of Media
http://www.kathleensworld.com/kidmedia.html

TeensHealth © 1995-2006 The Nemours Foundation.
http://www.kidshealth.org/

The Teacher Centre Frontline PBS web site © 1995-2005 WGBH educational foundation http://www.pbs.org/wgbh/pages/frontline/teach/cool

Canadian Media Research Consortium www.cmrcccrm.ca Report Card on Canadian News Media http://www.cmrcccrm.ca/english/report-card2004/01.html

University of Maine Cooperative Extension Bulletin #4100*Prepared by Judith Graham,* How Television Viewing Affects Children http://www.umext.maine.edu/onlinepubs/htmpubs/4100.htm

Communication, Cultural and Media Matters CCMS February 6, 2000 06:01:03 © Mick Underwood http://www.cultsock.ndirect.co.uk/MUHome/cshtml/index.html

Just an Hour of TV a Day Leads to Violence Study
Thu Mar 28,10:15 AM ET By Maggie Fox, Health and Science Correspondent http://www.trivision.ca/documents/Television%20Violence%20Study_March2002.pdf.

Television's Impact on Kids © 2005 Media Awareness Network
http://www.media-awareness.ca/english/parents/television/tv_impact_kids.cfm

Media Violence. The mainstream of reports discuss how TV affects children's development and how to use TV as an educational tool for children. TV-Free America http://campus.murraystate.edu/academic/faculty/j.dillon/violent.htm.

What Kids Get From TV: Some Things We Do Know That Can Help Us Understand How TV Affects Children. What People—Young or Old—Get From the Television www.thirteen.org/readytolearn/pdf/2_view readdo/view_pdf/what_kids_get_from_tv.pdf

Index

Nettler, G., 83
Neutralization Techniques, 70
New Brunswick, 244
Newfoundland, 241, 244
Newspapers, 99, 101, 105, 108, 110, 116,
    118, 119, 120, 121, 125, 127, 129,
    131, 132
Nietzsche, F., 27, 182, 241, 249
Nordentoft, K., 24
Normative Youth Cultures, 62
Nova Scotia, 244

O

O'Neill, J., 110, 155
O'Sullivan, C., 118
Oakes, J., 222, 227
Objectivation, 182
Office of Juvenile Justice and Delinquency
    Prevention, 151
Ogbu, J.U., 230
Ohlin, L., 66
Ontario Code of Conduct, 237
Ontario Human Rights Commission, 202
Ontario, 224, 229, 233, 234, 235, 236, 237,
    238, 239, 240, 241, 242, 244, 267
Organization for Economic Cooperation
    and Development, 243

P

Pakistan, 102
Parenti, M., 98, 125
Parsons, T., 64
Pasquino, P., 171
Peel Region, 95
Pennington, J., 231
Pepinsky, H.E., 179, 180, 181
Pew Research Center, 109
Pfohl, S., 31, 32, 33, 82
Phenomenology of Youth Crime, 29
Phenomenology, 86
Podolski, L., 124, 125
Police, 72, 73, 84, 116, 138, 148, 157, 161,
    162, 163, 164, 165, 166, 170, 171,
    186, 190, 192, 194, 197, 198, 202,
    237, 238, 239, 240, 266, 268
Political Economy, 1, 7, 8, 9, 37
Pollard, D., 225
Polytextures of Identity, 29
Possessiveness, 2
Poverty, 27, 34, 68, 69, 78, 218, 219, 221,
    222, 228, 232, 241, 257, 259, 266, 267

Powell, B., 164
Presdee, M., 265
Prince Edward Island, 244
Procacci, G., 171
Progressive Pedagogy, 251
Prostitution, 192, 197, 198, 199, 200
Prus, R., 191

Q

Quebec, 244
Quinney, R., 75, 180, 181

R

Race, 10, 29, 95, 113, 124, 143, 205, 211,
    224, 228, 230, 231, 232, 238, 244, 266
Racial Relations, 58
Racism, 124, 132, 135, 204, 222, 225, 226,
    227, 229, 230, 231, 233, 240, 258, 266
Radical Criminology, 82, 83
Radwanski, G., 227
Rankin, J., 209, 210, 229, 268
Rap, 121, 124, 127, 130, 132, 133, 134, 135
Rape, 150
Rawls, J., 155
Rayner, B., 202
Reaction Formations, 64
Reckless, W., 68, 69
Rée, J., 24
Refexivity, 32
Regulating Youth, 232
Rehabilitation, 159, 160, 165, 167, 168
Reiman, J., 118
Reinforcement and Opportunities, 69
Reintegration, 159, 160, 161, 167
Rezai-Rashti, G., 256
Riceour, P., 262
Risk of Resistance, 173, 175, 177, 179, 181,
    183, 185, 187, 189, 191, 193, 195,
    197, 199, 201, 203, 205, 207, 209, 211
Rist, R.C., 228
Robbery, 149, 150, 239
Roberts, J.V., 127
Robinson, C., 185
Rock, P., 82, 98, 124, 127, 133, 134
Rocker, R., 180
Rogers, C., 19, 20, 40
Rosch, E., 20
Rose, G., 140
Rosen, S., 252
Ross, D.P., 218, 219
Russia, 102

Unemployment, 69
United Kingdom, 102
United Nations, 163
United States, 102, 104, 109, 122, 123, 176,
    227, 229, 240, 243
USA Today, 229

V

Valverde, M., 94
Vanzetti, B., 179
Velasquez, E., 267
Video Games, 95, 122, 123, 127, 128, 130,
    134, 140
Violence, 11, 34, 36, 40, 46, 55, 65, 66, 67,
    78, 110, 116, 118, 120, 121, 122, 123,
    124, 126, 130, 133, 134, 135, 137,
    138, 144, 153, 157, 161, 163, 164,
    165, 166, 181, 187, 197, 198, 199,
    202, 203, 206, 209, 210, 211, 213,
    215, 232, 240, 257, 258, 260, 266,
    267, 269
Violent Crime Index, 150
Violent Youth Crime, 149, 150, 157, 159
Virilio, P., 98
Visano, L., 34, 93, 157, 158, 161, 187, 189,
    192, 193, 195, 198, 201, 220, 266
Vold, G., 73, 82

W

Walcott, R., 230
Walker, J., 224
Walton, P., 74, 82
Ward, L.M., 127
Wartella, W., 121
Weber, M., 93, 152
Weiss, J., 142
Welfare, 156, 166, 168, 170, 220, 221, 225,
    245, 267
West, W.G., 192, 208
Westhead, R., 110
Whitney, C., 121
Wiles, P., 82
Williamson, H., 185
Willinsky 231
Willis, P., 34, 183, 241
Winks, R., 222
Wiseman, M.B., 50, 55
Wood, A., 87
Woodruff, K., 121
Woollacott, J., 92, 99, 107

World Almanac Education Group, 102, 105,
    123

Y

York Region, 95, 110
Young Offenders Act, 157, 158, 159, 160,
    161
Young, J., 74, 82
Youth Court, 148, 149, 150, 160
Youth Crime, 1, 2, 3, 5, 6, 7, 8, 9, 29, 31,
    37, 55, 64, 78, 83, 84, 93, 94, 108,
    113, 114, 115, 118, 120, 132, 133,
    142, 145, 147, 148, 149, 150, 151,
    154, 157, 158, 159, 161, 162, 163,
    164, 165, 166, 169, 172, 182, 208,
    211, 213, 261, 263, 264, 265, 266,
    267, 268
Youth Criminal Justice Act, 96, 233, 267
Youth Criminal Justice, 7
Youth Culture, 59
Youth Cultures, 49, 51, 58, 59, 60, 62, 93,
    94, 134
Youth Gangs, 66, 67, 79, 208
Youth Hostels, 95
Youth Identity, 1, 2, 3, 5, 7, 8, 9, 10, 11, 13,
    15, 17, 19, 21, 23, 25, 27, 29, 31, 33,
    35, 37, 38, 39, 40, 59, 83
Youth Justice Renewal Fund, 159
Youth Justice System, 158, 159
Youth Resistance, 173, 182, 183, 184, 202,
    211
Youth Unemployment, 220
Youth Values, 60
Yukon, 244

Z

Zatz, M., 153

Printed in the United States
42641LVS00007B/91-182

9 781897 160220